VOLUME 07

the AMAZING SPIDER-MAN

Armed and Dangerous

[redacted]

SPIDER-MAN

THE EMISSARY, a mad mathematician who tried to become a god of death (and nearly succeeded), has been defeated once and for all. But at what cost? MS. MARVEL made the ultimate sacrifice, giving her life to stop the evil plan. As she died in Spider-Man's arms, she removed her mask revealing her identity as Oscorp intern KAMALA KHAN. The devastating blow was felt doubly by NORMAN OSBORN, who realized the young hero had interned at Oscorp to keep an eye on him.

But Peter and Norman don't have time to sit with their grief and guilt when New York City needs the protection of Spider-Man and Gold Goblin.

Jennifer Grünwald COLLECTION EDITOR

Daniel Kirchhoffer ASSISTANT EDITOR

Lisa Montalbano ASSOCIATE MANAGER, TALENT RELATIONS

Jeff Youngquist VP PRODUCTION & SPECIAL PROJECTS

Jay Bowen BOOK DESIGNER

Adam Del Re MANAGER & SENIOR DESIGNER

David Gabriel SVP PRINT, SALES & MARKETING

C.B. Cebulski EDITOR IN CHIEF

AMAZING SPIDER-MAN BY ZEB WELLS VOL. 7: ARMED AND DANGEROUS. Contains material originally published in magazine form as AMAZING SPIDER-MAN (2022) #27-31 and FREE COMIC BOOK DAY 2023: SPIDER-MAN/VENOM #1. First printing 2023. ISBN 978-1-302-94739-2. Published by MARVEL WORLDWIDE, INC., a subsidiary of MARVEL ENTERTAINMENT, LLC. OFFICE OF PUBLICATION: 1290 Avenue of the Americas, New York, NY 10104. © 2023 MARVEL No similarity between any of the names, characters, persons, and/or institutions in this book with those of any living or dead person or institution is intended, and any such similarity which may exist is purely coincidental. **Printed in the U.S.A.** KEVIN FEIGE, Chief Creative Officer; DAN BUCKLEY, President, Marvel Entertainment; DAVID BOGART, Associate Publisher & SVP of Talent Affairs; TOM BREVOORT, VP, Executive Editor; NICK LOWE, Executive Editor, VP of Content, Digital Publishing; DAVID GABRIEL, VP of Print & Digital Publishing; SVEN LARSEN, VP of Licensed Publishing; MARK ANNUNZIATO, VP of Planning & Forecasting; JEFF YOUNGQUIST, VP of Production & Special Projects; ALEX MORALES, Director of Publishing Operations; DAN EDINGTON, Director of Editorial Operations; RICKEY PURDIN, Director of Talent Relations; JENNIFER GRÜNWALD, Director of Production & Special Projects; SUSAN CRESPI, Production Manager; STAN LEE, Chairman Emeritus. For information regarding advertising in Marvel Comics or on Marvel.com, please contact Vit DeBellis, Custom Solutions & Integrated Advertising Manager, at vdebellis@marvel.com. For Marvel subscription inquiries, please call 888-511-5480. **Manufactured between 9/1/2023 and 10/3/2023 by SEAWAY PRINTING, GREEN BAY, WI, USA.**

10 9 8 7 6 5 4 3 2 1

VOLUME 07

the AMAZING SPIDER-MAN

Armed and Dangerous

Zeb Wells WRITER

FREE COMIC BOOK DAY: SPIDER-MAN/VENOM

Patrick Gleason ARTIST
Marcio Menyz COLOR ARTIST
VC's **Joe Caramagna** LETTERER
Patrick Gleason & **Bryan Valenza** COVER ART

AMAZING SPIDER-MAN #27-30

Ed McGuinness PENCILER
Mark Farmer WITH Cliff Rathburn (#30) & Ed McGuinness (#30) INKERS
Marcio Menyz COLOR ARTIST
VC's **Joe Caramagna** LETTERER
Ed McGuinness & **Marcio Menyz** COVER ART

AMAZING SPIDER-MAN #31

JOHN ROMITA JR. & **EMILIO LAISO** WITH Zé Carlos PENCILERS
Scott Hanna & **Emilio Laiso** WITH Zé Carlos INKERS
Marcio Menyz & **Bryan Valenza** COLOR ARTISTS
VC's **Joe Caramagna** LETTERER
John Romita Jr., **Scott Hanna** & **Marcio Menyz** COVER ART

Kaeden McGahey ASSISTANT EDITOR
Tom Groneman ASSISTANT EDITOR
Nick Lowe EDITOR

SPIDER-MAN CREATED BY STAN LEE & STEVE DITKO

THERE MUST ALSO COME GREAT RESPONSIBILITY

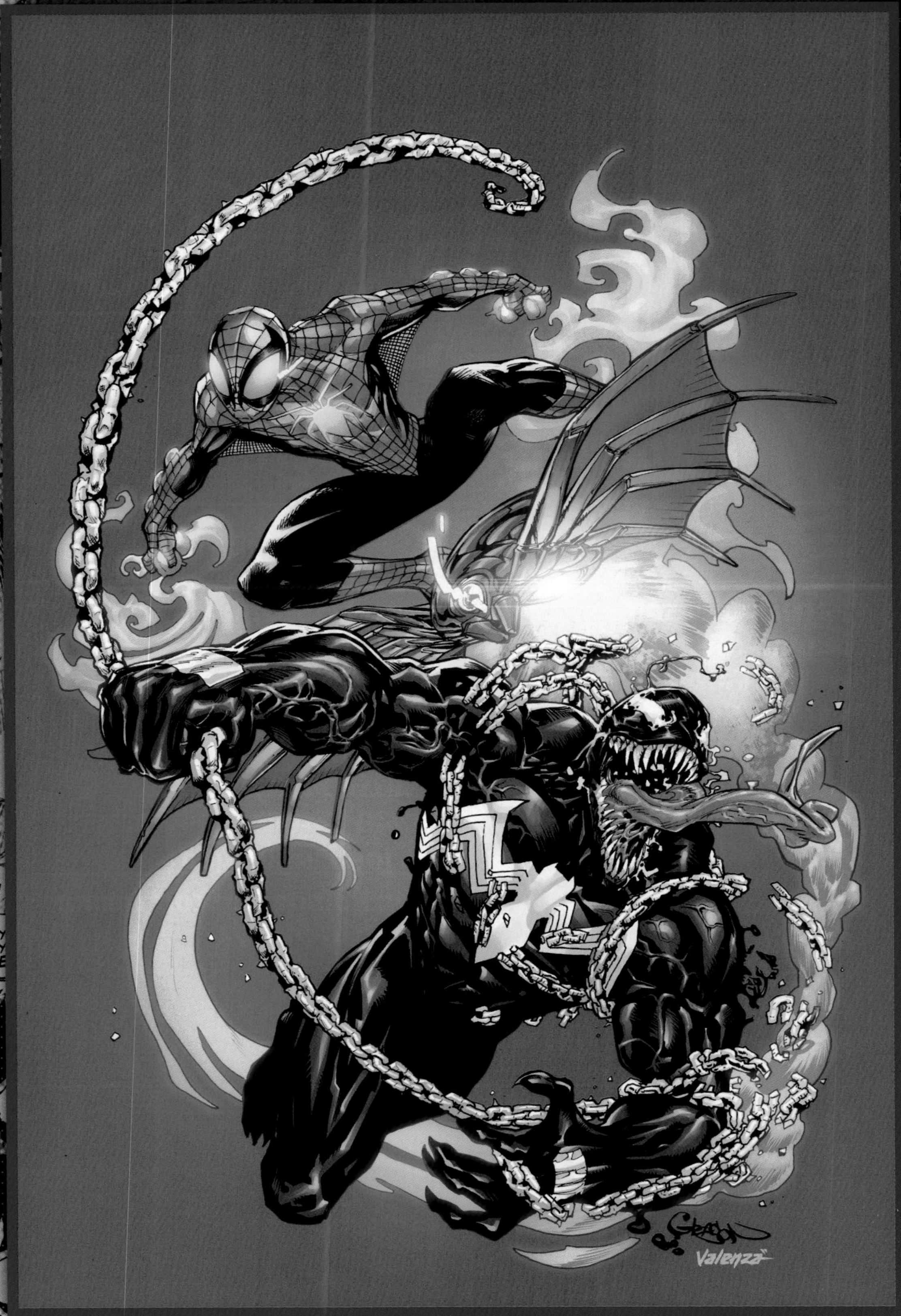
Valenza

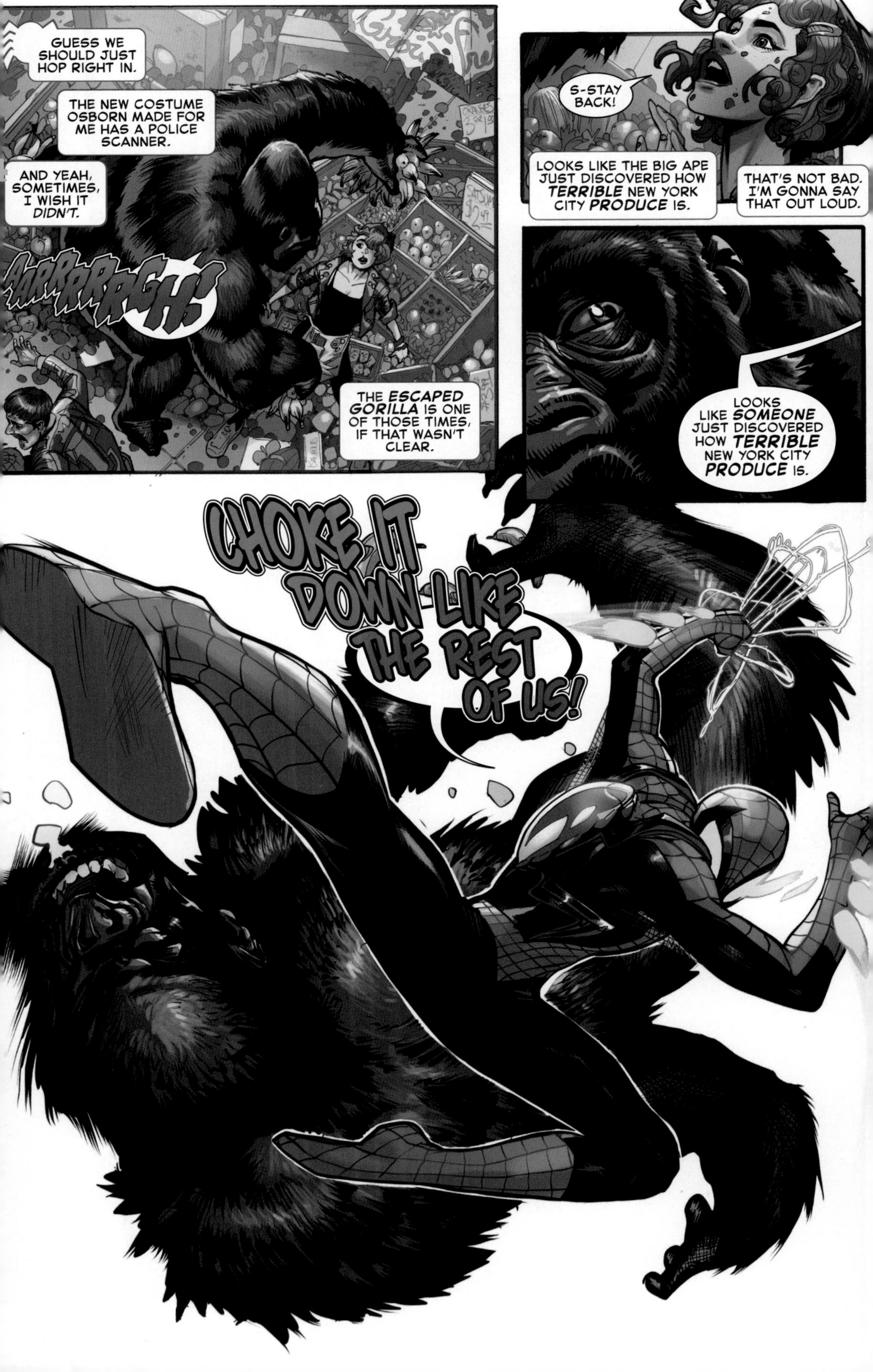

GUESS WE SHOULD JUST HOP RIGHT IN.
THE NEW COSTUME OSBORN MADE FOR ME HAS A POLICE SCANNER.
AND YEAH, SOMETIMES, I WISH IT *DIDN'T.*
AARRRRRGH!
THE *ESCAPED GORILLA* IS ONE OF THOSE TIMES, IF THAT WASN'T CLEAR.
S-STAY BACK!
LOOKS LIKE THE BIG APE JUST DISCOVERED HOW *TERRIBLE* NEW YORK CITY *PRODUCE* IS.
THAT'S NOT BAD. I'M GONNA SAY THAT OUT LOUD.
LOOKS LIKE *SOMEONE* JUST DISCOVERED HOW *TERRIBLE* NEW YORK CITY *PRODUCE* IS.
CHOKE IT DOWN LIKE THE REST OF US!

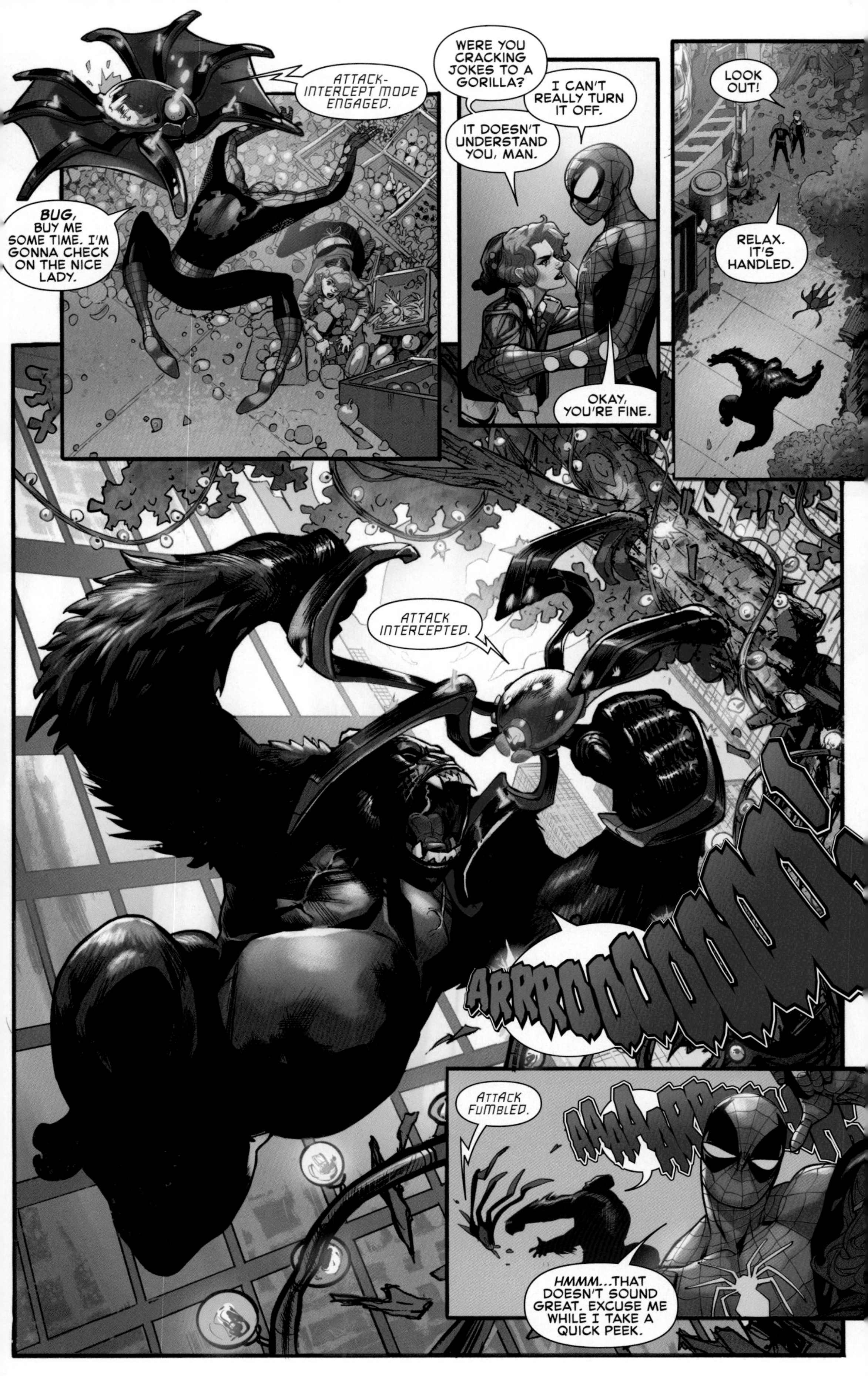
ATTACK-INTERCEPT MODE ENGAGED.
BUG, BUY ME SOME TIME. I'M GONNA CHECK ON THE NICE LADY.
WERE YOU CRACKING JOKES TO A GORILLA?
I CAN'T REALLY TURN IT OFF.
IT DOESN'T UNDERSTAND YOU, MAN.
OKAY, YOU'RE FINE.
LOOK OUT!
RELAX. IT'S HANDLED.
ATTACK INTERCEPTED.
ARRROOOOOO!
ATTACK FUMBLED.
HMMM...THAT DOESN'T SOUND GREAT. EXCUSE ME WHILE I TAKE A QUICK PEEK.

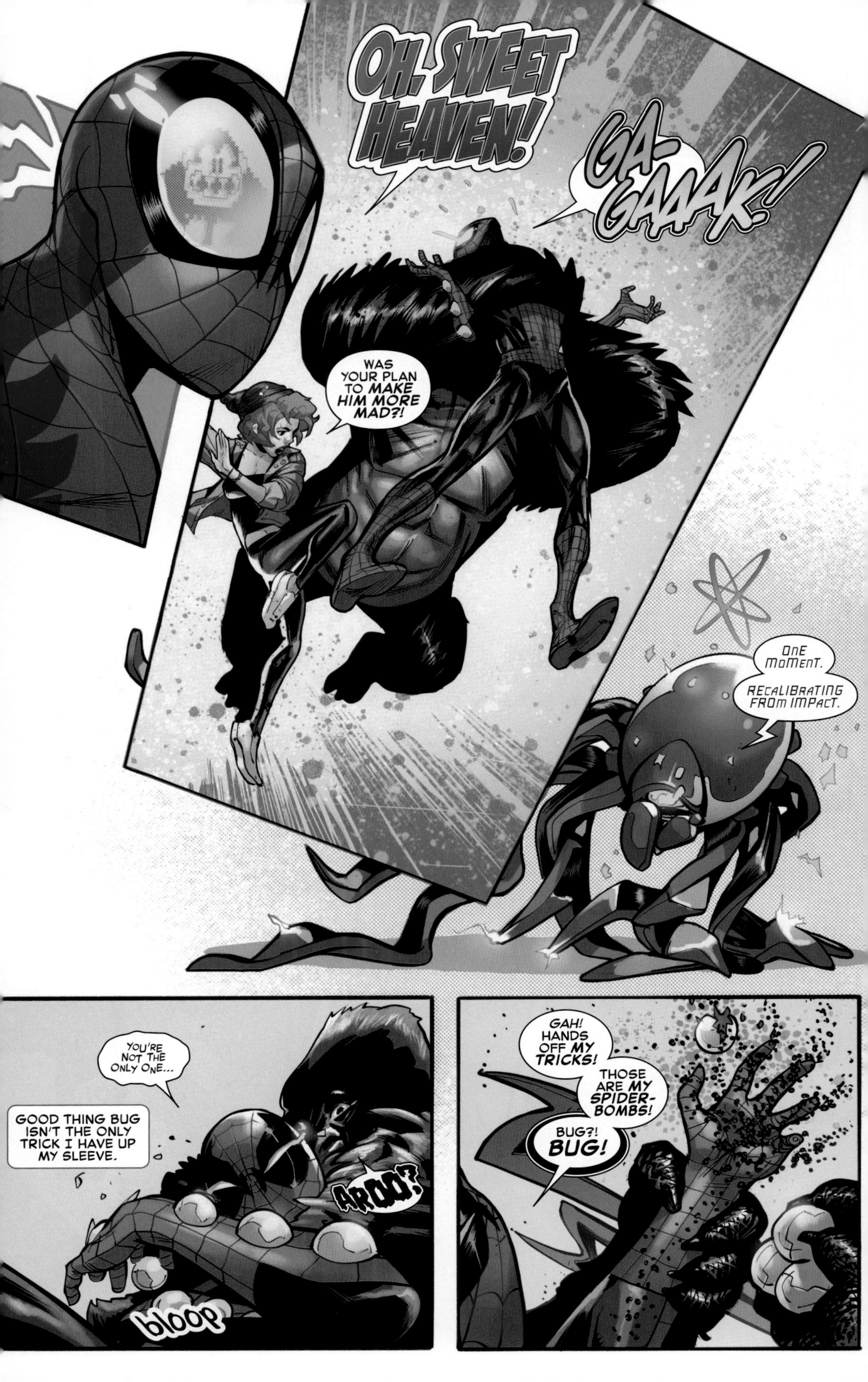
OH, SWEET HEAVEN!
GA-GAAAK!
WAS YOUR PLAN TO MAKE HIM MORE MAD?!
ONE MOMENT.
RECALIBRATING FROM IMPACT.
YOU'RE NOT THE ONLY ONE...
GOOD THING BUG ISN'T THE ONLY TRICK I HAVE UP MY SLEEVE.
AROO?
bloop
GAH! HANDS OFF MY TRICKS!
THOSE ARE MY SPIDER-BOMBS!
BUG?! BUG!

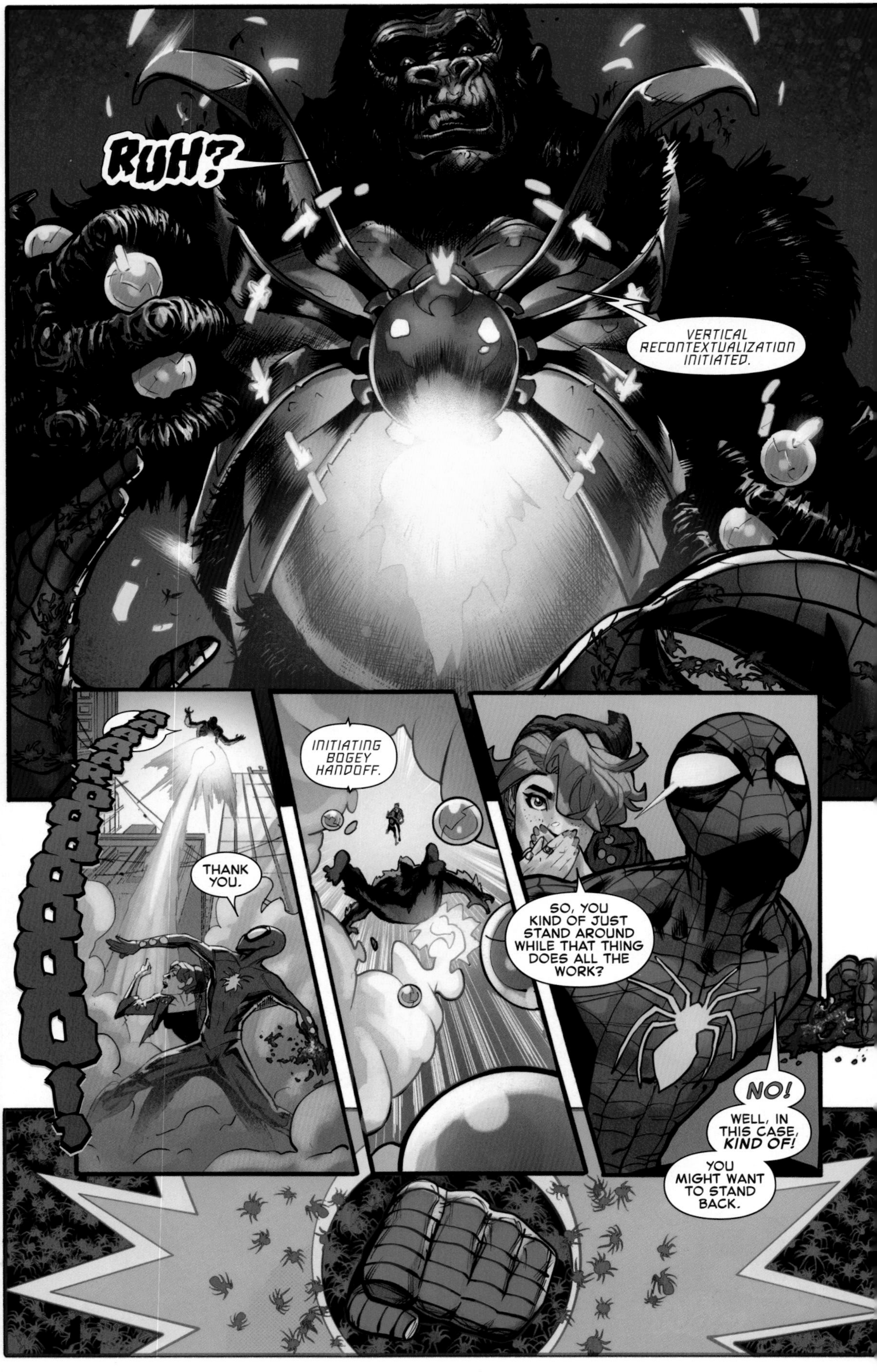
RUH?
VERTICAL RECONTEXTUALIZATION INITIATED.
THANK YOU.
INITIATING BOGEY HANDOFF.
SO, YOU KIND OF JUST STAND AROUND WHILE THAT THING DOES ALL THE WORK?
NO!
WELL, IN THIS CASE, KIND OF!
YOU MIGHT WANT TO STAND BACK.

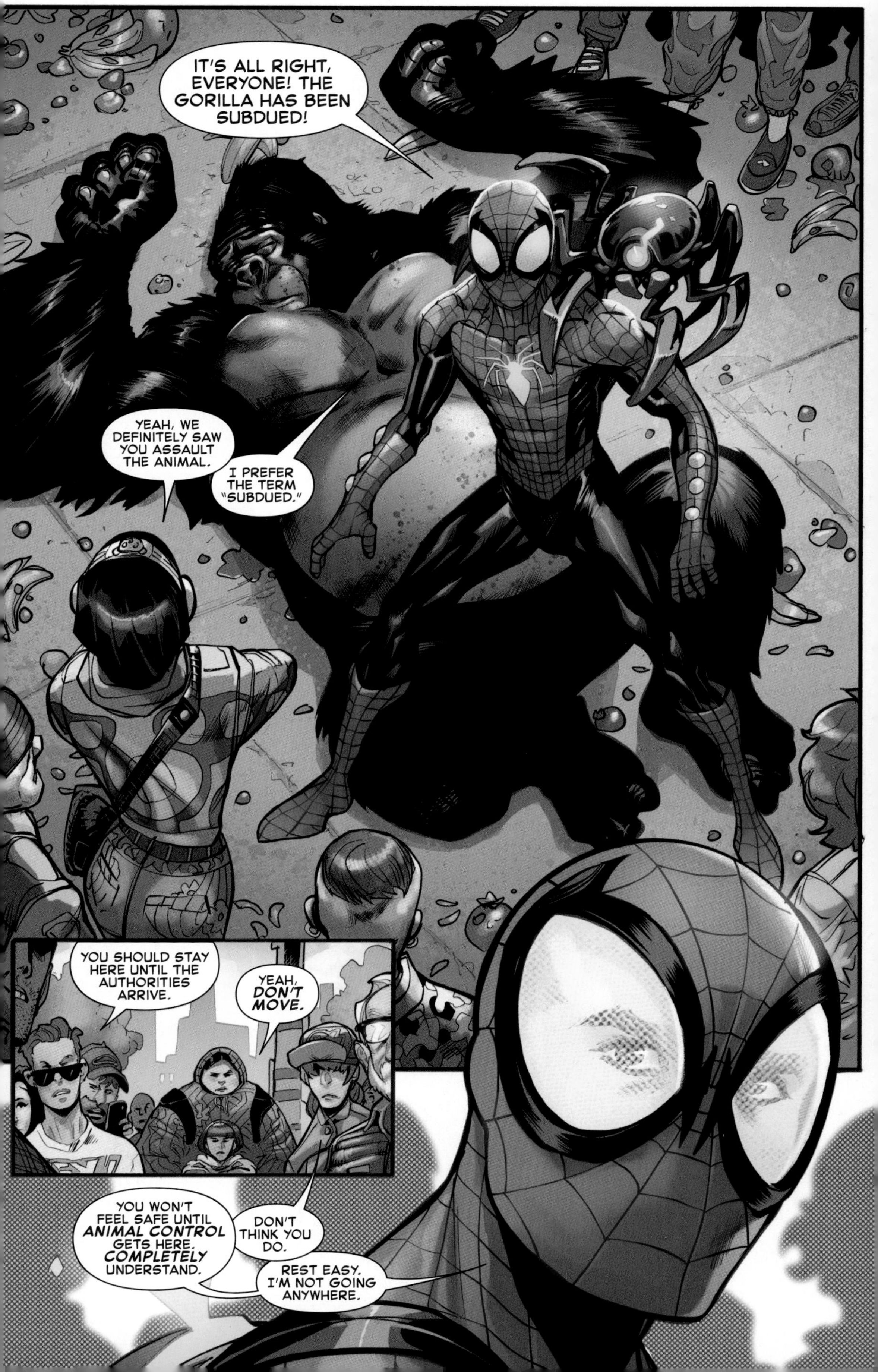
IT'S ALL RIGHT, EVERYONE! THE GORILLA HAS BEEN SUBDUED!
YEAH, WE DEFINITELY SAW YOU ASSAULT THE ANIMAL.
I PREFER THE TERM "SUBDUED."
YOU SHOULD STAY HERE UNTIL THE AUTHORITIES ARRIVE.
YEAH, DON'T MOVE.
YOU WON'T FEEL SAFE UNTIL ANIMAL CONTROL GETS HERE. COMPLETELY UNDERSTAND.
DON'T THINK YOU DO.
REST EASY. I'M NOT GOING ANYWHERE.

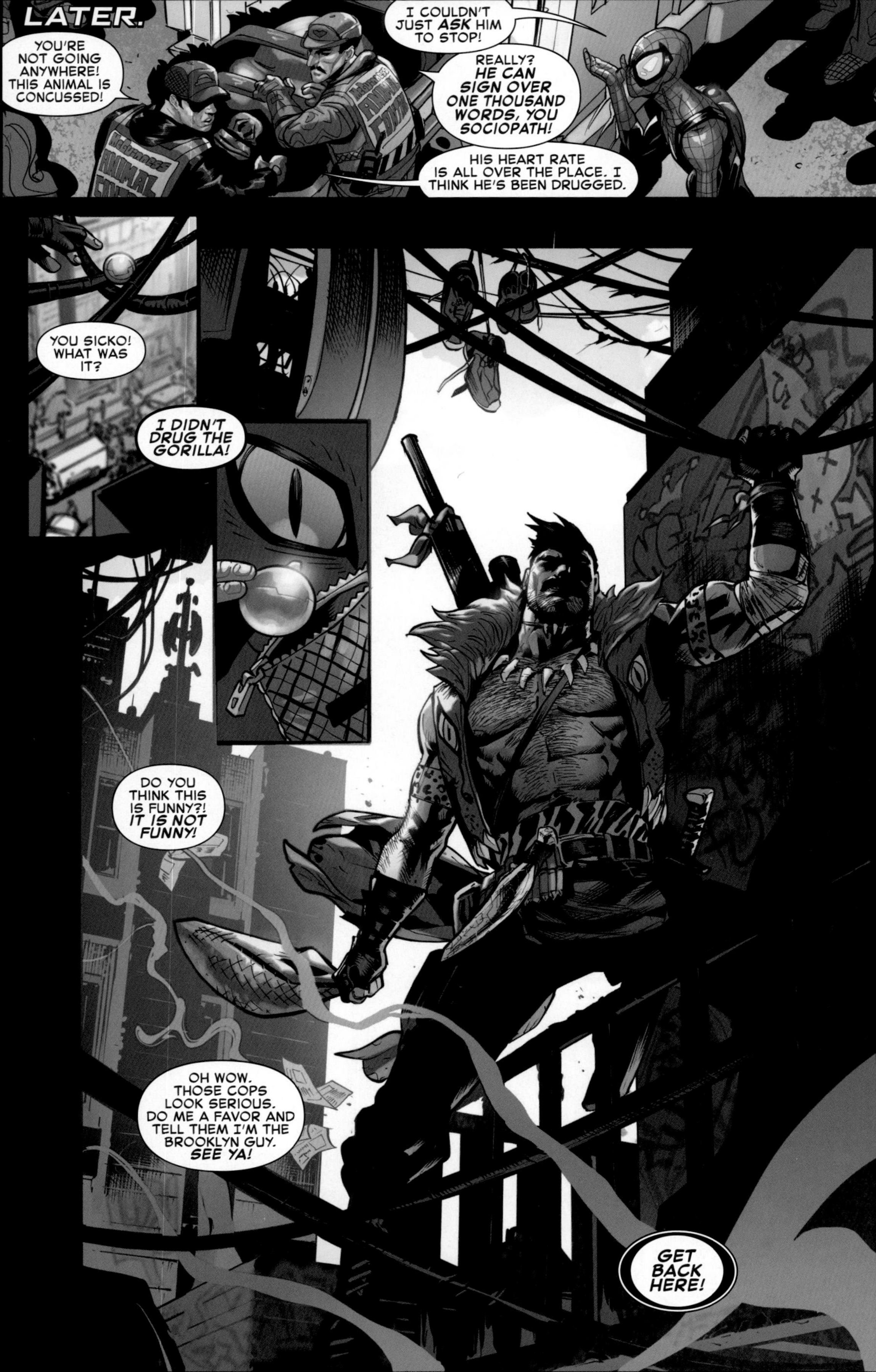
LATER.
YOU'RE NOT GOING ANYWHERE! THIS ANIMAL IS CONCUSSED!
I COULDN'T JUST ASK HIM TO STOP!
REALLY? HE CAN SIGN OVER ONE THOUSAND WORDS, YOU SOCIOPATH!
HIS HEART RATE IS ALL OVER THE PLACE. I THINK HE'S BEEN DRUGGED.
YOU SICKO! WHAT WAS IT?
I DIDN'T DRUG THE GORILLA!
DO YOU THINK THIS IS FUNNY?! IT IS NOT FUNNY!
OH WOW. THOSE COPS LOOK SERIOUS. DO ME A FAVOR AND TELL THEM I'M THE BROOKLYN GUY. SEE YA!
GET BACK HERE!

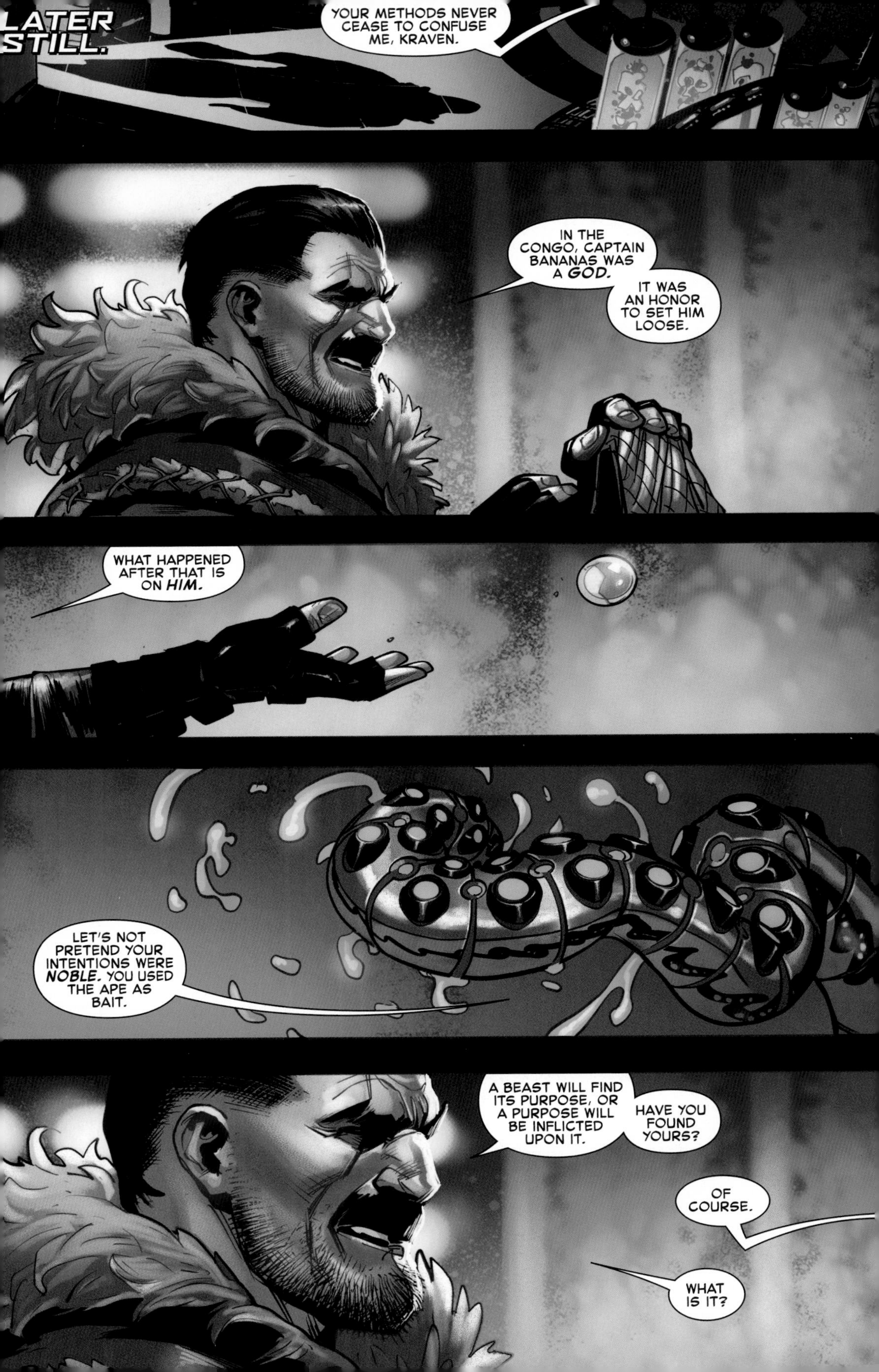
LATER STILL.
YOUR METHODS NEVER CEASE TO CONFUSE ME, KRAVEN.
IN THE CONGO, CAPTAIN BANANAS WAS A **GOD.**
IT WAS AN HONOR TO SET HIM LOOSE.
WHAT HAPPENED AFTER THAT IS ON ***HIM.***
LET'S NOT PRETEND YOUR INTENTIONS WERE ***NOBLE.*** YOU USED THE APE AS BAIT.
A BEAST WILL FIND ITS PURPOSE, OR A PURPOSE WILL BE INFLICTED UPON IT.
HAVE YOU FOUND YOURS?
OF COURSE.
WHAT IS IT?

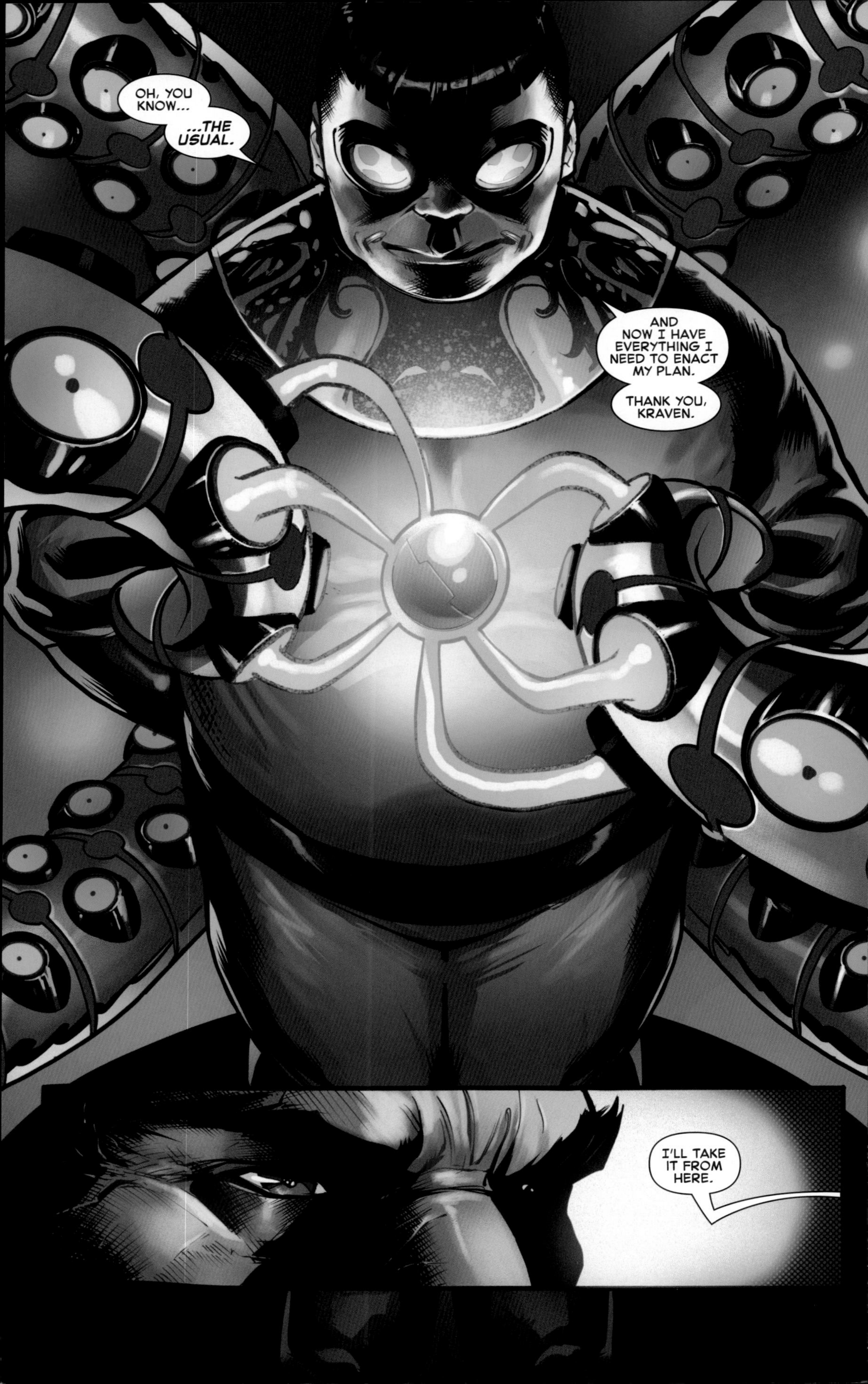
OH, YOU KNOW...
...THE USUAL.
AND NOW I HAVE EVERYTHING I NEED TO ENACT MY PLAN.
THANK YOU, KRAVEN.
I'LL TAKE IT FROM HERE.

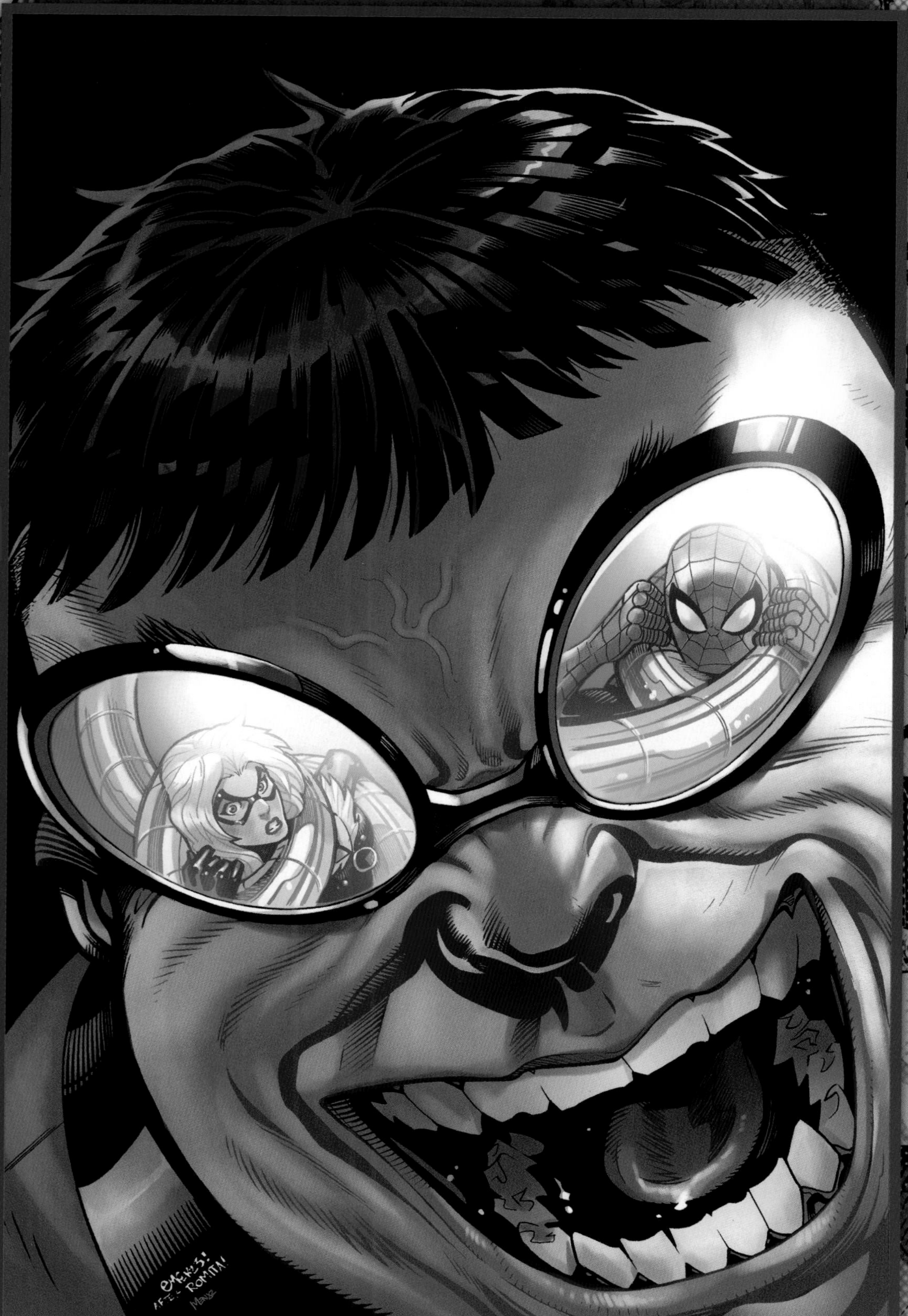

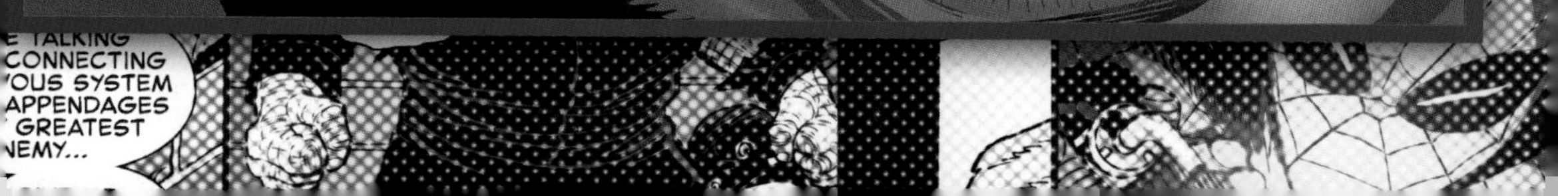
E TALKING
CONNECTING
VOUS SYSTEM
APPENDAGES
GREATEST
NEMY...

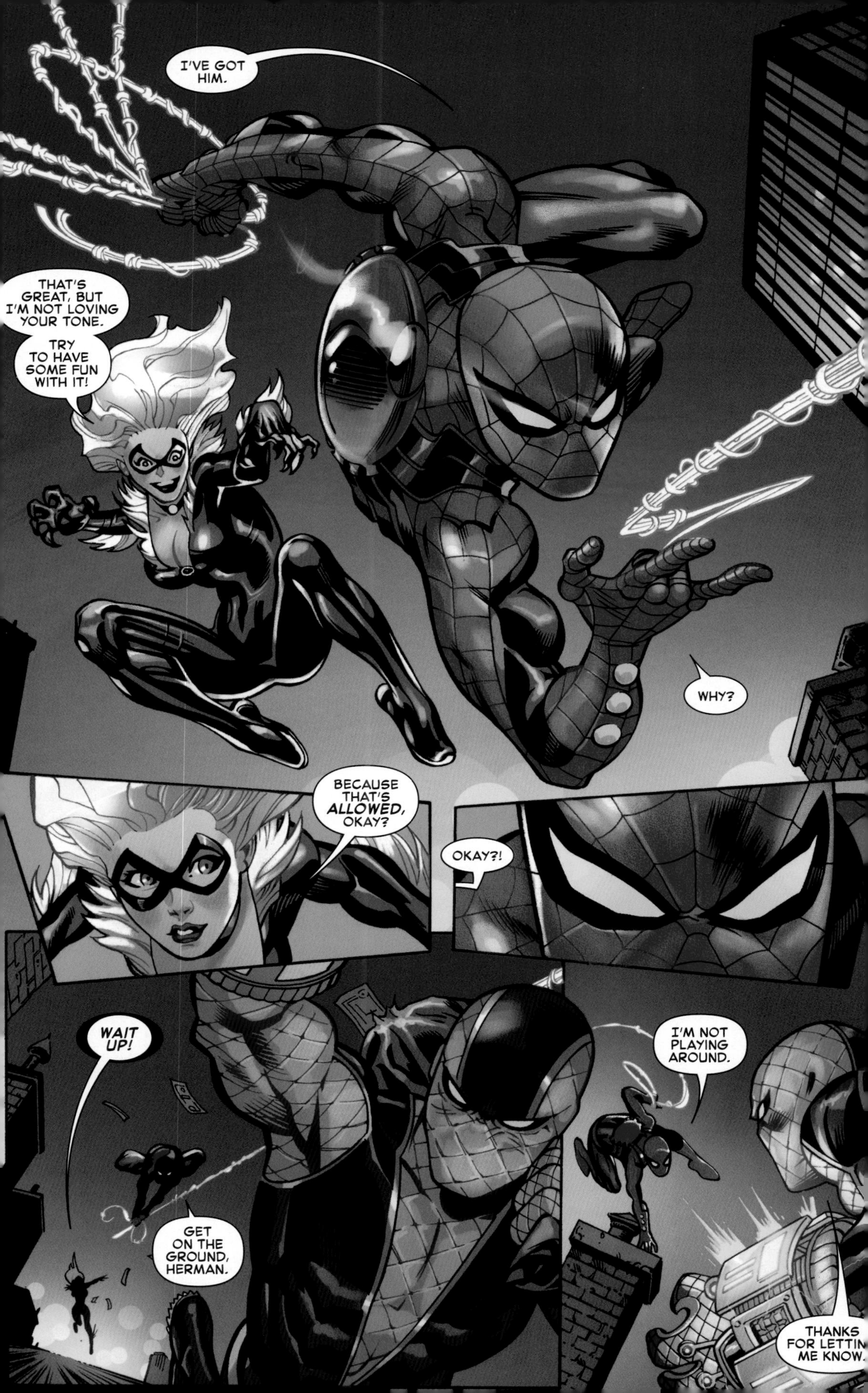

I'VE GOT HIM.
THAT'S GREAT, BUT I'M NOT LOVING YOUR TONE.
TRY TO HAVE SOME FUN WITH IT!
WHY?
BECAUSE THAT'S ALLOWED, OKAY?
OKAY?!
WAIT UP!
GET ON THE GROUND, HERMAN.
I'M NOT PLAYING AROUND.
THANKS FOR LETTIN ME KNOW.

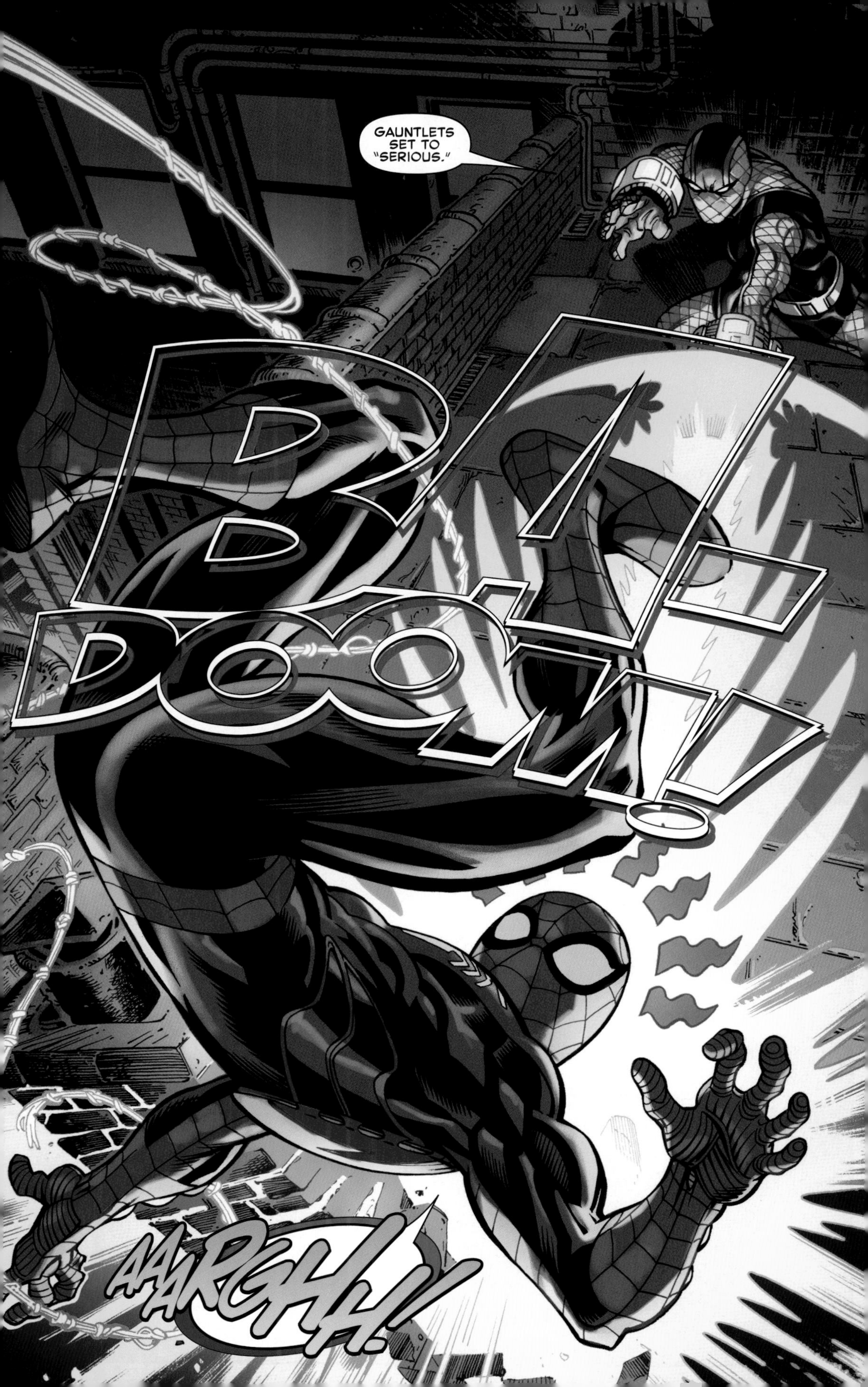
GAUNTLETS SET TO "SERIOUS."
BA-DOOM!!
AAARGHH!!

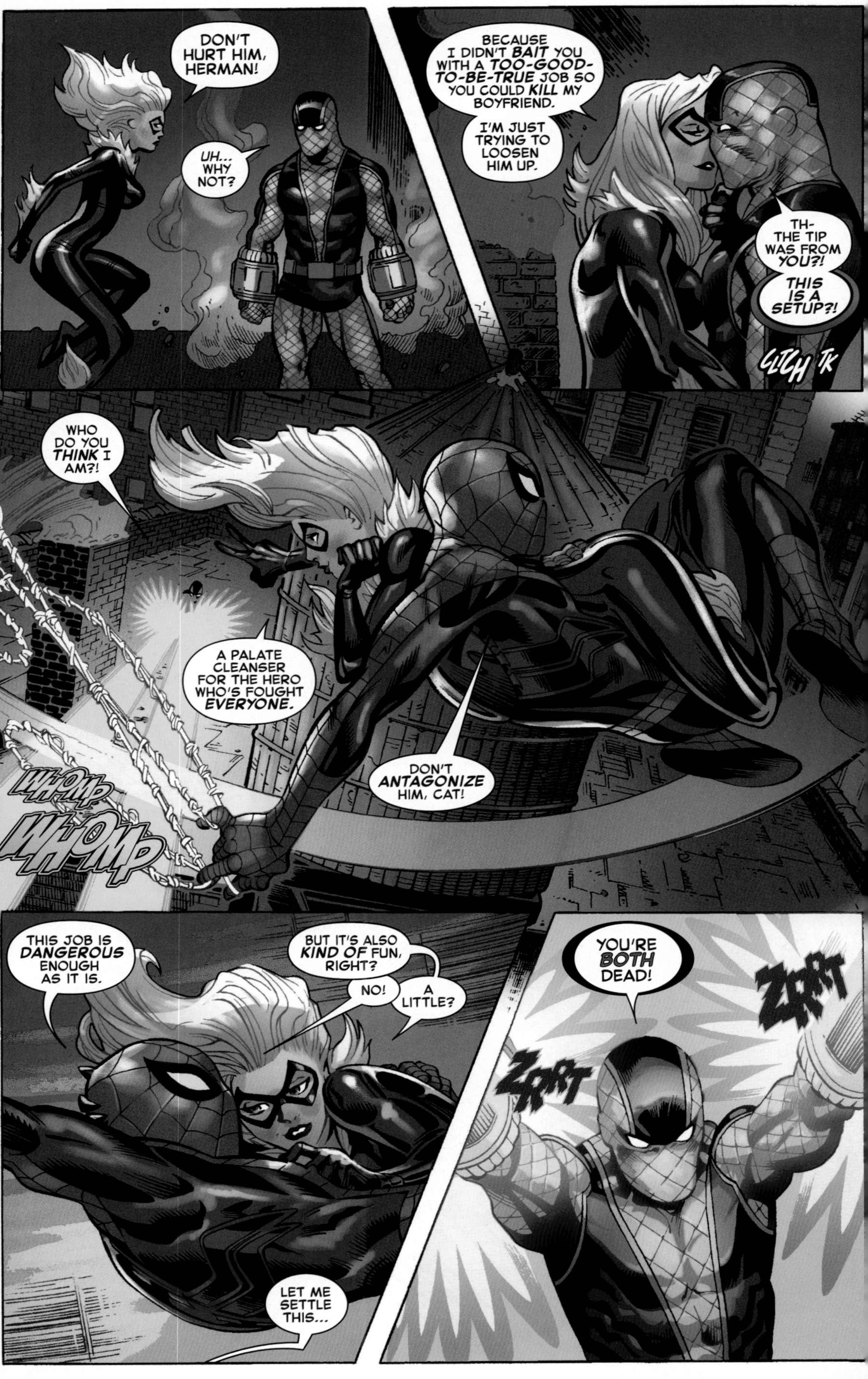
DON'T HURT HIM, HERMAN!
UH... WHY NOT?
BECAUSE I DIDN'T BAIT YOU WITH A TOO-GOOD-TO-BE-TRUE JOB SO YOU COULD KILL MY BOYFRIEND.
I'M JUST TRYING TO LOOSEN HIM UP.
TH- THE TIP WAS FROM YOU?!
THIS IS A SETUP?!
CLTCH
TK
WHO DO YOU THINK I AM?!
A PALATE CLEANSER FOR THE HERO WHO'S FOUGHT EVERYONE.
DON'T ANTAGONIZE HIM, CAT!
WHOMP
WHOMP
THIS JOB IS DANGEROUS ENOUGH AS IT IS.
BUT IT'S ALSO KIND OF FUN, RIGHT?
NO!
A LITTLE?
LET ME SETTLE THIS...
YOU'RE BOTH DEAD!
ZRRT
ZRRT

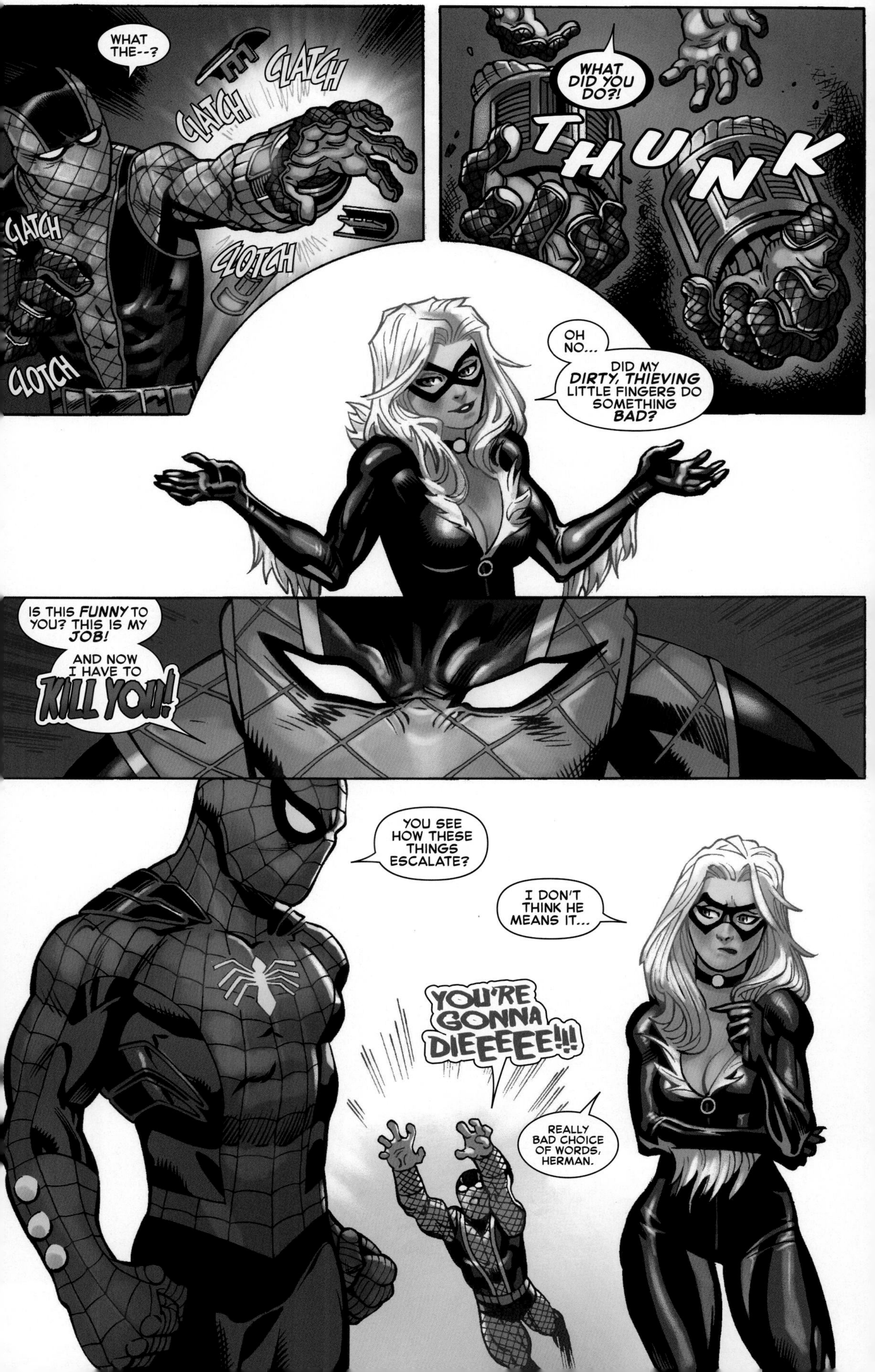
WHAT THE--?
CLATCH
CLATCH
CLATCH
CLOTCH
CLOTCH
WHAT DID YOU DO?!
THUNK
OH NO...
DID MY DIRTY, THIEVING LITTLE FINGERS DO SOMETHING BAD?
IS THIS FUNNY TO YOU? THIS IS MY JOB!
AND NOW I HAVE TO KILL YOU!
YOU SEE HOW THESE THINGS ESCALATE?
I DON'T THINK HE MEANS IT...
YOU'RE GONNA DIEEEEE!!!
REALLY BAD CHOICE OF WORDS, HERMAN.

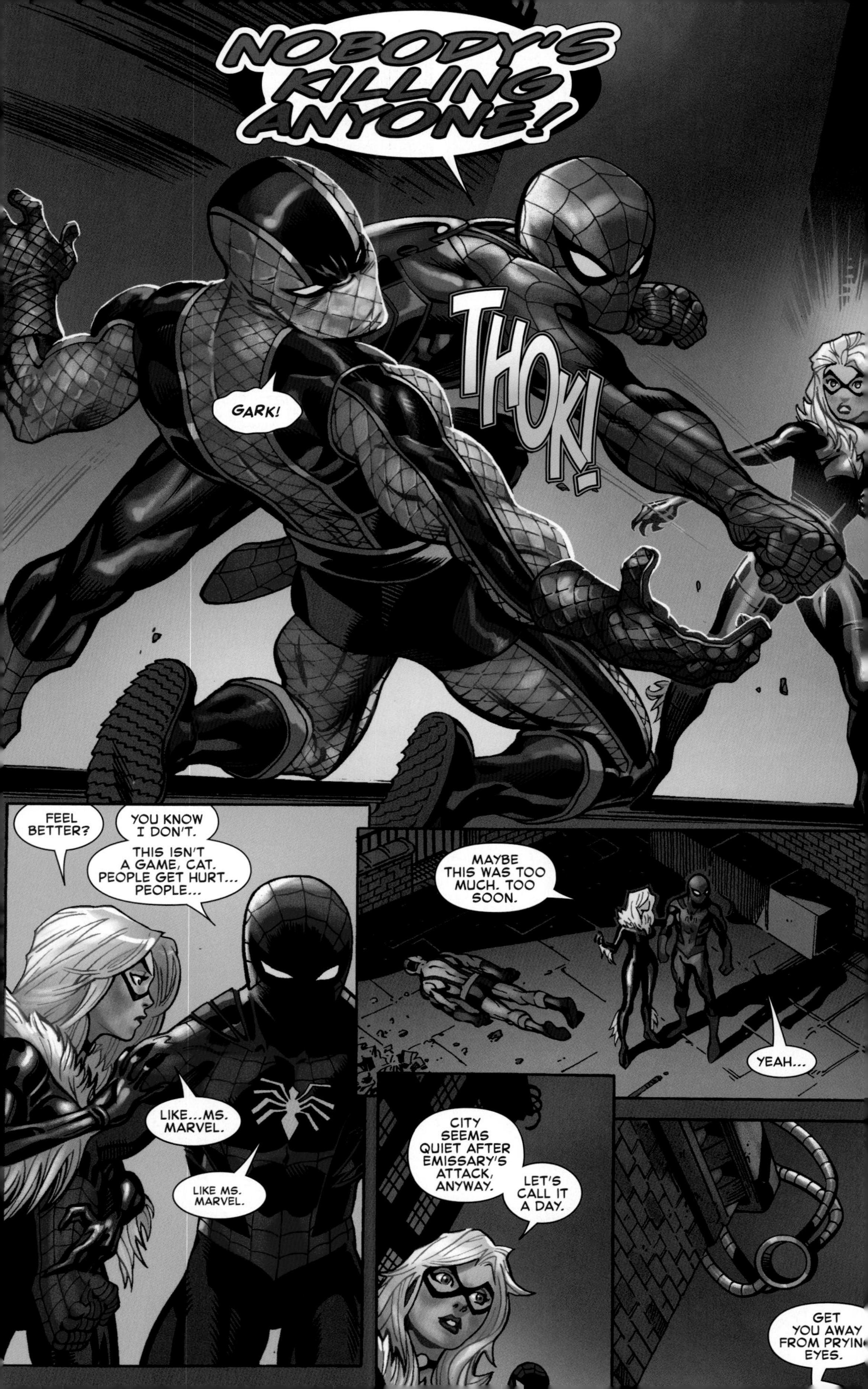
NOBODY'S KILLING ANYONE!
THOK!
GARK!
FEEL BETTER?
YOU KNOW I DON'T.
THIS ISN'T A GAME, CAT. PEOPLE GET HURT... PEOPLE...
LIKE...MS. MARVEL.
LIKE MS. MARVEL.
MAYBE THIS WAS TOO MUCH. TOO SOON.
YEAH...
CITY SEEMS QUIET AFTER EMISSARY'S ATTACK, ANYWAY.
LET'S CALL IT A DAY.
GET YOU AWAY FROM PRYIN EYES.

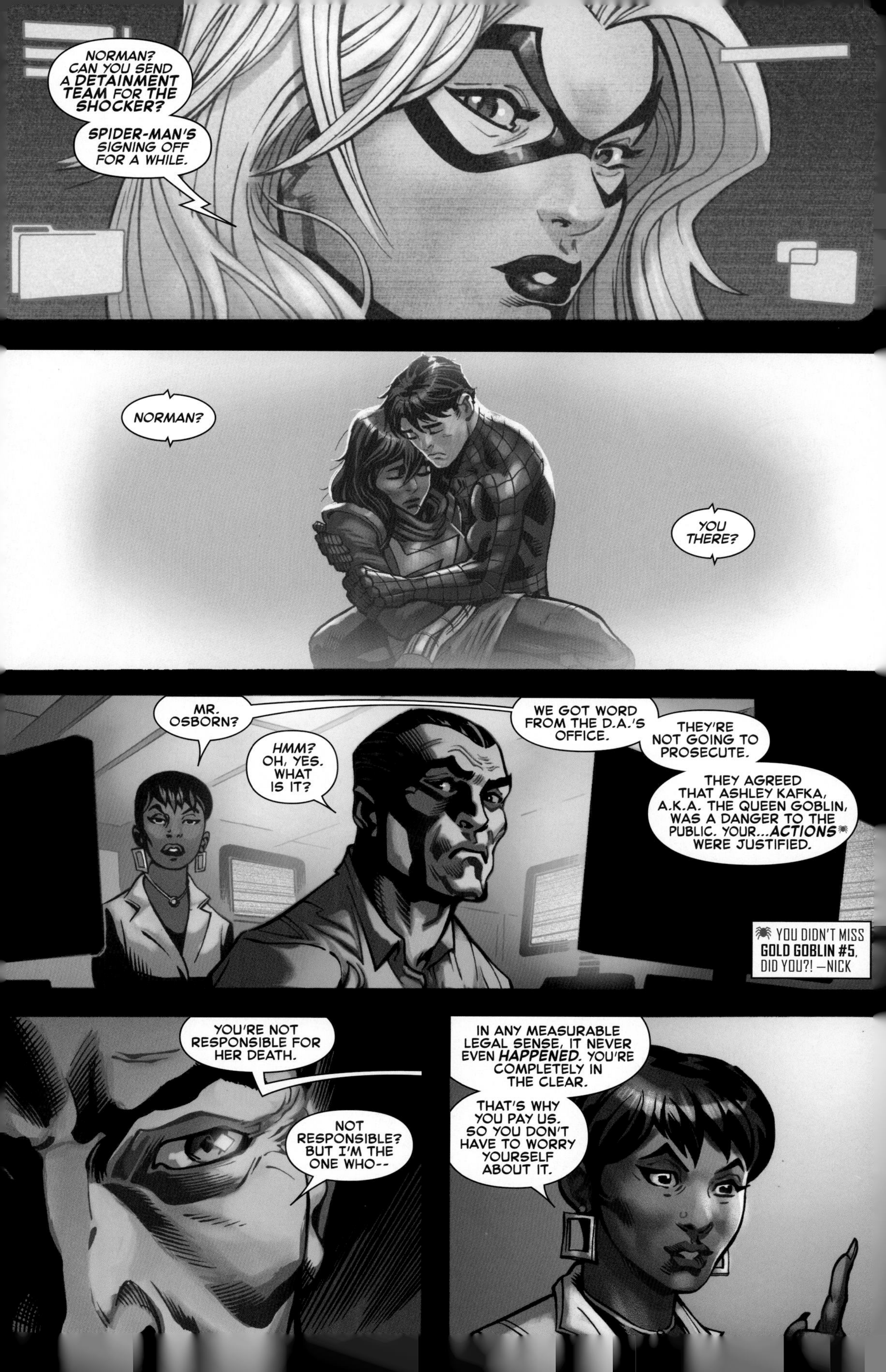
NORMAN? CAN YOU SEND A DETAINMENT TEAM FOR THE SHOCKER?
SPIDER-MAN'S SIGNING OFF FOR A WHILE.
NORMAN?
YOU THERE?
MR. OSBORN?
HMM? OH, YES. WHAT IS IT?
WE GOT WORD FROM THE D.A.'S OFFICE.
THEY'RE NOT GOING TO PROSECUTE.
THEY AGREED THAT ASHLEY KAFKA, A.K.A. THE QUEEN GOBLIN, WAS A DANGER TO THE PUBLIC. YOUR...ACTIONS WERE JUSTIFIED.
YOU DIDN'T MISS GOLD GOBLIN #5, DID YOU?! —NICK
YOU'RE NOT RESPONSIBLE FOR HER DEATH.
NOT RESPONSIBLE? BUT I'M THE ONE WHO--
IN ANY MEASURABLE LEGAL SENSE, IT NEVER EVEN HAPPENED. YOU'RE COMPLETELY IN THE CLEAR.
THAT'S WHY YOU PAY US. SO YOU DON'T HAVE TO WORRY YOURSELF ABOUT IT.

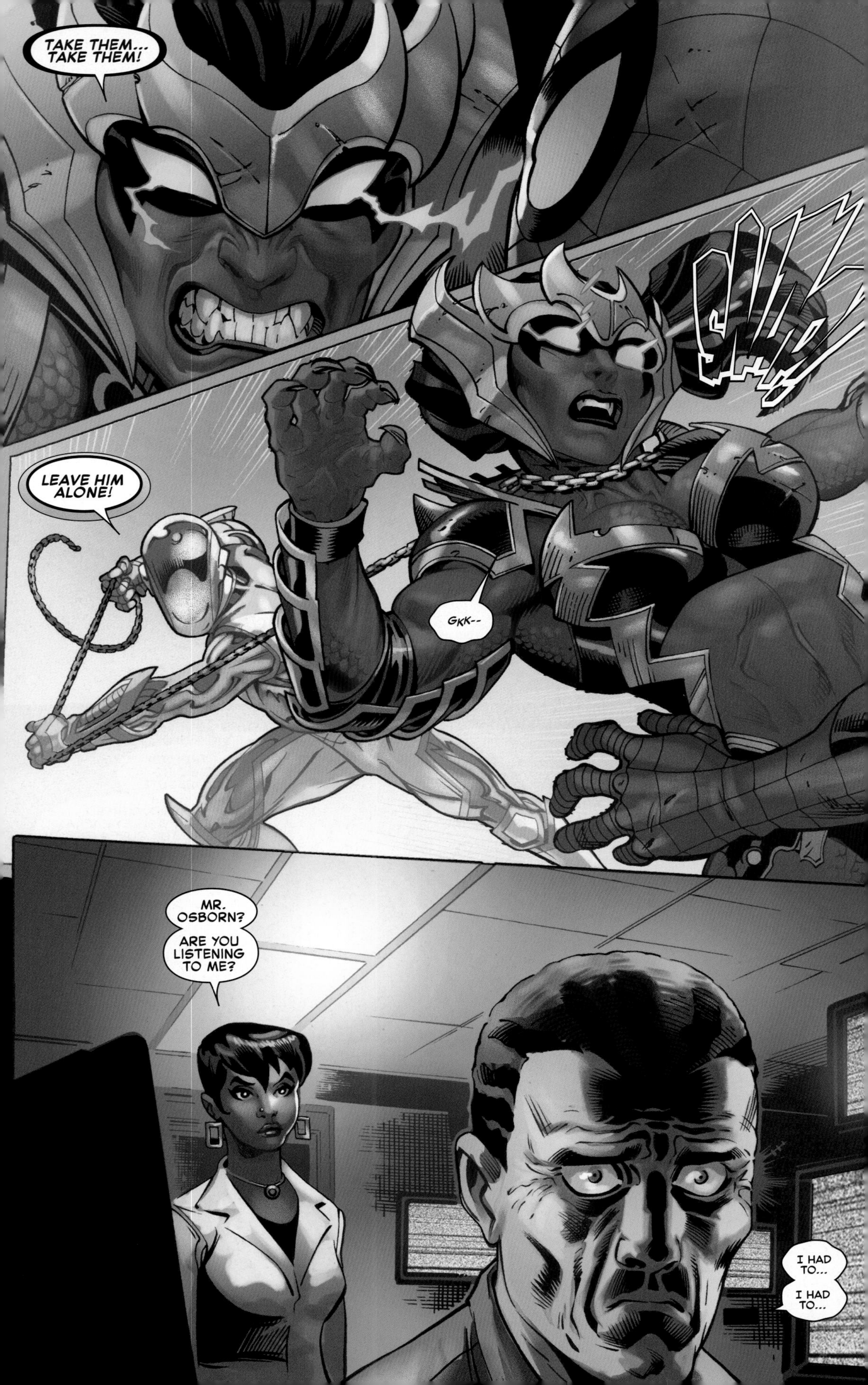
TAKE THEM... TAKE THEM!
SHZZZ
LEAVE HIM ALONE!
GKK--
MR. OSBORN?
ARE YOU LISTENING TO ME?
I HAD TO...
I HAD TO...

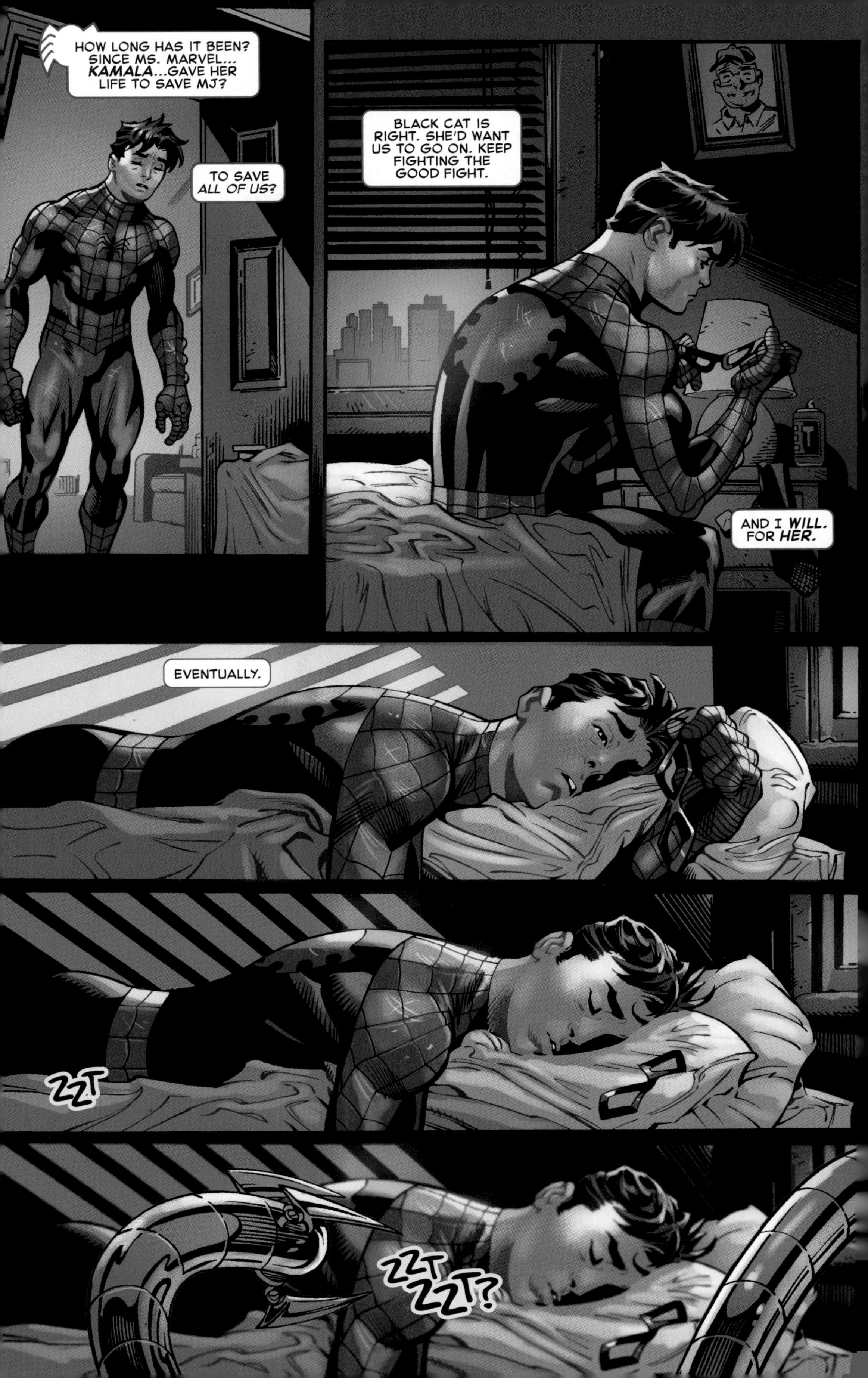
HOW LONG HAS IT BEEN? SINCE MS. MARVEL... KAMALA...GAVE HER LIFE TO SAVE MJ?
TO SAVE ALL OF US?
BLACK CAT IS RIGHT. SHE'D WANT US TO GO ON. KEEP FIGHTING THE GOOD FIGHT.
AND I WILL. FOR HER.
EVENTUALLY.
ZZT
ZZT
ZZT?

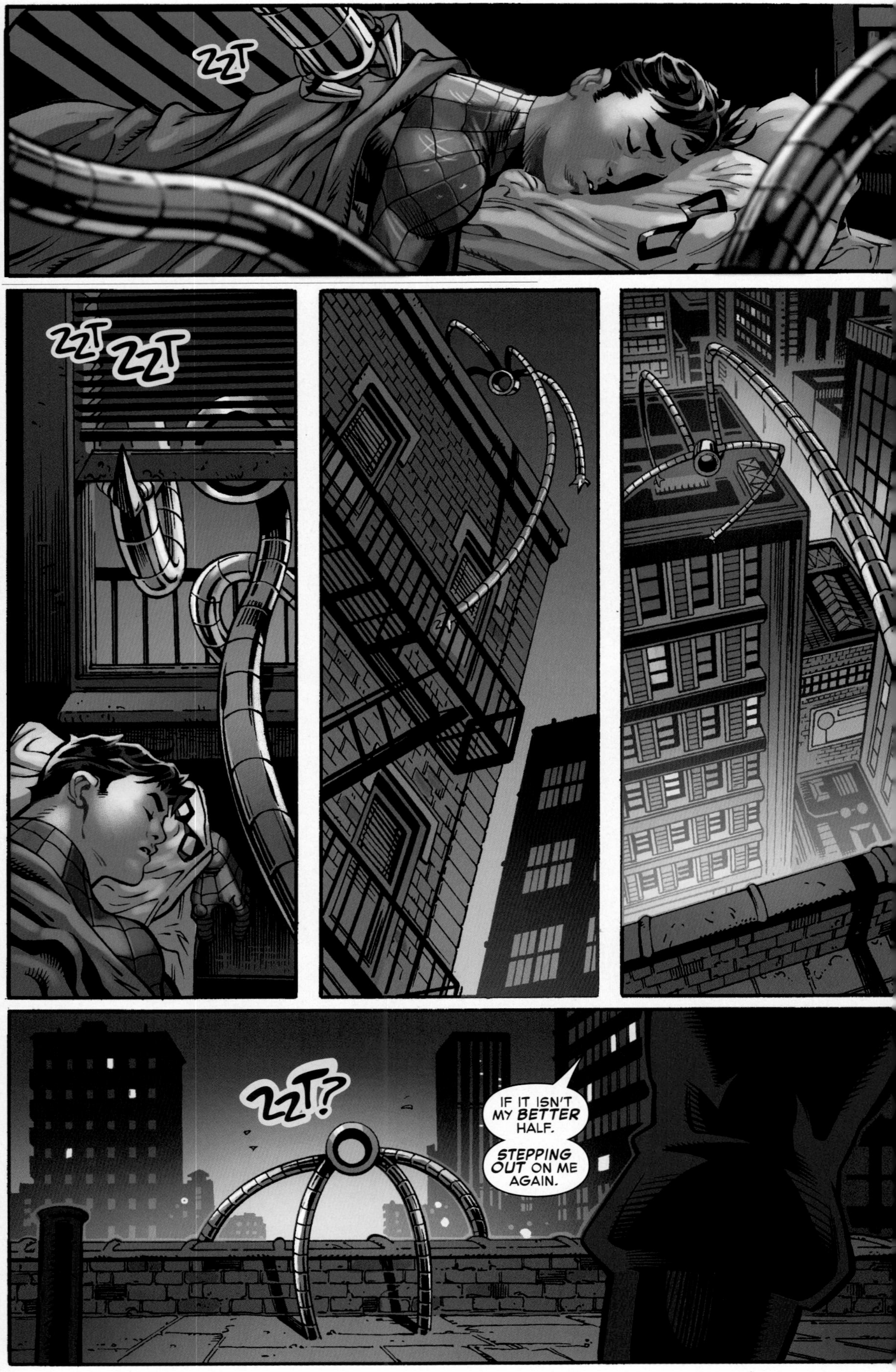

ZZT
ZZT ZZT
ZZT?
IF IT ISN'T MY BETTER HALF.
STEPPING OUT ON ME AGAIN.

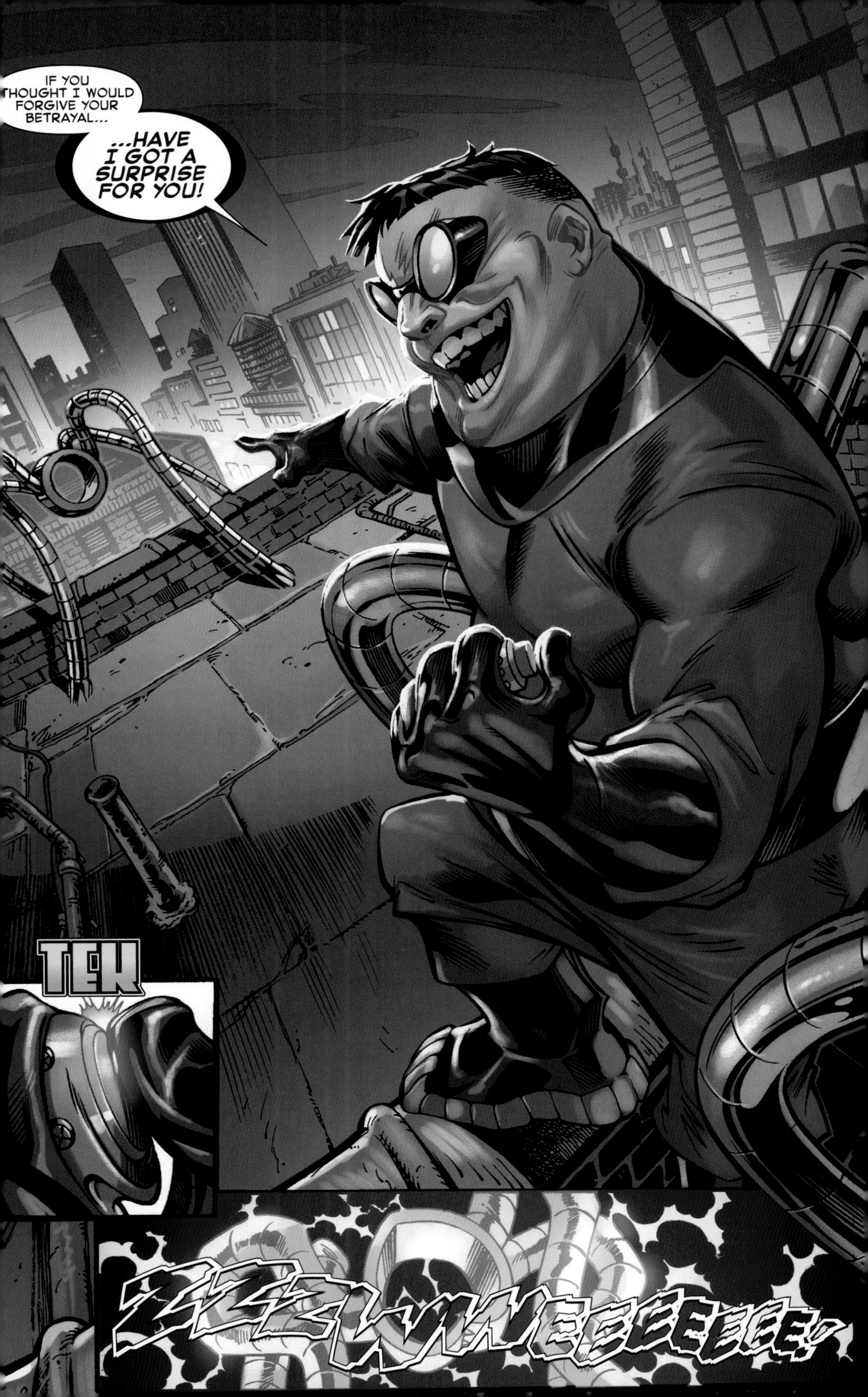
IF YOU THOUGHT I WOULD FORGIVE YOUR BETRAYAL...
...HAVE I GOT A SURPRISE FOR YOU!
TEK

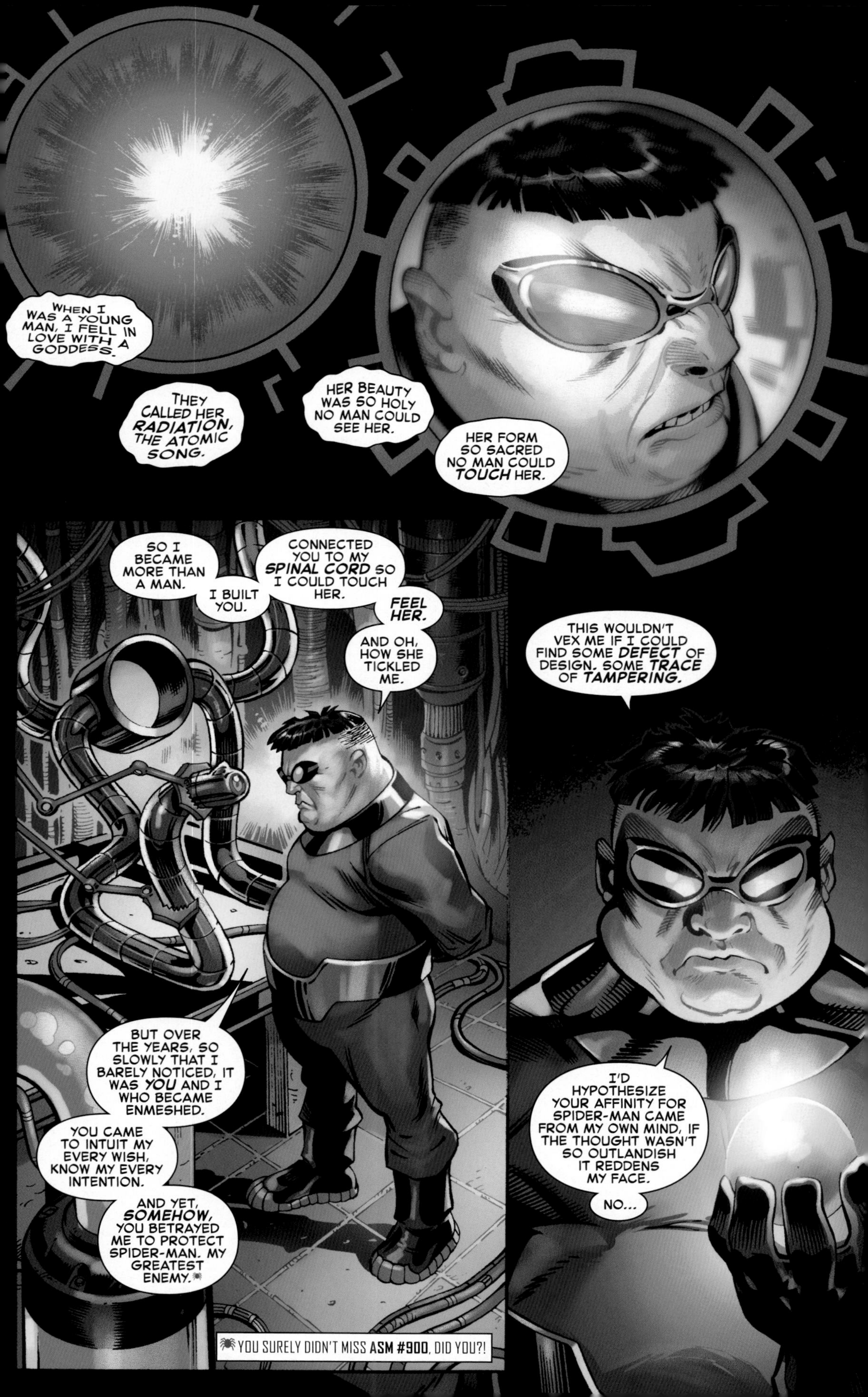
WHEN I WAS A YOUNG MAN, I FELL IN LOVE WITH A GODDESS.
THEY CALLED HER RADIATION, THE ATOMIC SONG.
HER BEAUTY WAS SO HOLY NO MAN COULD SEE HER.
HER FORM SO SACRED NO MAN COULD TOUCH HER.
SO I BECAME MORE THAN A MAN.
I BUILT YOU.
CONNECTED YOU TO MY SPINAL CORD SO I COULD TOUCH HER.
FEEL HER.
AND OH, HOW SHE TICKLED ME.
BUT OVER THE YEARS, SO SLOWLY THAT I BARELY NOTICED, IT WAS YOU AND I WHO BECAME ENMESHED.
YOU CAME TO INTUIT MY EVERY WISH, KNOW MY EVERY INTENTION.
AND YET, SOMEHOW, YOU BETRAYED ME TO PROTECT SPIDER-MAN. MY GREATEST ENEMY.
YOU SURELY DIDN'T MISS ASM #900, DID YOU?!
THIS WOULDN'T VEX ME IF I COULD FIND SOME DEFECT OF DESIGN. SOME TRACE OF TAMPERING.
I'D HYPOTHESIZE YOUR AFFINITY FOR SPIDER-MAN CAME FROM MY OWN MIND, IF THE THOUGHT WASN'T SO OUTLANDISH IT REDDENS MY FACE.
NO...

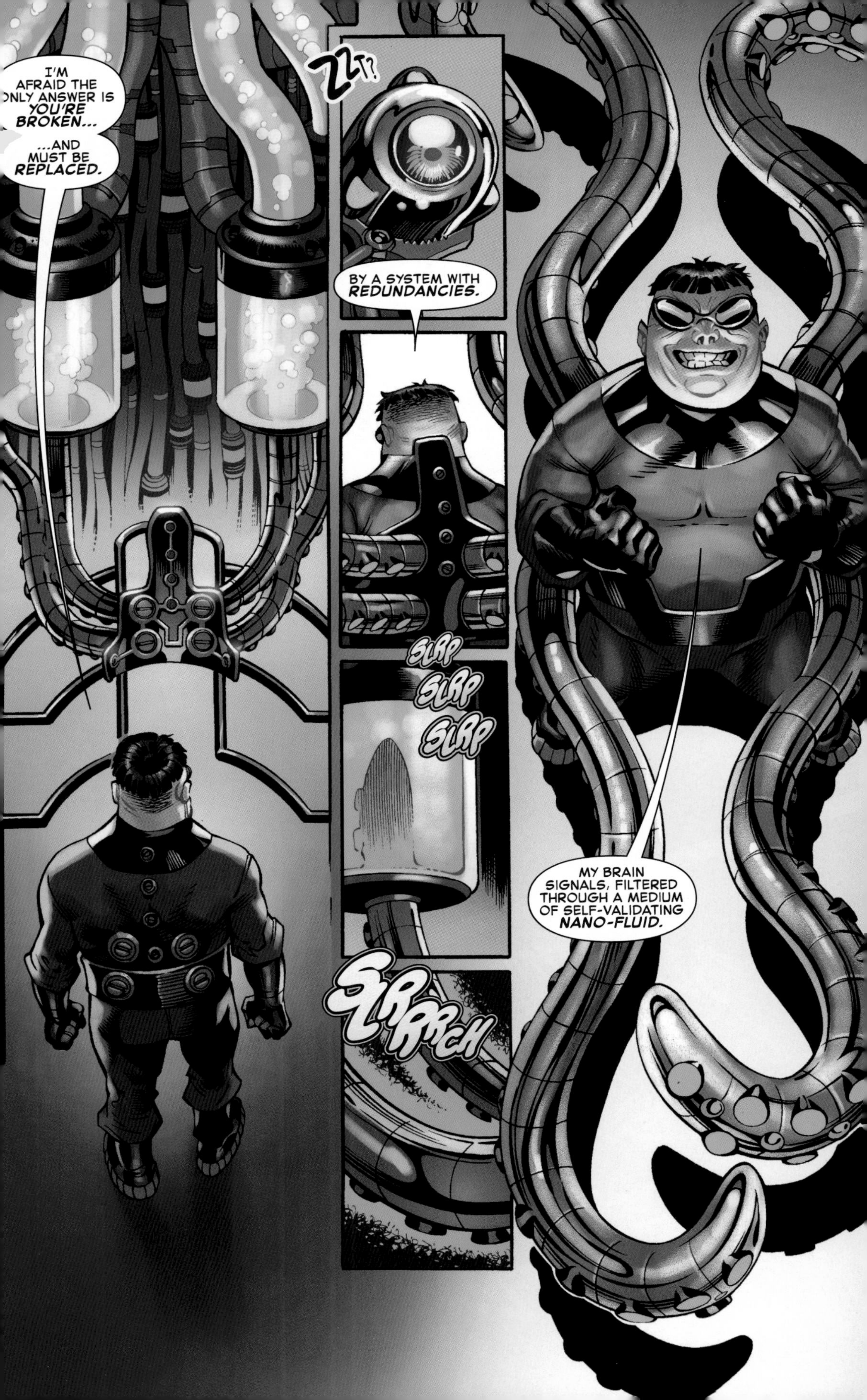
I'M AFRAID THE ONLY ANSWER IS YOU'RE BROKEN...
...AND MUST BE REPLACED.
ZZT?
BY A SYSTEM WITH REDUNDANCIES.
SLRP
SLRP
SLRP
SKRRRCH
MY BRAIN SIGNALS, FILTERED THROUGH A MEDIUM OF SELF-VALIDATING NANO-FLUID.

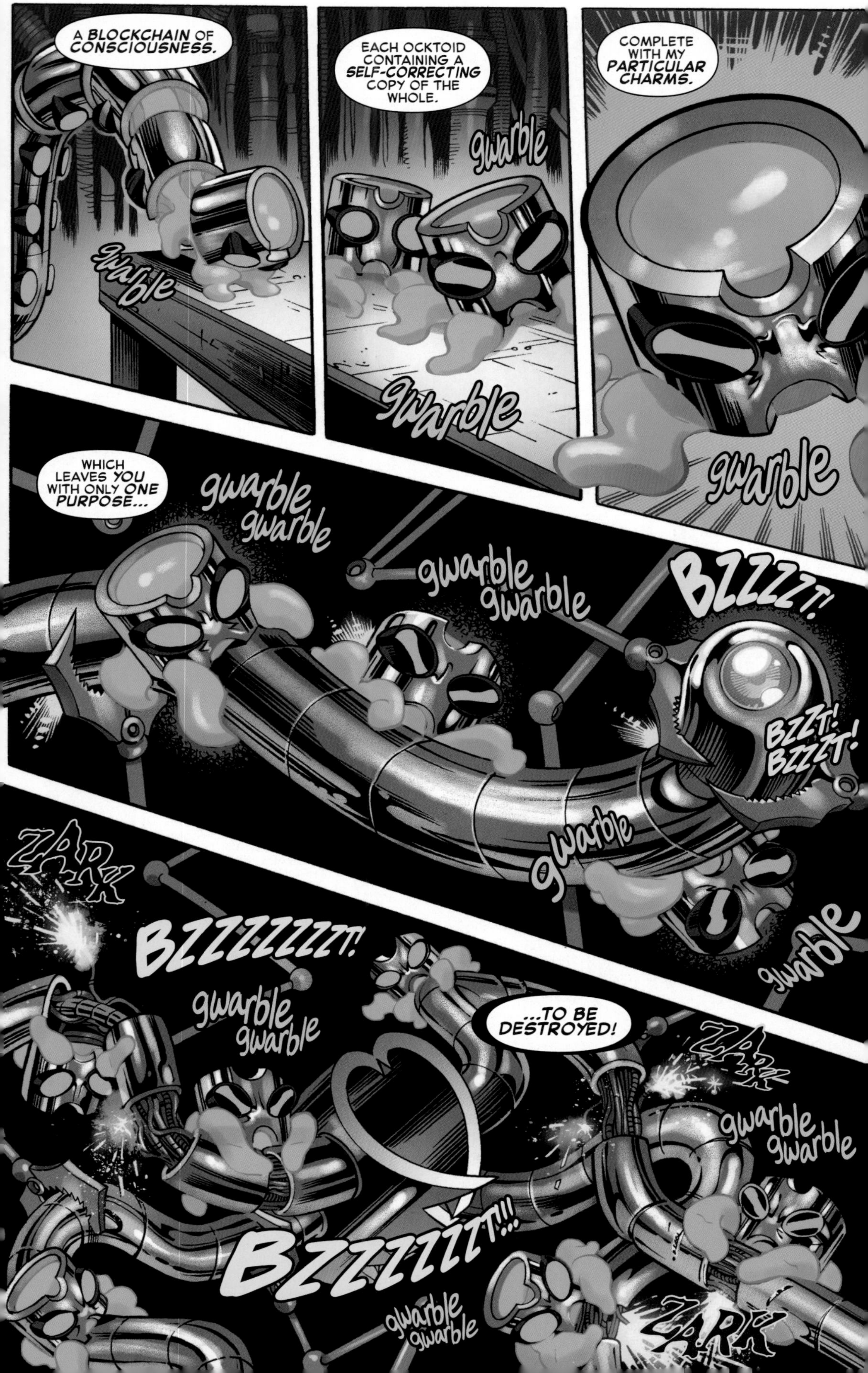
A BLOCKCHAIN OF CONSCIOUSNESS.
gwarble
EACH OCKTOID CONTAINING A SELF-CORRECTING COPY OF THE WHOLE.
gwarble
gwarble
COMPLETE WITH MY PARTICULAR CHARMS.
gwarble
WHICH LEAVES YOU WITH ONLY ONE PURPOSE...
gwarble gwarble
gwarble gwarble
BZZZZT!
BZZT! BZZZT!
gwarble
gwarble
ZARK
BZZZZZZZZT!
gwarble gwarble
...TO BE DESTROYED!
ZARK
gwarble gwarble
BZZZZZZZT!!!
gwarble gwarble
ZARK

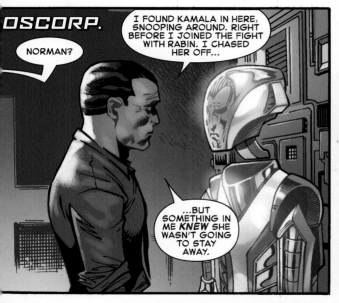

NORMAN?

I FOUND KAMALA IN HERE, SNOOPING AROUND. RIGHT BEFORE I JOINED THE FIGHT WITH RABIN. I CHASED HER OFF...

...BUT SOMETHING IN ME *KNEW* SHE WASN'T GOING TO STAY AWAY.

I RECOGNIZED SOMETHING IN HER. THE SAME THING I ALWAYS SAW IN YOU.

THE DAMN *HEROISM.*

AND NOW I RECOGNIZE SOMETHING FAR LESS FLATTERING IN MYSELF. A *BODY COUNT* THAT SEEMS TO FOLLOW ME AROUND.

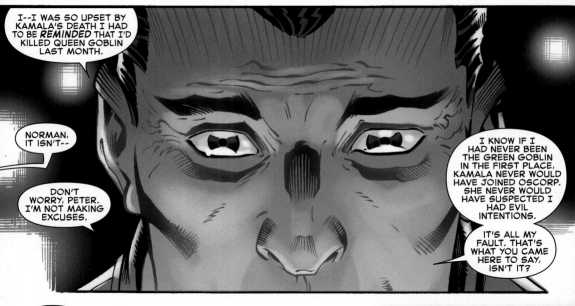

I--I WAS SO UPSET BY KAMALA'S DEATH I HAD TO BE *REMINDED* THAT I'D KILLED QUEEN GOBLIN LAST MONTH.

NORMAN, IT ISN'T--

DON'T WORRY, PETER. I'M NOT MAKING EXCUSES.

I KNOW IF I HAD NEVER BEEN THE GREEN GOBLIN IN THE FIRST PLACE, KAMALA NEVER WOULD HAVE JOINED OSCORP. SHE NEVER WOULD HAVE SUSPECTED I HAD EVIL INTENTIONS.

IT'S ALL MY FAULT. THAT'S WHAT YOU CAME HERE TO SAY, ISN'T IT?

NO, NORMAN. NOT AT ALL.

I CAME HERE TO MAKE SURE YOU'RE OKAY. TO MAKE SURE YOU CAN HANDLE ALL THIS. TO MAKE SURE YOU DON'T...

YOU KNOW.

OH.

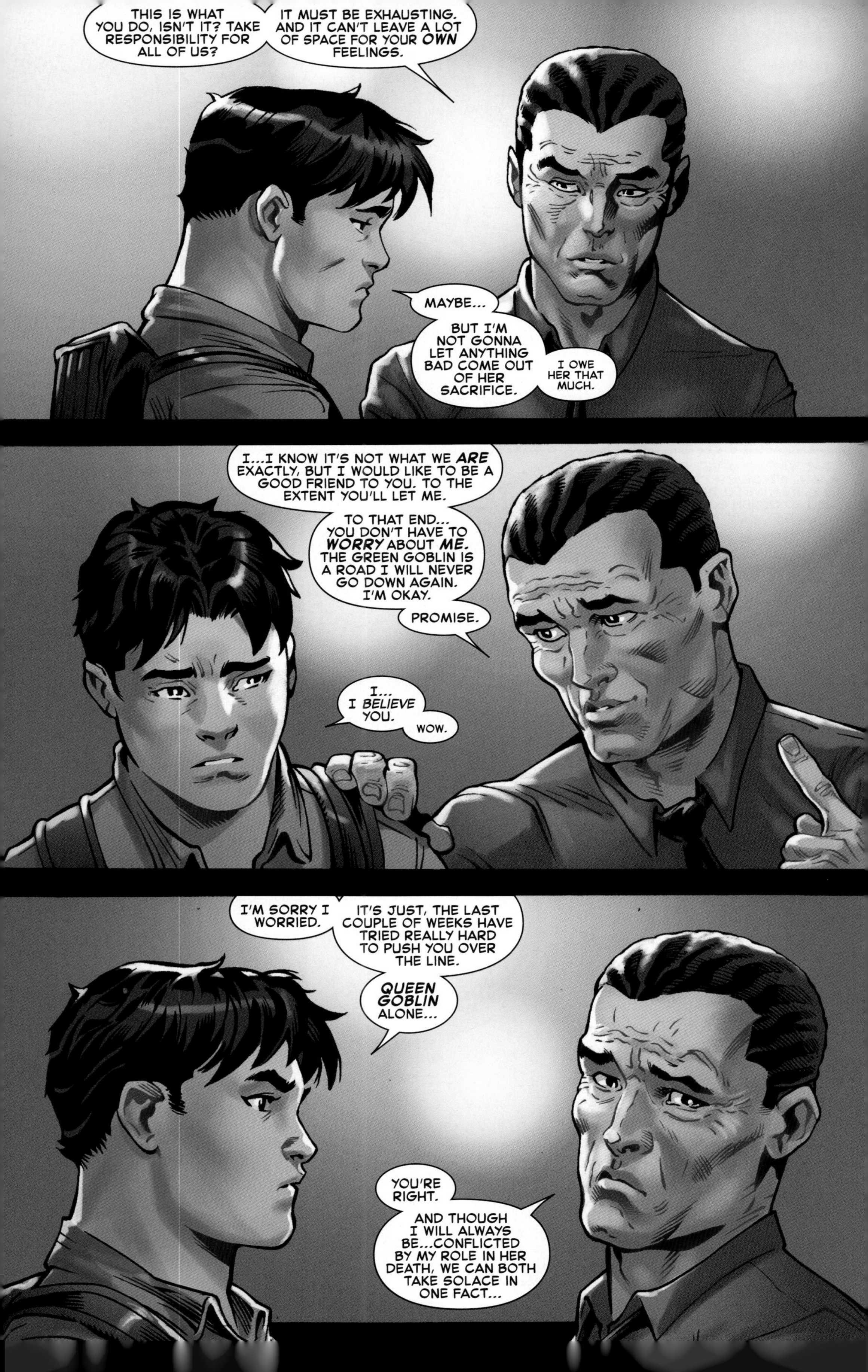
THIS IS WHAT YOU DO, ISN'T IT? TAKE RESPONSIBILITY FOR ALL OF US?
IT MUST BE EXHAUSTING. AND IT CAN'T LEAVE A LOT OF SPACE FOR YOUR *OWN* FEELINGS.
MAYBE...
BUT I'M NOT GONNA LET ANYTHING BAD COME OUT OF HER SACRIFICE.
I OWE HER THAT MUCH.
I...I KNOW IT'S NOT WHAT WE *ARE* EXACTLY, BUT I WOULD LIKE TO BE A GOOD FRIEND TO YOU. TO THE EXTENT YOU'LL LET ME.
TO THAT END... YOU DON'T HAVE TO *WORRY* ABOUT *ME.* THE GREEN GOBLIN IS A ROAD I WILL NEVER GO DOWN AGAIN. I'M OKAY.
PROMISE.
I... I *BELIEVE* YOU.
WOW.
I'M SORRY I WORRIED.
IT'S JUST, THE LAST COUPLE OF WEEKS HAVE TRIED REALLY HARD TO PUSH YOU OVER THE LINE.
QUEEN GOBLIN ALONE...
YOU'RE RIGHT.
AND THOUGH I WILL ALWAYS BE...CONFLICTED BY MY ROLE IN HER DEATH, WE CAN BOTH TAKE SOLACE IN ONE FACT...

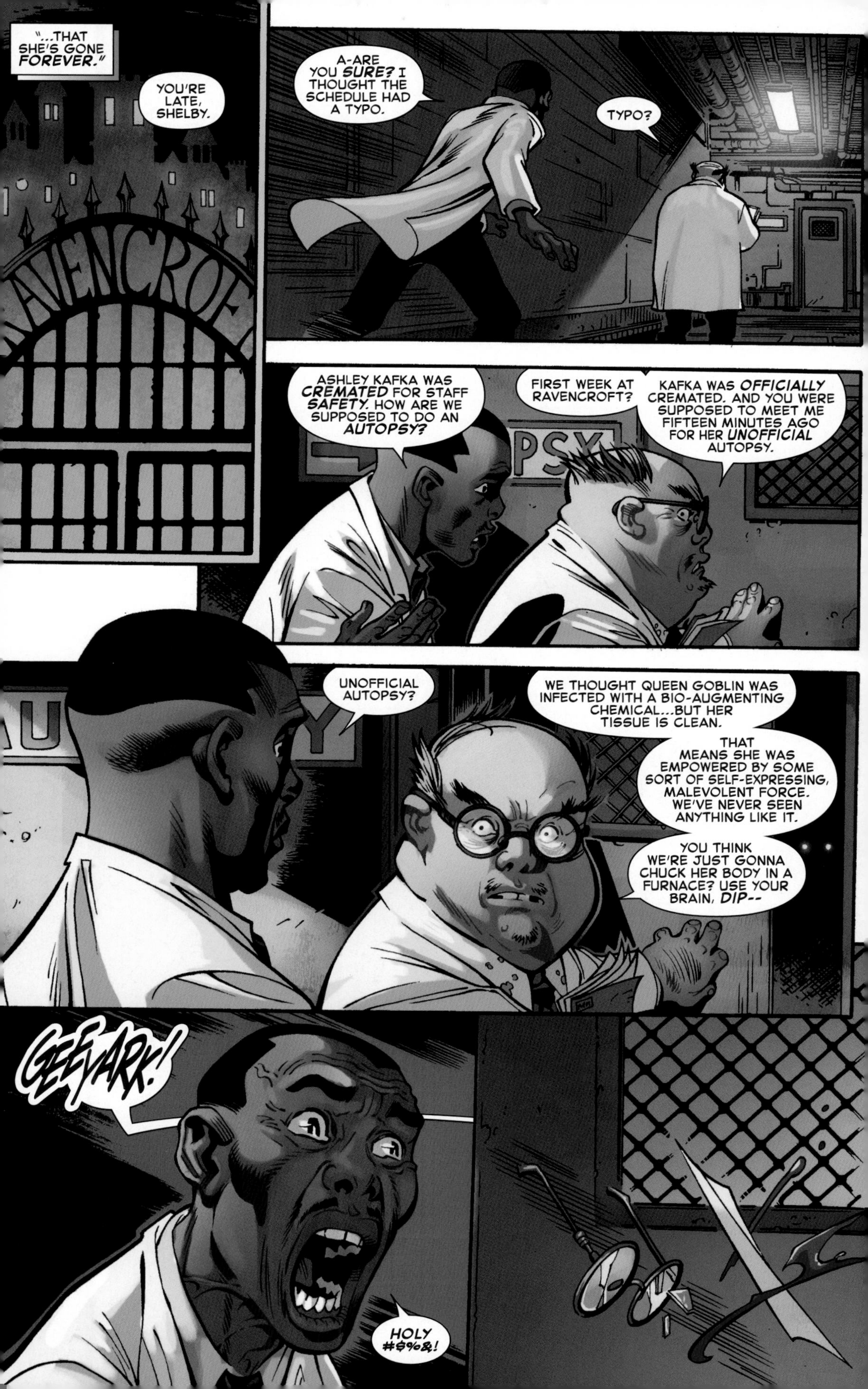
"...THAT SHE'S GONE FOREVER."
YOU'RE LATE, SHELBY.
RAVENCROFT
A-ARE YOU SURE? I THOUGHT THE SCHEDULE HAD A TYPO.
TYPO?
ASHLEY KAFKA WAS CREMATED FOR STAFF SAFETY. HOW ARE WE SUPPOSED TO DO AN AUTOPSY?
FIRST WEEK AT RAVENCROFT?
KAFKA WAS OFFICIALLY CREMATED. AND YOU WERE SUPPOSED TO MEET ME FIFTEEN MINUTES AGO FOR HER UNOFFICIAL AUTOPSY.
UNOFFICIAL AUTOPSY?
WE THOUGHT QUEEN GOBLIN WAS INFECTED WITH A BIO-AUGMENTING CHEMICAL...BUT HER TISSUE IS CLEAN.
THAT MEANS SHE WAS EMPOWERED BY SOME SORT OF SELF-EXPRESSING, MALEVOLENT FORCE. WE'VE NEVER SEEN ANYTHING LIKE IT.
YOU THINK WE'RE JUST GONNA CHUCK HER BODY IN A FURNACE? USE YOUR BRAIN, DIP--
GEEYARK!
HOLY #$%&!

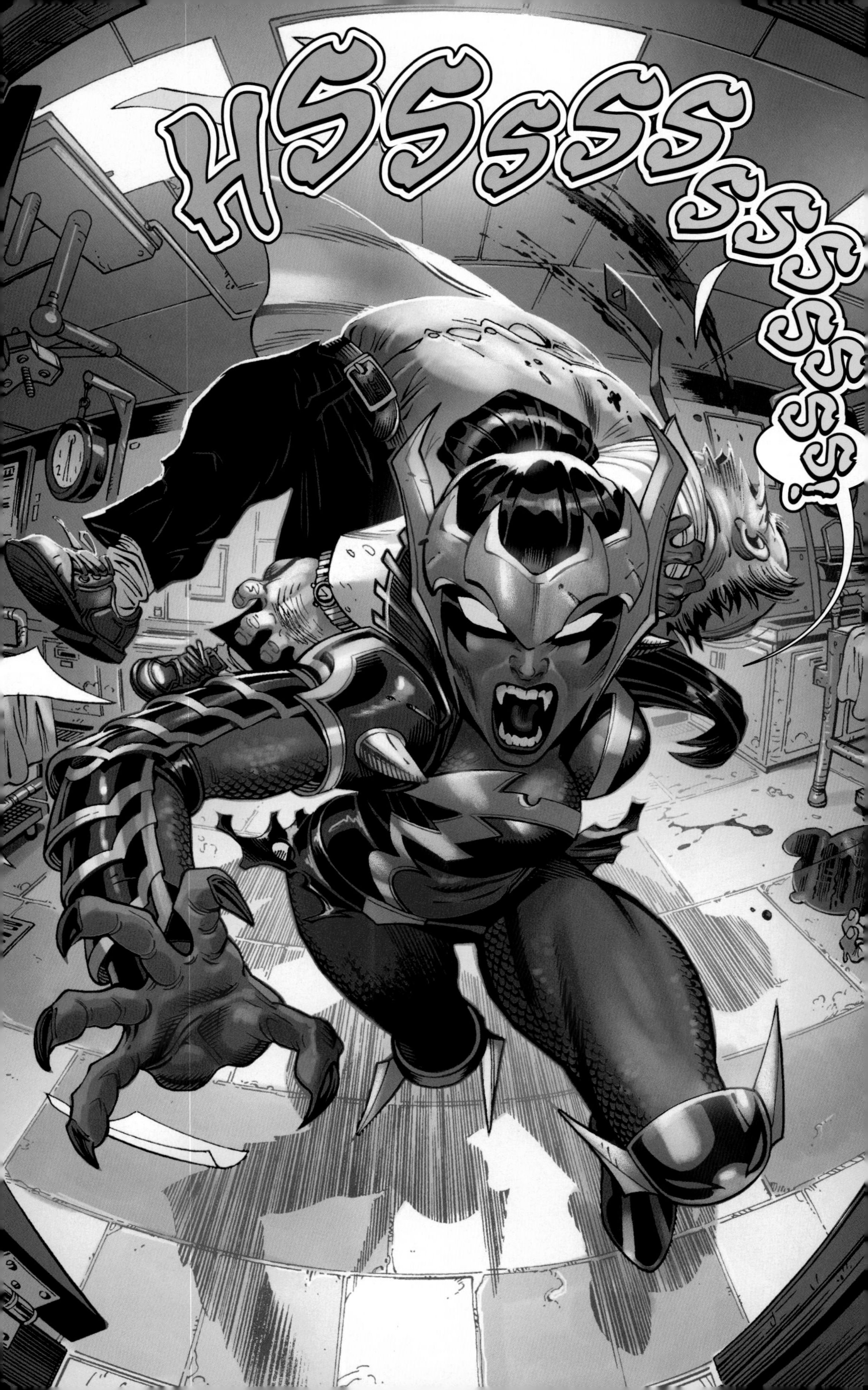
HSSssSSSSSSSS!

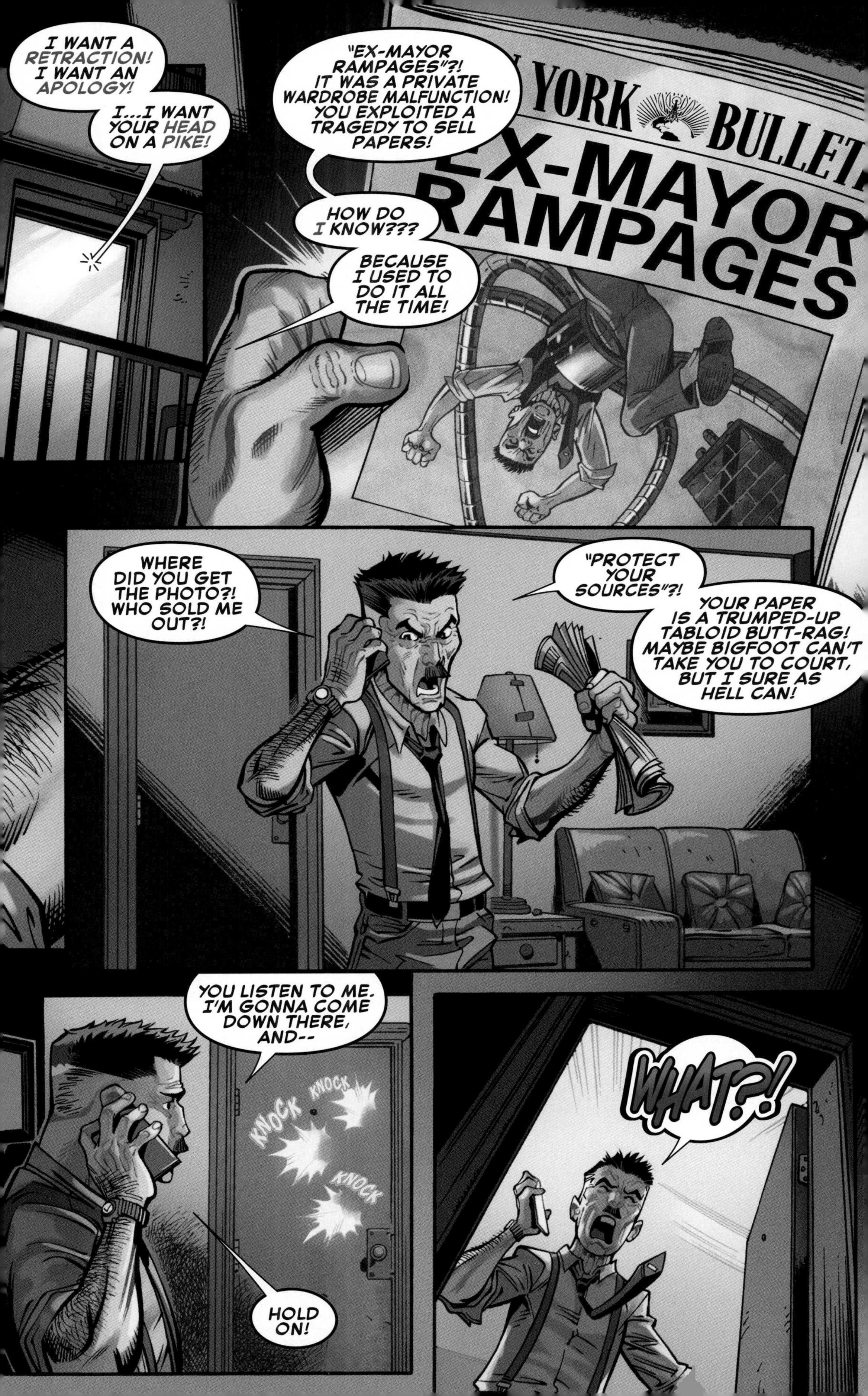
I WANT A RETRACTION! I WANT AN APOLOGY!
I...I WANT YOUR HEAD ON A PIKE!
"EX-MAYOR RAMPAGES"?! IT WAS A PRIVATE WARDROBE MALFUNCTION! YOU EXPLOITED A TRAGEDY TO SELL PAPERS!
YORK BULLET
EX-MAYOR RAMPAGES
HOW DO I KNOW???
BECAUSE I USED TO DO IT ALL THE TIME!
WHERE DID YOU GET THE PHOTO?! WHO SOLD ME OUT?!
"PROTECT YOUR SOURCES"?!
YOUR PAPER IS A TRUMPED-UP TABLOID BUTT-RAG! MAYBE BIGFOOT CAN'T TAKE YOU TO COURT, BUT I SURE AS HELL CAN!
YOU LISTEN TO ME. I'M GONNA COME DOWN THERE, AND--
KNOCK
KNOCK
KNOCK
HOLD ON!
WHAT?!

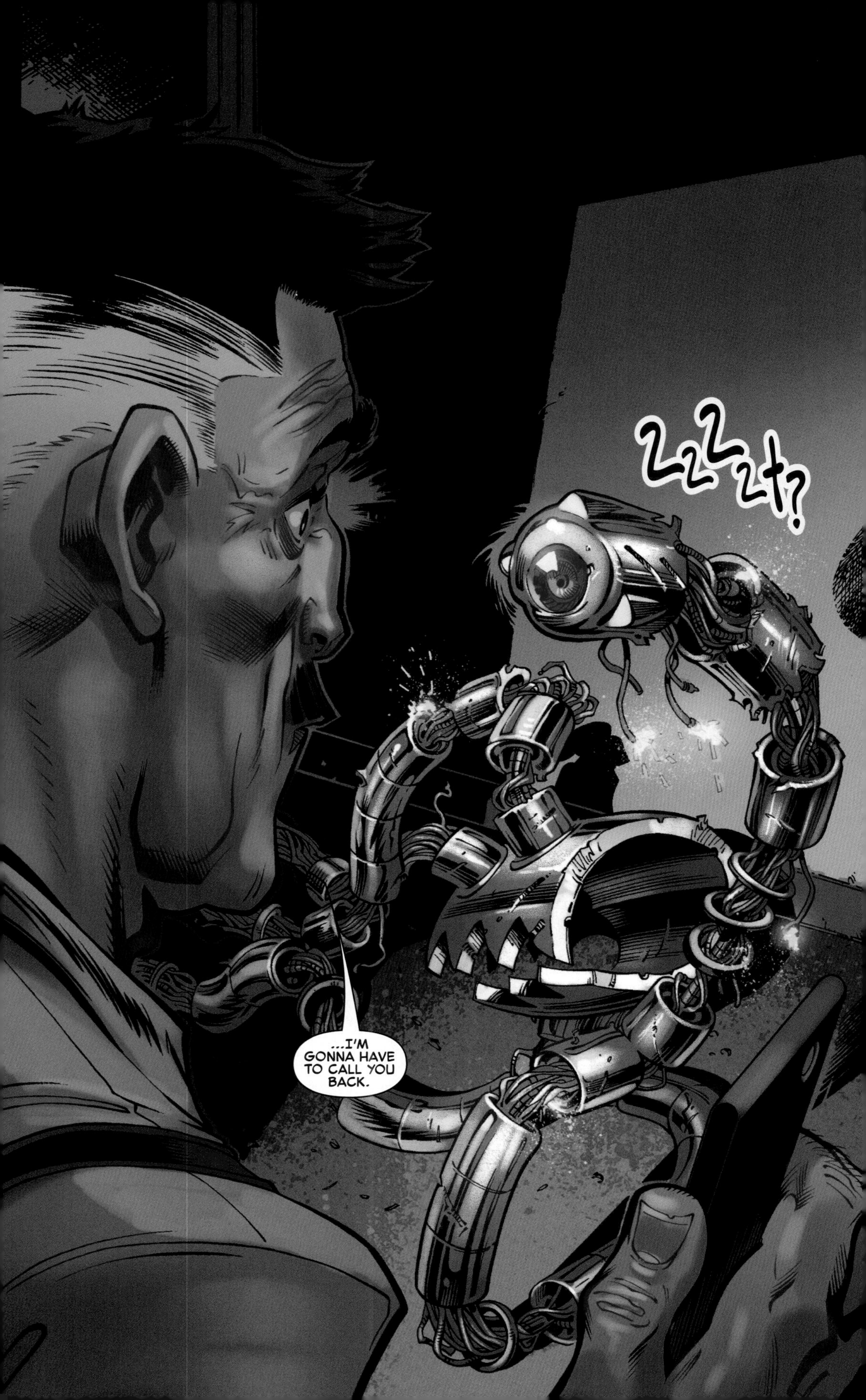
ZzZzt?
...I'M GONNA HAVE TO CALL YOU BACK.

E TALKING
CONNECTING
OUS SYSTEM
APPENDAGES
GREATEST
NEMY...

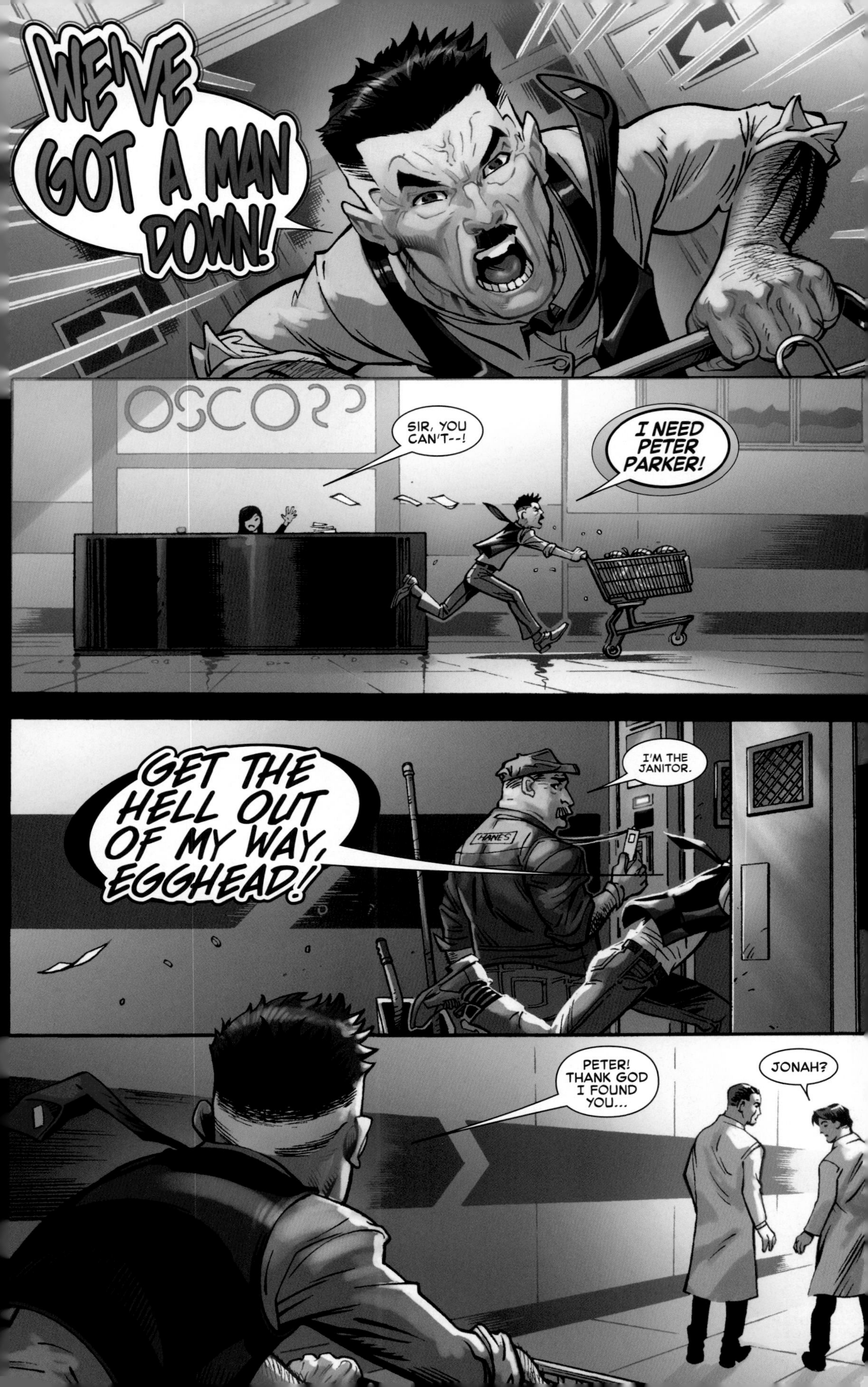
WE'VE GOT A MAN DOWN!
OSCORP
SIR, YOU CAN'T--!
I NEED PETER PARKER!
GET THE HELL OUT OF MY WAY, EGGHEAD!
I'M THE JANITOR.
HANES
PETER! THANK GOD I FOUND YOU...
JONAH?

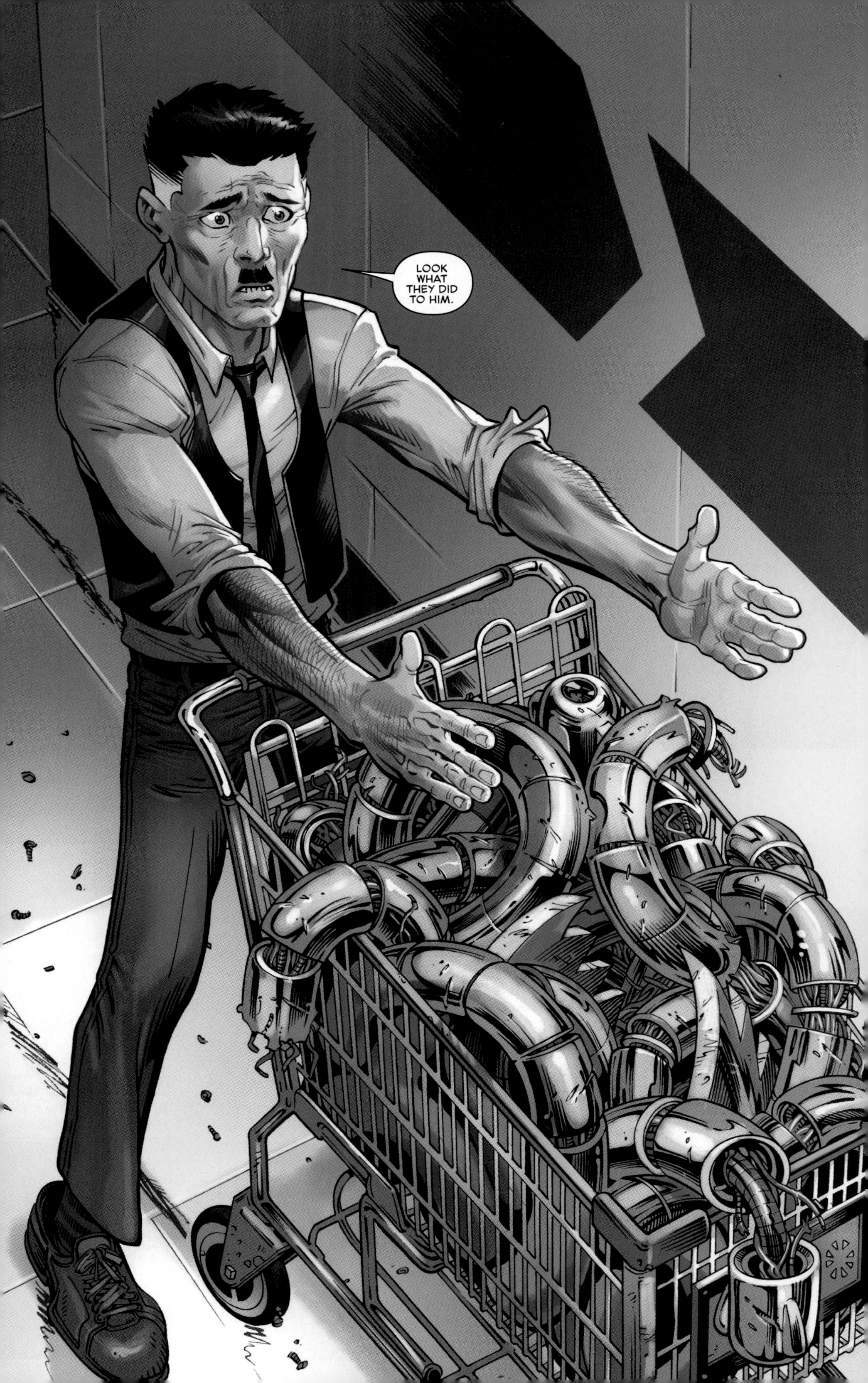
LOOK WHAT THEY DID TO HIM.

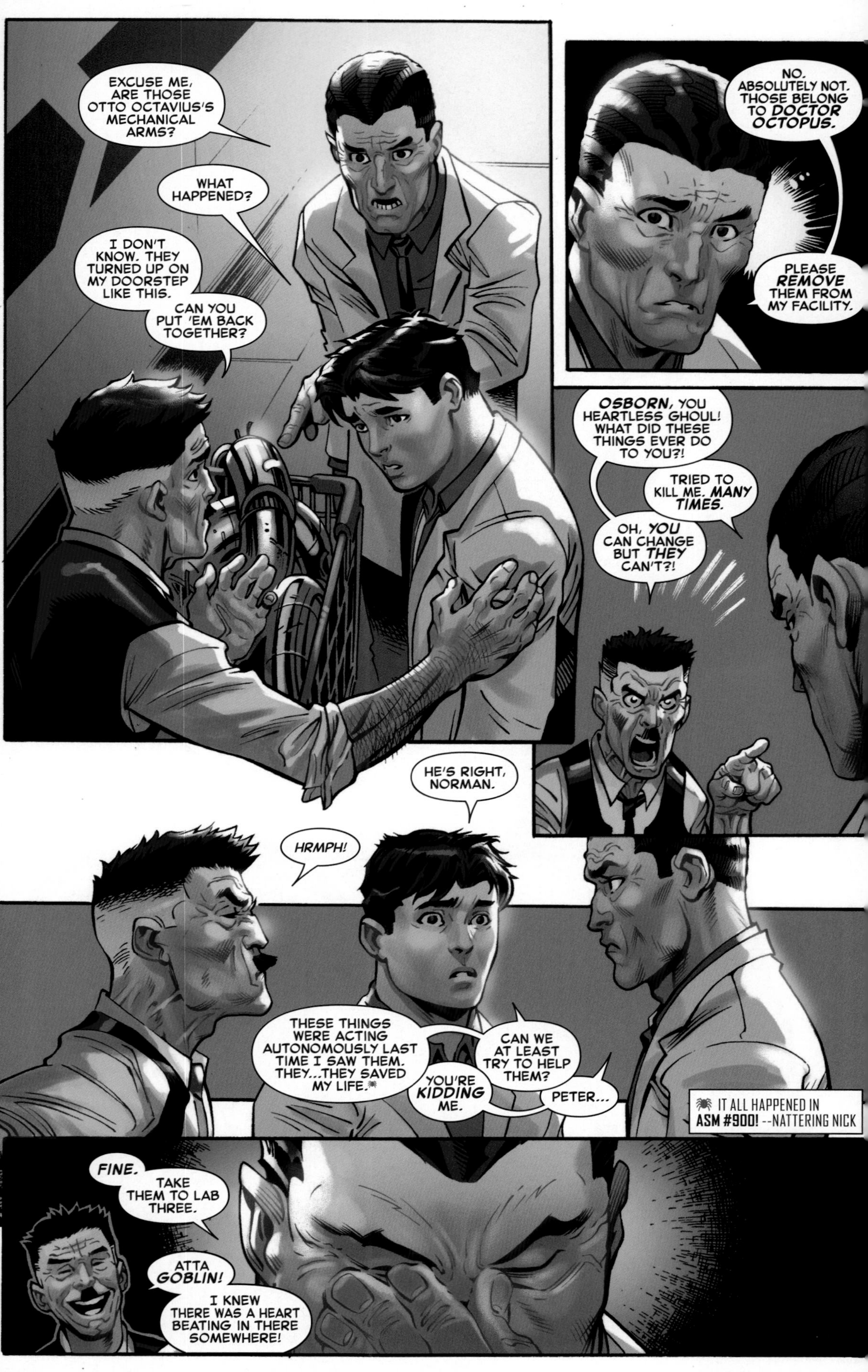
EXCUSE ME, ARE THOSE OTTO OCTAVIUS'S MECHANICAL ARMS?
WHAT HAPPENED?
I DON'T KNOW. THEY TURNED UP ON MY DOORSTEP LIKE THIS.
CAN YOU PUT 'EM BACK TOGETHER?
NO. ABSOLUTELY NOT. THOSE BELONG TO DOCTOR OCTOPUS.
PLEASE REMOVE THEM FROM MY FACILITY.
OSBORN, YOU HEARTLESS GHOUL! WHAT DID THESE THINGS EVER DO TO YOU?!
TRIED TO KILL ME. MANY TIMES.
OH, YOU CAN CHANGE BUT THEY CAN'T?!
HE'S RIGHT, NORMAN.
HRMPH!
THESE THINGS WERE ACTING AUTONOMOUSLY LAST TIME I SAW THEM. THEY...THEY SAVED MY LIFE.
CAN WE AT LEAST TRY TO HELP THEM?
YOU'RE KIDDING ME.
PETER...
IT ALL HAPPENED IN ASM #900! --NATTERING NICK
FINE.
TAKE THEM TO LAB THREE.
ATTA GOBLIN!
I KNEW THERE WAS A HEART BEATING IN THERE SOMEWHERE!

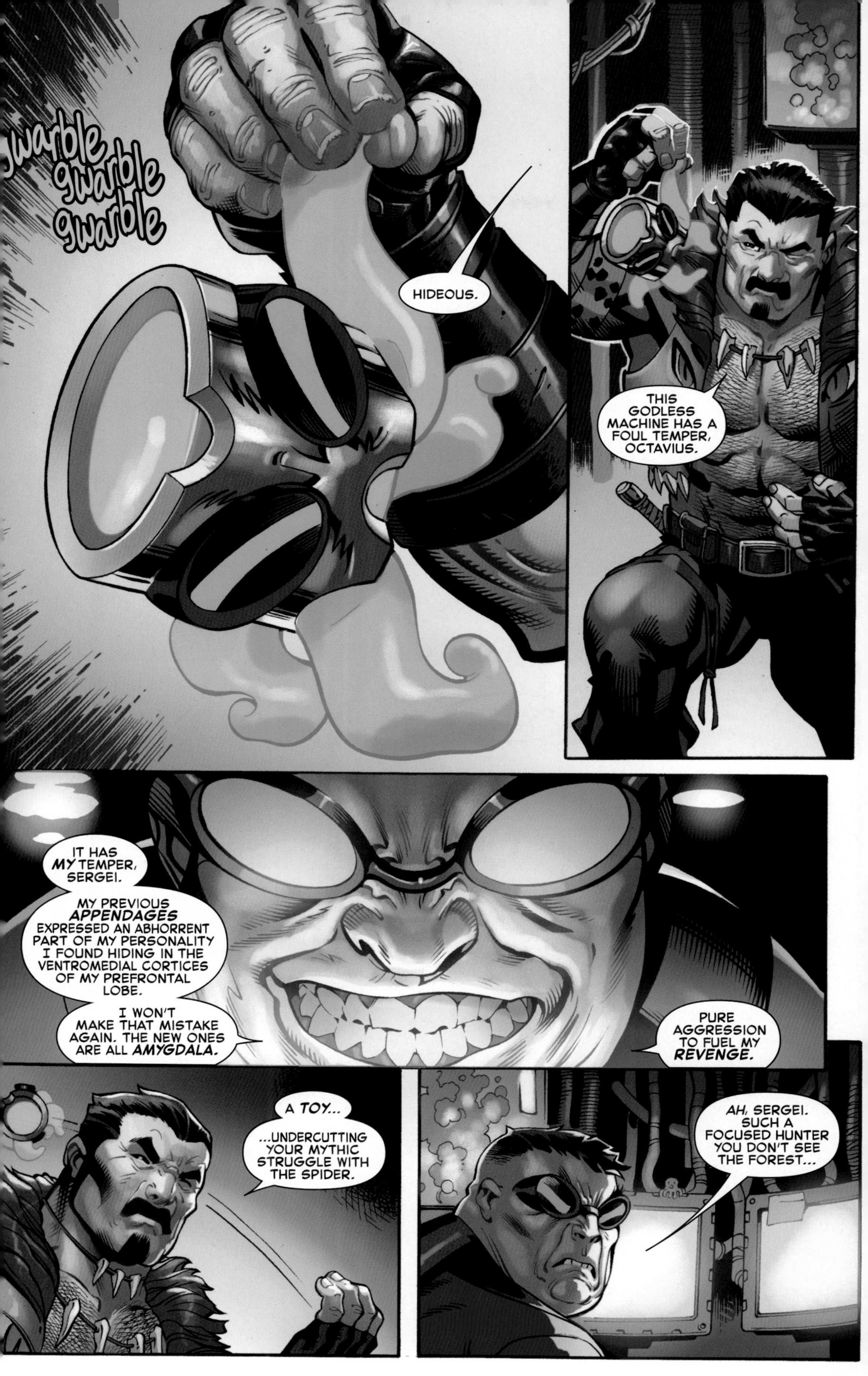
gwarble gwarble gwarble
HIDEOUS.
THIS GODLESS MACHINE HAS A FOUL TEMPER, OCTAVIUS.
IT HAS MY TEMPER, SERGEI.
MY PREVIOUS APPENDAGES EXPRESSED AN ABHORRENT PART OF MY PERSONALITY I FOUND HIDING IN THE VENTROMEDIAL CORTICES OF MY PREFRONTAL LOBE.
I WON'T MAKE THAT MISTAKE AGAIN. THE NEW ONES ARE ALL AMYGDALA.
PURE AGGRESSION TO FUEL MY REVENGE.
A TOY...
...UNDERCUTTING YOUR MYTHIC STRUGGLE WITH THE SPIDER.
AH, SERGEI. SUCH A FOCUSED HUNTER YOU DON'T SEE THE FOREST...

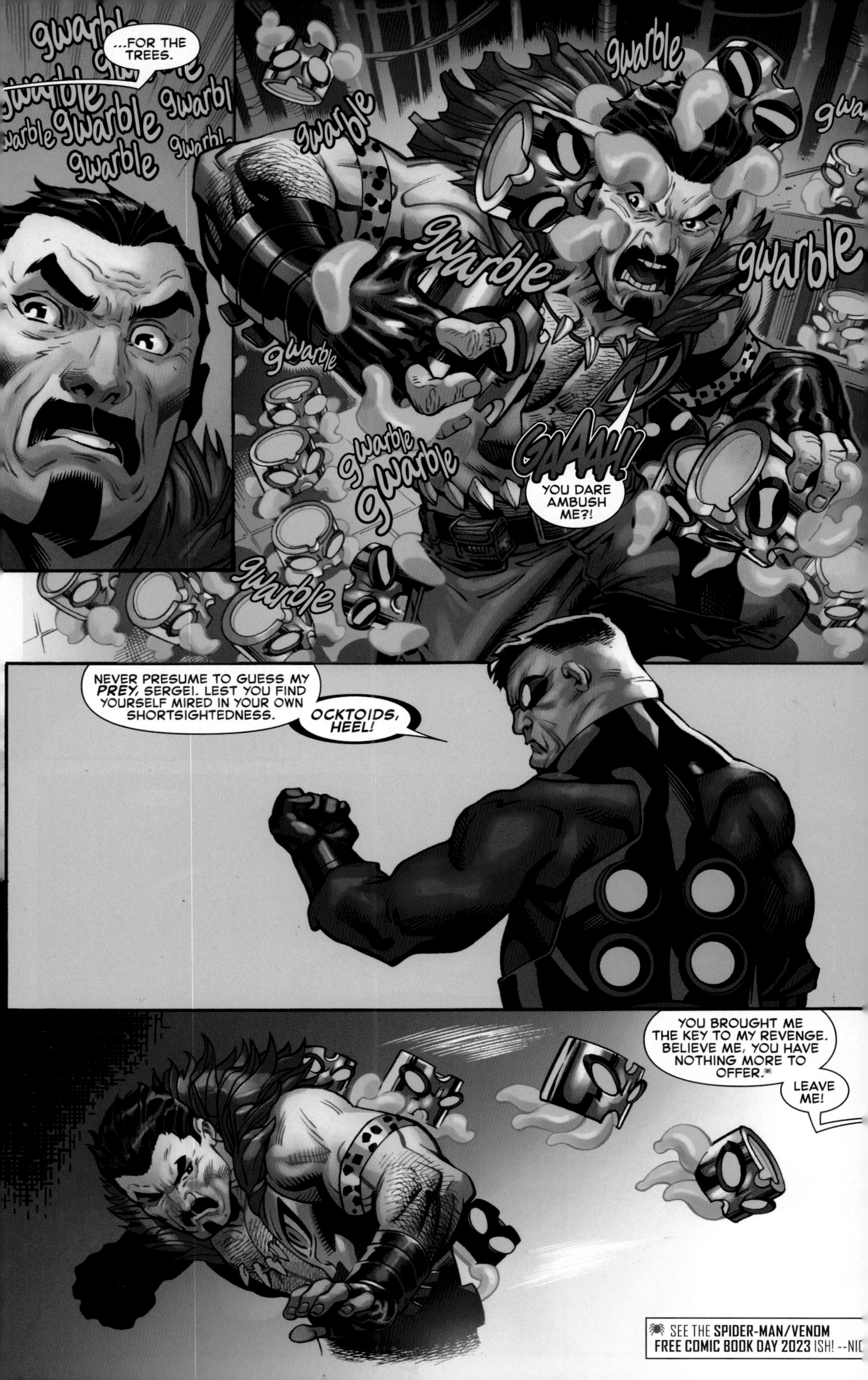

GWARBLE GWARBLE GWARBLE GWARBLE GWARBLE GWARBLE
...FOR THE TREES.
GWARBLE GWARBLE GWARBLE GWARBLE GWARBLE GWARBLE GWARBLE GWARBLE GWARBLE
GAAAH!
YOU DARE AMBUSH ME?!
NEVER PRESUME TO GUESS MY PREY, SERGEI. LEST YOU FIND YOURSELF MIRED IN YOUR OWN SHORTSIGHTEDNESS.
OCKTOIDS, HEEL!
YOU BROUGHT ME THE KEY TO MY REVENGE. BELIEVE ME, YOU HAVE NOTHING MORE TO OFFER.*
LEAVE ME!
*SEE THE SPIDER-MAN/VENOM FREE COMIC BOOK DAY 2023 ISH! --NIC

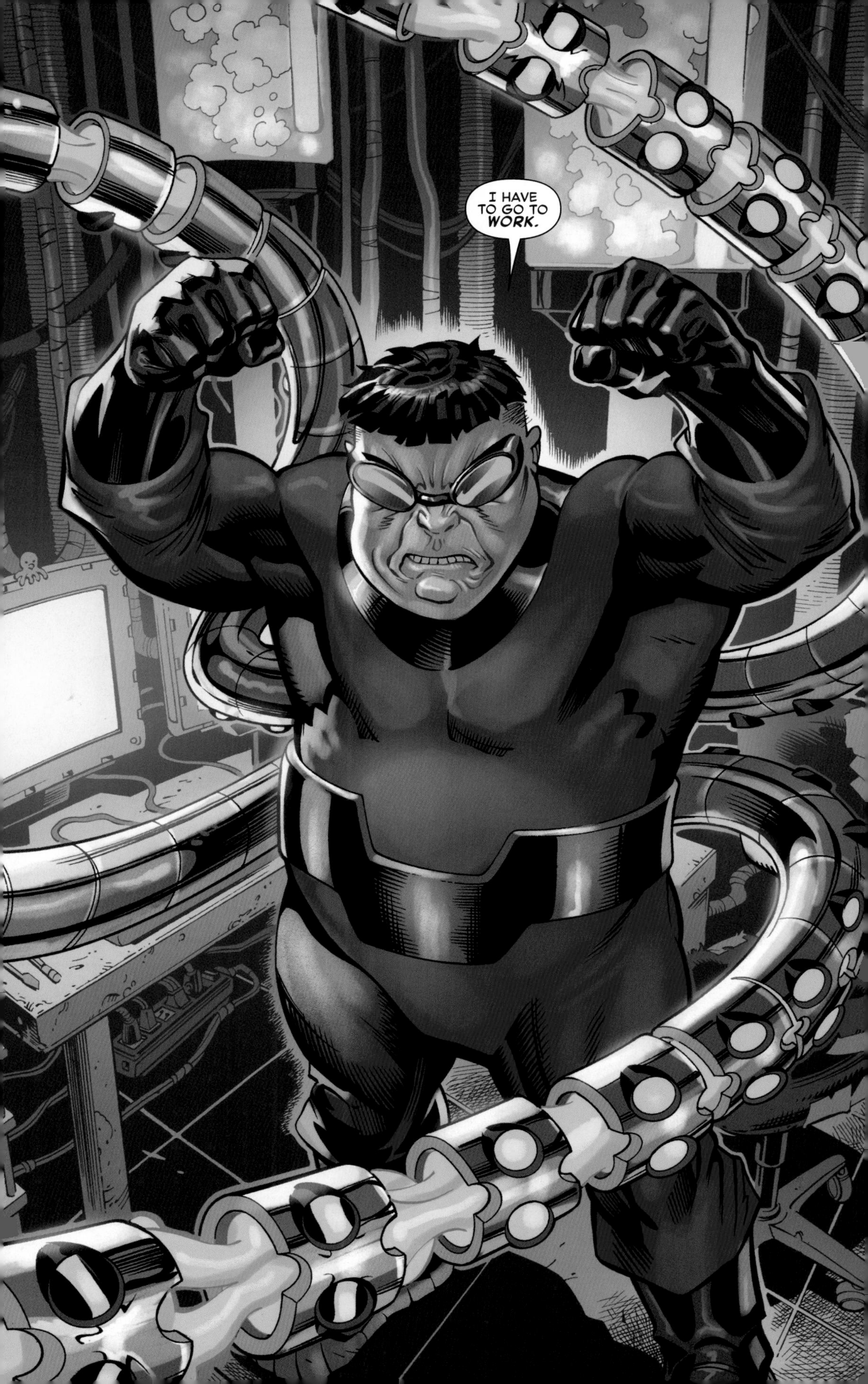
I HAVE TO GO TO WORK.

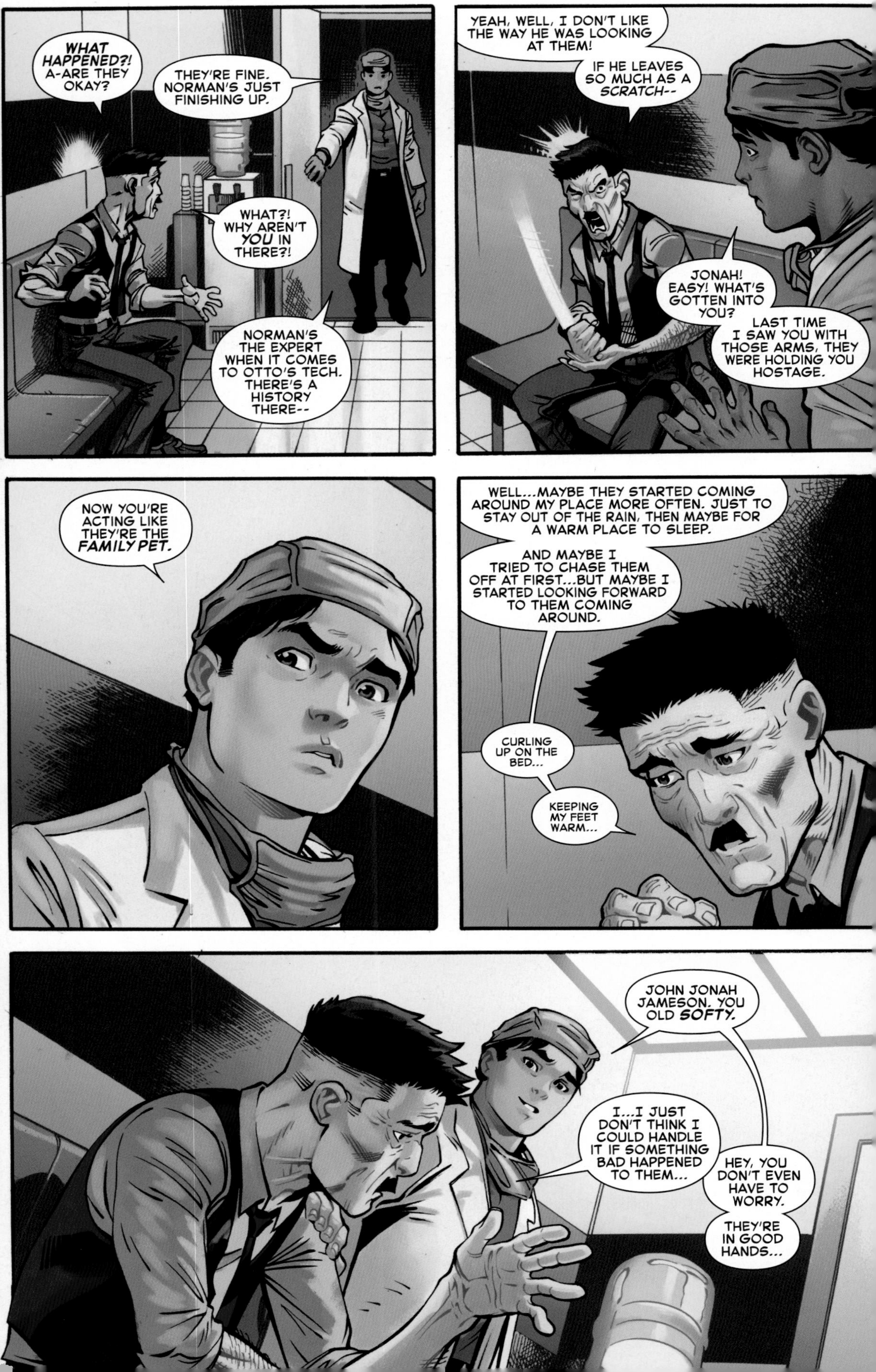
WHAT HAPPENED?! A-ARE THEY OKAY?
THEY'RE FINE. NORMAN'S JUST FINISHING UP.
WHAT?! WHY AREN'T YOU IN THERE?!
NORMAN'S THE EXPERT WHEN IT COMES TO OTTO'S TECH. THERE'S A HISTORY THERE--
YEAH, WELL, I DON'T LIKE THE WAY HE WAS LOOKING AT THEM!
IF HE LEAVES SO MUCH AS A SCRATCH--
JONAH! EASY! WHAT'S GOTTEN INTO YOU?
LAST TIME I SAW YOU WITH THOSE ARMS, THEY WERE HOLDING YOU HOSTAGE.
NOW YOU'RE ACTING LIKE THEY'RE THE FAMILY PET.
WELL...MAYBE THEY STARTED COMING AROUND MY PLACE MORE OFTEN. JUST TO STAY OUT OF THE RAIN, THEN MAYBE FOR A WARM PLACE TO SLEEP.
AND MAYBE I TRIED TO CHASE THEM OFF AT FIRST...BUT MAYBE I STARTED LOOKING FORWARD TO THEM COMING AROUND.
CURLING UP ON THE BED...
KEEPING MY FEET WARM...
JOHN JONAH JAMESON. YOU OLD SOFTY.
I...I JUST DON'T THINK I COULD HANDLE IT IF SOMETHING BAD HAPPENED TO THEM...
HEY, YOU DON'T EVEN HAVE TO WORRY.
THEY'RE IN GOOD HANDS...

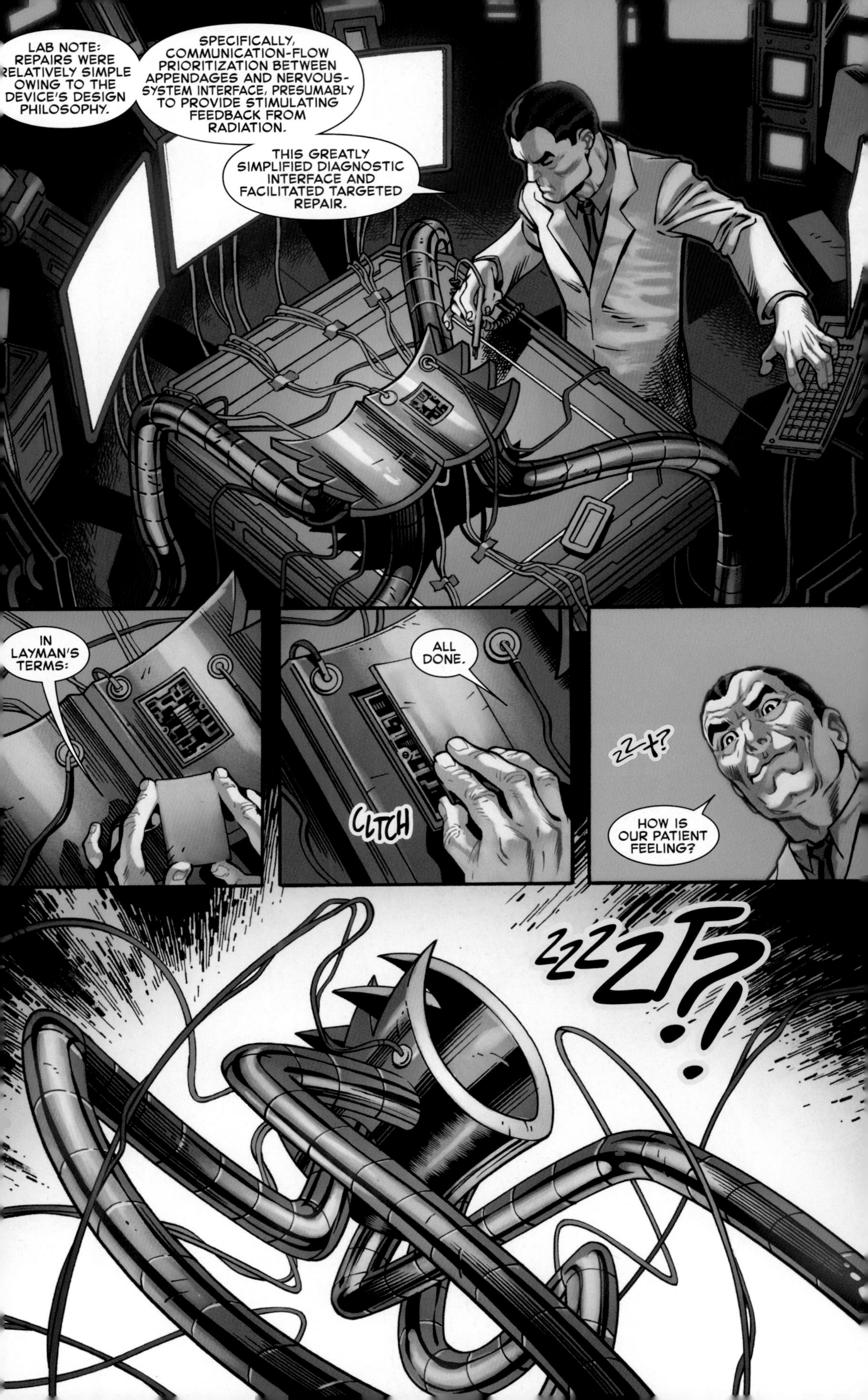
LAB NOTE: REPAIRS WERE RELATIVELY SIMPLE OWING TO THE DEVICE'S DESIGN PHILOSOPHY.
SPECIFICALLY, COMMUNICATION-FLOW PRIORITIZATION BETWEEN APPENDAGES AND NERVOUS-SYSTEM INTERFACE, PRESUMABLY TO PROVIDE STIMULATING FEEDBACK FROM RADIATION.
THIS GREATLY SIMPLIFIED DIAGNOSTIC INTERFACE AND FACILITATED TARGETED REPAIR.
IN LAYMAN'S TERMS:
ALL DONE.
CLTCH
HOW IS OUR PATIENT FEELING?
ZZZZT?!

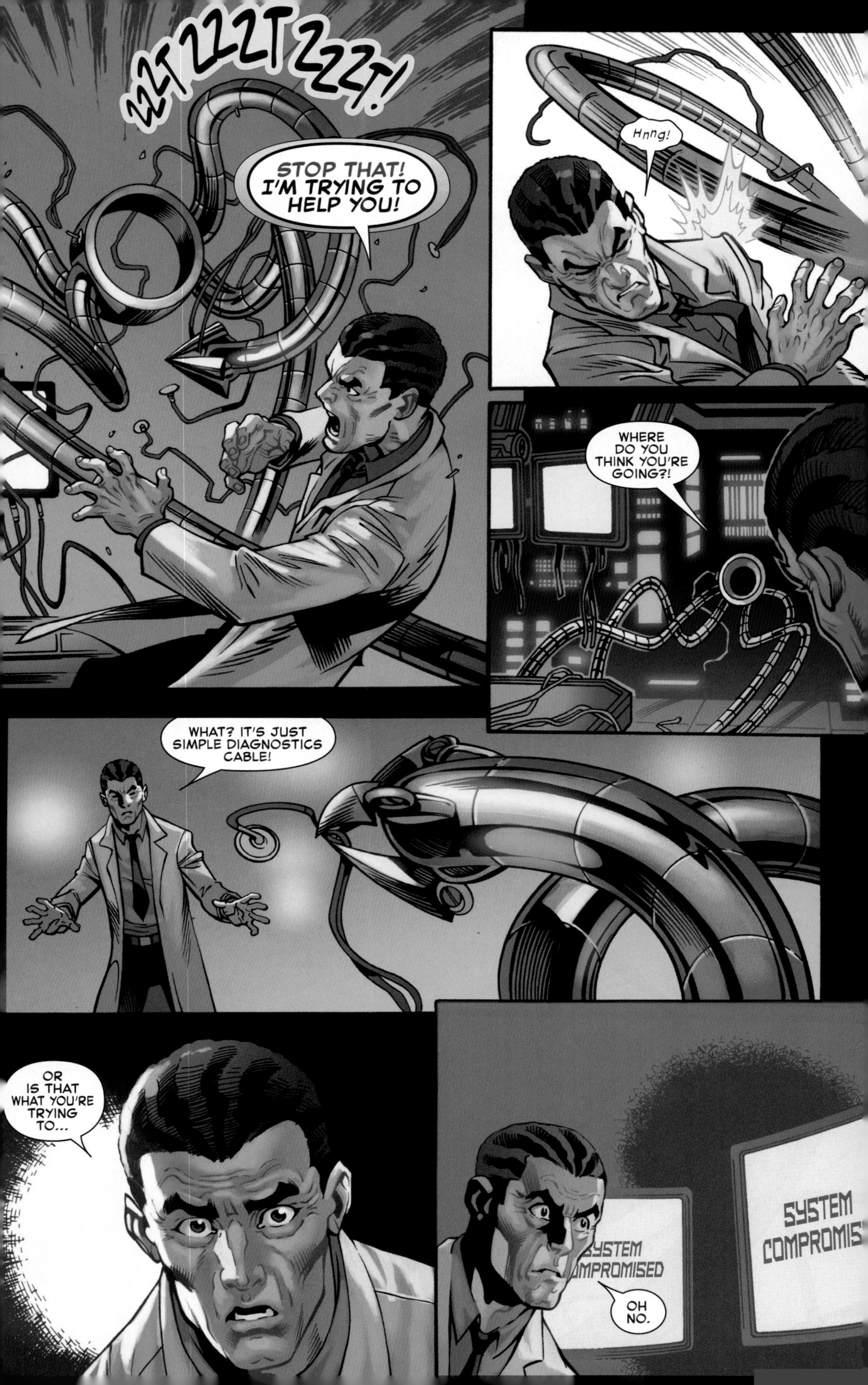
ZZZT ZZZT ZZZT!
STOP THAT! I'M TRYING TO HELP YOU!
Hnng!
WHERE DO YOU THINK YOU'RE GOING?!
WHAT? IT'S JUST SIMPLE DIAGNOSTICS CABLE!
OR IS THAT WHAT YOU'RE TRYING TO...
SYSTEM COMPROMIS
OH NO.

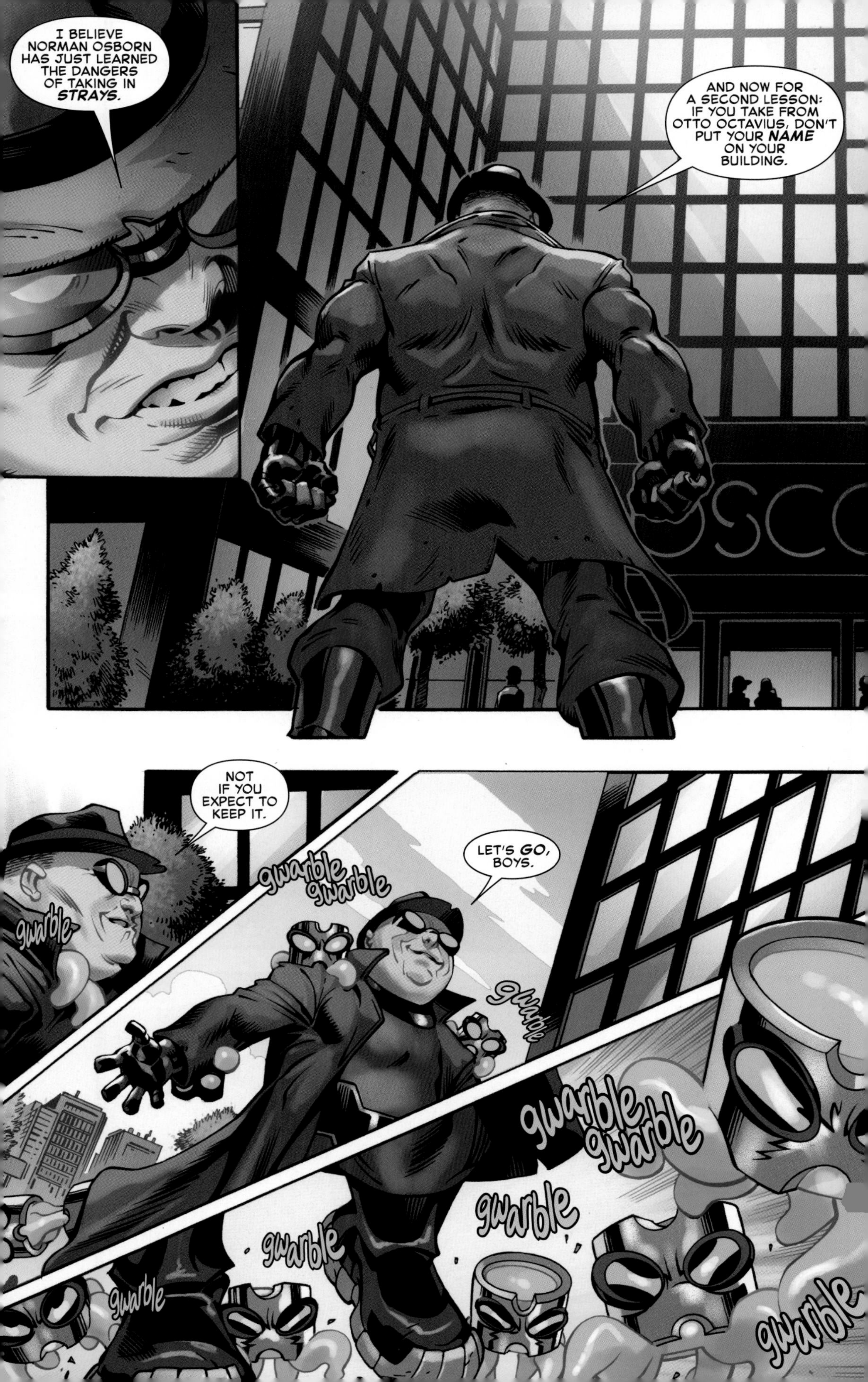
I BELIEVE NORMAN OSBORN HAS JUST LEARNED THE DANGERS OF TAKING IN STRAYS.
AND NOW FOR A SECOND LESSON: IF YOU TAKE FROM OTTO OCTAVIUS, DON'T PUT YOUR NAME ON YOUR BUILDING.
OSCO
NOT IF YOU EXPECT TO KEEP IT.
LET'S GO, BOYS.
gwarble gwarble
gwarble
gwarble
gwarble gwarble
gwarble
gwarble
gwarble
gwarble

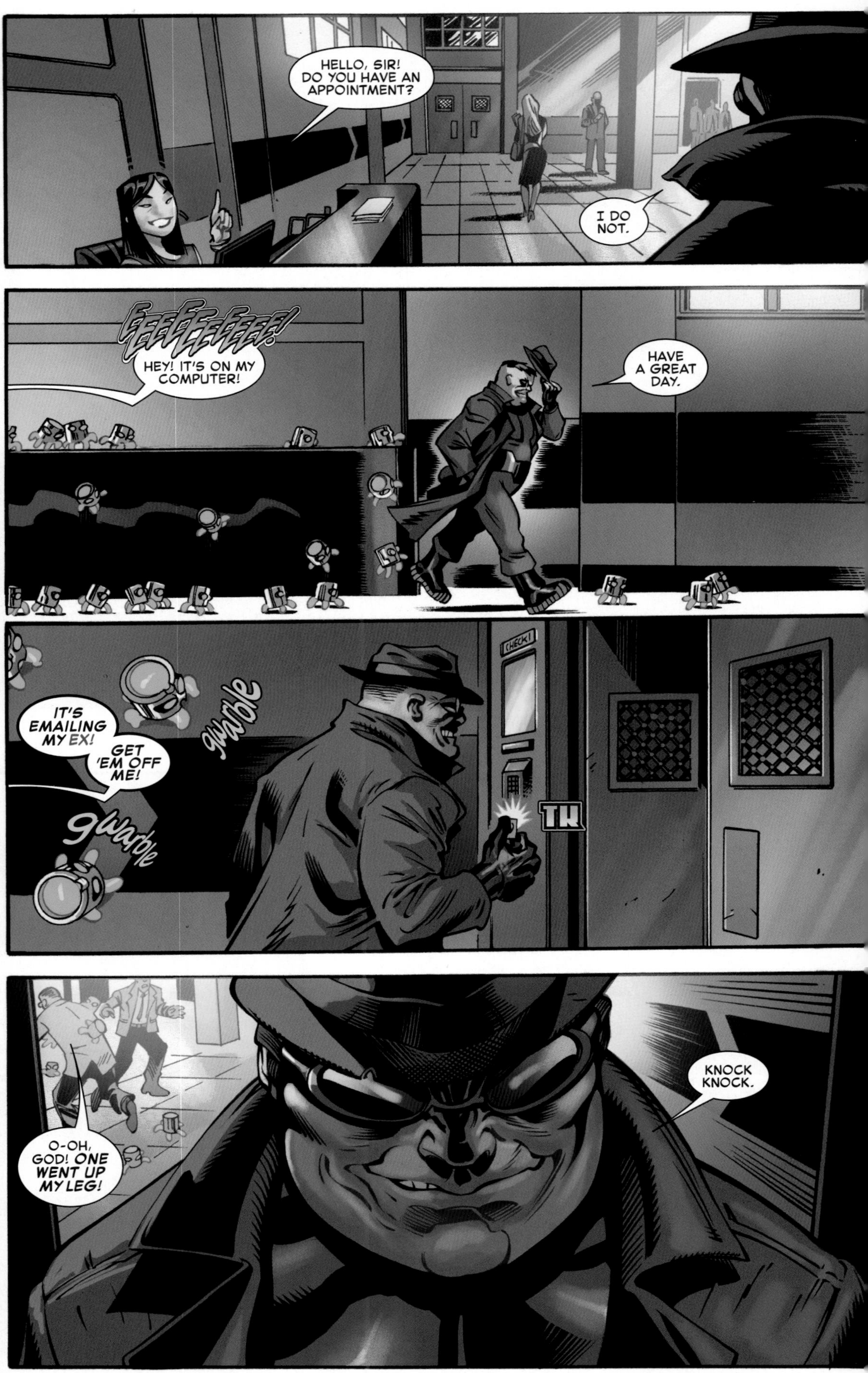
HELLO, SIR! DO YOU HAVE AN APPOINTMENT?
I DO NOT.
EEEEEEEEEEE!
HEY! IT'S ON MY COMPUTER!
HAVE A GREAT DAY.
IT'S EMAILING MY EX!
GET 'EM OFF ME!
gwarble
CHECK!
TK
gwarble
KNOCK KNOCK.
O-OH, GOD! ONE WENT UP MY LEG!

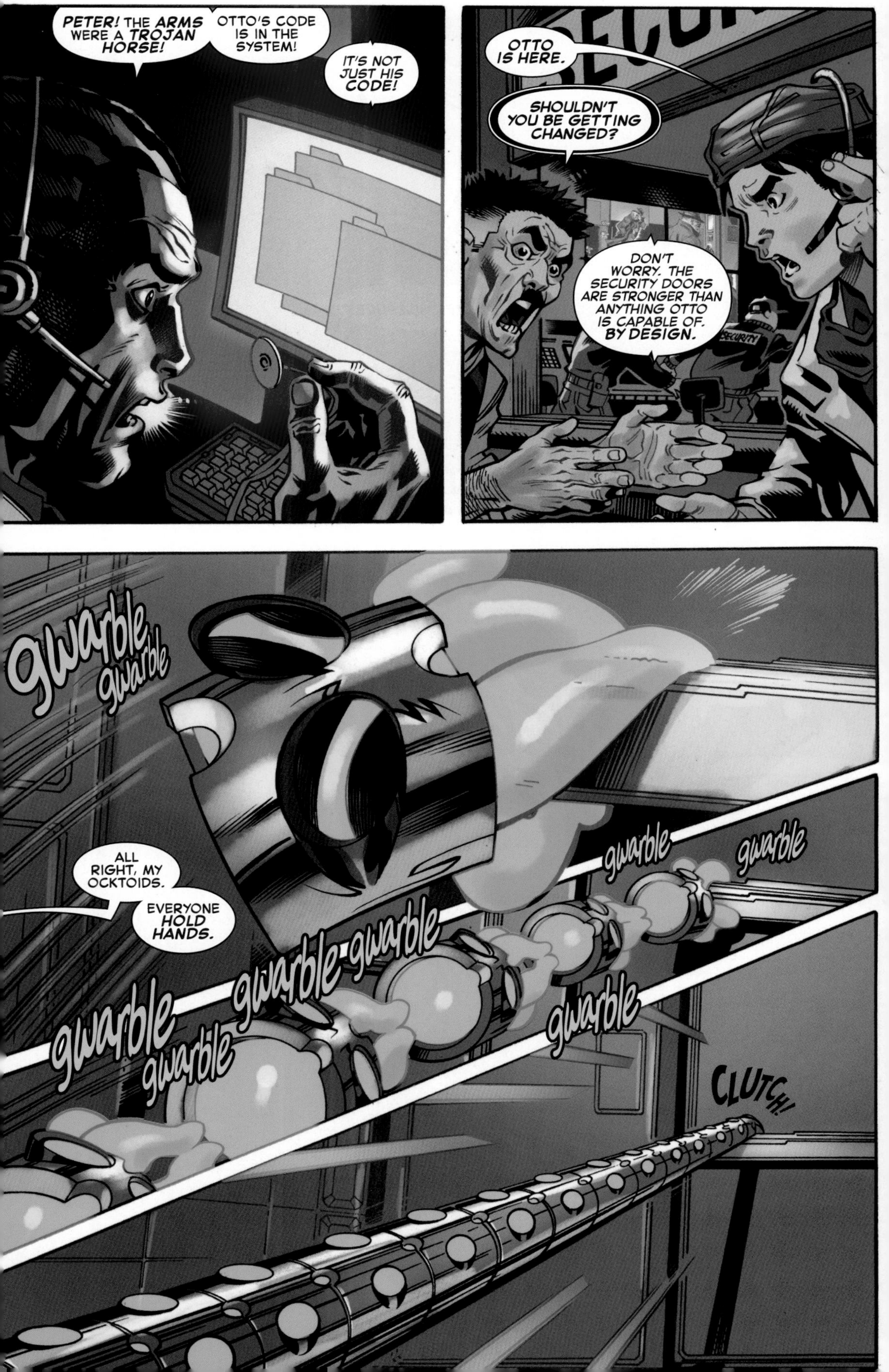
PETER! THE ARMS WERE A TROJAN HORSE!
OTTO'S CODE IS IN THE SYSTEM!
IT'S NOT JUST HIS CODE!
OTTO IS HERE.
SHOULDN'T YOU BE GETTING CHANGED?
DON'T WORRY. THE SECURITY DOORS ARE STRONGER THAN ANYTHING OTTO IS CAPABLE OF. BY DESIGN.
SECURITY
gwarble gwarble
ALL RIGHT, MY OCKTOIDS.
EVERYONE HOLD HANDS.
gwarble
gwarble
gwarble gwarble gwarble
gwarble gwarble
gwarble
CLUTCH!

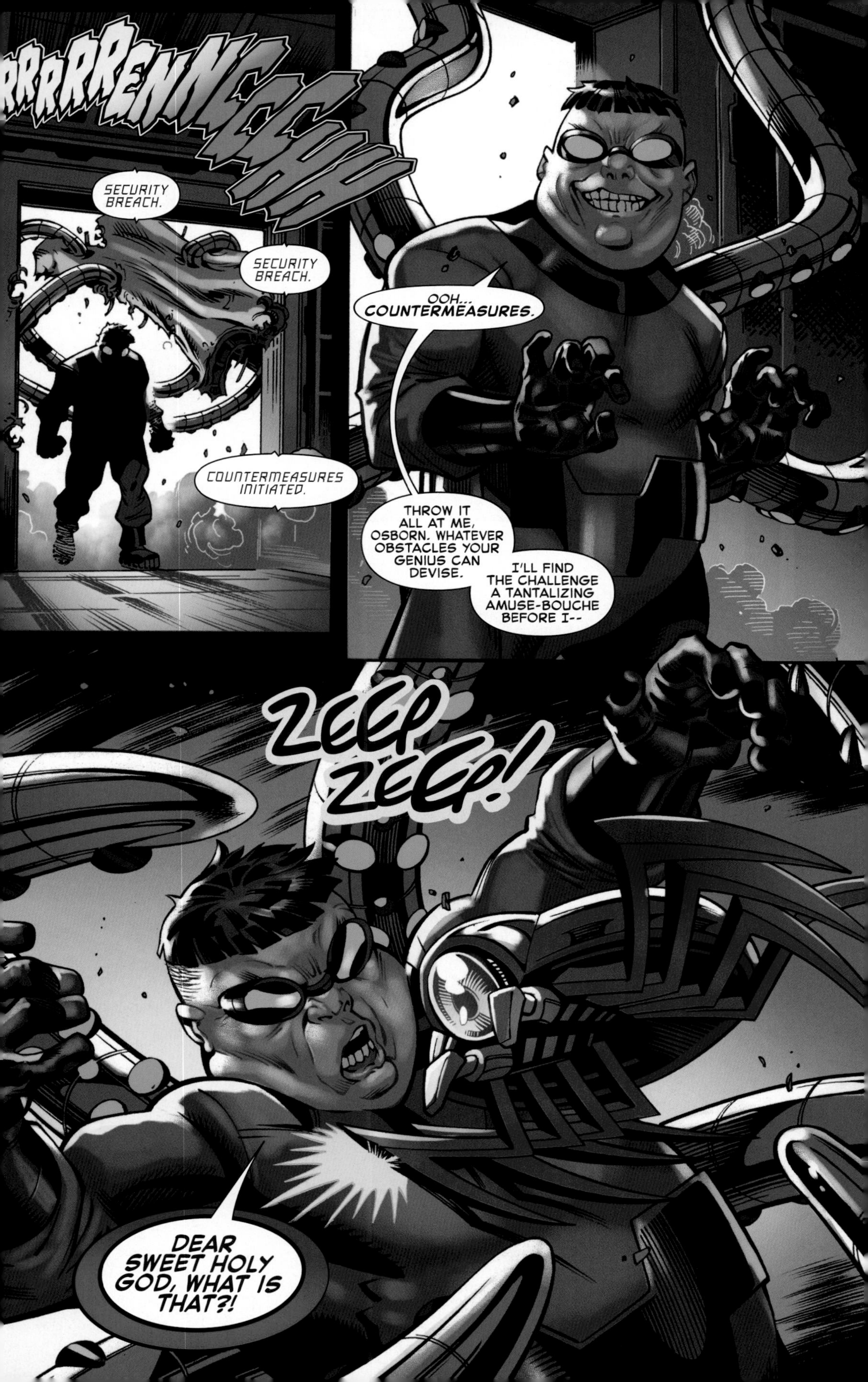
RRRRRRENNNCCHHH
SECURITY BREACH.
SECURITY BREACH.
COUNTERMEASURES INITIATED.
OOH... COUNTERMEASURES.
THROW IT ALL AT ME, OSBORN. WHATEVER OBSTACLES YOUR GENIUS CAN DEVISE.
I'LL FIND THE CHALLENGE A TANTALIZING AMUSE-BOUCHE BEFORE I--
ZEEP ZEEP!
DEAR SWEET HOLY GOD, WHAT IS THAT?!

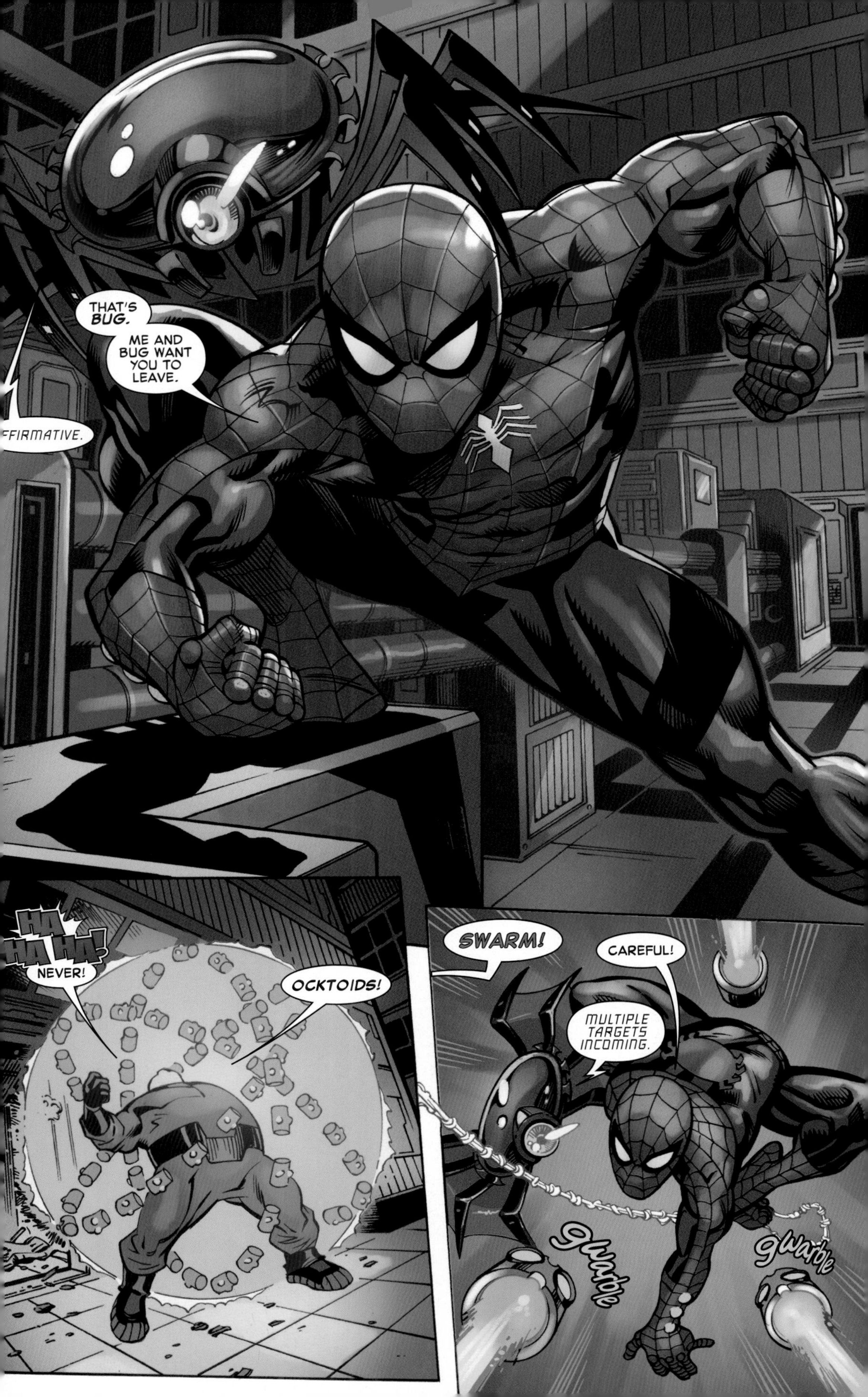
THAT'S BUG.
ME AND BUG WANT YOU TO LEAVE.
FFIRMATIVE.
HA HA HA!
NEVER!
OCKTOIDS!
SWARM!
CAREFUL!
MULTIPLE TARGETS INCOMING.
gwarble
gwarble

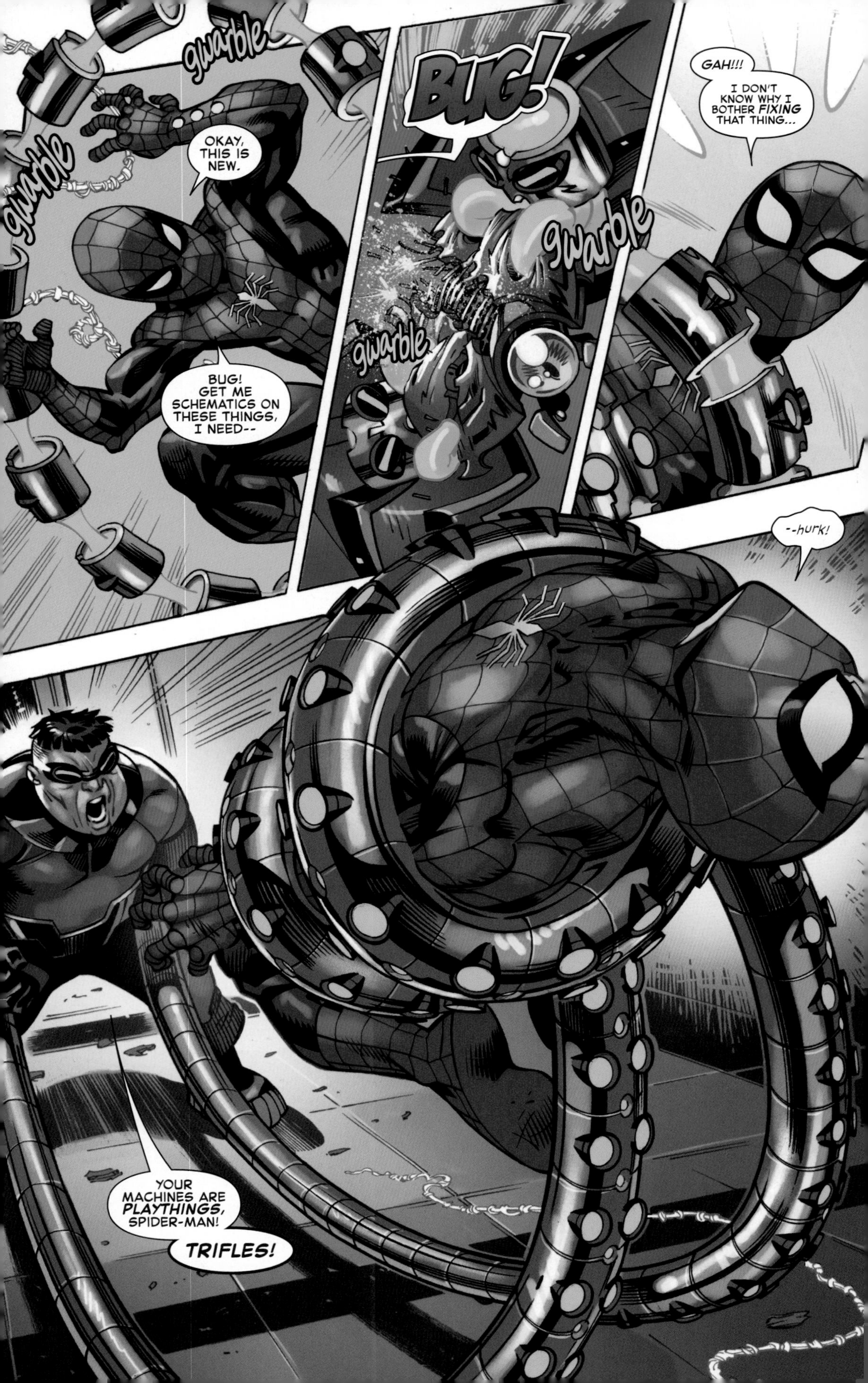
gwarble
gwarble
gwarble
OKAY, THIS IS NEW.
BUG! GET ME SCHEMATICS ON THESE THINGS, I NEED--
BUG!
gwarble
gwarble
GAH!!!
I DON'T KNOW WHY I BOTHER FIXING THAT THING...
--hurk!
YOUR MACHINES ARE PLAYTHINGS, SPIDER-MAN!
TRIFLES!

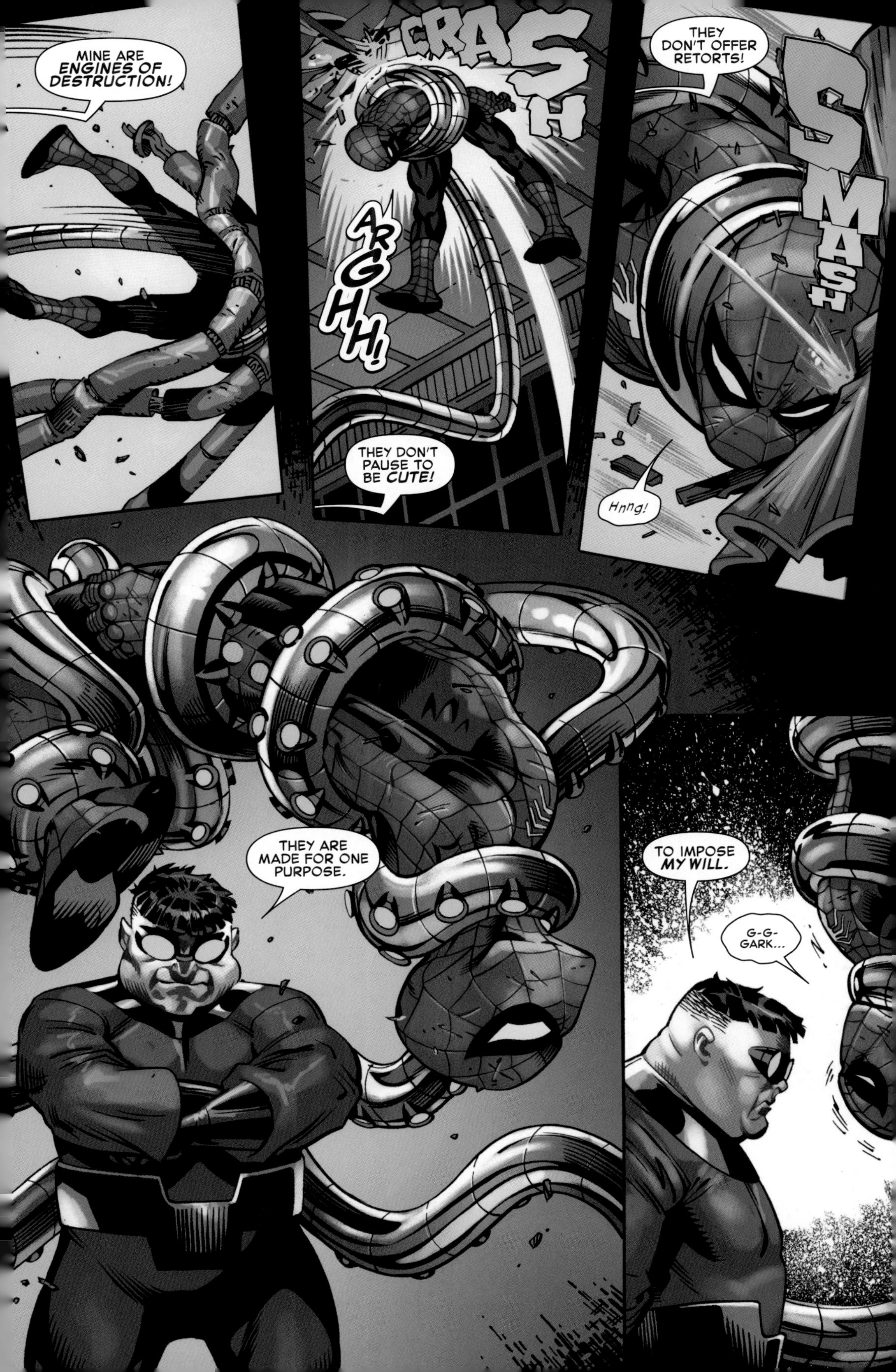
MINE ARE ENGINES OF DESTRUCTION!
CRASH
ARGHH!
THEY DON'T PAUSE TO BE CUTE!
THEY DON'T OFFER RETORTS!
SMASH
Hnng!
THEY ARE MADE FOR ONE PURPOSE.
TO IMPOSE MY WILL.
G-G-GARK...

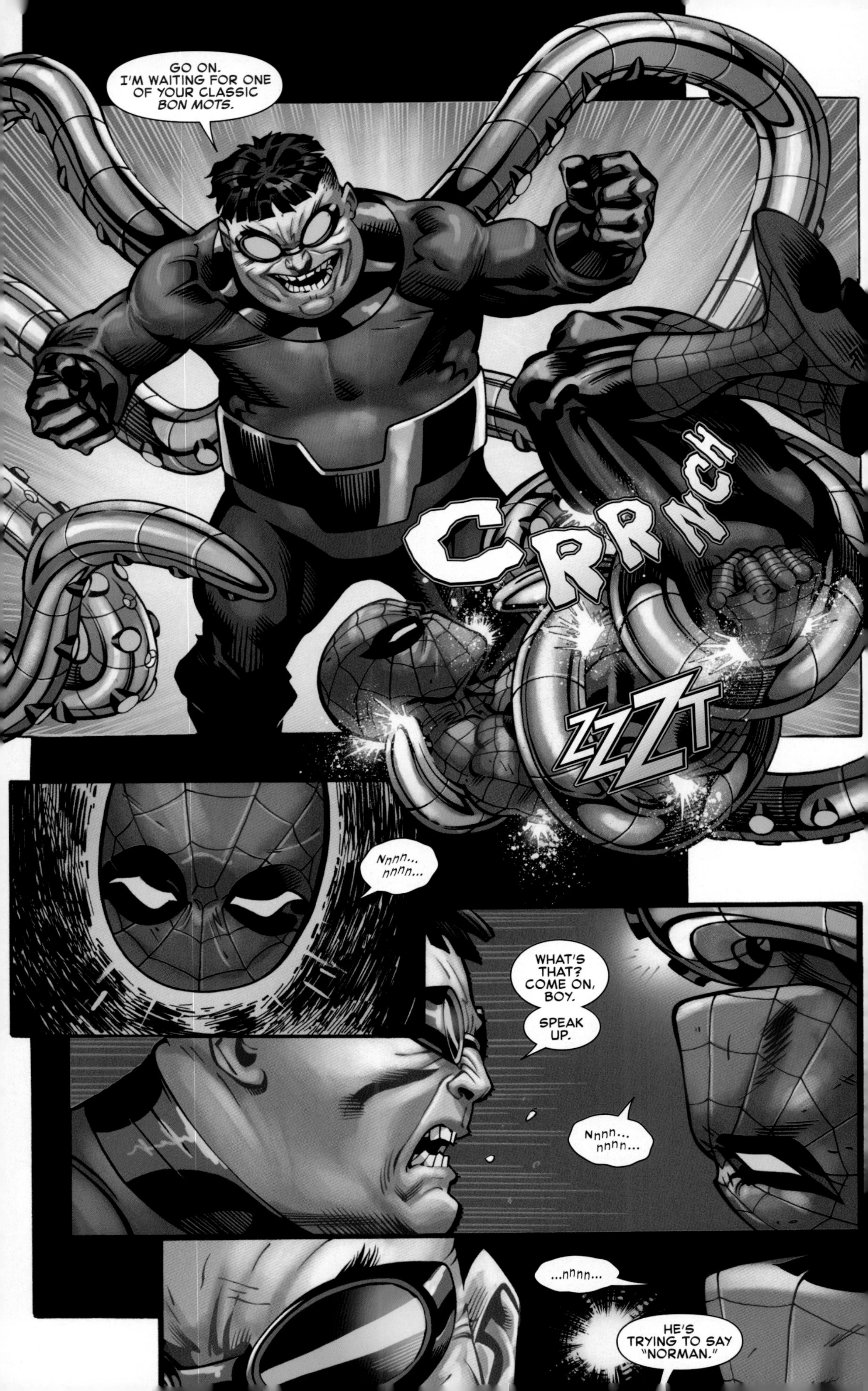
GO ON. I'M WAITING FOR ONE OF YOUR CLASSIC BON MOTS.
CRRNCH
ZZZT
Nnnn... nnnn...
WHAT'S THAT? COME ON, BOY.
SPEAK UP.
Nnnn... nnnn...
...nnnn...
HE'S TRYING TO SAY "NORMAN."

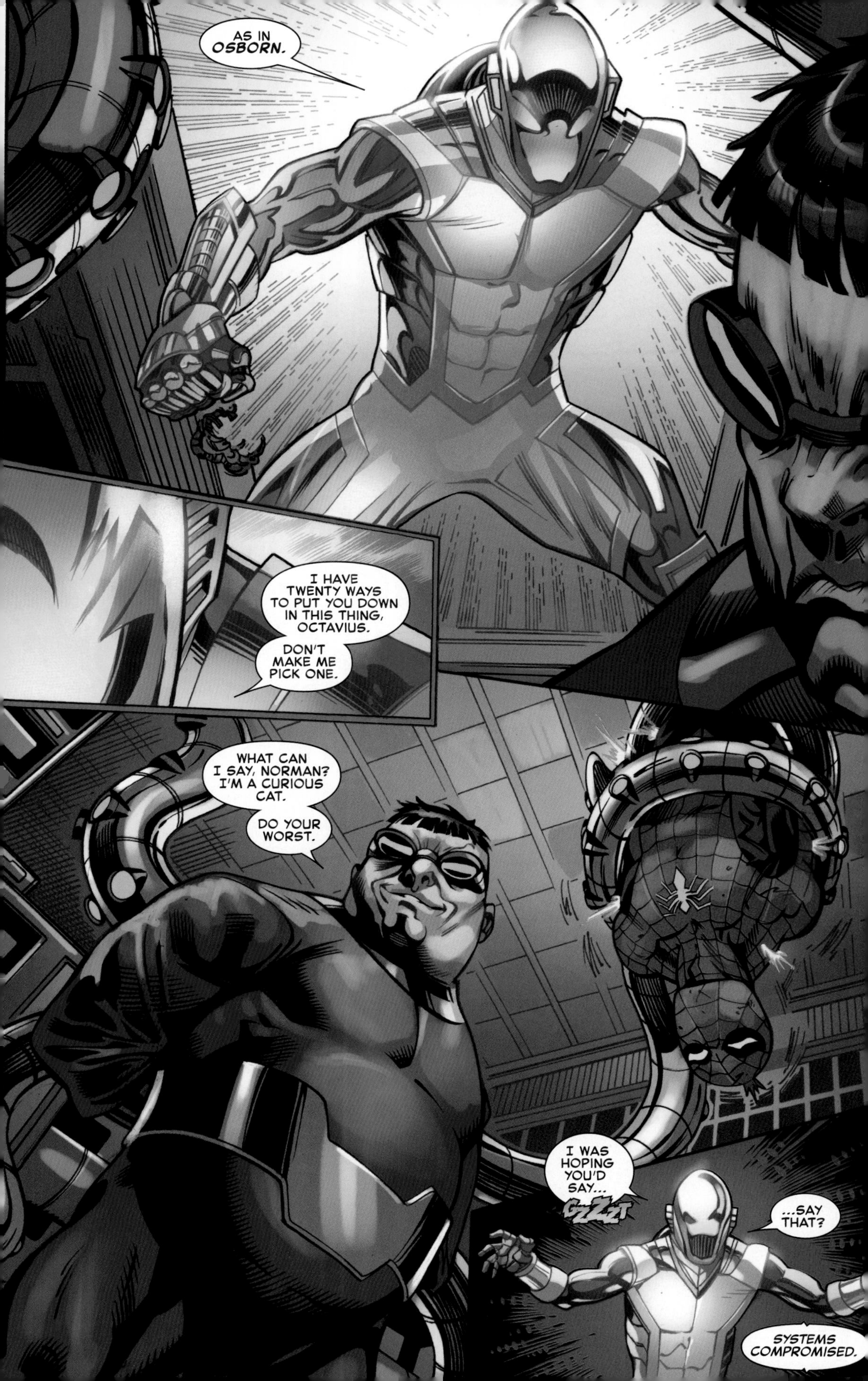
AS IN OSBORN.
I HAVE TWENTY WAYS TO PUT YOU DOWN IN THIS THING, OCTAVIUS.
DON'T MAKE ME PICK ONE.
WHAT CAN I SAY, NORMAN? I'M A CURIOUS CAT.
DO YOUR WORST.
I WAS HOPING YOU'D SAY...
GZZZZT
...SAY THAT?
SYSTEMS COMPROMISED.

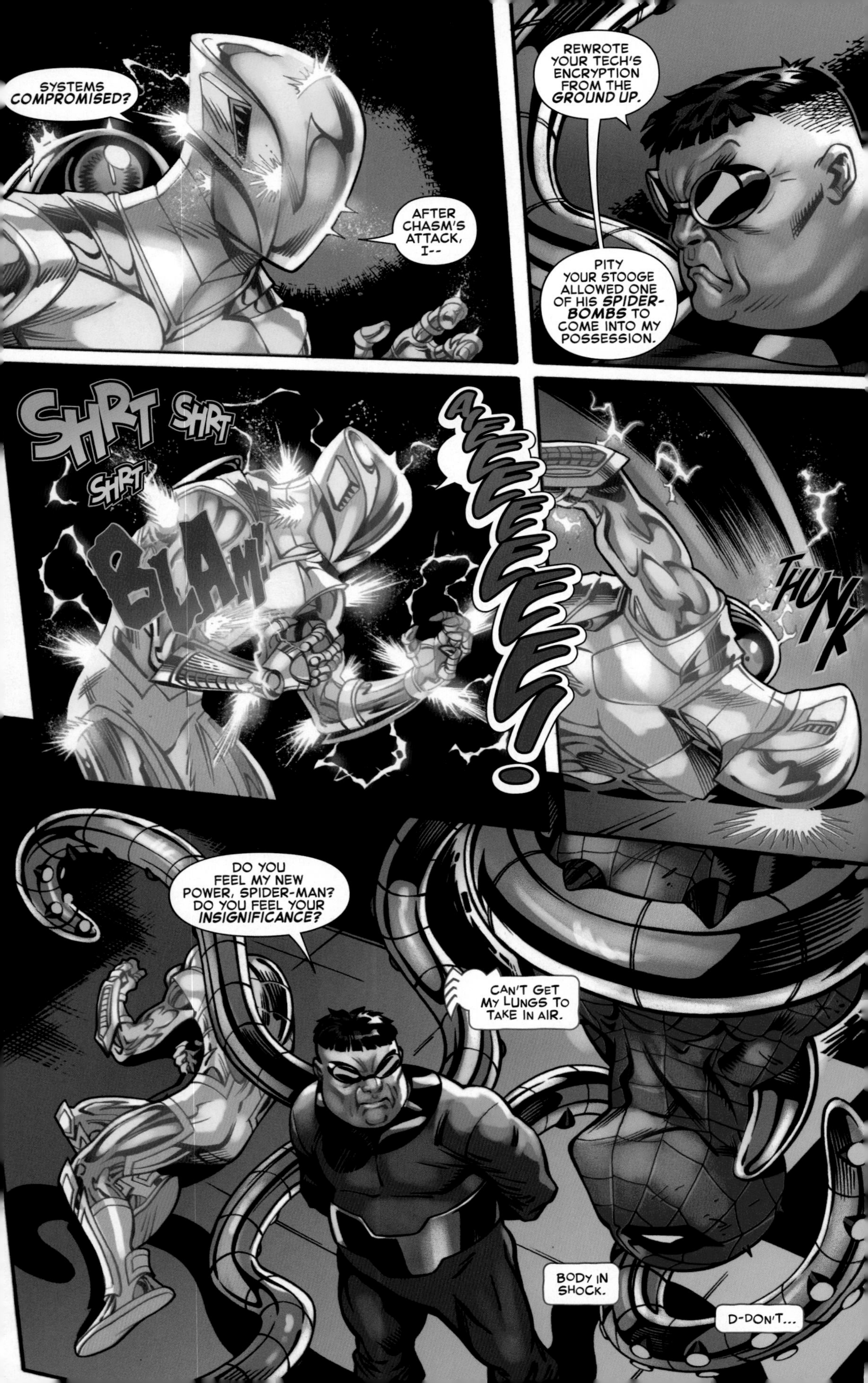
SYSTEMS COMPROMISED?
AFTER CHASM'S ATTACK, I--
REWROTE YOUR TECH'S ENCRYPTION FROM THE GROUND UP.
PITY YOUR STOOGE ALLOWED ONE OF HIS SPIDER-BOMBS TO COME INTO MY POSSESSION.
SHRT SHRT
SHRT
BLAM!
AEEEEEEE!
THUNK
DO YOU FEEL MY NEW POWER, SPIDER-MAN? DO YOU FEEL YOUR INSIGNIFICANCE?
CAN'T GET MY LUNGS TO TAKE IN AIR.
BODY IN SHOCK.
D-DON'T...

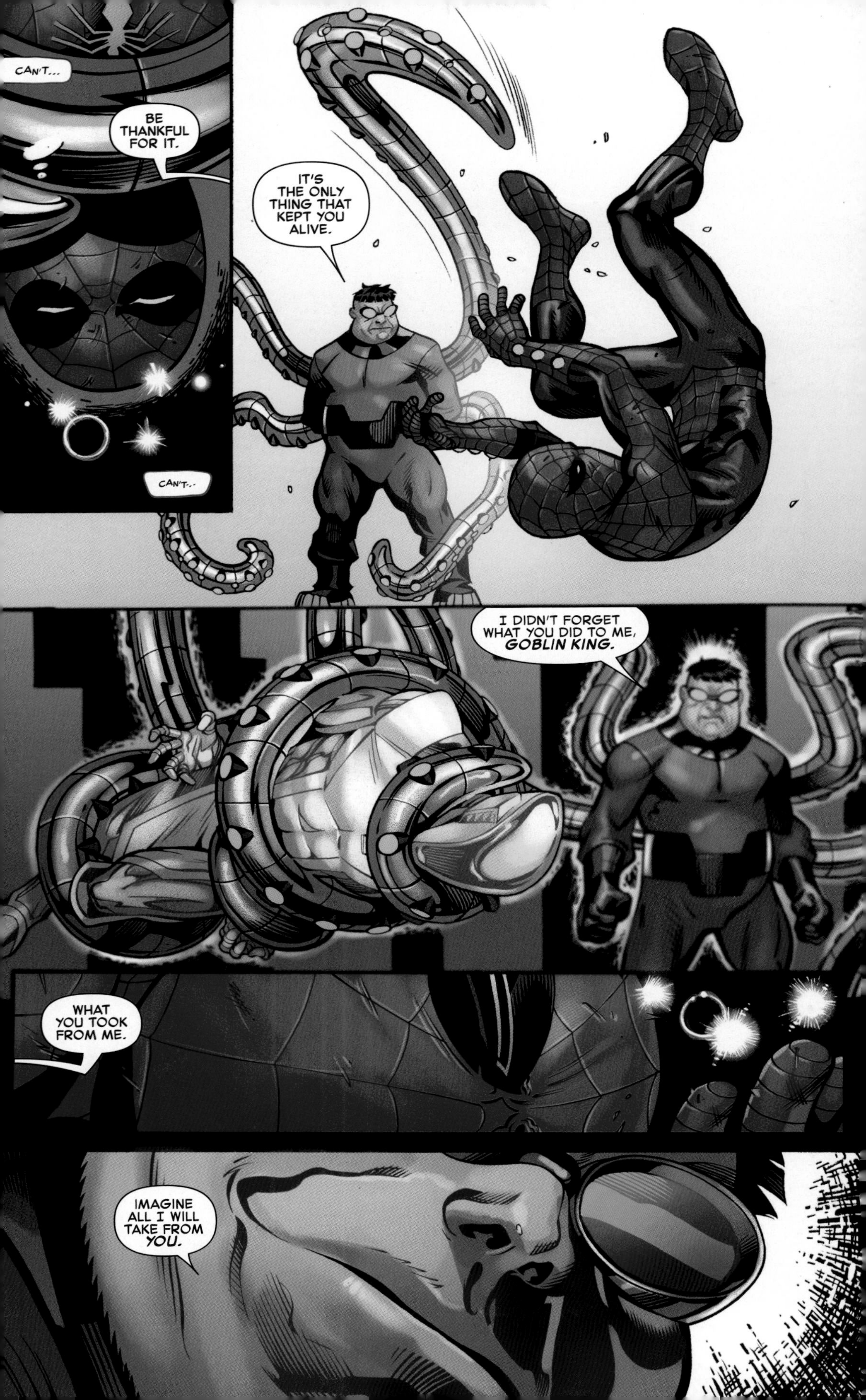
CAN'T...
BE THANKFUL FOR IT.
IT'S THE ONLY THING THAT KEPT YOU ALIVE.
CAN'T...
I DIDN'T FORGET WHAT YOU DID TO ME, GOBLIN KING.
WHAT YOU TOOK FROM ME.
IMAGINE ALL I WILL TAKE FROM YOU.

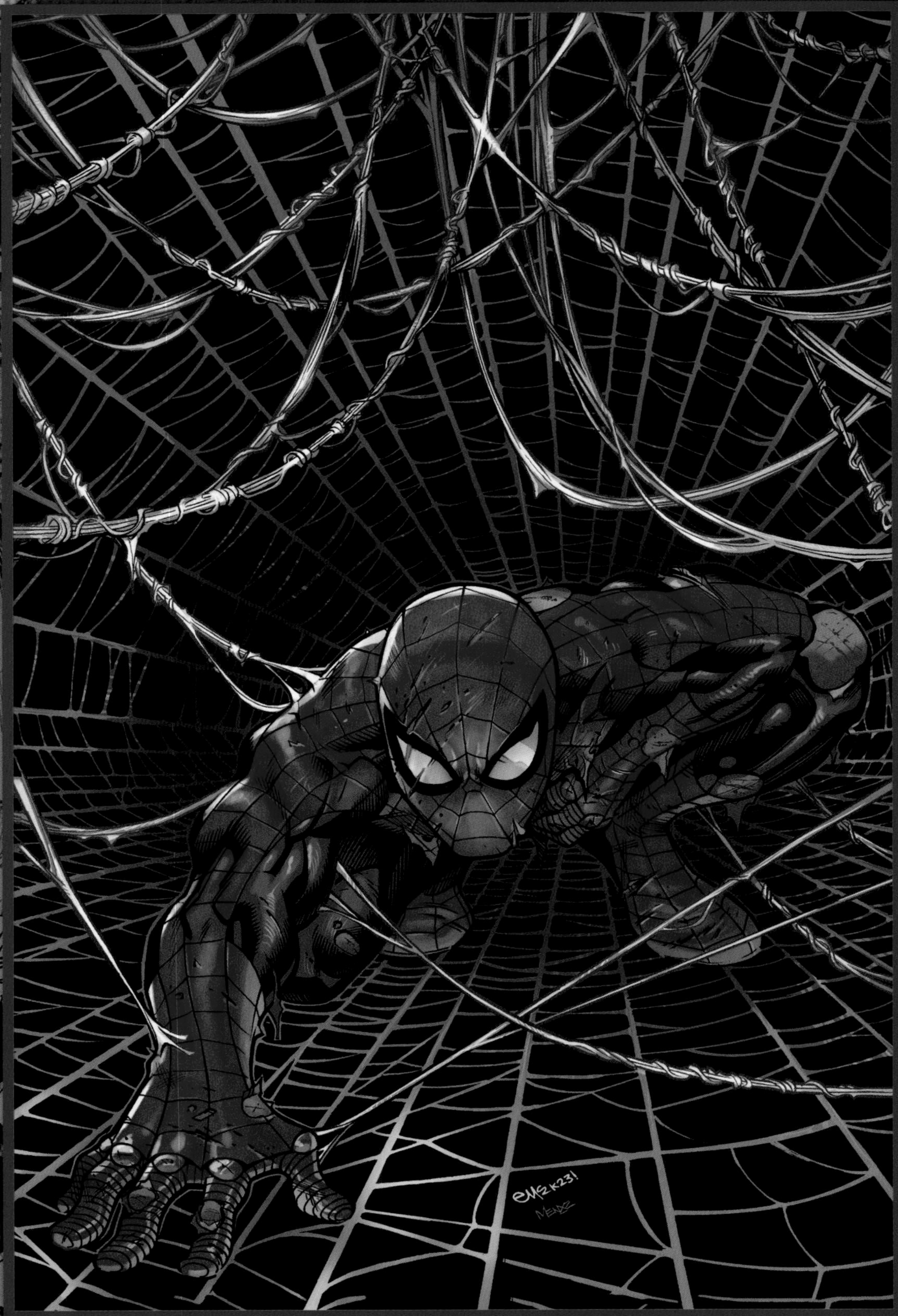

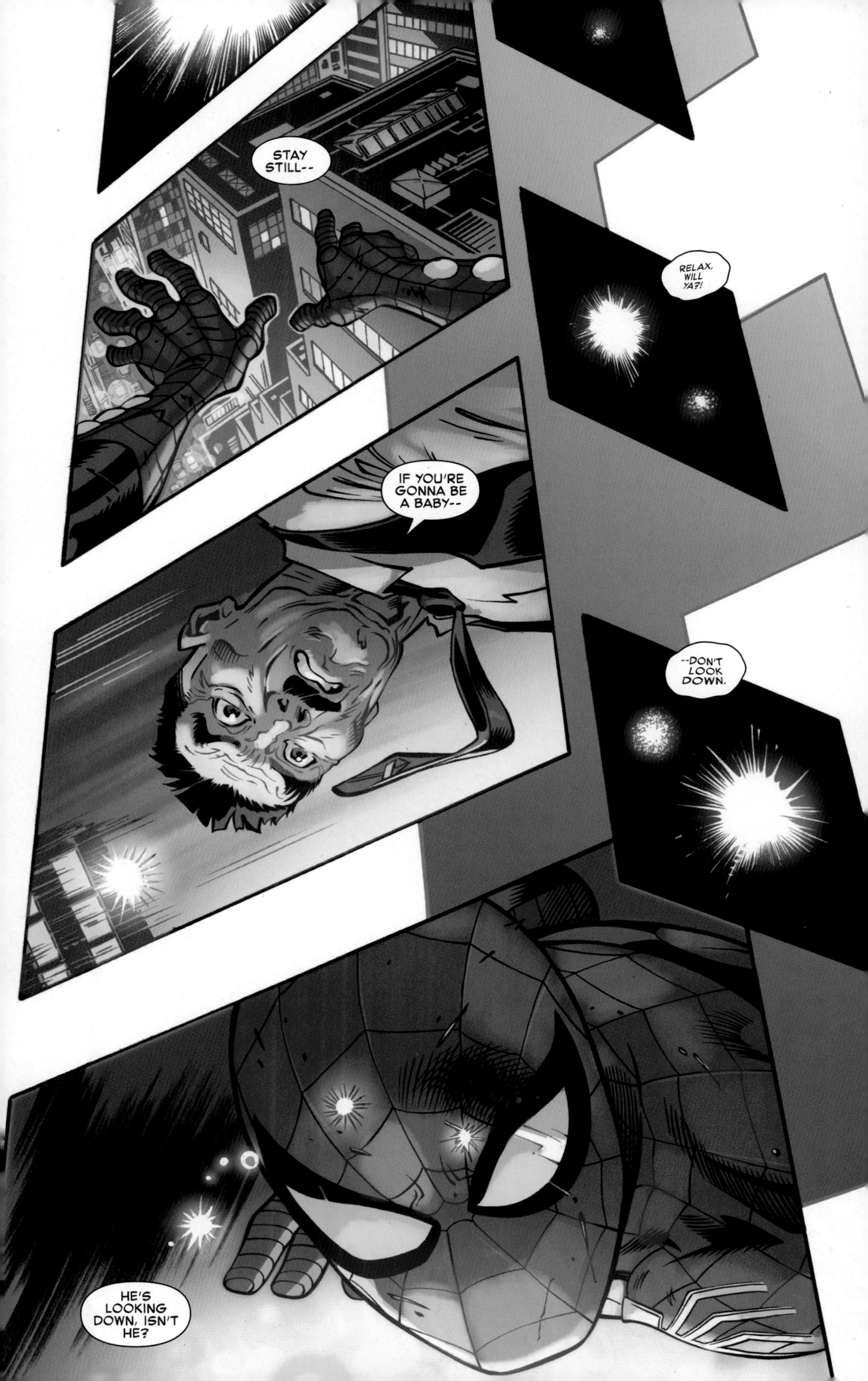
STAY STILL--
RELAX, WILL YA?!
IF YOU'RE GONNA BE A BABY--
--DON'T LOOK DOWN.
HE'S LOOKING DOWN, ISN'T HE?

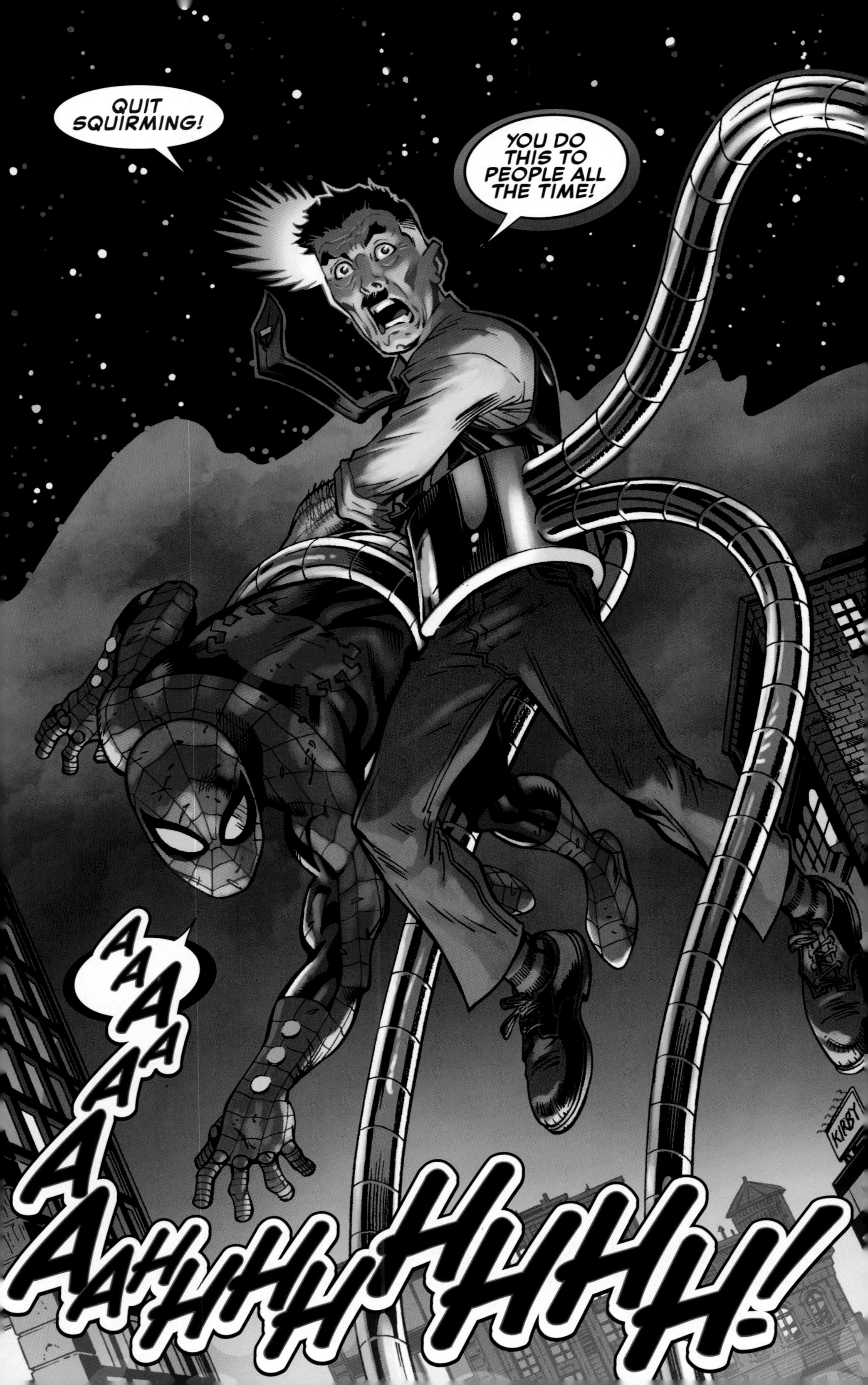
QUIT SQUIRMING!
YOU DO THIS TO PEOPLE ALL THE TIME!
AAAAAAAAAAHHHHHHHHHH!
KIRBY!

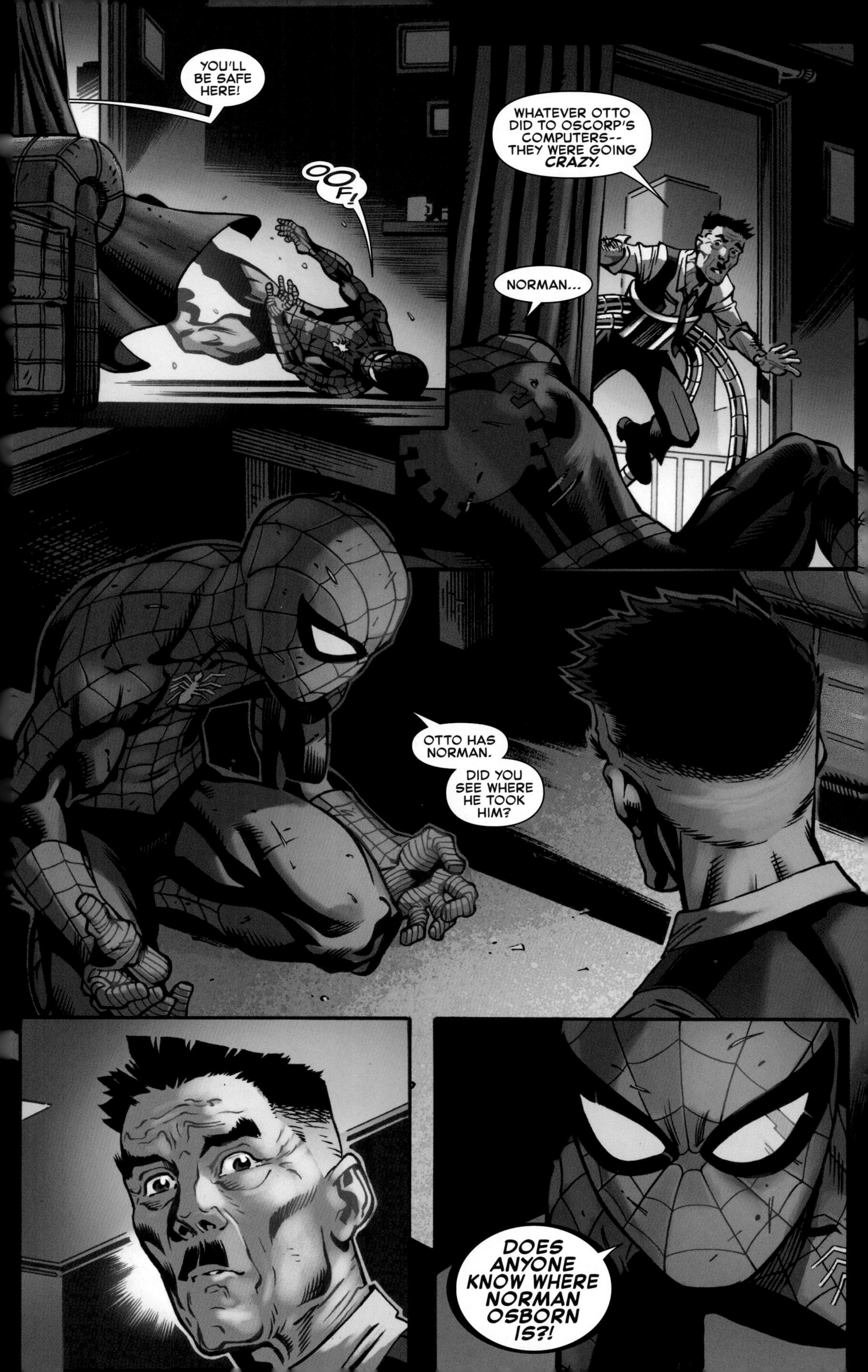
YOU'LL BE SAFE HERE!
OOF!
WHATEVER OTTO DID TO OSCORP'S COMPUTERS-- THEY WERE GOING CRAZY.
NORMAN...
OTTO HAS NORMAN.
DID YOU SEE WHERE HE TOOK HIM?
DOES ANYONE KNOW WHERE NORMAN OSBORN IS?!

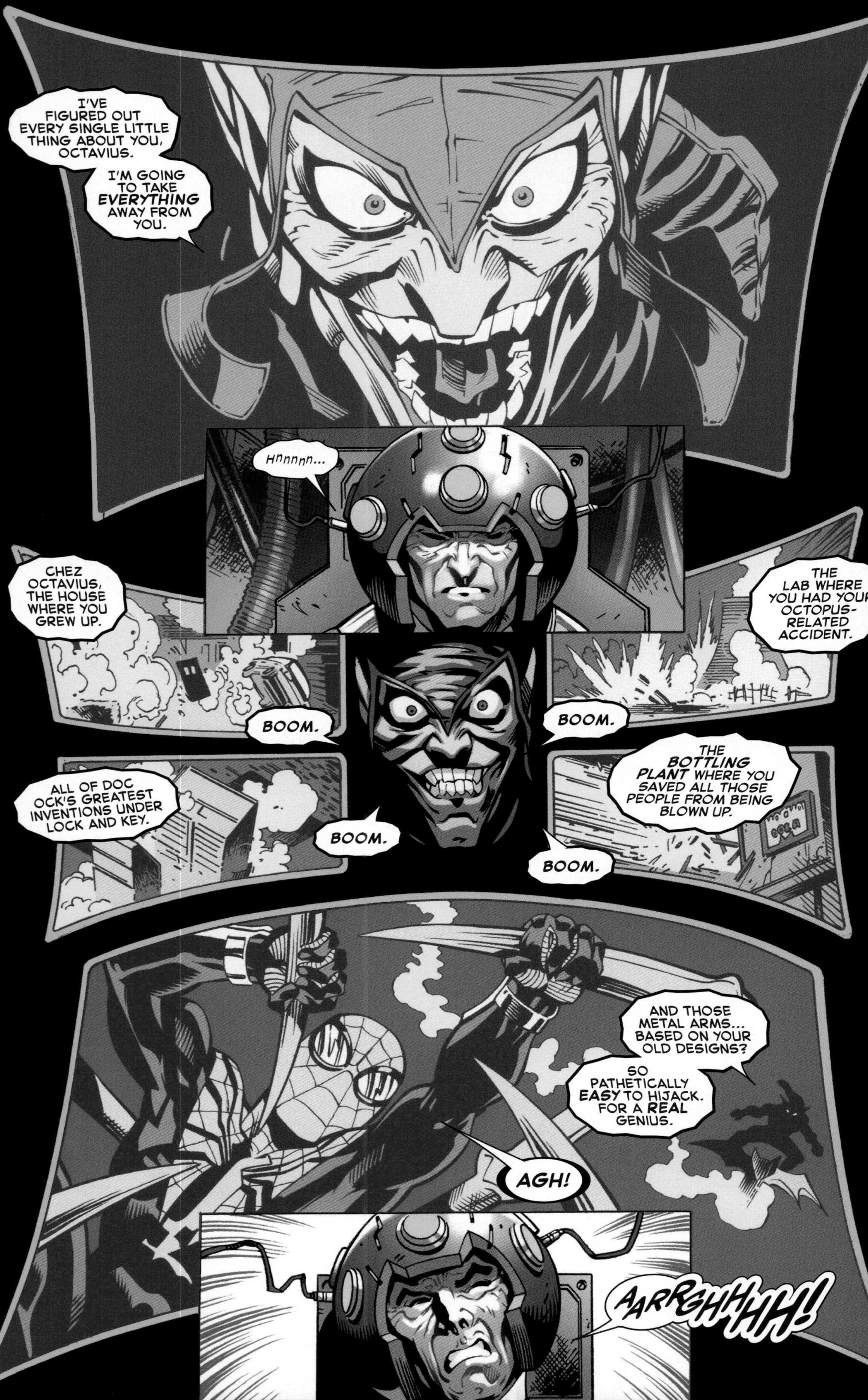

I'VE FIGURED OUT EVERY SINGLE LITTLE THING ABOUT YOU, OCTAVIUS.
I'M GOING TO TAKE **EVERYTHING** AWAY FROM YOU.
Hnnnnn...
CHEZ OCTAVIUS, THE HOUSE WHERE YOU GREW UP.
BOOM.
THE LAB WHERE YOU HAD YOUR OCTOPUS-RELATED ACCIDENT.
BOOM.
ALL OF DOC OCK'S GREATEST INVENTIONS UNDER LOCK AND KEY.
BOOM.
THE **BOTTLING PLANT** WHERE YOU SAVED ALL THOSE PEOPLE FROM BEING BLOWN UP.
BOOM.
AND THOSE METAL ARMS... BASED ON YOUR OLD DESIGNS?
SO PATHETICALLY **EASY** TO HIJACK. FOR A **REAL** GENIUS.
AGH!
AARRGHHHHH!

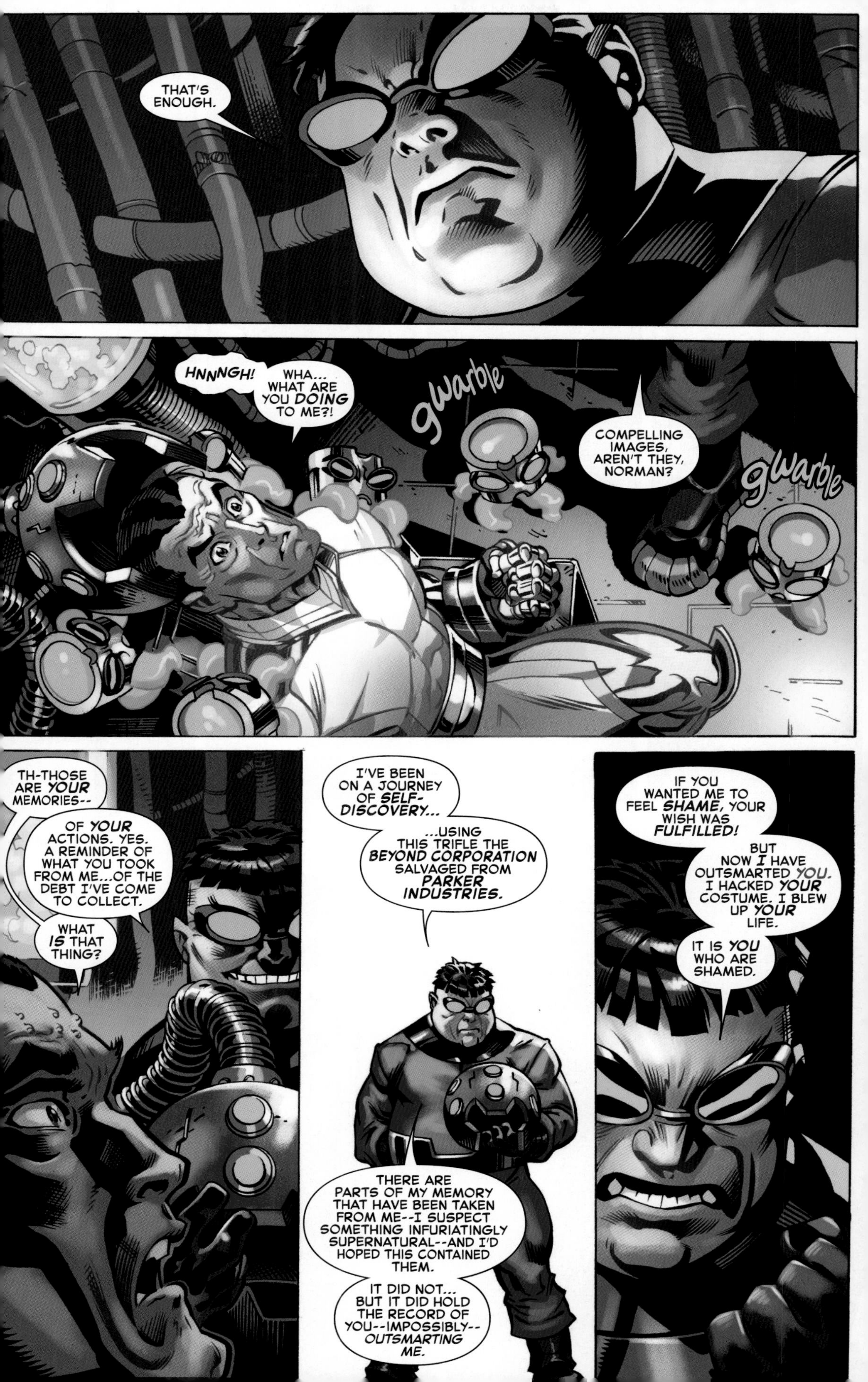
THAT'S ENOUGH.
HNNNGH!
WHA... WHAT ARE YOU DOING TO ME?!
gwarble
COMPELLING IMAGES, AREN'T THEY, NORMAN?
gwarble
TH-THOSE ARE YOUR MEMORIES--
OF YOUR ACTIONS. YES. A REMINDER OF WHAT YOU TOOK FROM ME...OF THE DEBT I'VE COME TO COLLECT.
WHAT IS THAT THING?
I'VE BEEN ON A JOURNEY OF SELF-DISCOVERY...
...USING THIS TRIFLE THE BEYOND CORPORATION SALVAGED FROM PARKER INDUSTRIES.
THERE ARE PARTS OF MY MEMORY THAT HAVE BEEN TAKEN FROM ME--I SUSPECT SOMETHING INFURIATINGLY SUPERNATURAL--AND I'D HOPED THIS CONTAINED THEM.
IT DID NOT... BUT IT DID HOLD THE RECORD OF YOU--IMPOSSIBLY--OUTSMARTING ME.
IF YOU WANTED ME TO FEEL SHAME, YOUR WISH WAS FULFILLED!
BUT NOW I HAVE OUTSMARTED YOU. I HACKED YOUR COSTUME. I BLEW UP YOUR LIFE.
IT IS YOU WHO ARE SHAMED.

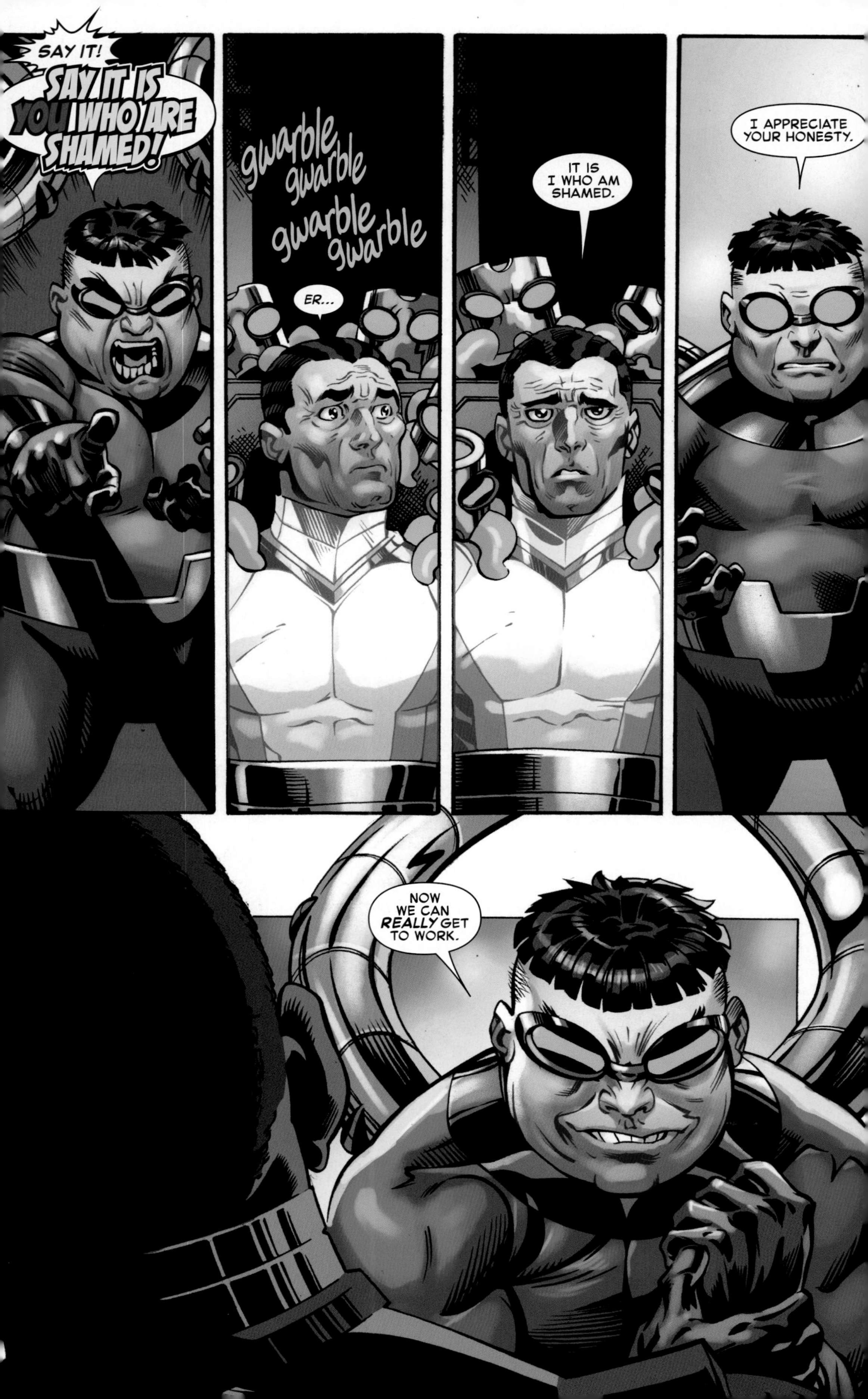
SAY IT!
SAY IT IS YOU WHO ARE SHAMED!
gwarble gwarble gwarble gwarble
ER...
IT IS I WHO AM SHAMED.
I APPRECIATE YOUR HONESTY.
NOW WE CAN *REALLY* GET TO WORK.

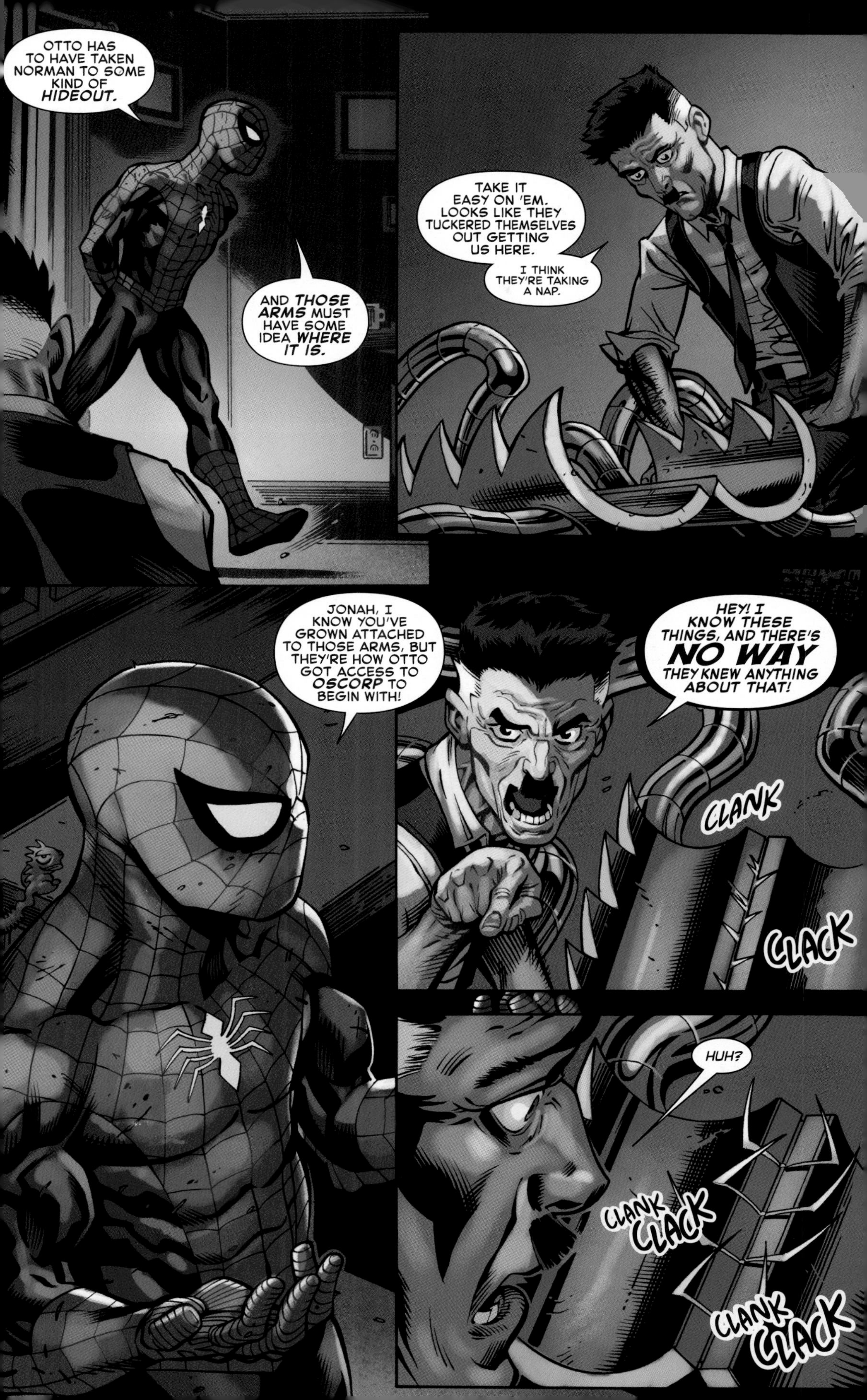

OTTO HAS TO HAVE TAKEN NORMAN TO SOME KIND OF HIDEOUT.
AND THOSE ARMS MUST HAVE SOME IDEA WHERE IT IS.
TAKE IT EASY ON 'EM. LOOKS LIKE THEY TUCKERED THEMSELVES OUT GETTING US HERE.
I THINK THEY'RE TAKING A NAP.
JONAH, I KNOW YOU'VE GROWN ATTACHED TO THOSE ARMS, BUT THEY'RE HOW OTTO GOT ACCESS TO OSCORP TO BEGIN WITH!
HEY! I KNOW THESE THINGS, AND THERE'S NO WAY THEY KNEW ANYTHING ABOUT THAT!
CLANK
CLACK
HUH?
CLANK
CLACK
CLANK
CLACK

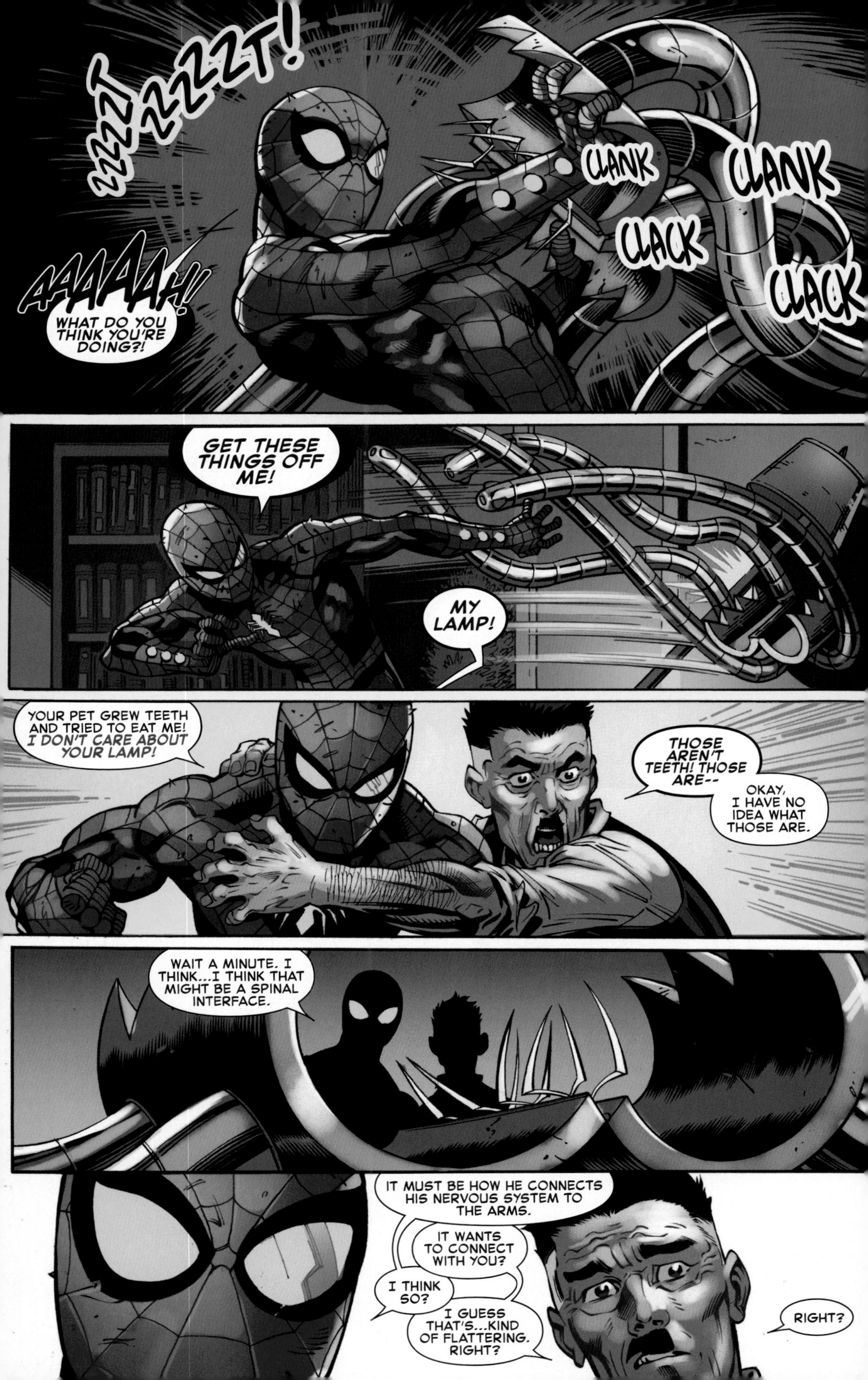
ZZZZZT ZZZZZT!
AAAAAAH!!
WHAT DO YOU THINK YOU'RE DOING?!
CLANK
CLANK
CLACK
CLACK
GET THESE THINGS OFF ME!
MY LAMP!
YOUR PET GREW TEETH AND TRIED TO EAT ME! I DON'T CARE ABOUT YOUR LAMP!
THOSE AREN'T TEETH! THOSE ARE--
OKAY, I HAVE NO IDEA WHAT THOSE ARE.
WAIT A MINUTE. I THINK...I THINK THAT MIGHT BE A SPINAL INTERFACE.
IT MUST BE HOW HE CONNECTS HIS NERVOUS SYSTEM TO THE ARMS.
IT WANTS TO CONNECT WITH YOU?
I THINK SO?
I GUESS THAT'S...KIND OF FLATTERING. RIGHT?
RIGHT?

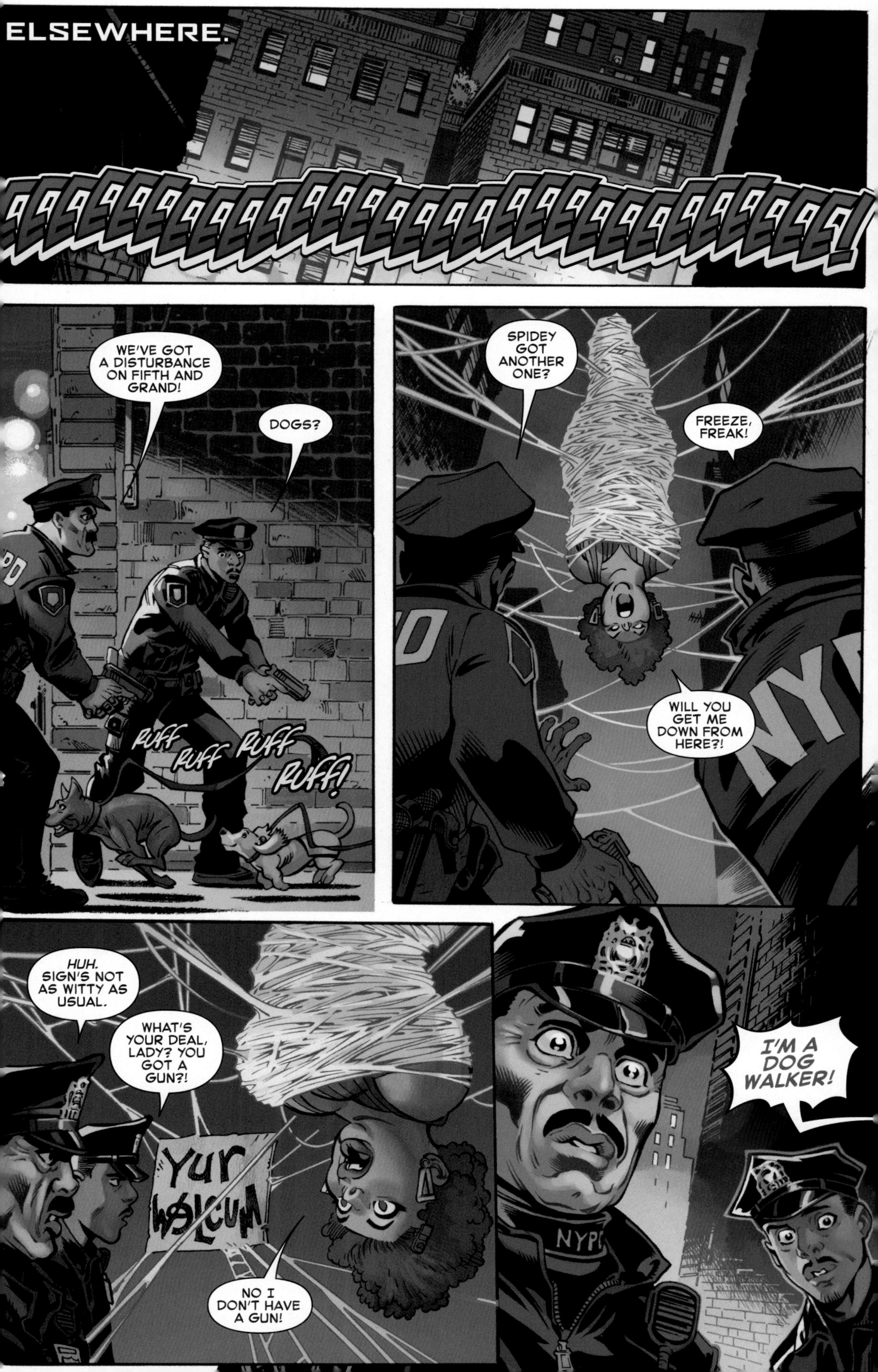

ELSEWHERE.
EEEEEEEEEEEEEEEEEEEEEEEEEE!
WE'VE GOT A DISTURBANCE ON FIFTH AND GRAND!
DOGS?
RUFF RUFF RUFF RUFF!
SPIDEY GOT ANOTHER ONE?
FREEZE, FREAK!
WILL YOU GET ME DOWN FROM HERE?!
HUH. SIGN'S NOT AS WITTY AS USUAL.
WHAT'S YOUR DEAL, LADY? YOU GOT A GUN?!
YUR WELCUM
NO I DON'T HAVE A GUN!
I'M A DOG WALKER!

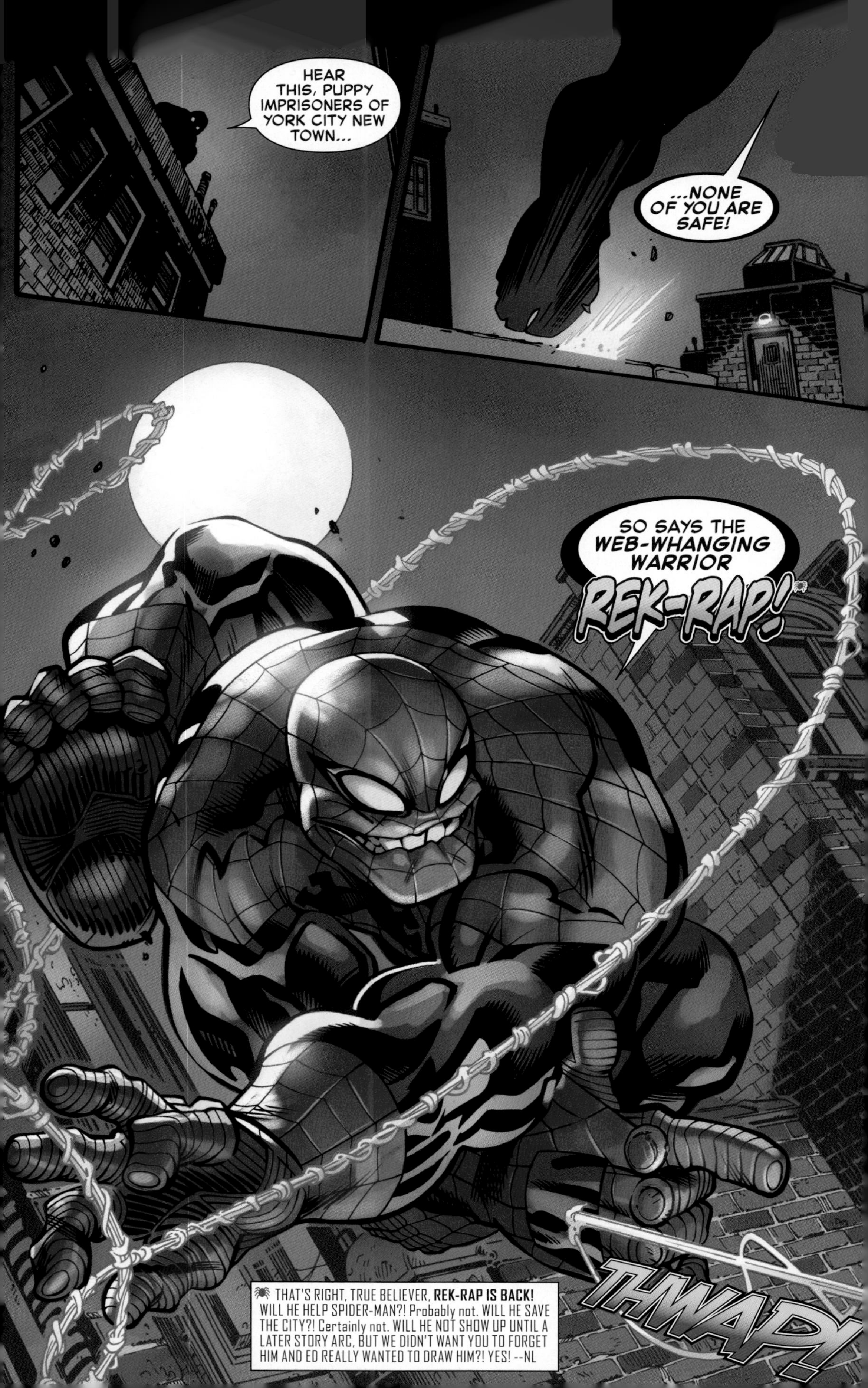
HEAR THIS, PUPPY IMPRISONERS OF YORK CITY NEW TOWN...
...NONE OF YOU ARE SAFE!
SO SAYS THE WEB-WHANGING WARRIOR
REK-RAP!
THAT'S RIGHT, TRUE BELIEVER, REK-RAP IS BACK! WILL HE HELP SPIDER-MAN?! Probably not. WILL HE SAVE THE CITY?! Certainly not. WILL HE NOT SHOW UP UNTIL A LATER STORY ARC, BUT WE DIDN'T WANT YOU TO FORGET HIM AND ED REALLY WANTED TO DRAW HIM?! YES! --NL
THWAP!

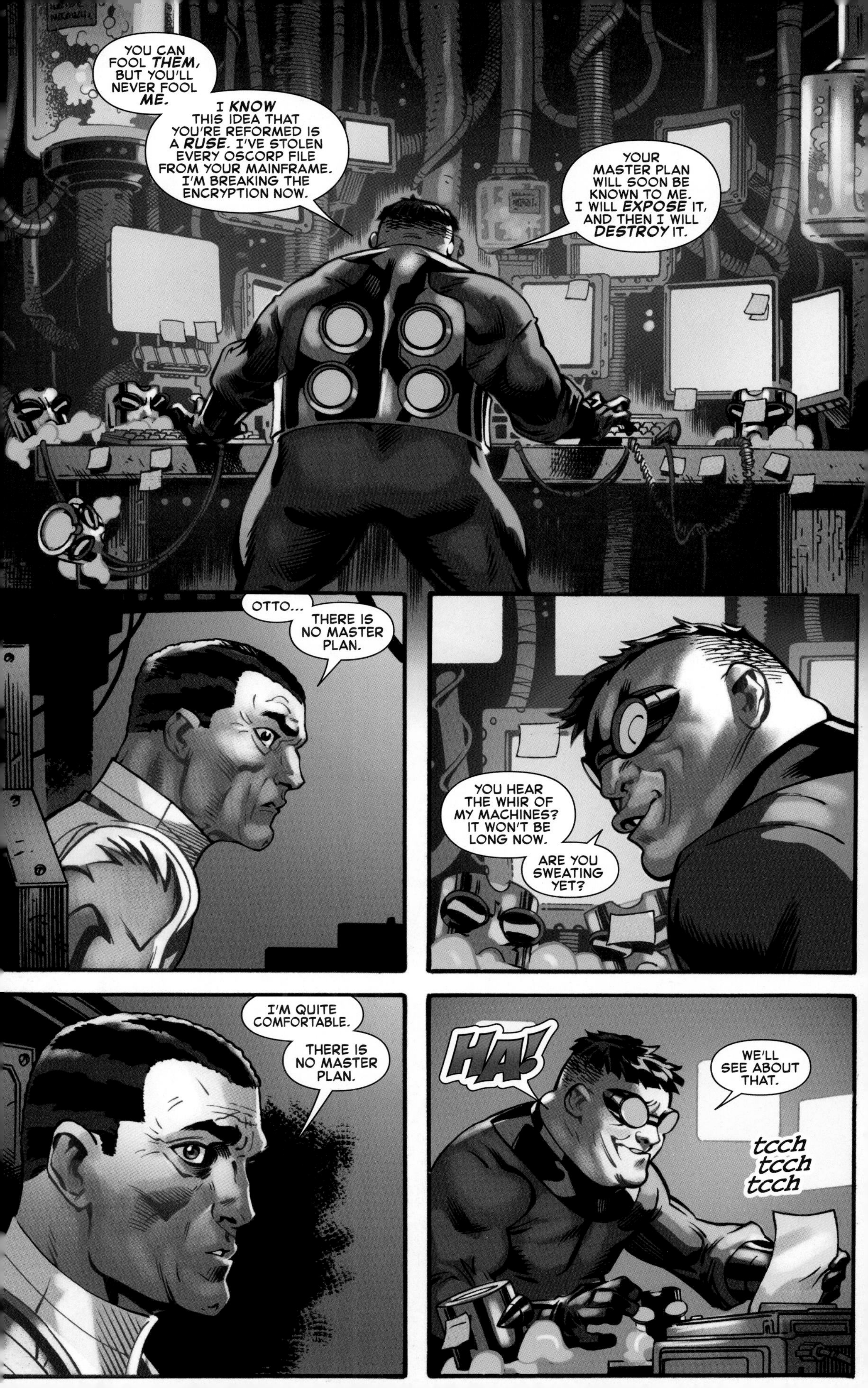
YOU CAN FOOL THEM, BUT YOU'LL NEVER FOOL ME.
I KNOW THIS IDEA THAT YOU'RE REFORMED IS A RUSE. I'VE STOLEN EVERY OSCORP FILE FROM YOUR MAINFRAME. I'M BREAKING THE ENCRYPTION NOW.
YOUR MASTER PLAN WILL SOON BE KNOWN TO ME. I WILL EXPOSE IT, AND THEN I WILL DESTROY IT.
OTTO...
THERE IS NO MASTER PLAN.
YOU HEAR THE WHIR OF MY MACHINES? IT WON'T BE LONG NOW.
ARE YOU SWEATING YET?
I'M QUITE COMFORTABLE.
THERE IS NO MASTER PLAN.
HA!
WE'LL SEE ABOUT THAT.
tcch tcch tcch

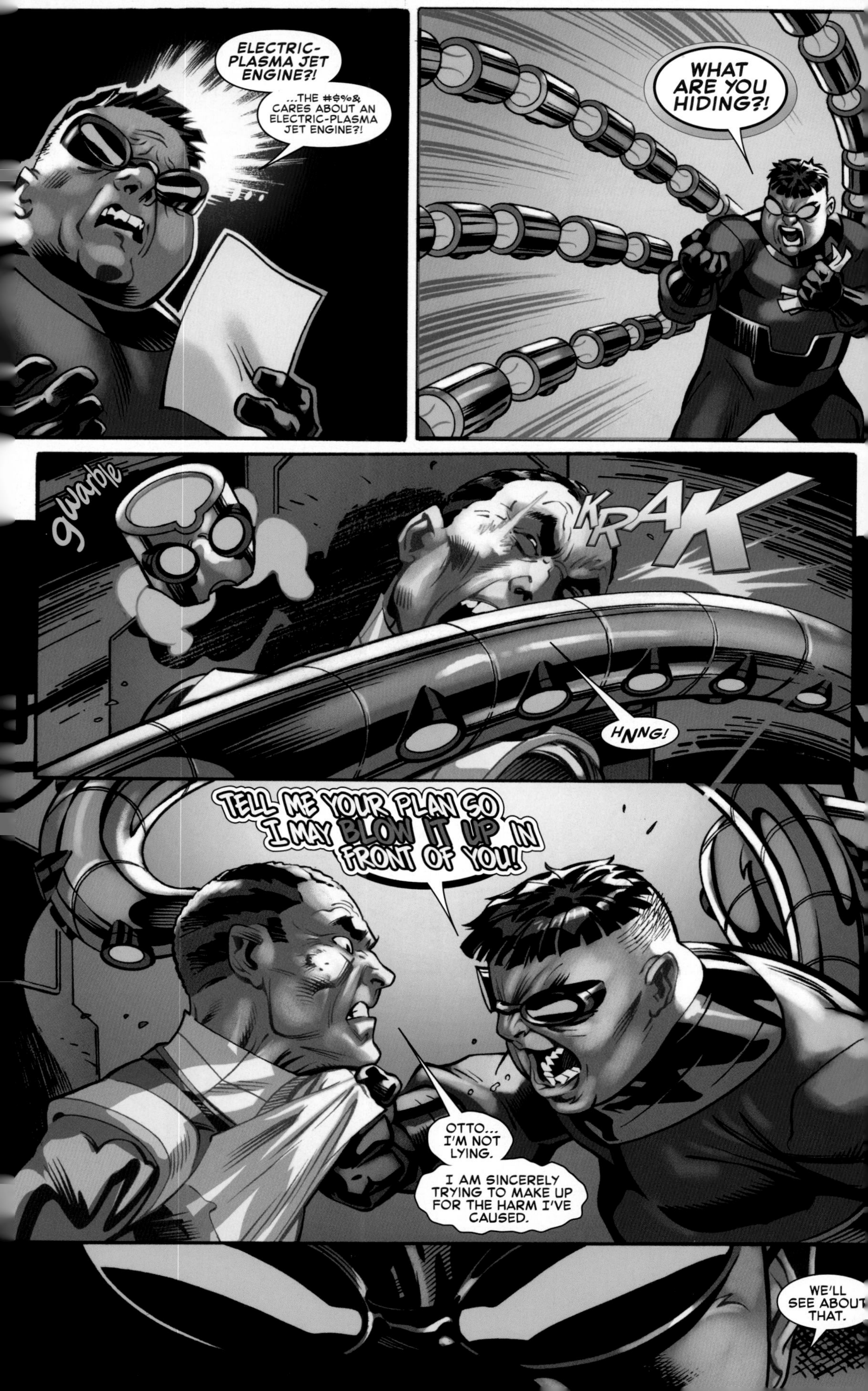
ELECTRIC-PLASMA JET ENGINE?!
...THE #$%& CARES ABOUT AN ELECTRIC-PLASMA JET ENGINE?!
WHAT ARE YOU HIDING?!
gwarble
KRAK
HNNG!
TELL ME YOUR PLAN SO I MAY BLOW IT UP IN FRONT OF YOU!
OTTO... I'M NOT LYING.
I AM SINCERELY TRYING TO MAKE UP FOR THE HARM I'VE CAUSED.
WE'LL SEE ABOUT THAT.

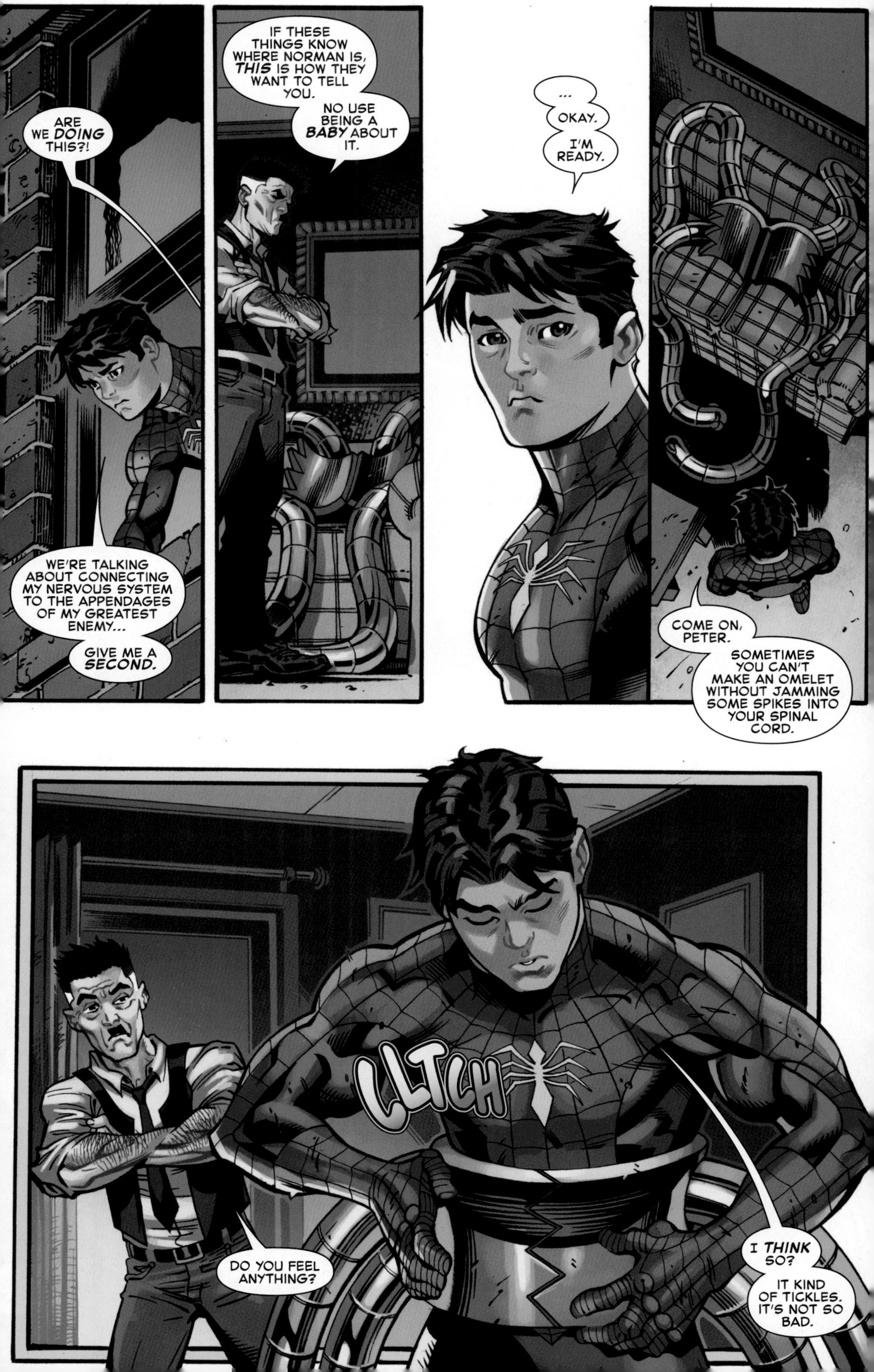
ARE WE DOING THIS?!
WE'RE TALKING ABOUT CONNECTING MY NERVOUS SYSTEM TO THE APPENDAGES OF MY GREATEST ENEMY...
GIVE ME A SECOND.
IF THESE THINGS KNOW WHERE NORMAN IS, THIS IS HOW THEY WANT TO TELL YOU.
NO USE BEING A BABY ABOUT IT.
...
OKAY.
I'M READY.
COME ON, PETER.
SOMETIMES YOU CAN'T MAKE AN OMELET WITHOUT JAMMING SOME SPIKES INTO YOUR SPINAL CORD.
LLTCH
DO YOU FEEL ANYTHING?
I THINK SO?
IT KIND OF TICKLES. IT'S NOT SO BAD.

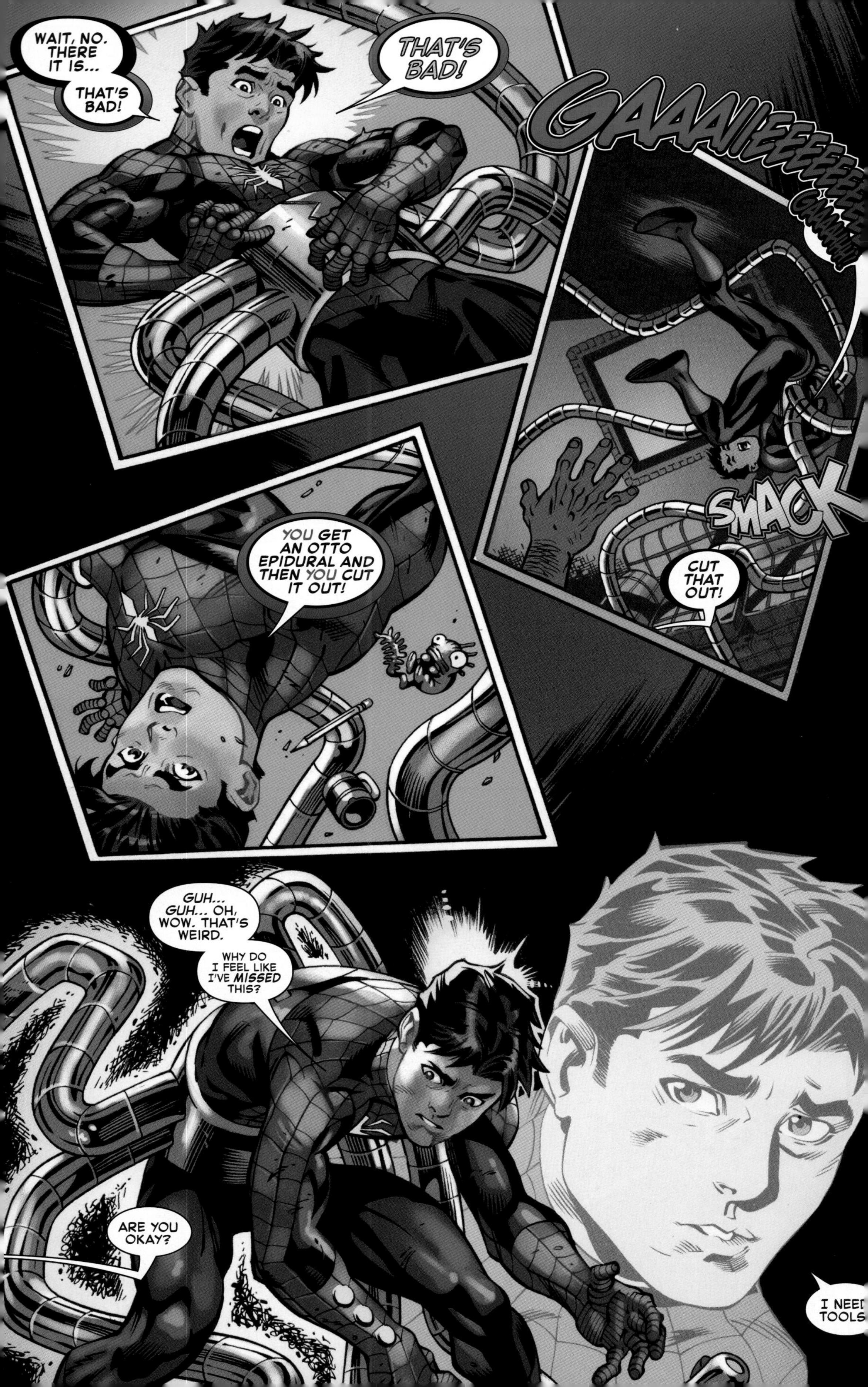
WAIT, NO. THERE IT IS...
THAT'S BAD!
THAT'S BAD!
GAAAIIEEEEEEE
YOU GET AN OTTO EPIDURAL AND THEN YOU CUT IT OUT!
SMACK
CUT THAT OUT!
GUH... GUH... OH, WOW. THAT'S WEIRD.
WHY DO I FEEL LIKE I'VE MISSED THIS?
ARE YOU OKAY?
I NEED TOOLS

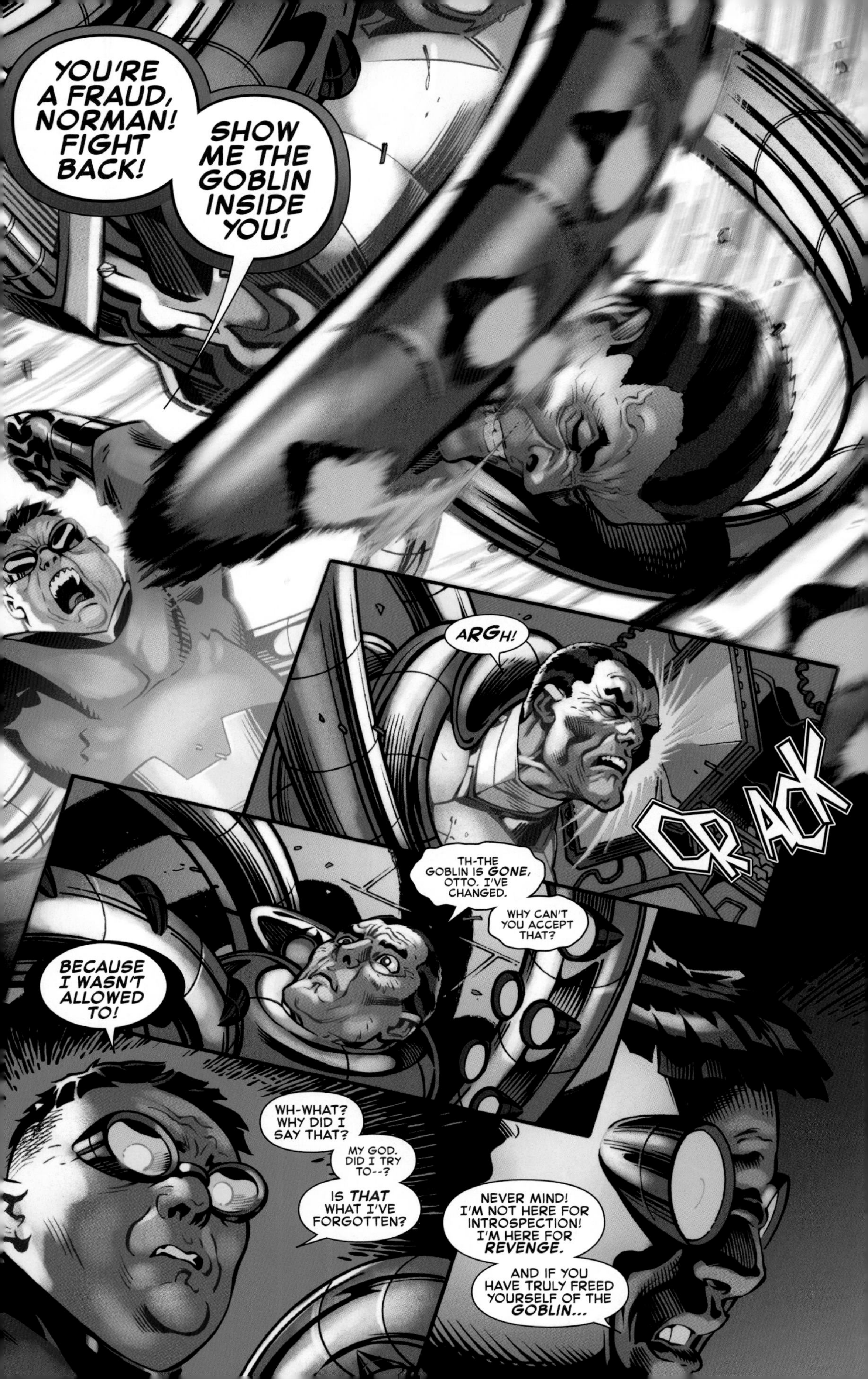
YOU'RE A FRAUD, NORMAN! FIGHT BACK!
SHOW ME THE GOBLIN INSIDE YOU!
ARGH!
CRACK
TH-THE GOBLIN IS GONE, OTTO. I'VE CHANGED.
WHY CAN'T YOU ACCEPT THAT?
BECAUSE I WASN'T ALLOWED TO!
WH-WHAT? WHY DID I SAY THAT?
MY GOD. DID I TRY TO--?
IS THAT WHAT I'VE FORGOTTEN?
NEVER MIND! I'M NOT HERE FOR INTROSPECTION! I'M HERE FOR REVENGE.
AND IF YOU HAVE TRULY FREED YOURSELF OF THE GOBLIN...

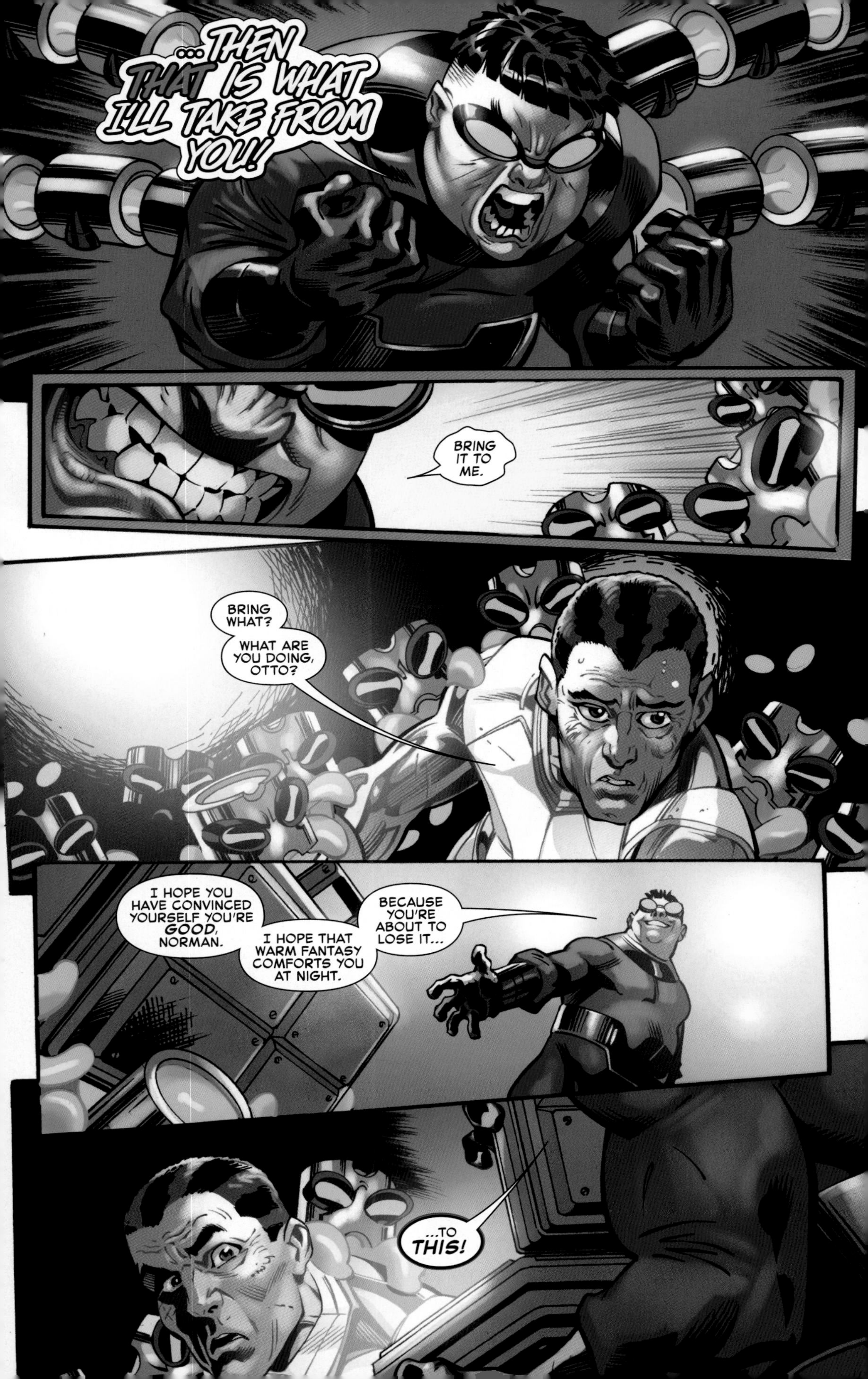
...THEN THAT IS WHAT I'LL TAKE FROM YOU!
BRING IT TO ME.
BRING WHAT?
WHAT ARE YOU DOING, OTTO?
I HOPE YOU HAVE CONVINCED YOURSELF YOU'RE GOOD, NORMAN.
I HOPE THAT WARM FANTASY COMFORTS YOU AT NIGHT.
BECAUSE YOU'RE ABOUT TO LOSE IT...
...TO THIS!

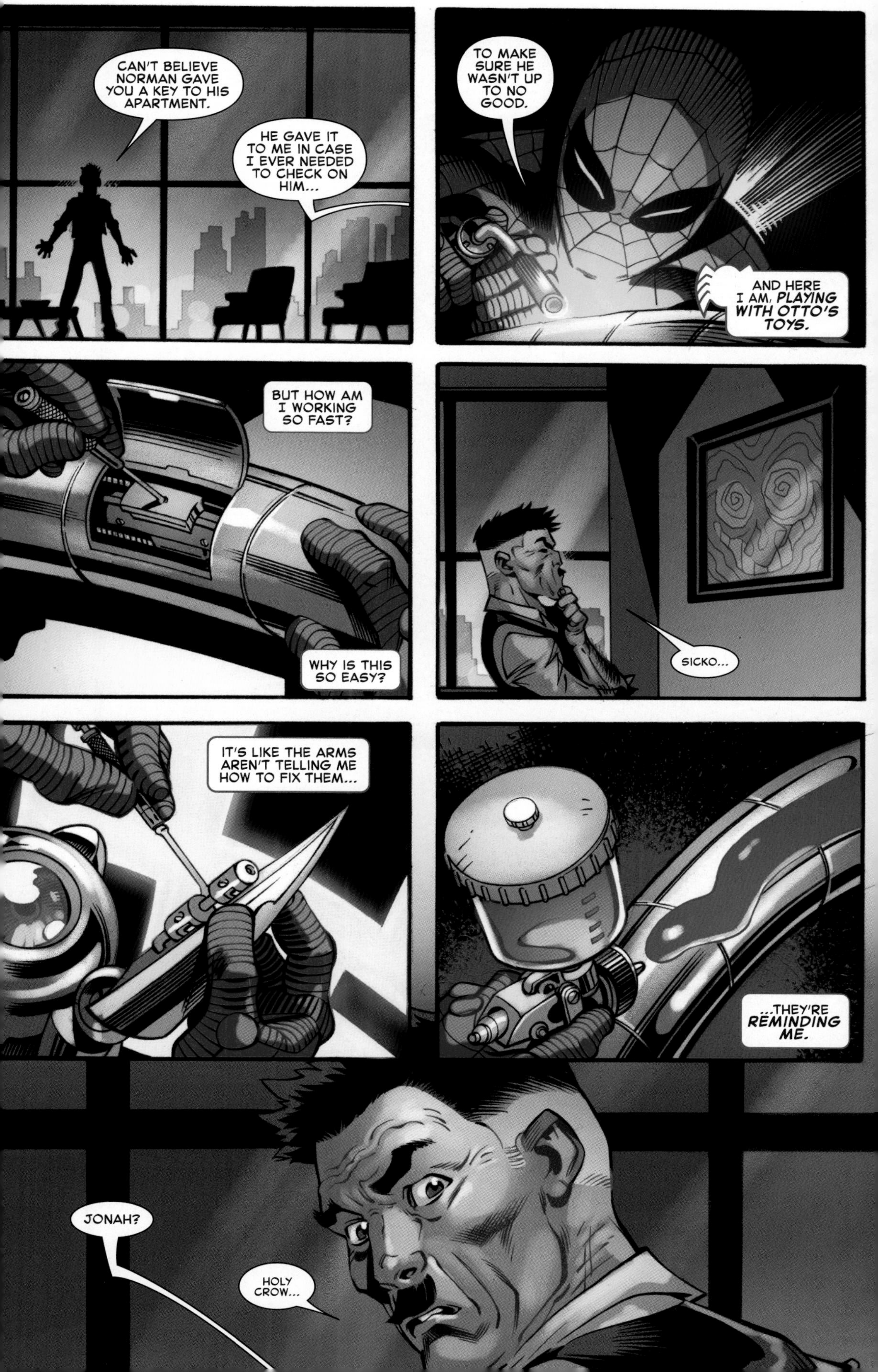
CAN'T BELIEVE NORMAN GAVE YOU A KEY TO HIS APARTMENT.
HE GAVE IT TO ME IN CASE I EVER NEEDED TO CHECK ON HIM...
TO MAKE SURE HE WASN'T UP TO NO GOOD.
AND HERE I AM, PLAYING WITH OTTO'S TOYS.
BUT HOW AM I WORKING SO FAST?
WHY IS THIS SO EASY?
SICKO...
IT'S LIKE THE ARMS AREN'T TELLING ME HOW TO FIX THEM...
...THEY'RE REMINDING ME.
JONAH?
HOLY CROW...

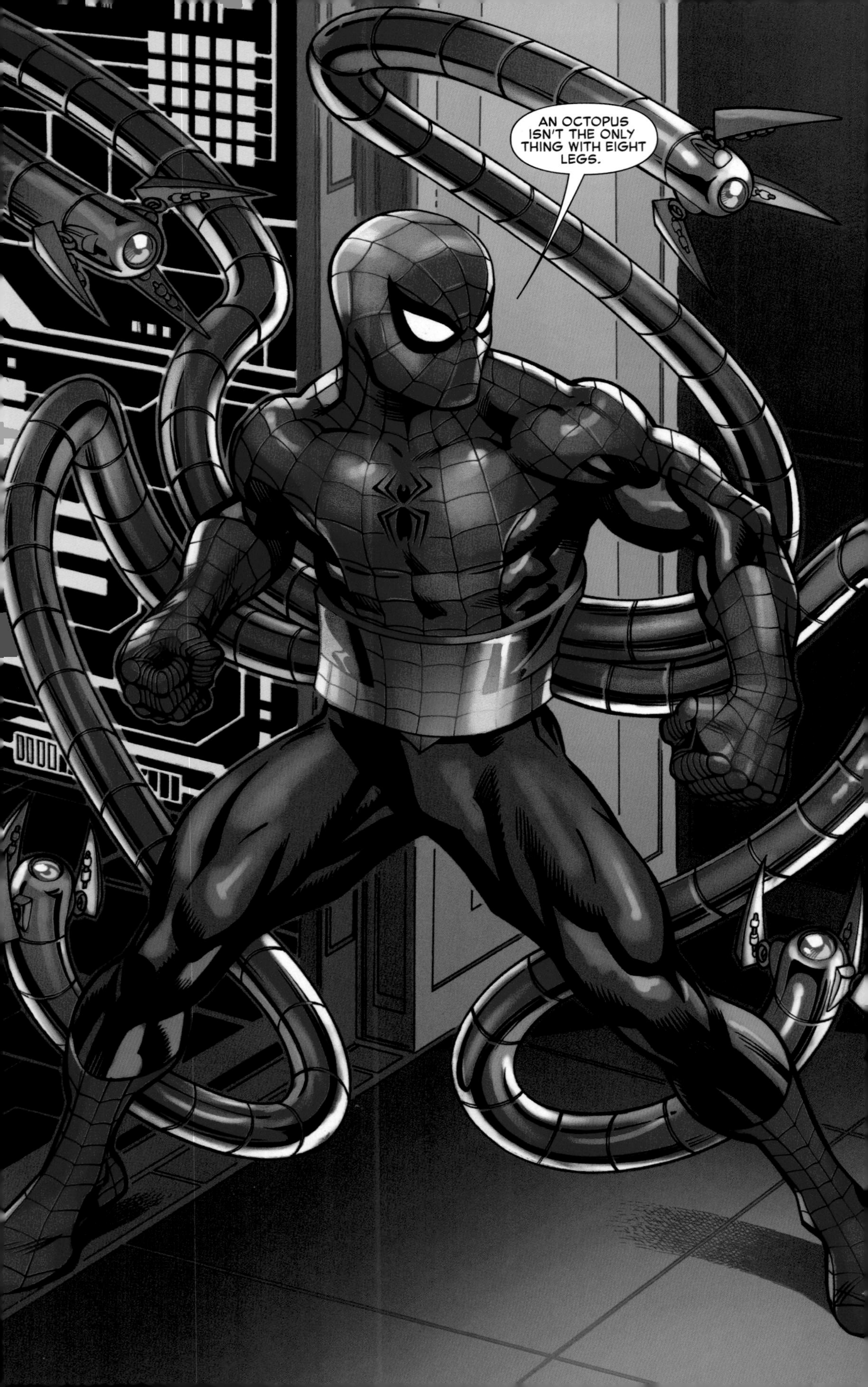
AN OCTOPUS ISN'T THE ONLY THING WITH EIGHT LEGS.

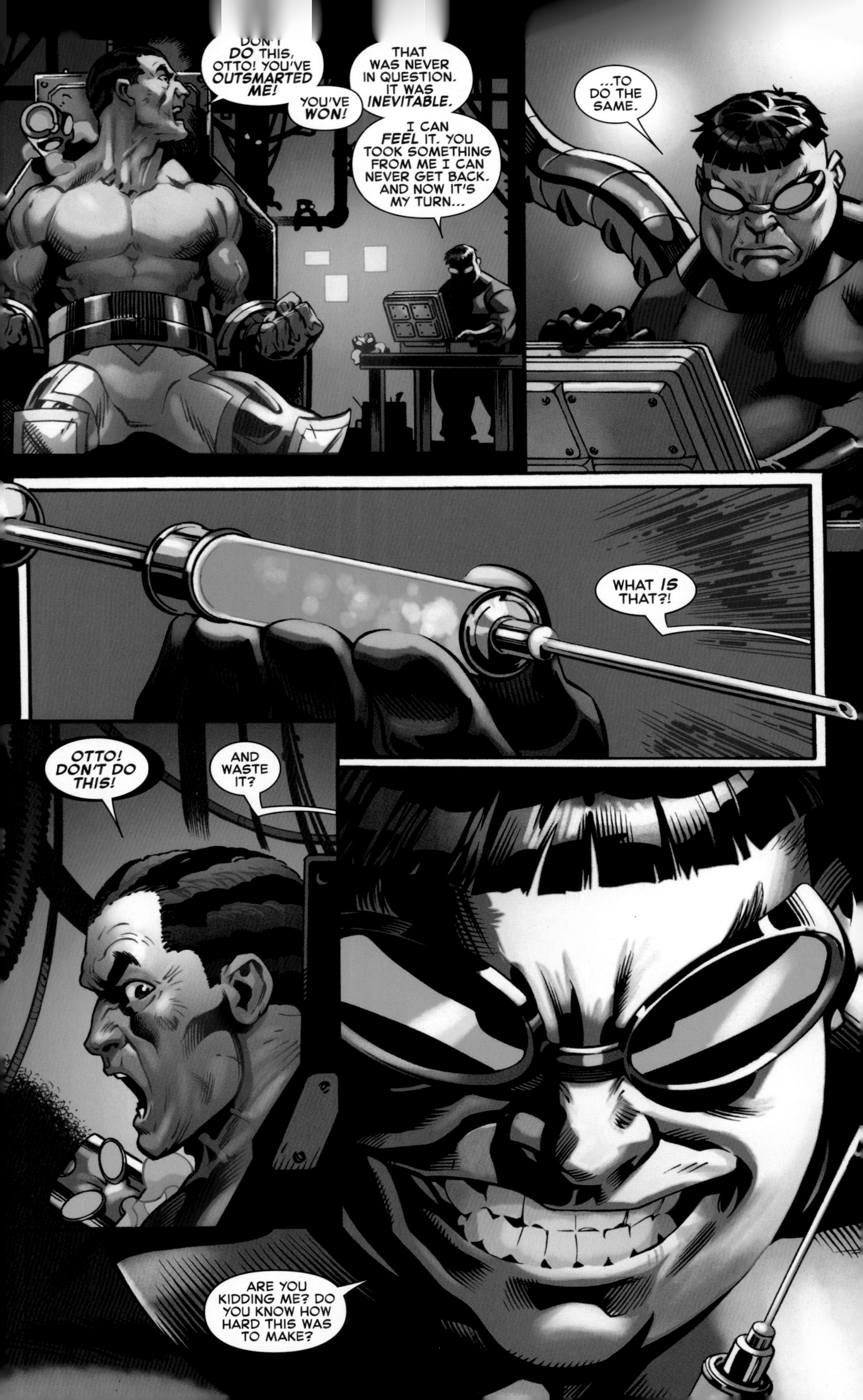
DON'T DO THIS, OTTO! YOU'VE OUTSMARTED ME!
YOU'VE WON!
THAT WAS NEVER IN QUESTION. IT WAS INEVITABLE.
I CAN FEEL IT. YOU TOOK SOMETHING FROM ME I CAN NEVER GET BACK. AND NOW IT'S MY TURN...
...TO DO THE SAME.
WHAT IS THAT?!
OTTO! DON'T DO THIS!
AND WASTE IT?
ARE YOU KIDDING ME? DO YOU KNOW HOW HARD THIS WAS TO MAKE?

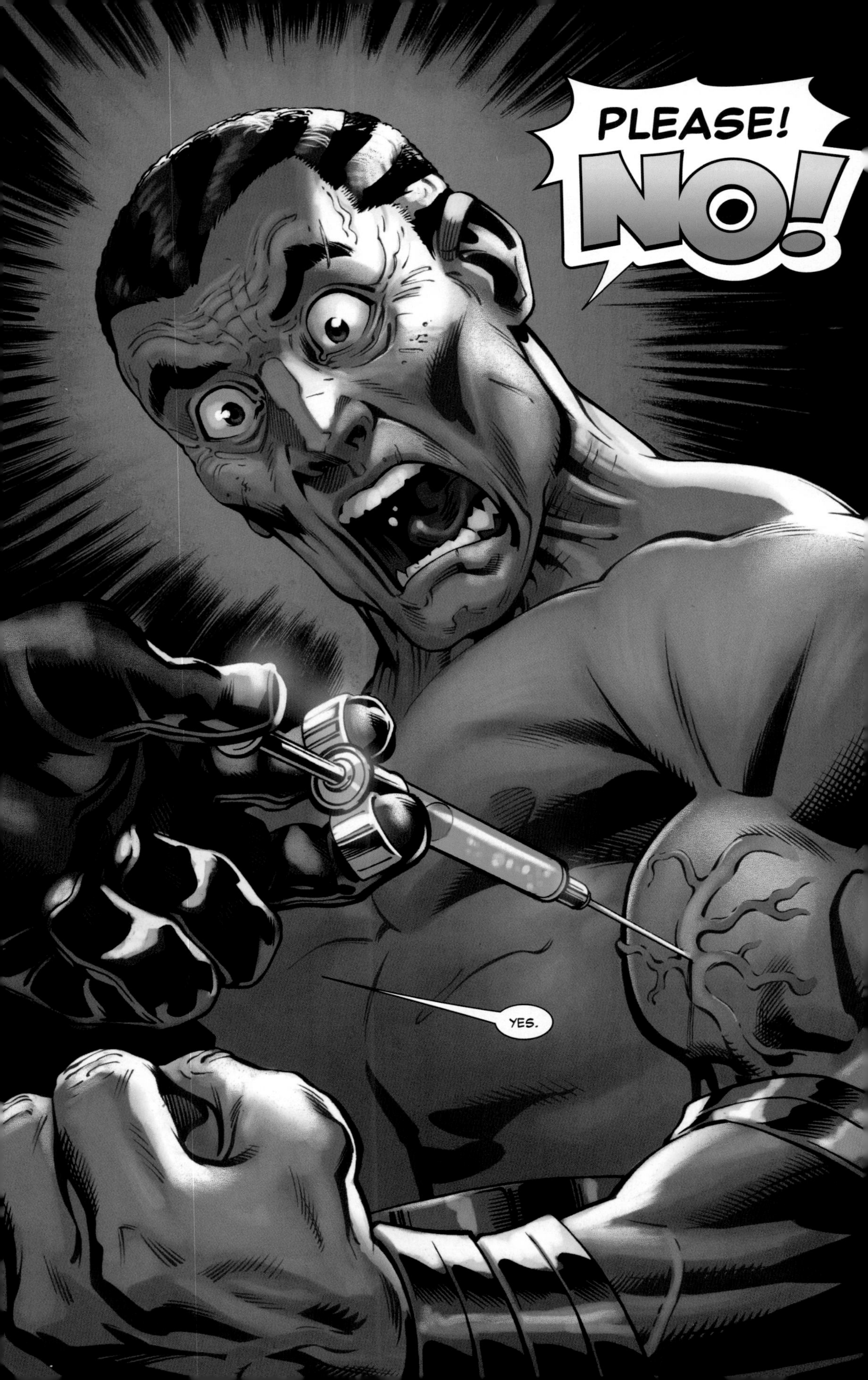
PLEASE! NO!
YES.

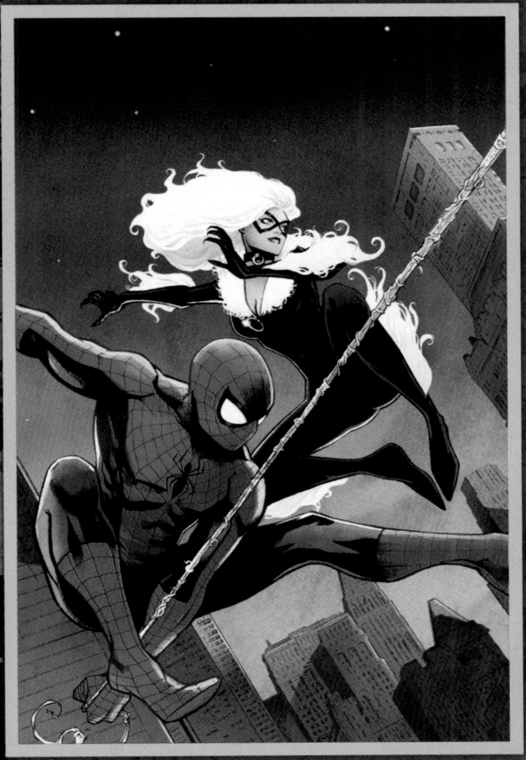

Lee Garbett
#27 VARIANT

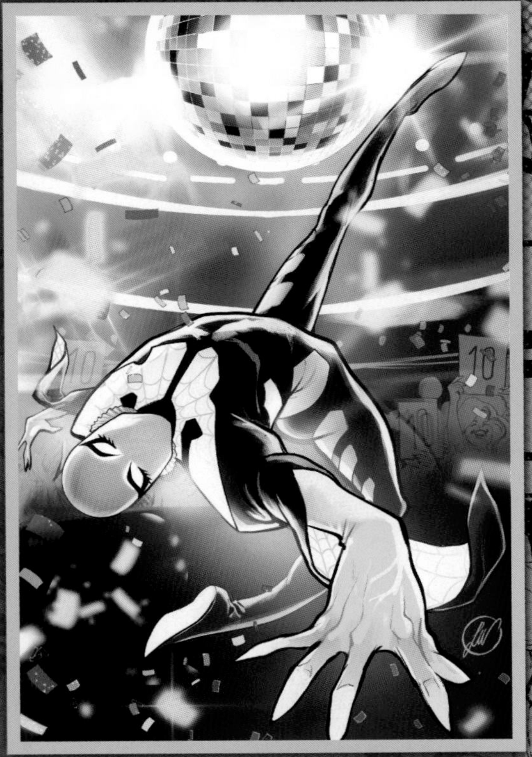

Lucas Werneck
#27 PRIDE VARIANT

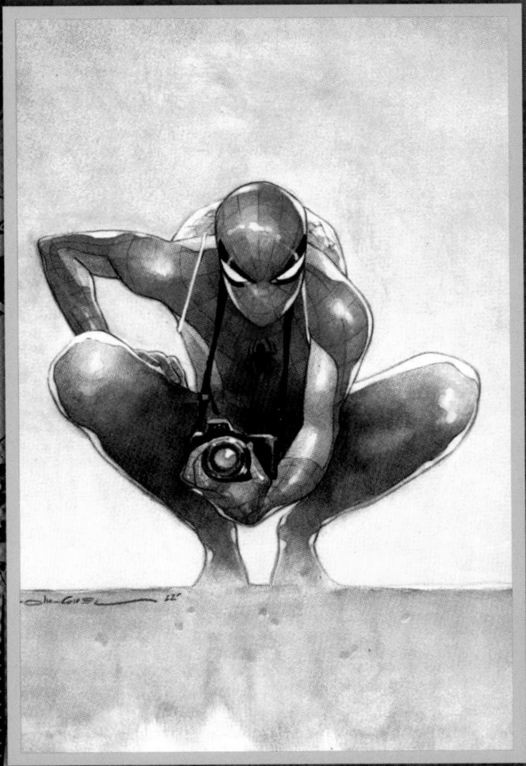

Olivier Coipel
#28 VARIANT

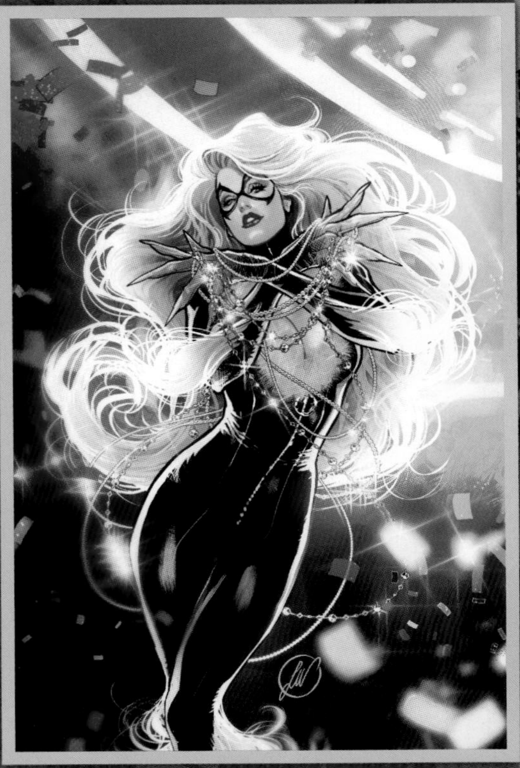

Lucas Werneck
#28 PRIDE VARIANT

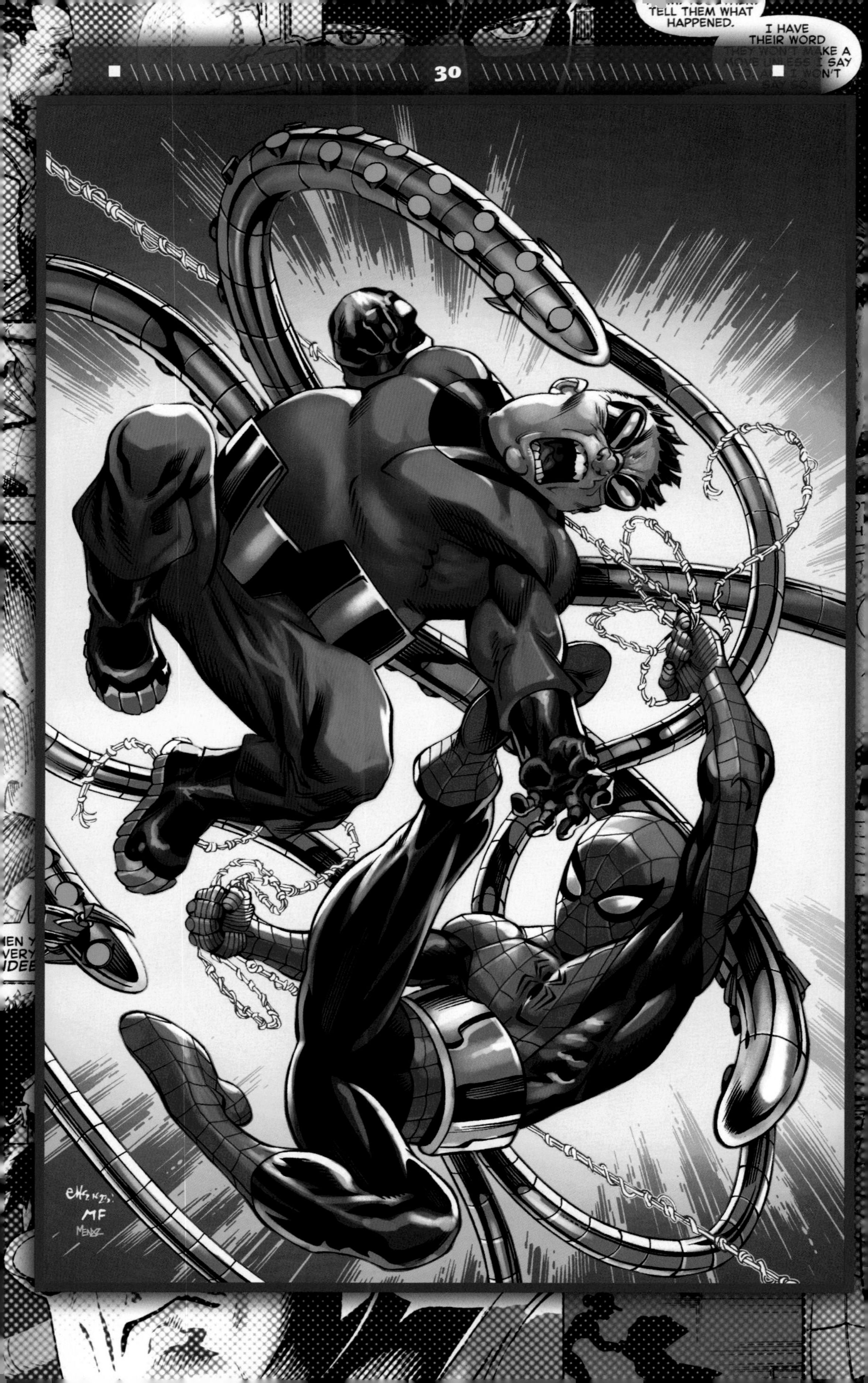
TELL THEM WHAT HAPPENED.
I HAVE THEIR WORD

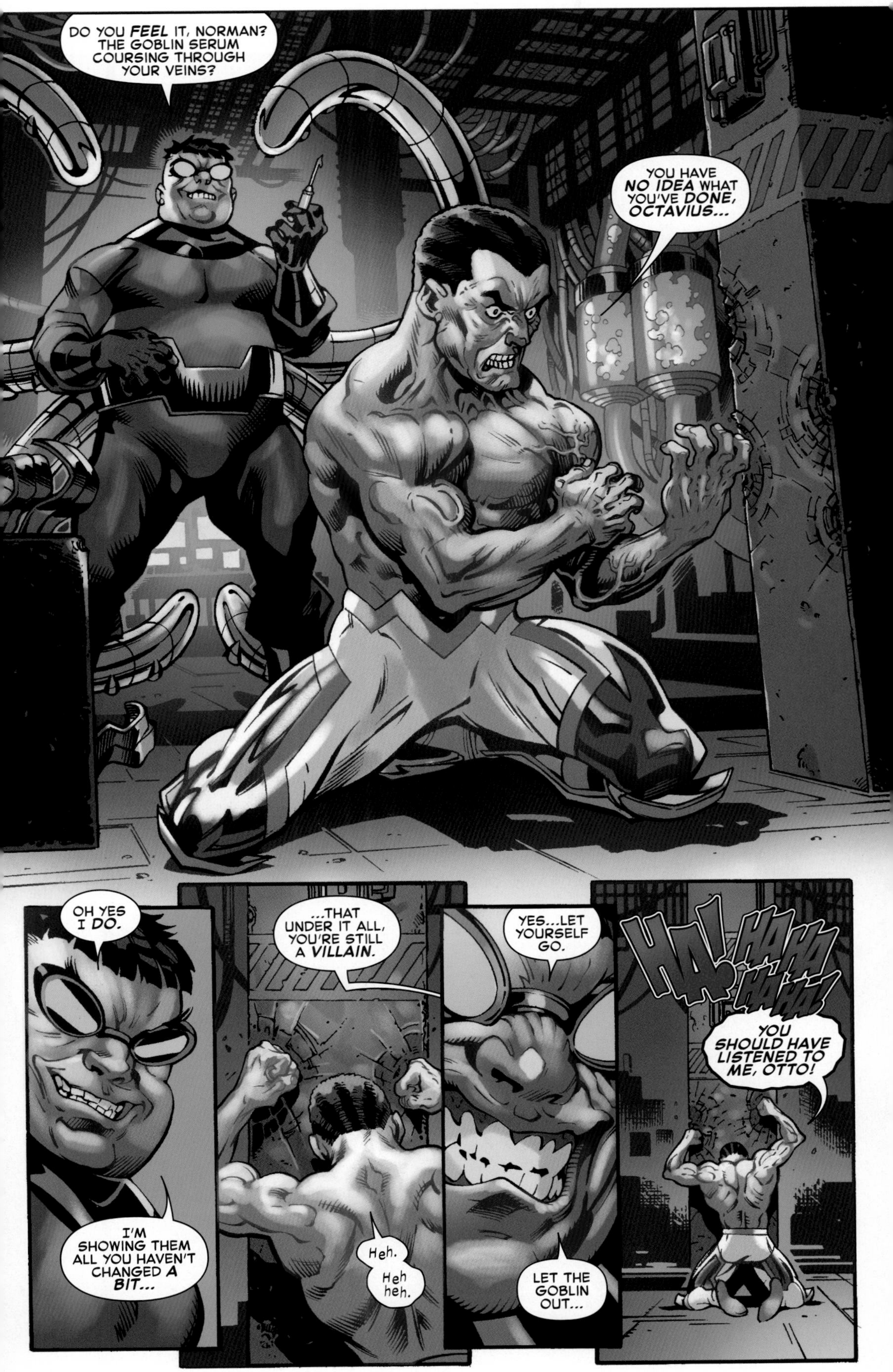
DO YOU FEEL IT, NORMAN? THE GOBLIN SERUM COURSING THROUGH YOUR VEINS?
YOU HAVE NO IDEA WHAT YOU'VE DONE, OCTAVIUS...
OH YES I DO.
I'M SHOWING THEM ALL YOU HAVEN'T CHANGED A BIT...
...THAT UNDER IT ALL, YOU'RE STILL A VILLAIN.
Heh.
Heh heh.
YES...LET YOURSELF GO.
LET THE GOBLIN OUT...
HA! HA HA HA HA!
YOU SHOULD HAVE LISTENED TO ME, OTTO!

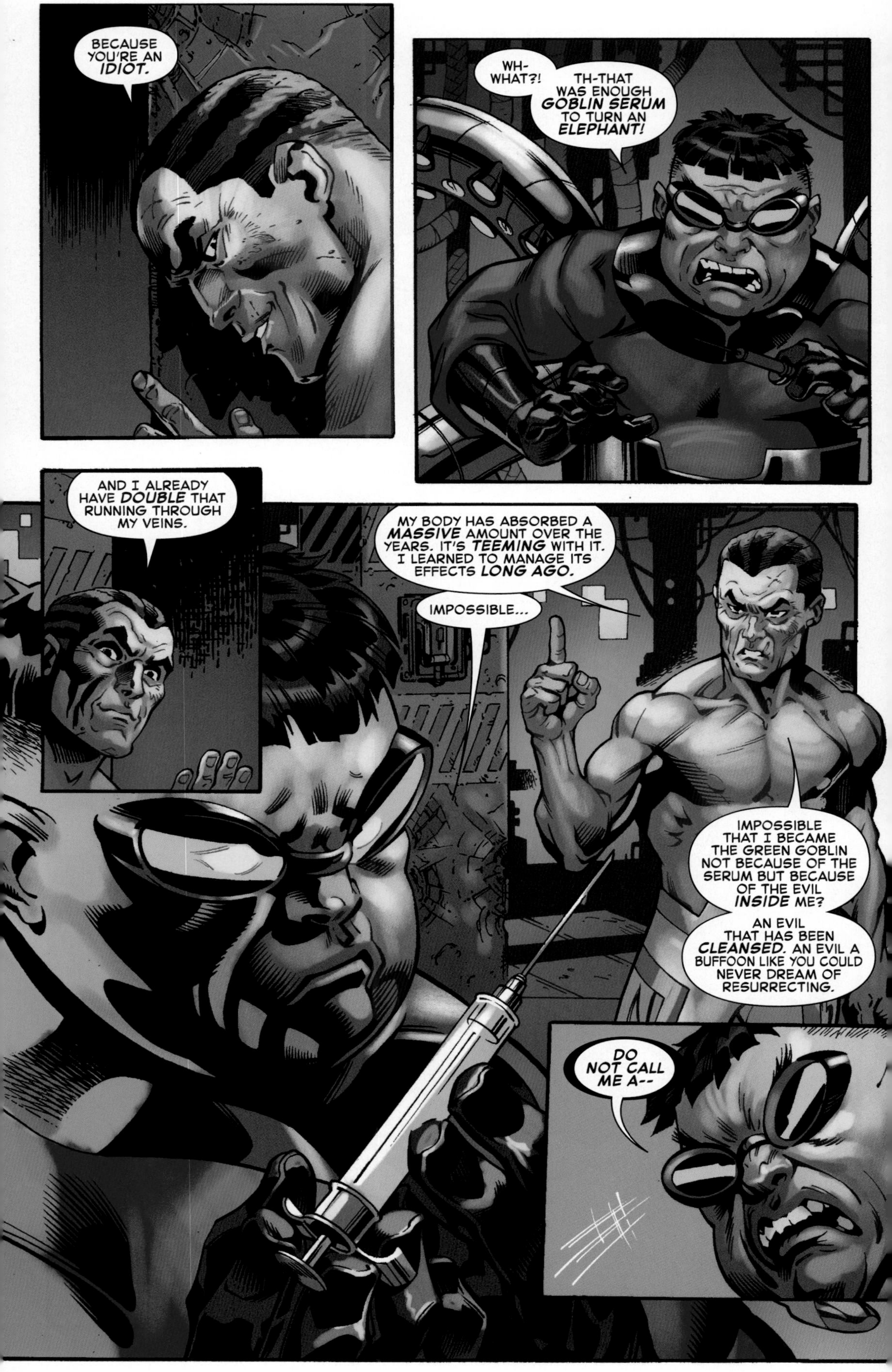
BECAUSE YOU'RE AN IDIOT.
WH-WHAT?!
TH-THAT WAS ENOUGH GOBLIN SERUM TO TURN AN ELEPHANT!
AND I ALREADY HAVE DOUBLE THAT RUNNING THROUGH MY VEINS.
MY BODY HAS ABSORBED A MASSIVE AMOUNT OVER THE YEARS. IT'S TEEMING WITH IT. I LEARNED TO MANAGE ITS EFFECTS LONG AGO.
IMPOSSIBLE...
IMPOSSIBLE THAT I BECAME THE GREEN GOBLIN NOT BECAUSE OF THE SERUM BUT BECAUSE OF THE EVIL INSIDE ME?
AN EVIL THAT HAS BEEN CLEANSED. AN EVIL A BUFFOON LIKE YOU COULD NEVER DREAM OF RESURRECTING.
DO NOT CALL ME A--

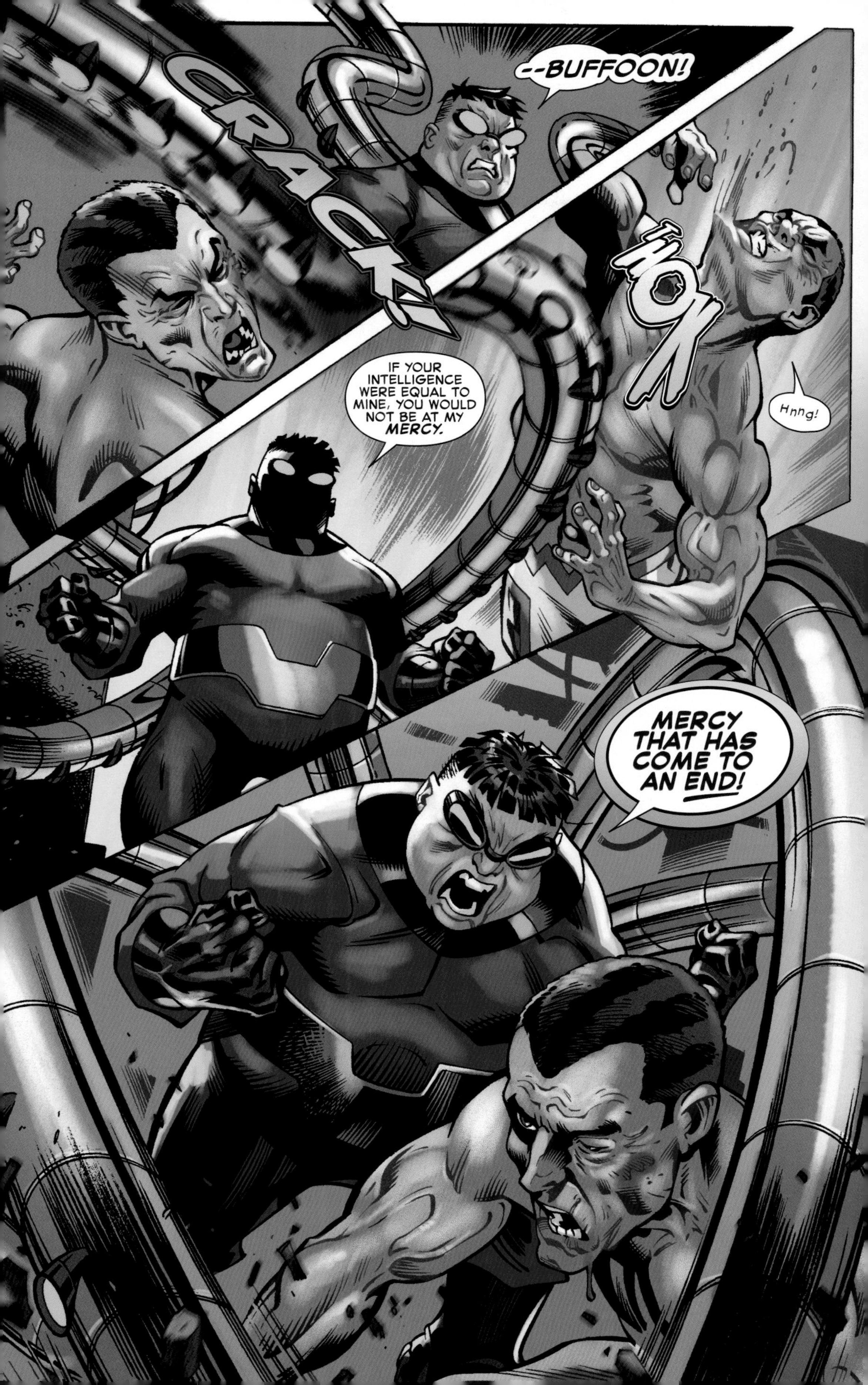
CRACK!!
--BUFFOON!
THOK
IF YOUR INTELLIGENCE WERE EQUAL TO MINE, YOU WOULD NOT BE AT MY MERCY.
Hnng!
MERCY THAT HAS COME TO AN END!

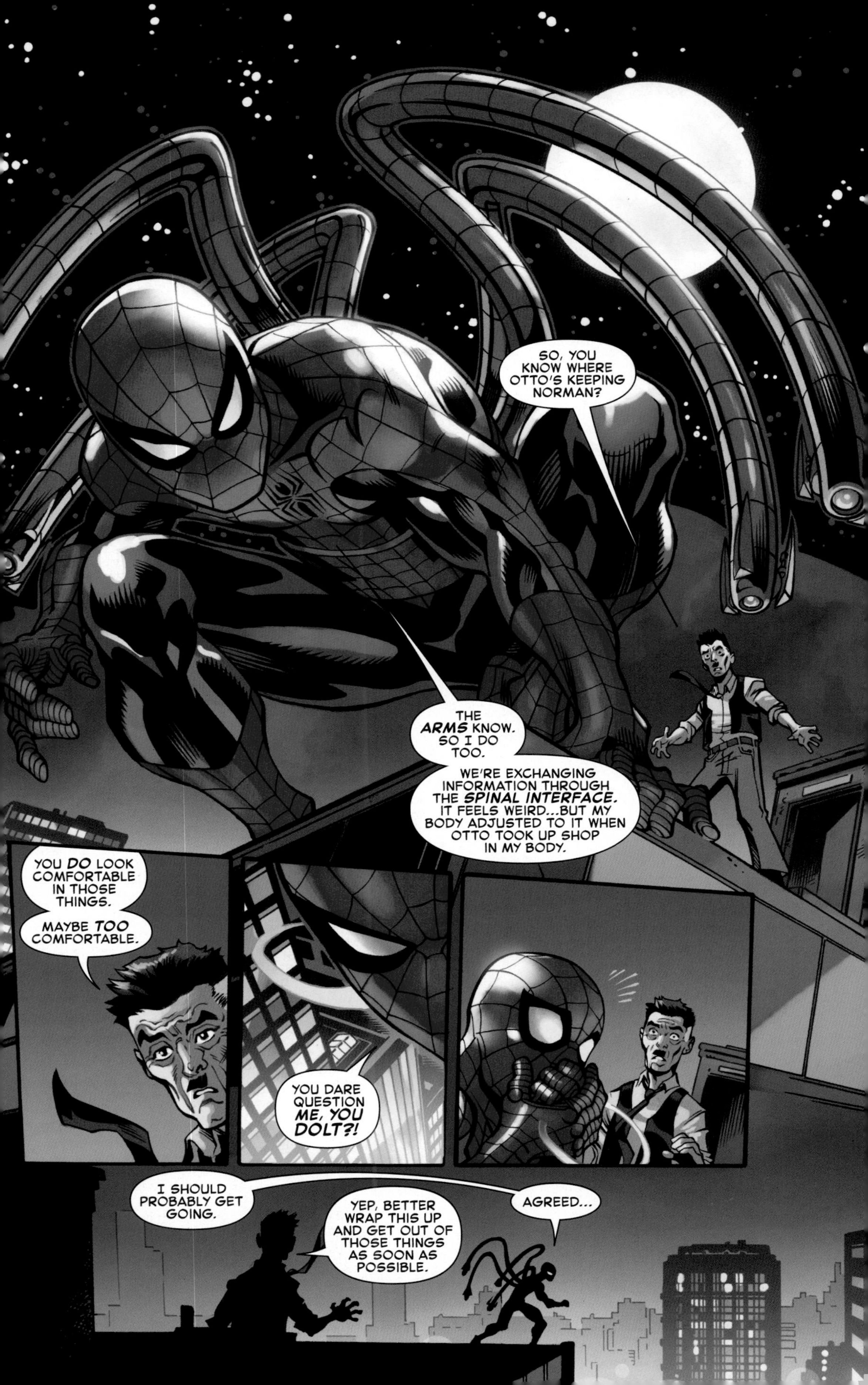
SO, YOU KNOW WHERE OTTO'S KEEPING NORMAN?
THE ARMS KNOW. SO I DO TOO.
WE'RE EXCHANGING INFORMATION THROUGH THE SPINAL INTERFACE. IT FEELS WEIRD...BUT MY BODY ADJUSTED TO IT WHEN OTTO TOOK UP SHOP IN MY BODY.
YOU DO LOOK COMFORTABLE IN THOSE THINGS.
MAYBE TOO COMFORTABLE.
YOU DARE QUESTION ME, YOU DOLT?!
I SHOULD PROBABLY GET GOING.
AGREED...
YEP, BETTER WRAP THIS UP AND GET OUT OF THOSE THINGS AS SOON AS POSSIBLE.

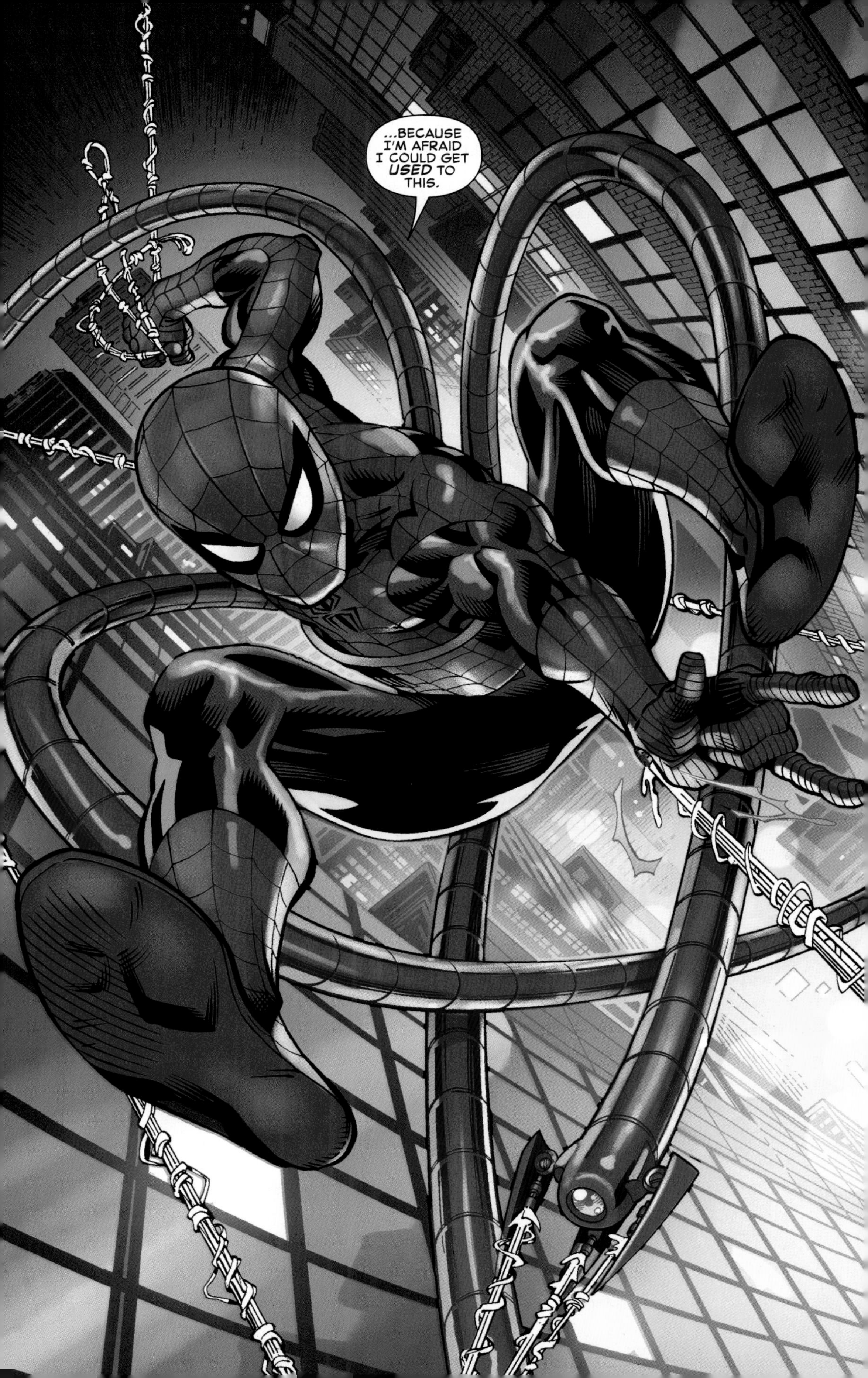
...BECAUSE I'M AFRAID I COULD GET USED TO THIS.

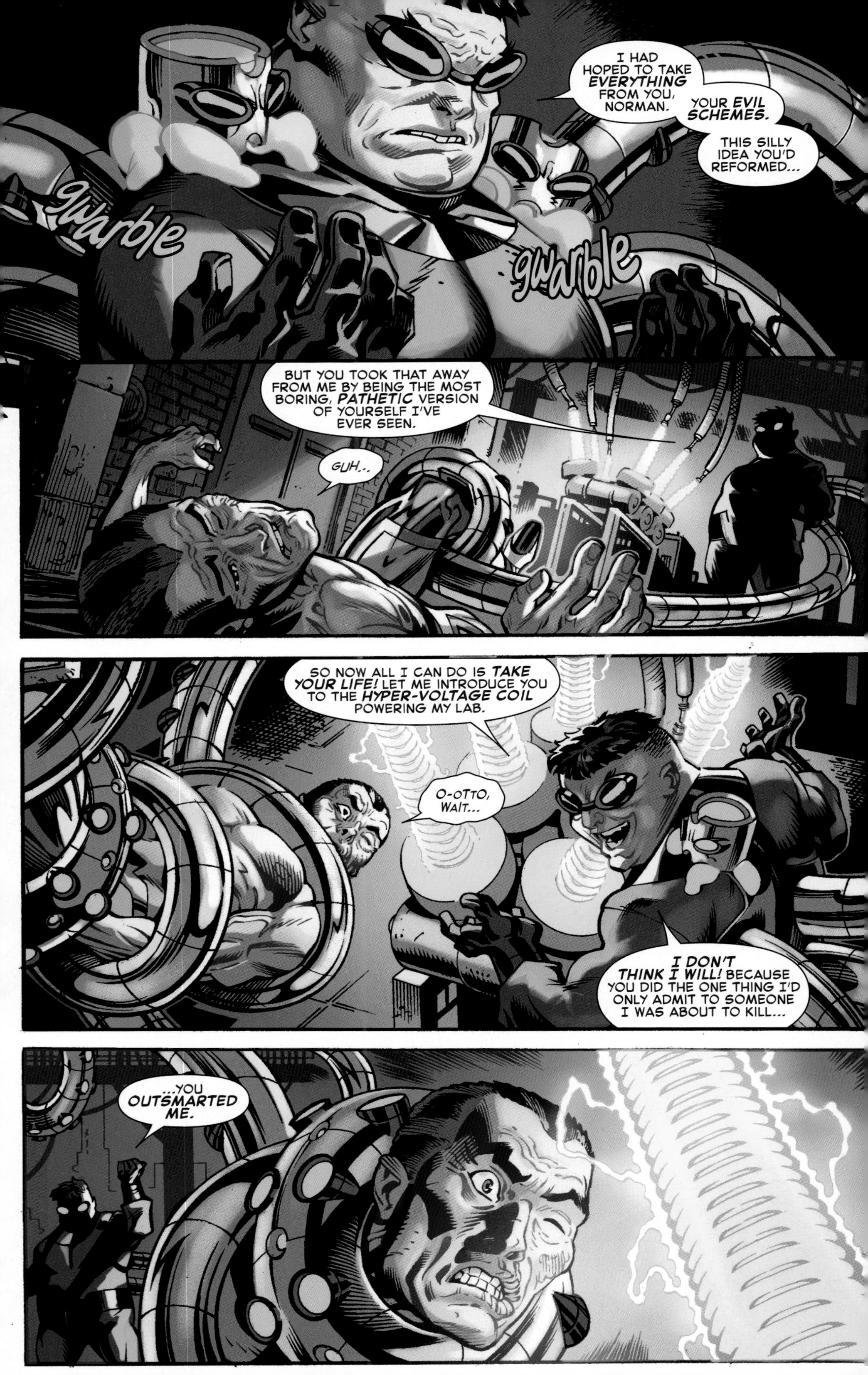
I HAD HOPED TO TAKE EVERYTHING FROM YOU, NORMAN.
YOUR EVIL SCHEMES.
THIS SILLY IDEA YOU'D REFORMED...
gwarble
gwarble
BUT YOU TOOK THAT AWAY FROM ME BY BEING THE MOST BORING, PATHETIC VERSION OF YOURSELF I'VE EVER SEEN.
GUH...
SO NOW ALL I CAN DO IS TAKE YOUR LIFE! LET ME INTRODUCE YOU TO THE HYPER-VOLTAGE COIL POWERING MY LAB.
O-OTTO, WAIT...
I DON'T THINK I WILL! BECAUSE YOU DID THE ONE THING I'D ONLY ADMIT TO SOMEONE I WAS ABOUT TO KILL...
...YOU OUTSMARTED ME.

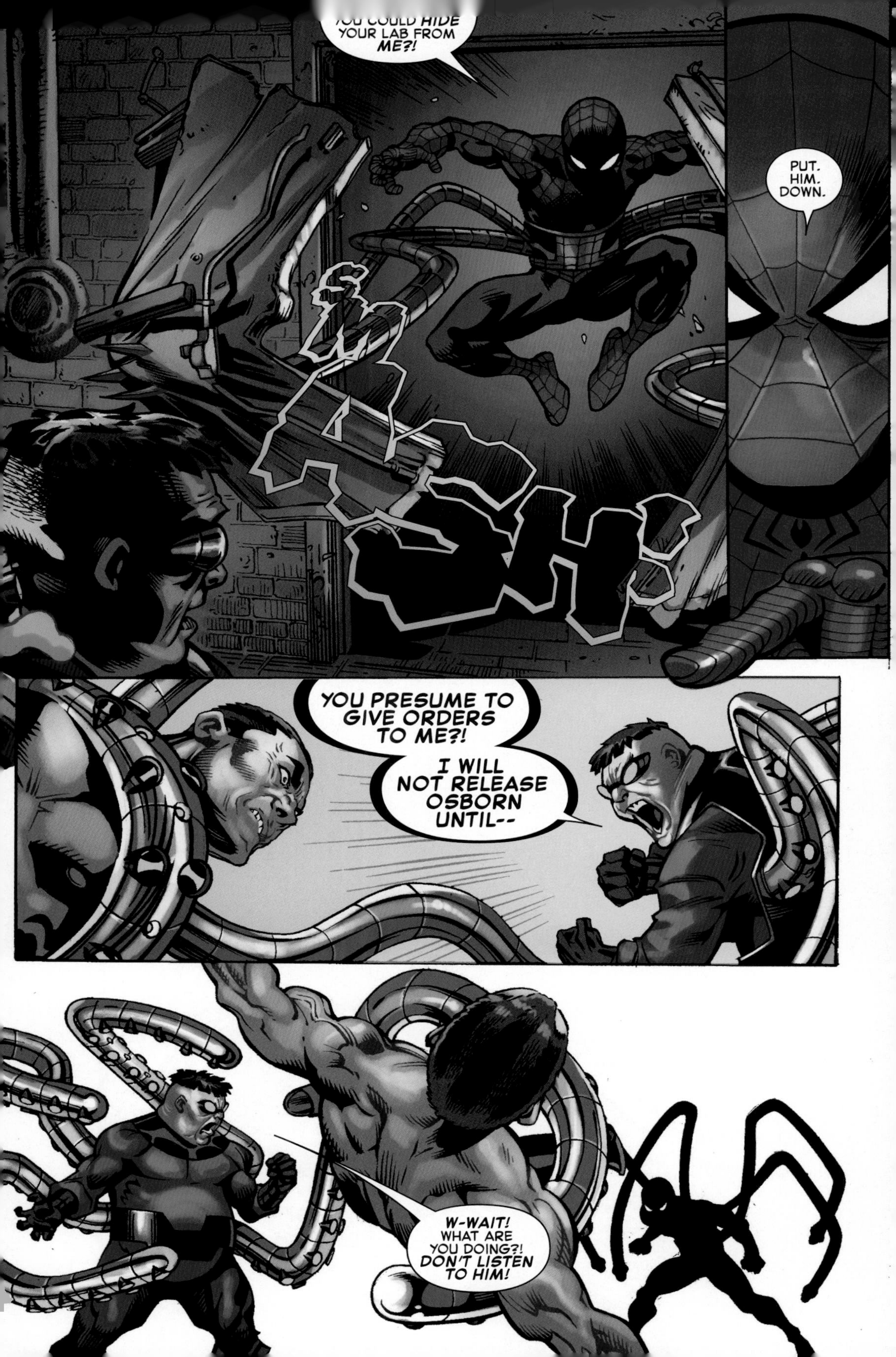

YOU COULD HIDE YOUR LAB FROM ME?!
PUT. HIM. DOWN.
YOU PRESUME TO GIVE ORDERS TO ME?!
I WILL NOT RELEASE OSBORN UNTIL--
W-WAIT! WHAT ARE YOU DOING?! DON'T LISTEN TO HIM!

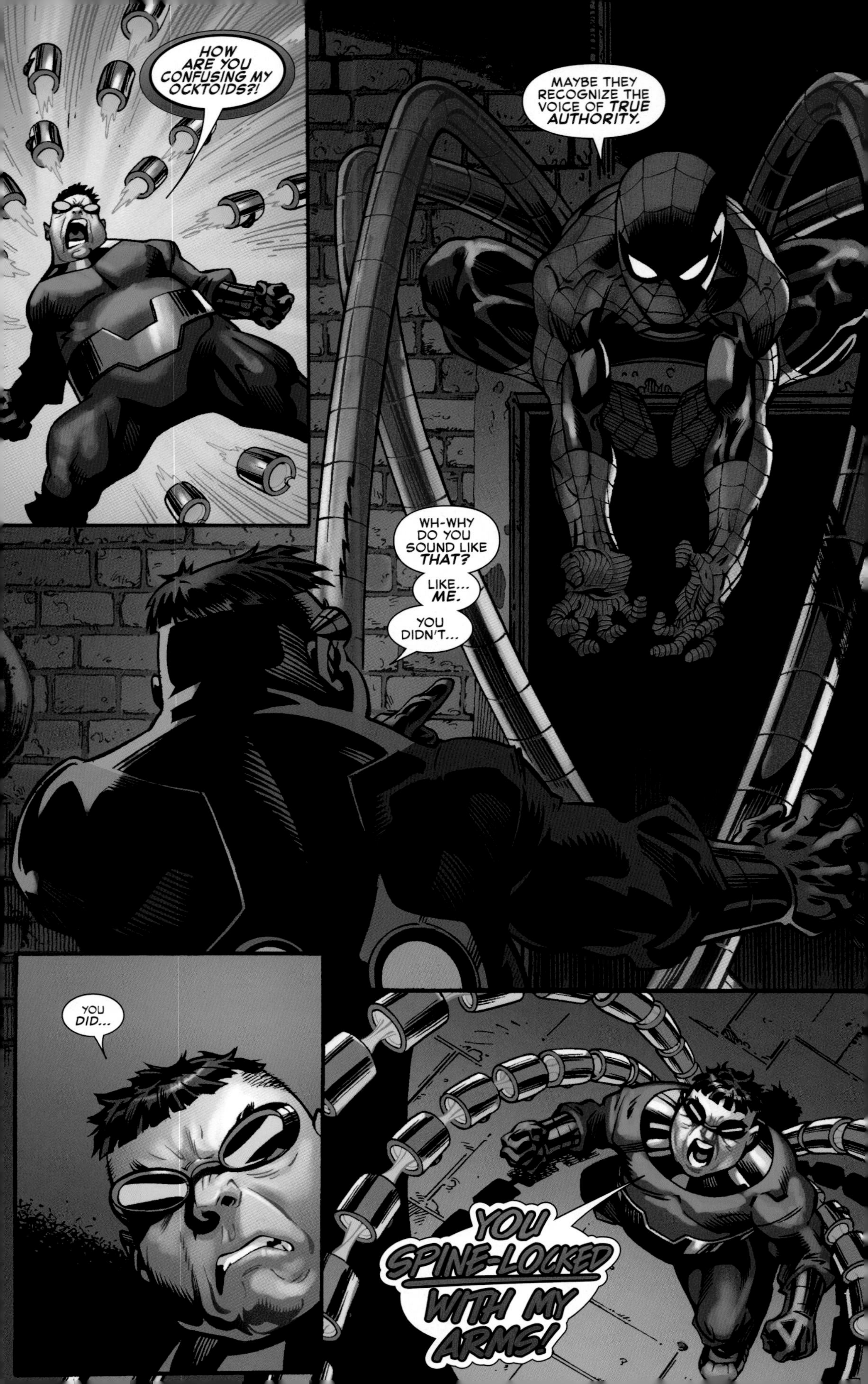

HOW ARE YOU CONFUSING MY OCKTOIDS?!
MAYBE THEY RECOGNIZE THE VOICE OF TRUE AUTHORITY.
WH-WHY DO YOU SOUND LIKE THAT?
LIKE... ME.
YOU DIDN'T...
YOU DID...
YOU SPINE-LOCKED WITH MY ARMS!

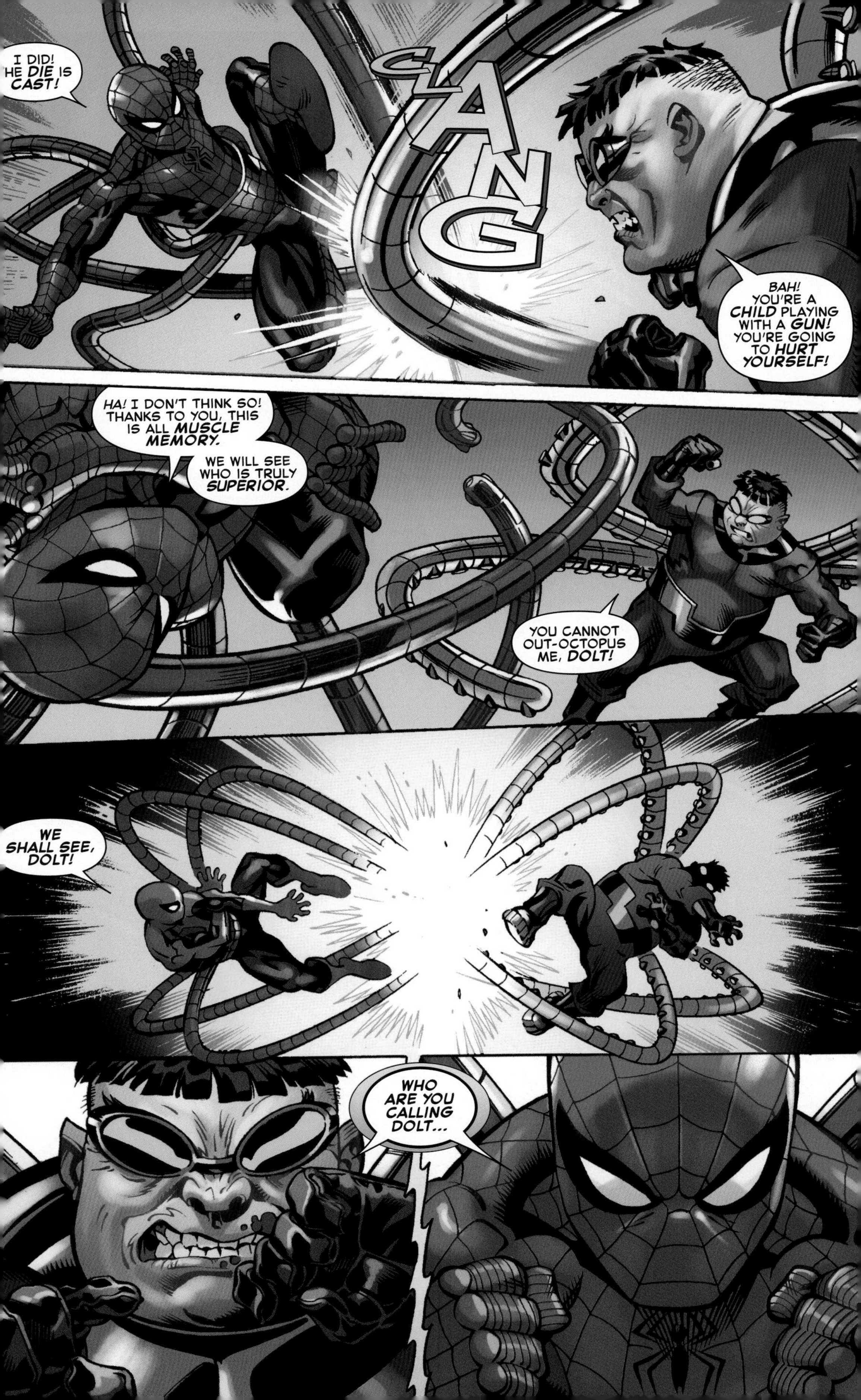
I DID! THE DIE IS CAST!
CLANG
BAH! YOU'RE A CHILD PLAYING WITH A GUN! YOU'RE GOING TO HURT YOURSELF!
HA! I DON'T THINK SO! THANKS TO YOU, THIS IS ALL MUSCLE MEMORY.
WE WILL SEE WHO IS TRULY SUPERIOR.
YOU CANNOT OUT-OCTOPUS ME, DOLT!
WE SHALL SEE, DOLT!
WHO ARE YOU CALLING DOLT...

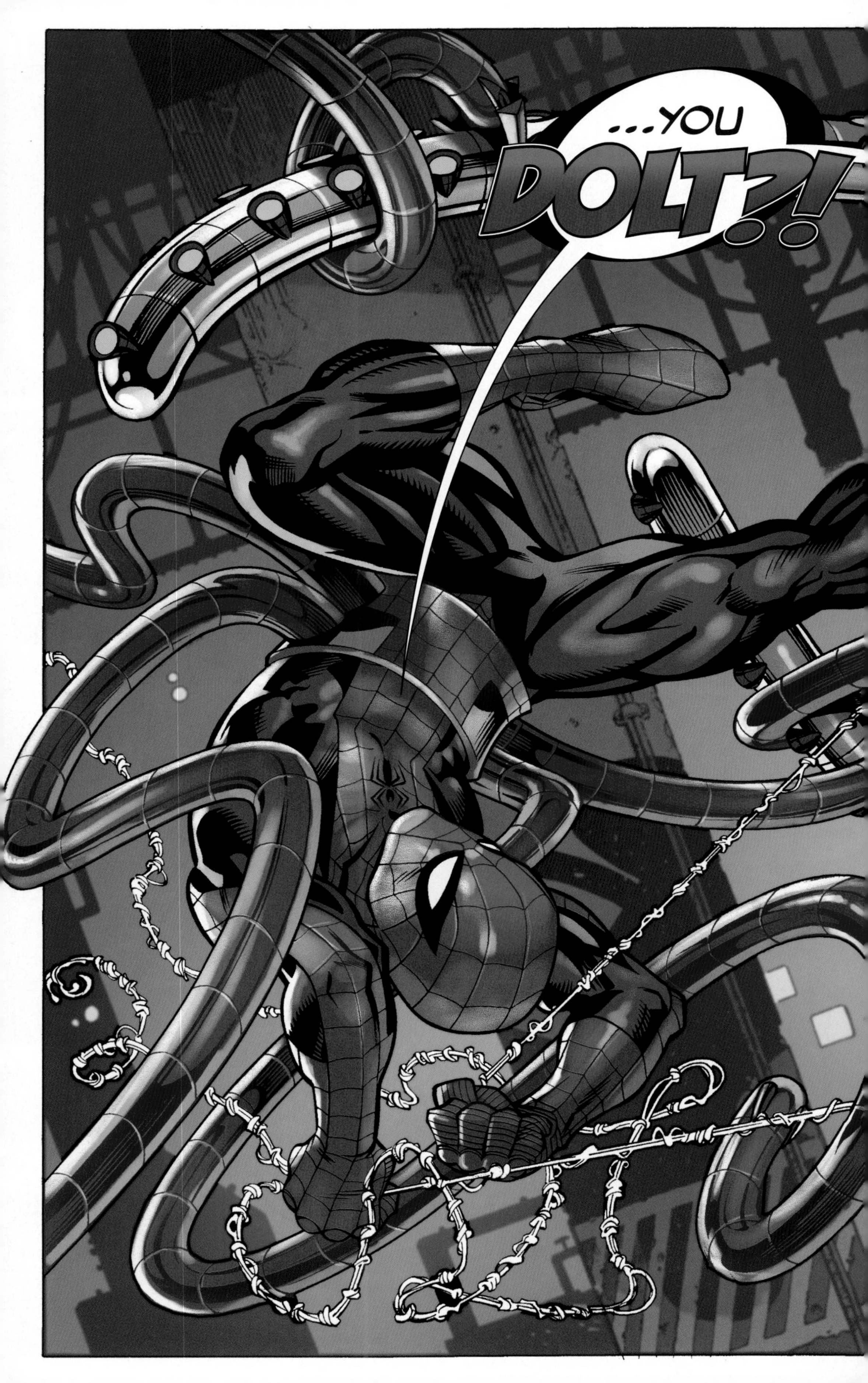
...YOU
DOLT?!

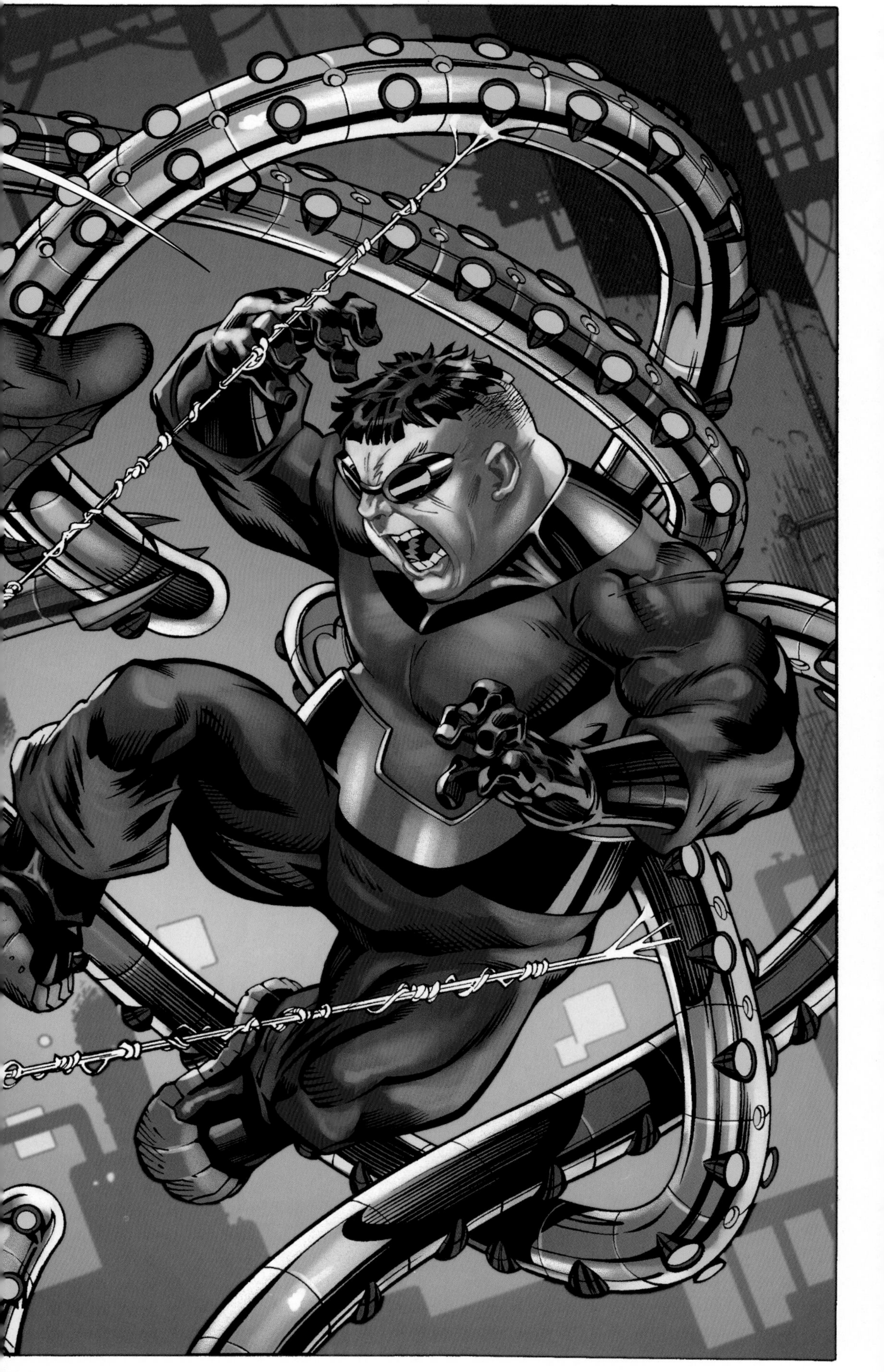

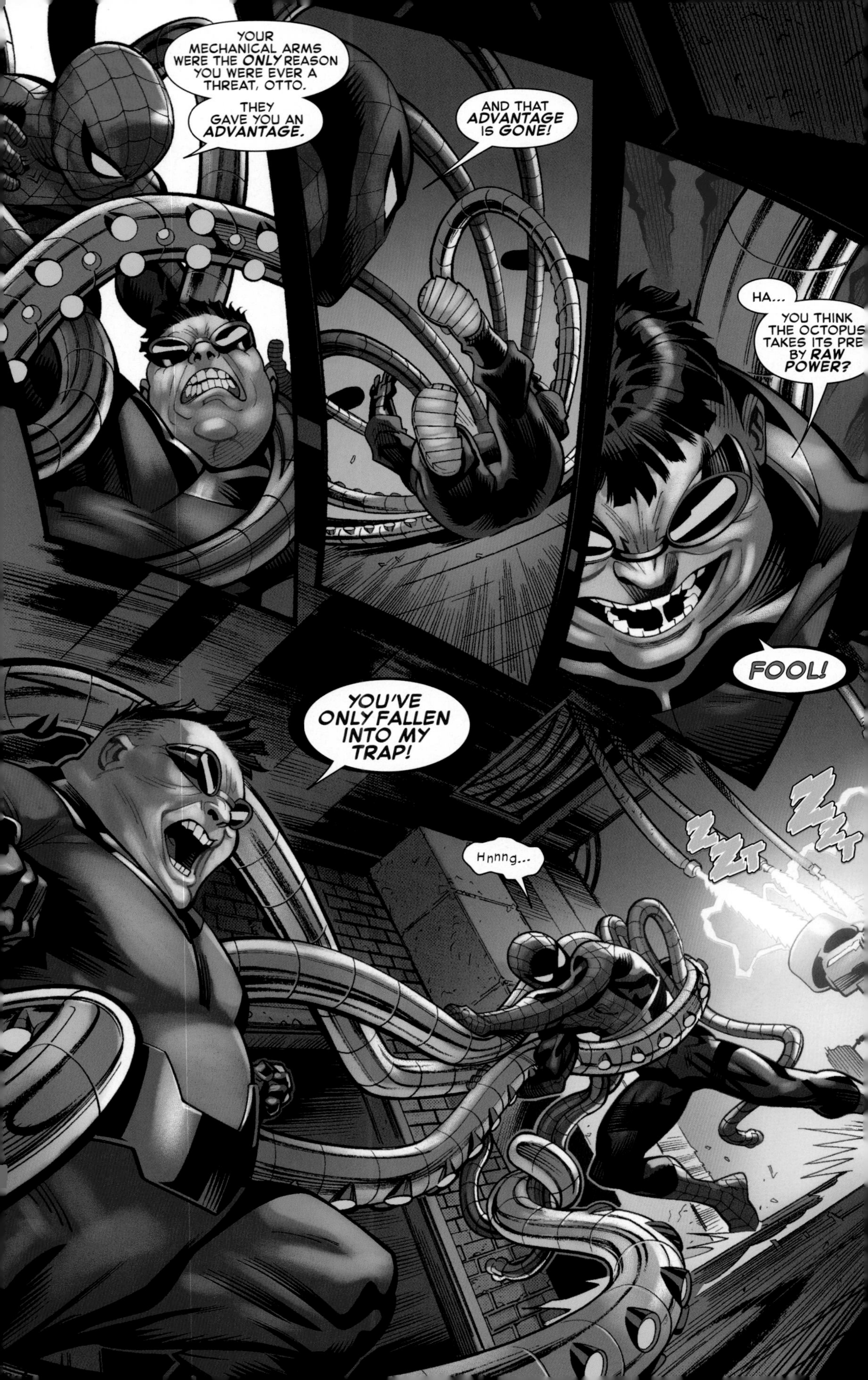
YOUR MECHANICAL ARMS WERE THE ONLY REASON YOU WERE EVER A THREAT, OTTO.
THEY GAVE YOU AN ADVANTAGE.
AND THAT ADVANTAGE IS GONE!
HA...
YOU THINK THE OCTOPUS TAKES ITS PRE BY RAW POWER?
FOOL!
YOU'VE ONLY FALLEN INTO MY TRAP!
Hnnng...
ZZT
ZZT

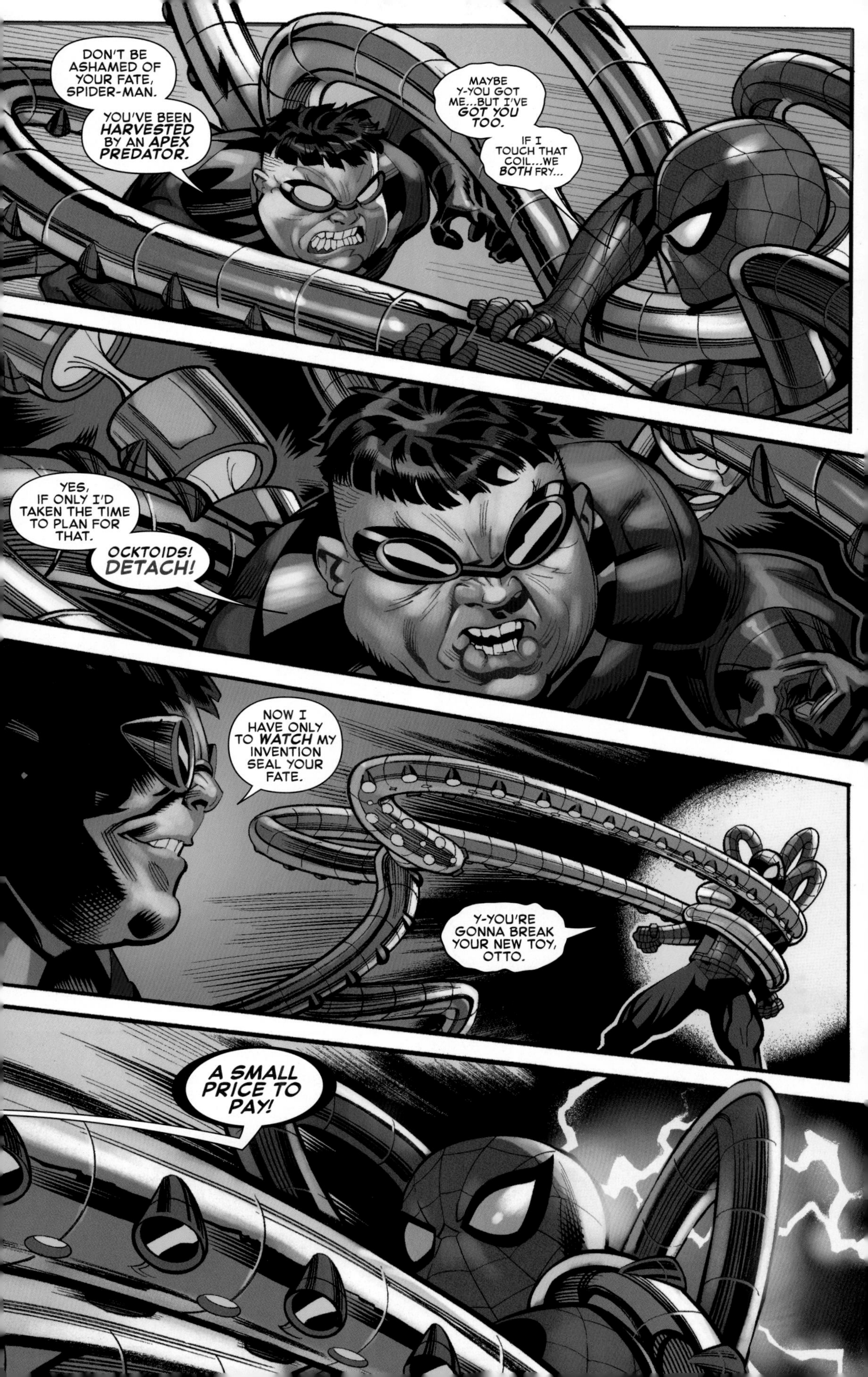
DON'T BE ASHAMED OF YOUR FATE, SPIDER-MAN.
YOU'VE BEEN HARVESTED BY AN APEX PREDATOR.
MAYBE Y-YOU GOT ME...BUT I'VE GOT YOU TOO.
IF I TOUCH THAT COIL...WE BOTH FRY...
YES, IF ONLY I'D TAKEN THE TIME TO PLAN FOR THAT.
OCKTOIDS! DETACH!
NOW I HAVE ONLY TO WATCH MY INVENTION SEAL YOUR FATE.
Y-YOU'RE GONNA BREAK YOUR NEW TOY, OTTO.
A SMALL PRICE TO PAY!

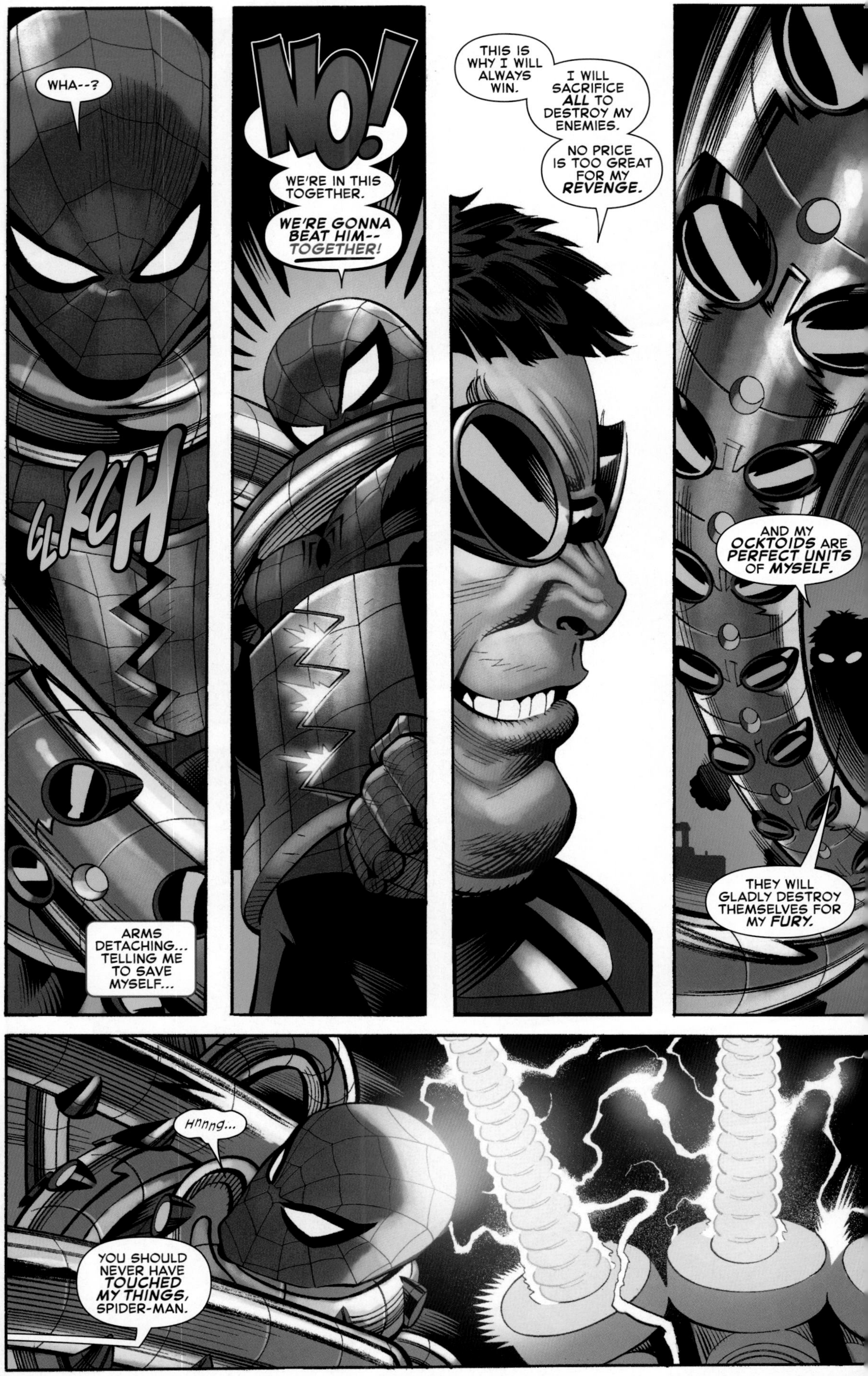
WHA--?
CLLRCH
ARMS DETACHING... TELLING ME TO SAVE MYSELF...
NO!
WE'RE IN THIS TOGETHER.
WE'RE GONNA BEAT HIM-- TOGETHER!
THIS IS WHY I WILL ALWAYS WIN.
I WILL SACRIFICE ALL TO DESTROY MY ENEMIES.
NO PRICE IS TOO GREAT FOR MY REVENGE.
AND MY OCKTOIDS ARE PERFECT UNITS OF MYSELF.
THEY WILL GLADLY DESTROY THEMSELVES FOR MY FURY.
Hnnng...
YOU SHOULD NEVER HAVE TOUCHED MY THINGS, SPIDER-MAN.

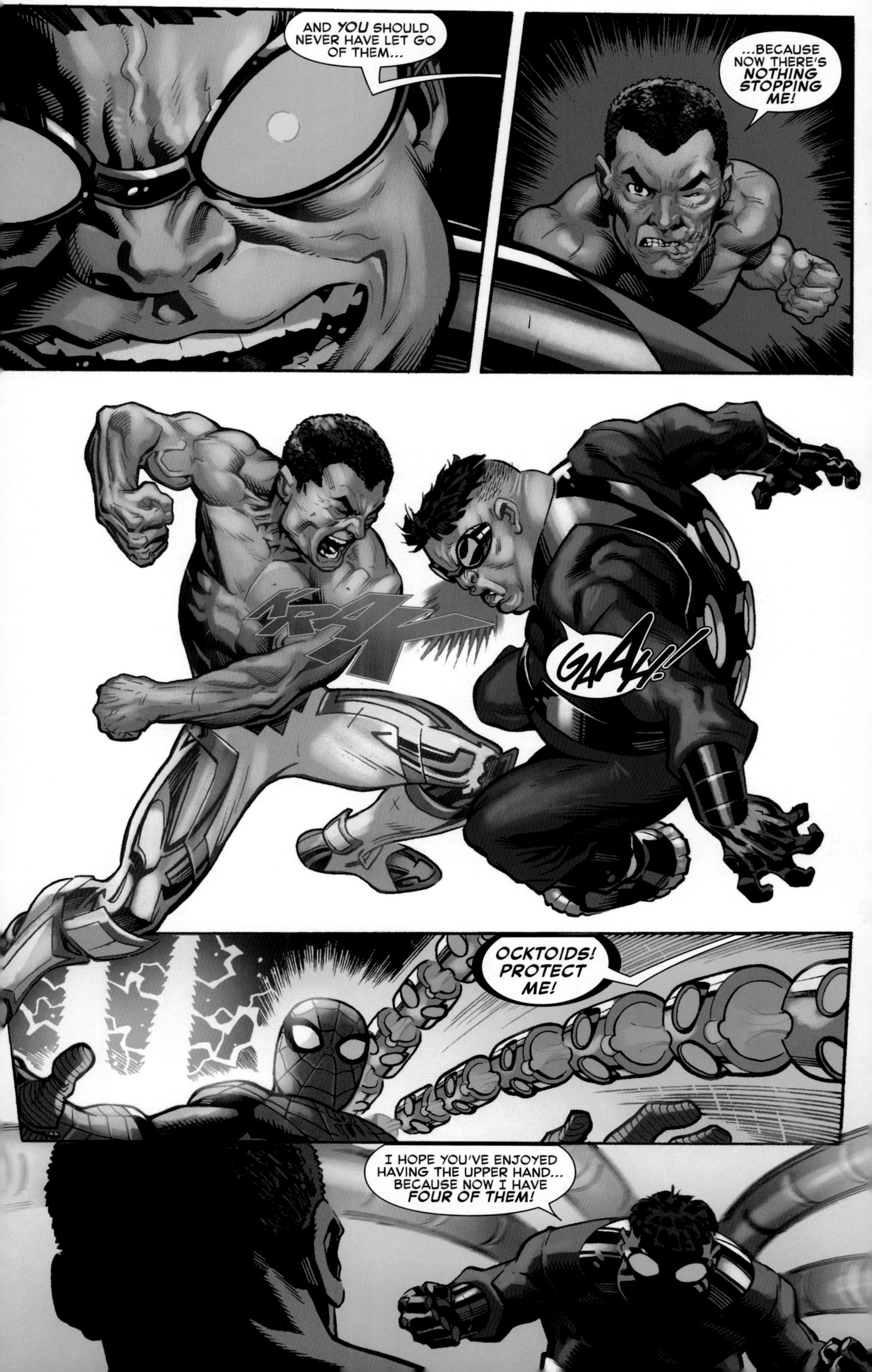
AND YOU SHOULD NEVER HAVE LET GO OF THEM...
...BECAUSE NOW THERE'S NOTHING STOPPING ME!
KRAK
GAAH!
OCKTOIDS! PROTECT ME!
I HOPE YOU'VE ENJOYED HAVING THE UPPER HAND... BECAUSE NOW I HAVE FOUR OF THEM!

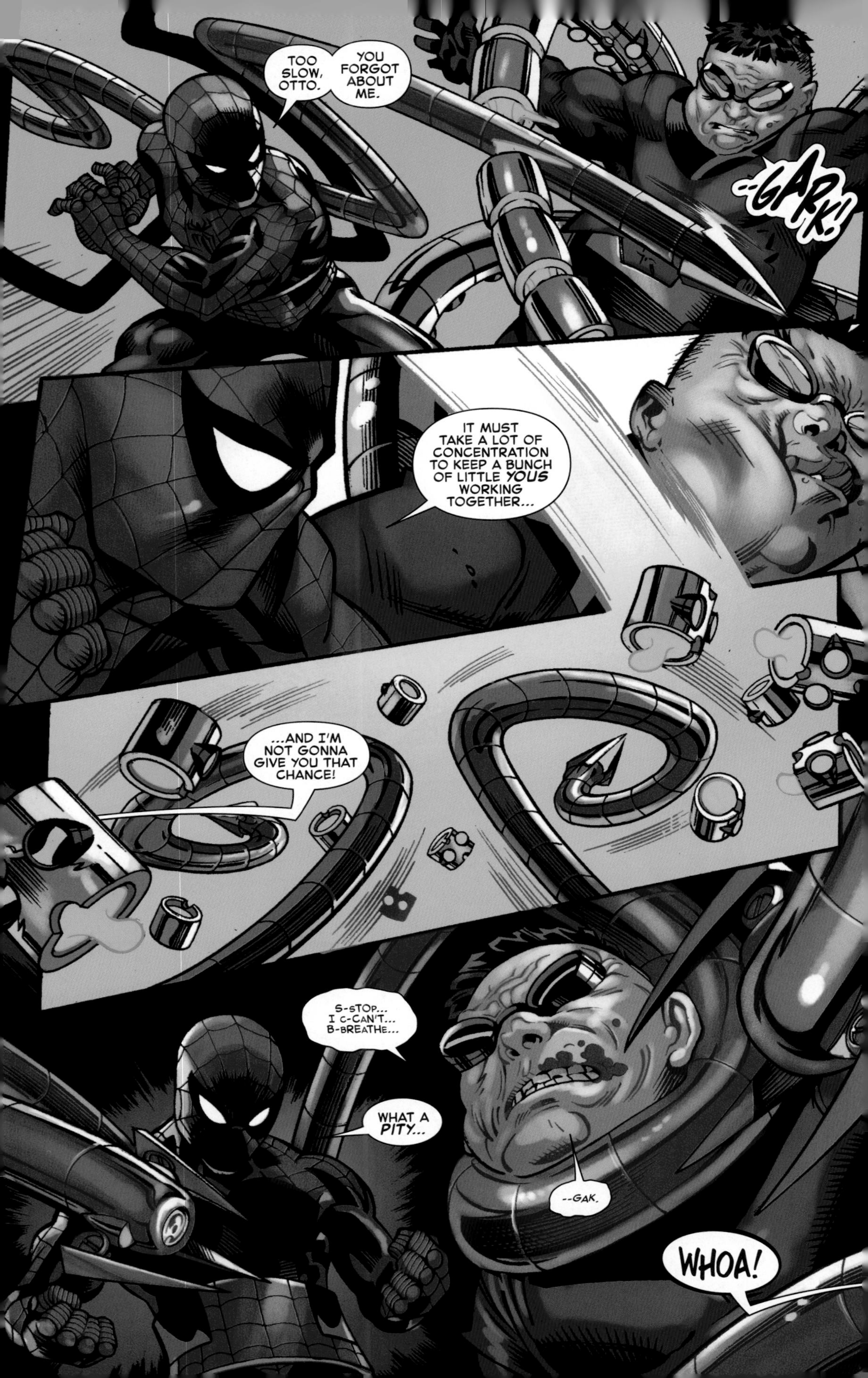
TOO SLOW, OTTO.
YOU FORGOT ABOUT ME.
--GARK!
IT MUST TAKE A LOT OF CONCENTRATION TO KEEP A BUNCH OF LITTLE YOUS WORKING TOGETHER...
...AND I'M NOT GONNA GIVE YOU THAT CHANCE!
S-STOP... I C-CAN'T... B-BREATHE...
WHAT A PITY...
--GAK.
WHOA!

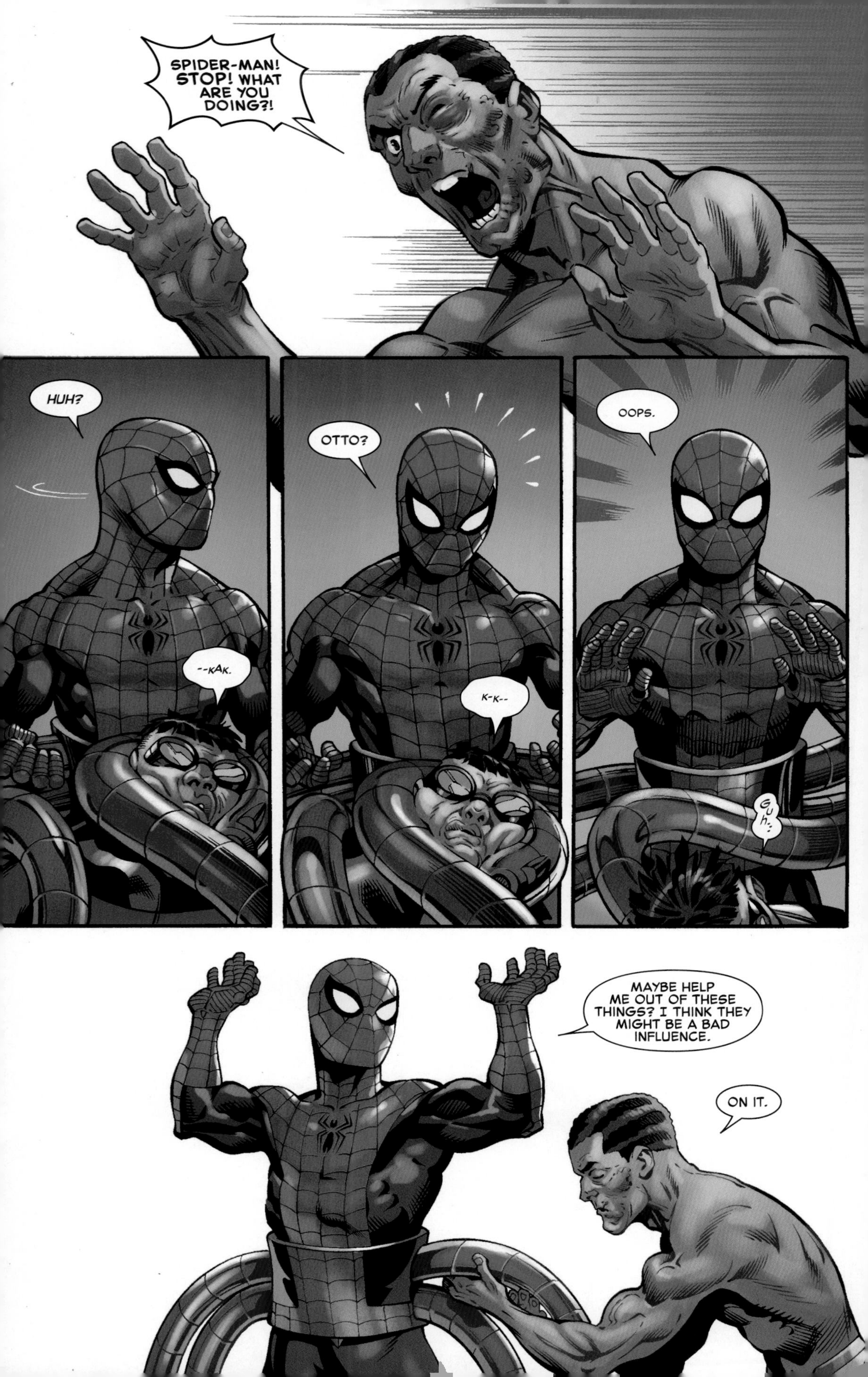
SPIDER-MAN! STOP! WHAT ARE YOU DOING?!
HUH?
--KAK.
OTTO?
K-K--
OOPS.
GUH..
MAYBE HELP ME OUT OF THESE THINGS? I THINK THEY MIGHT BE A BAD INFLUENCE.
ON IT.

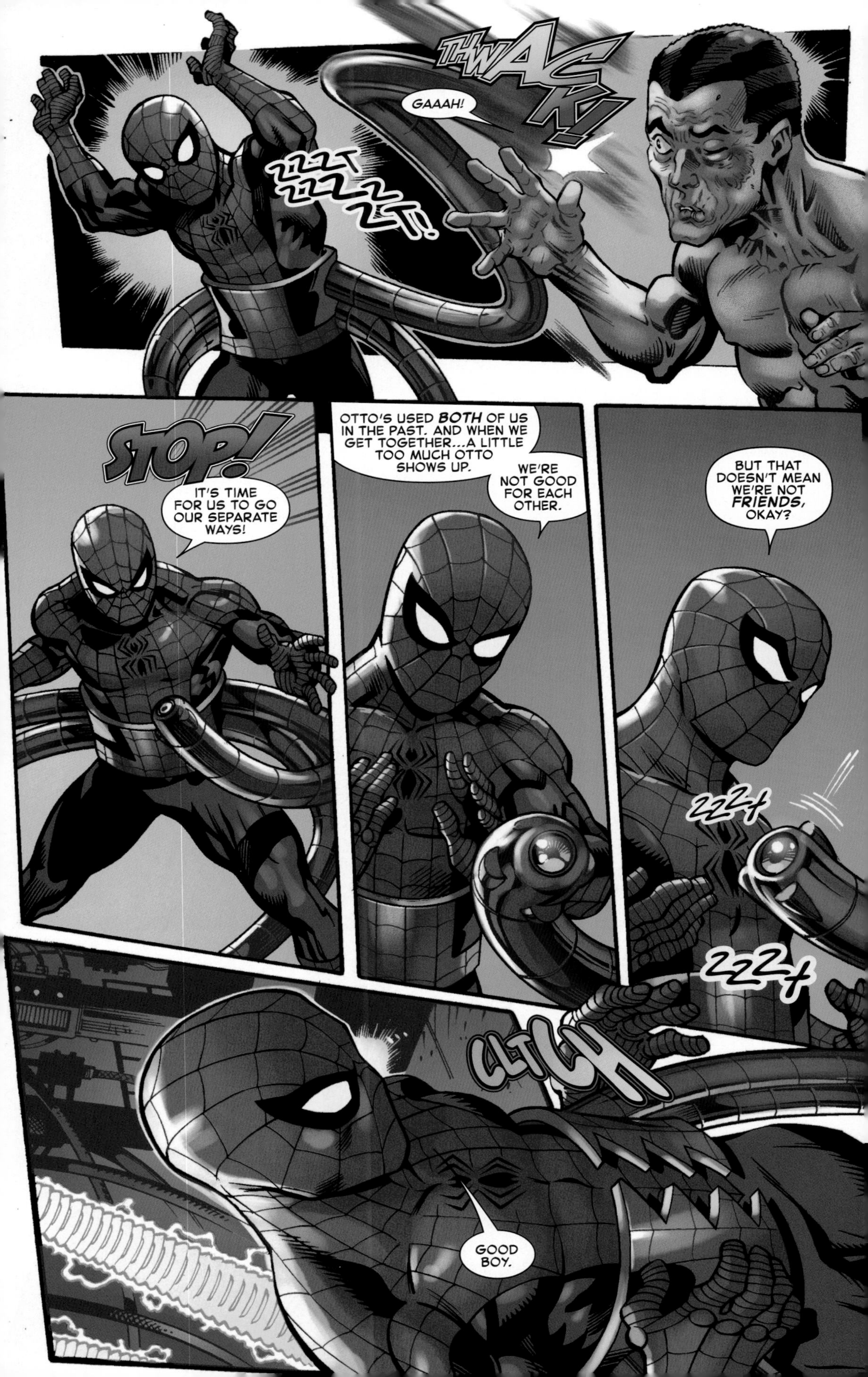
THWACK!
GAAAH!
ZZZT
ZZZZZZT!
STOP!
IT'S TIME FOR US TO GO OUR SEPARATE WAYS!
OTTO'S USED BOTH OF US IN THE PAST. AND WHEN WE GET TOGETHER...A LITTLE TOO MUCH OTTO SHOWS UP.
WE'RE NOT GOOD FOR EACH OTHER.
BUT THAT DOESN'T MEAN WE'RE NOT FRIENDS, OKAY?
ZZZT
ZZZT
CLTCH
GOOD BOY.

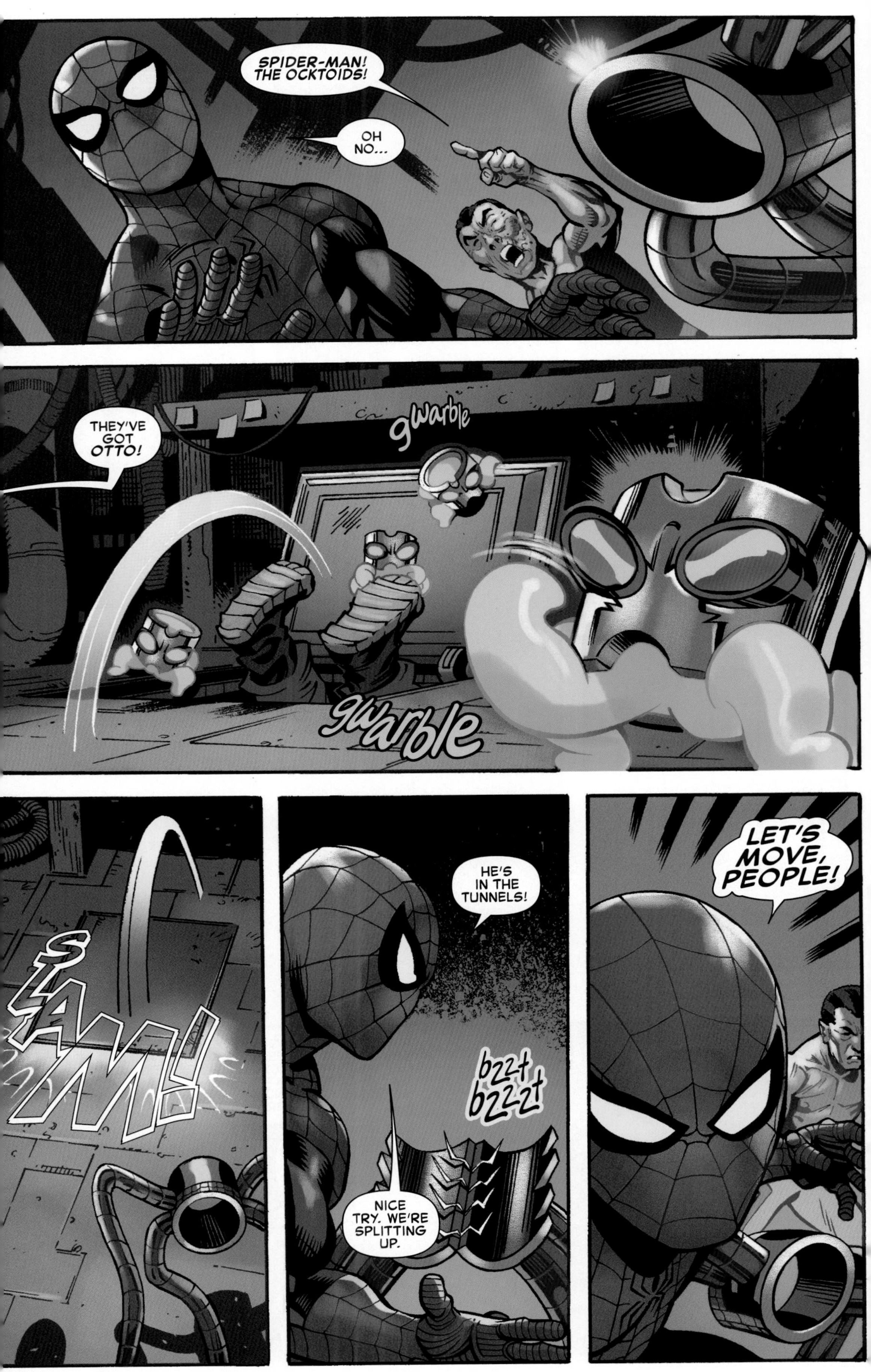
SPIDER-MAN! THE OCKTOIDS!
OH NO...
THEY'VE GOT OTTO!
gwarble
gwarble
SLAM!
HE'S IN THE TUNNELS!
bzzt bzzzt
NICE TRY. WE'RE SPLITTING UP.
LET'S MOVE, PEOPLE!

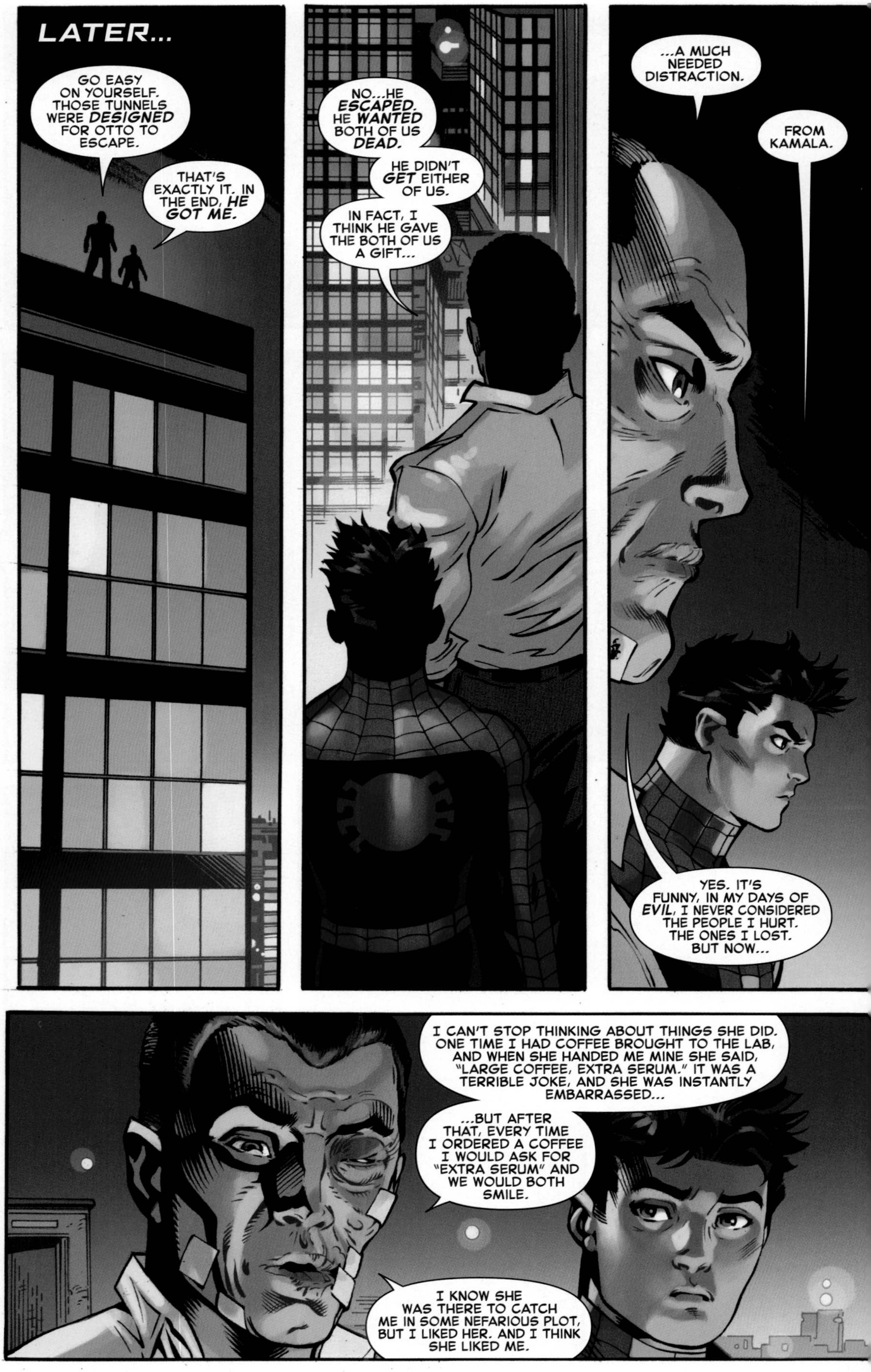
LATER...
GO EASY ON YOURSELF. THOSE TUNNELS WERE DESIGNED FOR OTTO TO ESCAPE.
THAT'S EXACTLY IT. IN THE END, HE GOT ME.
NO...HE ESCAPED. HE WANTED BOTH OF US DEAD.
HE DIDN'T GET EITHER OF US.
IN FACT, I THINK HE GAVE THE BOTH OF US A GIFT...
...A MUCH NEEDED DISTRACTION.
FROM KAMALA.
YES. IT'S FUNNY, IN MY DAYS OF EVIL, I NEVER CONSIDERED THE PEOPLE I HURT. THE ONES I LOST. BUT NOW...
I CAN'T STOP THINKING ABOUT THINGS SHE DID. ONE TIME I HAD COFFEE BROUGHT TO THE LAB, AND WHEN SHE HANDED ME MINE SHE SAID, "LARGE COFFEE, EXTRA SERUM." IT WAS A TERRIBLE JOKE, AND SHE WAS INSTANTLY EMBARRASSED...
...BUT AFTER THAT, EVERY TIME I ORDERED A COFFEE I WOULD ASK FOR "EXTRA SERUM" AND WE WOULD BOTH SMILE.
I KNOW SHE WAS THERE TO CATCH ME IN SOME NEFARIOUS PLOT, BUT I LIKED HER. AND I THINK SHE LIKED ME.

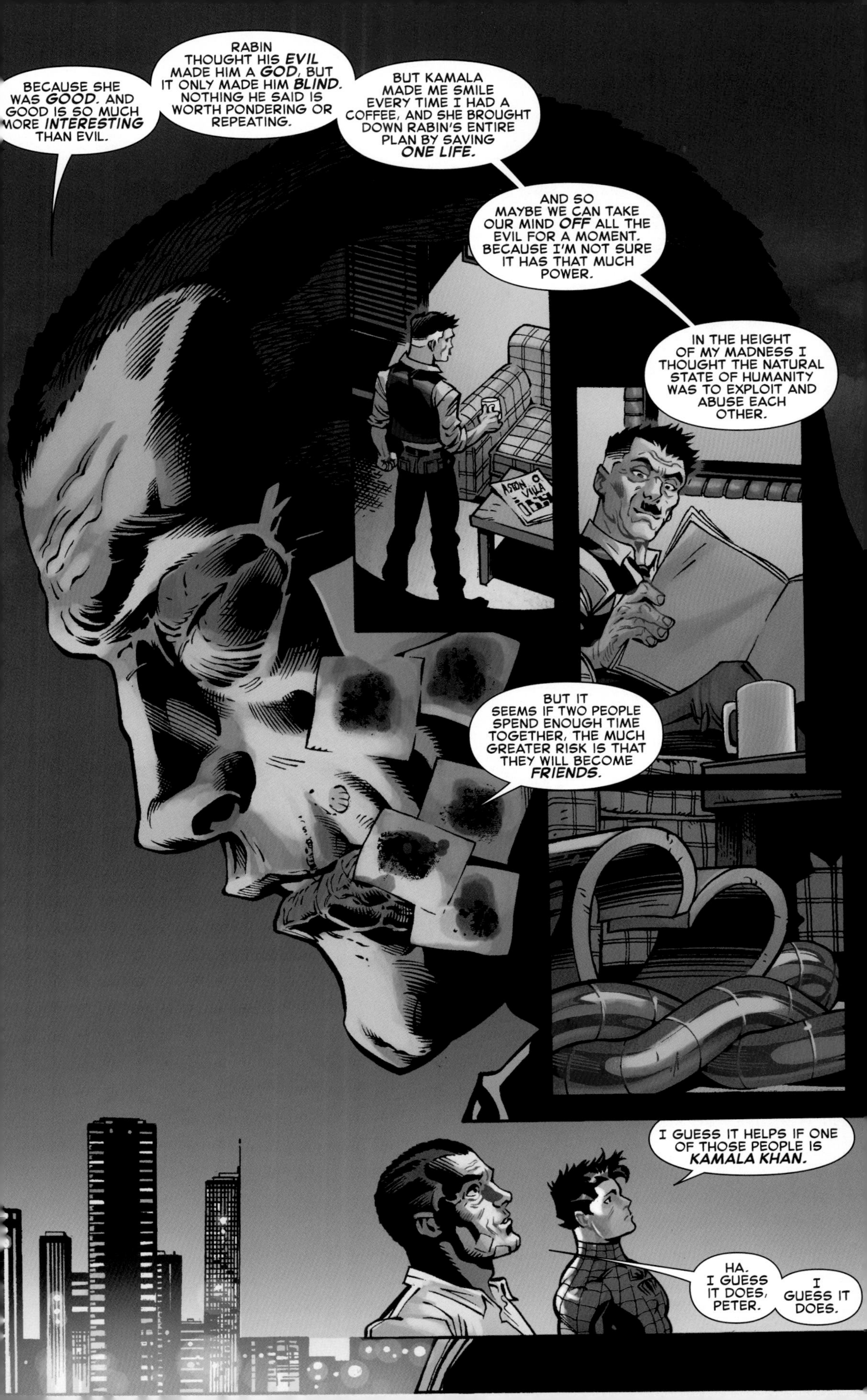
BECAUSE SHE WAS GOOD. AND GOOD IS SO MUCH MORE INTERESTING THAN EVIL.
RABIN THOUGHT HIS EVIL MADE HIM A GOD, BUT IT ONLY MADE HIM BLIND. NOTHING HE SAID IS WORTH PONDERING OR REPEATING.
BUT KAMALA MADE ME SMILE EVERY TIME I HAD A COFFEE, AND SHE BROUGHT DOWN RABIN'S ENTIRE PLAN BY SAVING ONE LIFE.
AND SO MAYBE WE CAN TAKE OUR MIND OFF ALL THE EVIL FOR A MOMENT. BECAUSE I'M NOT SURE IT HAS THAT MUCH POWER.
IN THE HEIGHT OF MY MADNESS I THOUGHT THE NATURAL STATE OF HUMANITY WAS TO EXPLOIT AND ABUSE EACH OTHER.
ASTON VILLA
BUT IT SEEMS IF TWO PEOPLE SPEND ENOUGH TIME TOGETHER, THE MUCH GREATER RISK IS THAT THEY WILL BECOME FRIENDS.
I GUESS IT HELPS IF ONE OF THOSE PEOPLE IS KAMALA KHAN.
HA. I GUESS IT DOES, PETER.
I GUESS IT DOES.

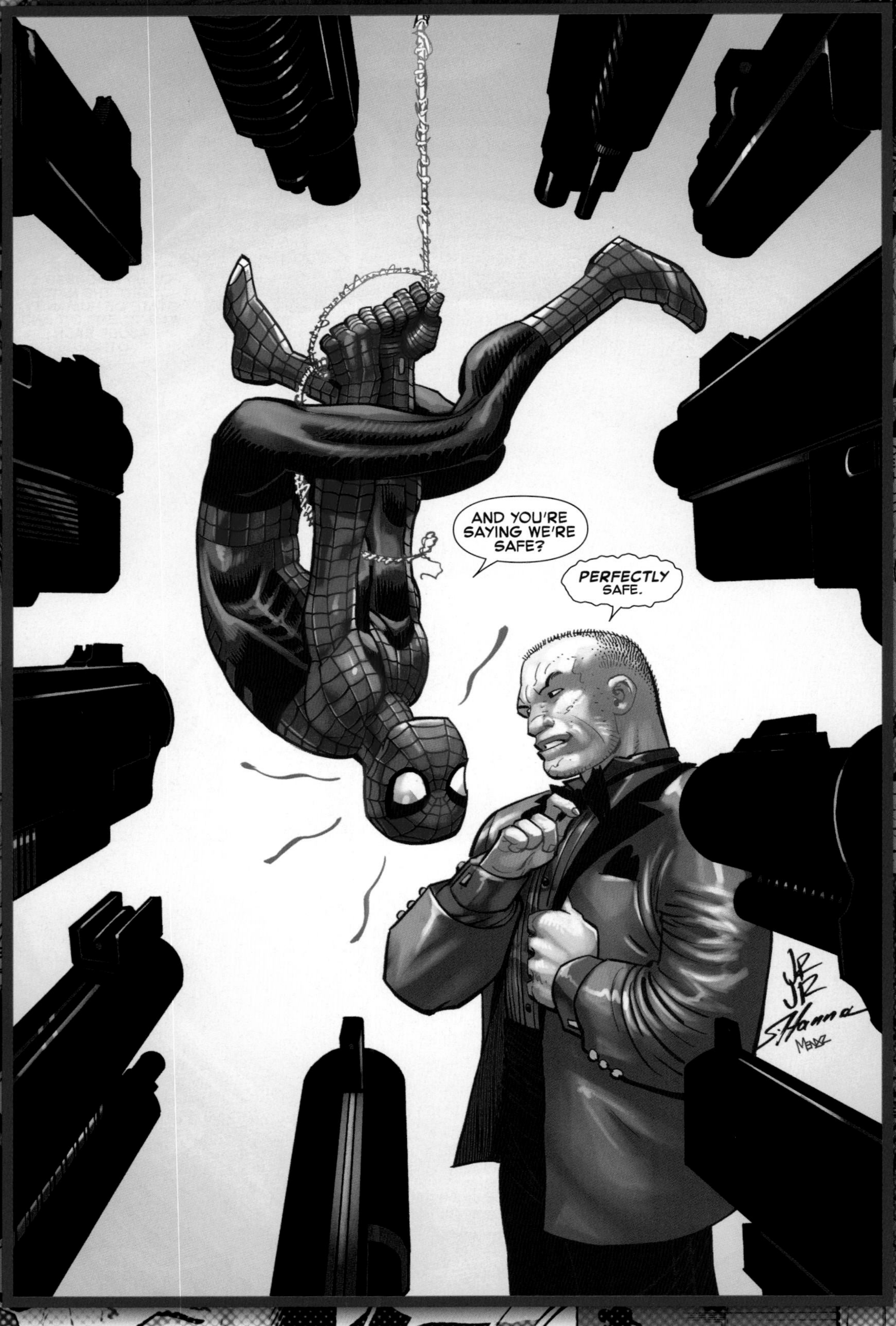
AND YOU'RE SAYING WE'RE SAFE?
PERFECTLY SAFE.

PRELUDE:

Your Presence Is Requested...

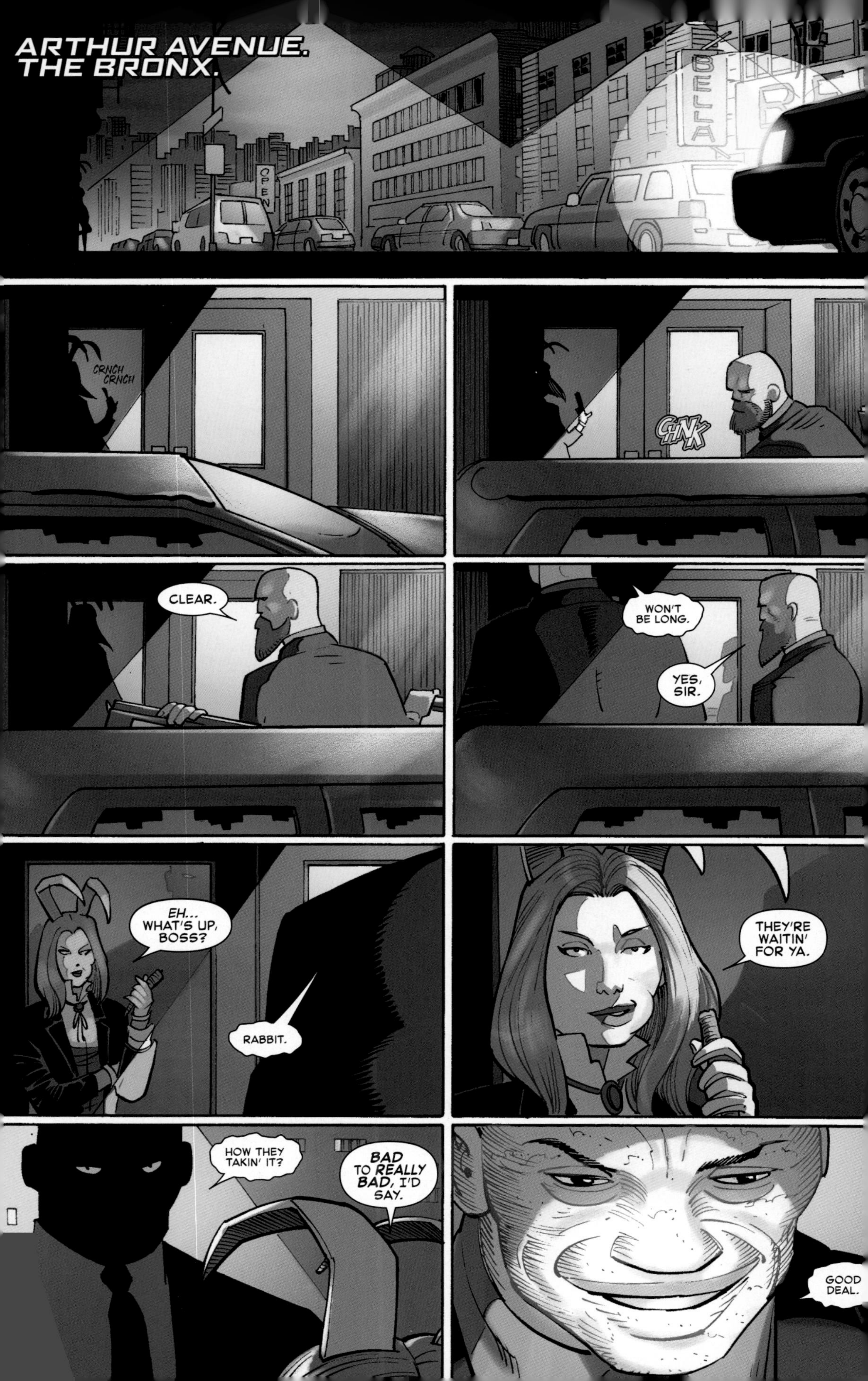
ARTHUR AVENUE.
THE BRONX.
BELLA
OPEN
CRNCH CRNCH
CHINK
CLEAR.
WON'T BE LONG.
YES, SIR.
EH... WHAT'S UP, BOSS?
RABBIT.
THEY'RE WAITIN' FOR YA.
HOW THEY TAKIN' IT?
BAD TO REALLY BAD, I'D SAY.
GOOD DEAL.

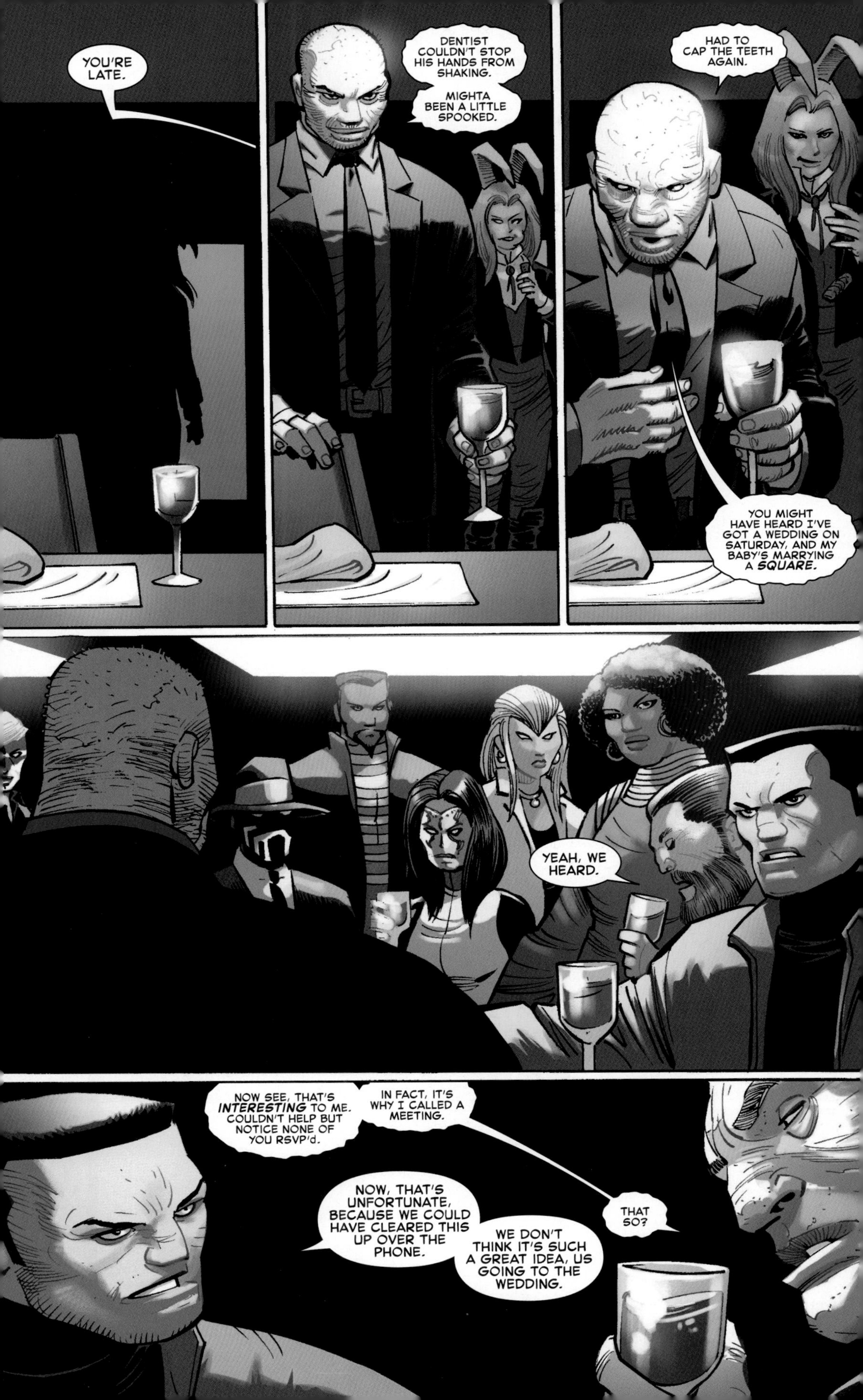
YOU'RE LATE.
DENTIST COULDN'T STOP HIS HANDS FROM SHAKING.
MIGHTA BEEN A LITTLE SPOOKED.
HAD TO CAP THE TEETH AGAIN.
YOU MIGHT HAVE HEARD I'VE GOT A WEDDING ON SATURDAY, AND MY BABY'S MARRYING A SQUARE.
YEAH, WE HEARD.
NOW SEE, THAT'S INTERESTING TO ME. COULDN'T HELP BUT NOTICE NONE OF YOU RSVP'd.
IN FACT, IT'S WHY I CALLED A MEETING.
THAT SO?
NOW, THAT'S UNFORTUNATE, BECAUSE WE COULD HAVE CLEARED THIS UP OVER THE PHONE.
WE DON'T THINK IT'S SUCH A GREAT IDEA, US GOING TO THE WEDDING.

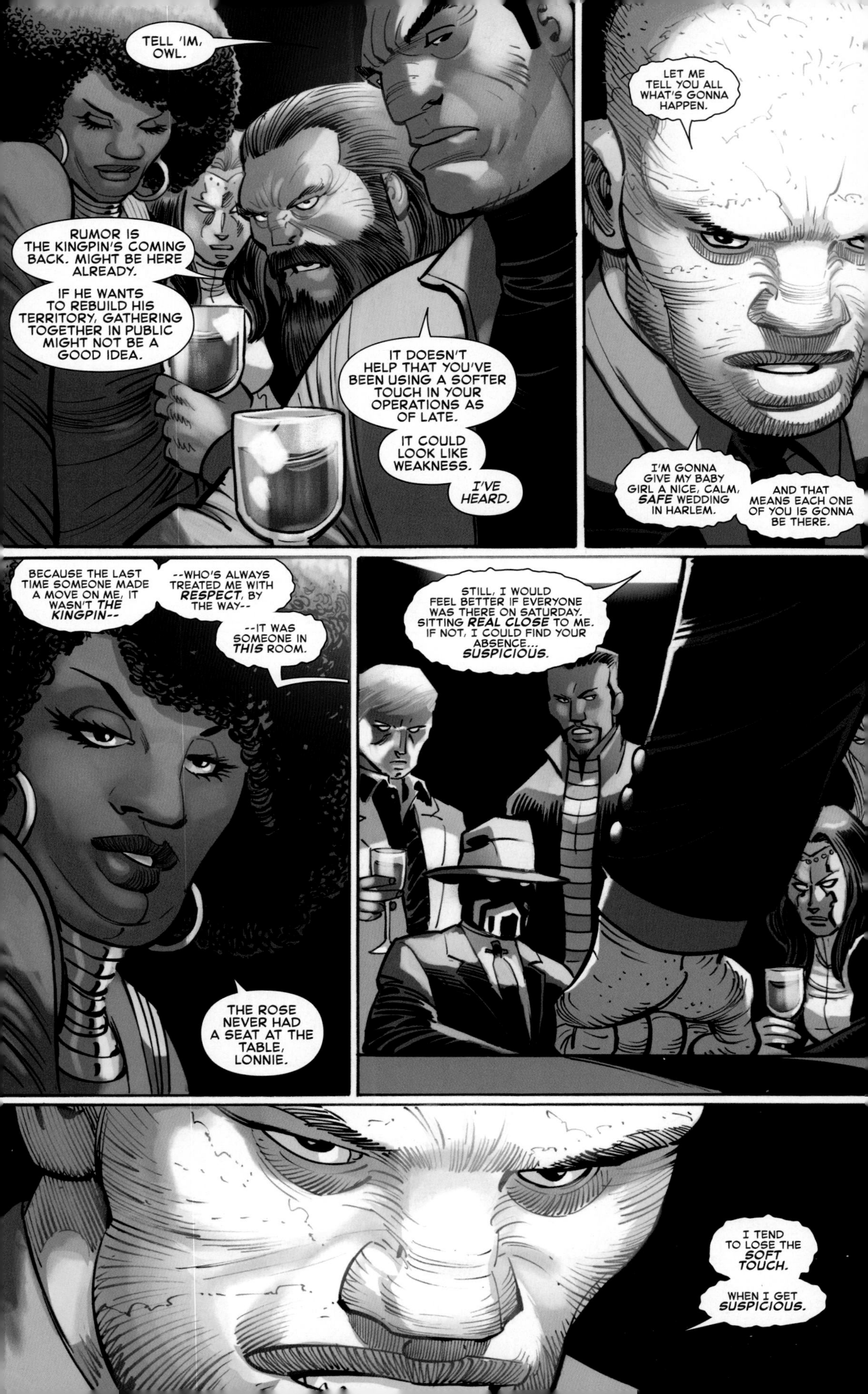
TELL 'IM, OWL.
RUMOR IS THE KINGPIN'S COMING BACK. MIGHT BE HERE ALREADY.
IF HE WANTS TO REBUILD HIS TERRITORY, GATHERING TOGETHER IN PUBLIC MIGHT NOT BE A GOOD IDEA.
IT DOESN'T HELP THAT YOU'VE BEEN USING A SOFTER TOUCH IN YOUR OPERATIONS AS OF LATE.
IT COULD LOOK LIKE WEAKNESS.
I'VE HEARD.
LET ME TELL YOU ALL WHAT'S GONNA HAPPEN.
I'M GONNA GIVE MY BABY GIRL A NICE, CALM, SAFE WEDDING IN HARLEM.
AND THAT MEANS EACH ONE OF YOU IS GONNA BE THERE.
BECAUSE THE LAST TIME SOMEONE MADE A MOVE ON ME, IT WASN'T THE KINGPIN--
--WHO'S ALWAYS TREATED ME WITH RESPECT, BY THE WAY--
--IT WAS SOMEONE IN THIS ROOM.
THE ROSE NEVER HAD A SEAT AT THE TABLE, LONNIE.
STILL, I WOULD FEEL BETTER IF EVERYONE WAS THERE ON SATURDAY. SITTING REAL CLOSE TO ME. IF NOT, I COULD FIND YOUR ABSENCE... SUSPICIOUS.
I TEND TO LOSE THE SOFT TOUCH.
WHEN I GET SUSPICIOUS.

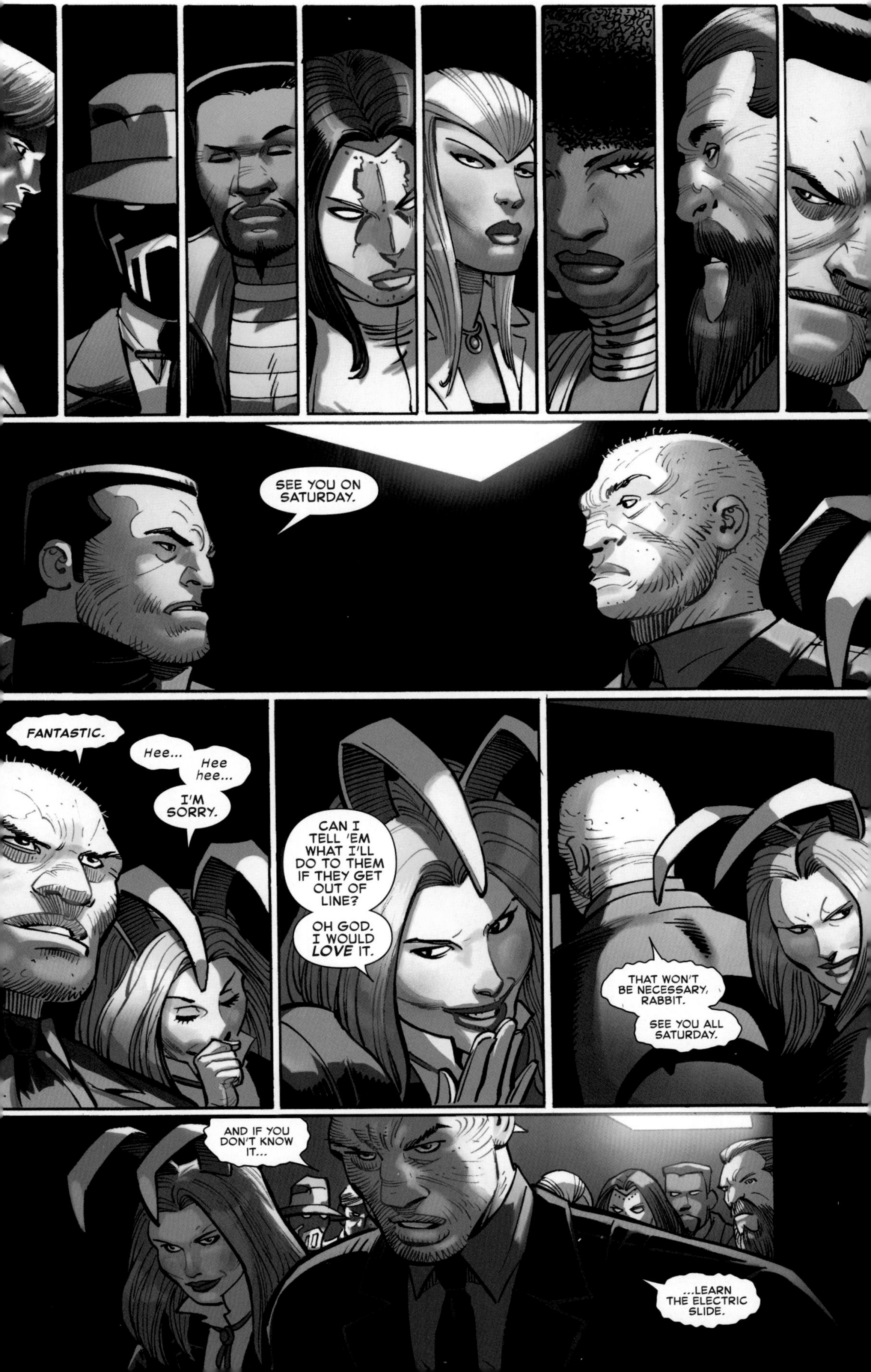
SEE YOU ON SATURDAY.
FANTASTIC.
Hee... Hee hee...
I'M SORRY.
CAN I TELL 'EM WHAT I'LL DO TO THEM IF THEY GET OUT OF LINE?
OH GOD. I WOULD LOVE IT.
THAT WON'T BE NECESSARY, RABBIT.
SEE YOU ALL SATURDAY.
AND IF YOU DON'T KNOW IT...
...LEARN THE ELECTRIC SLIDE.

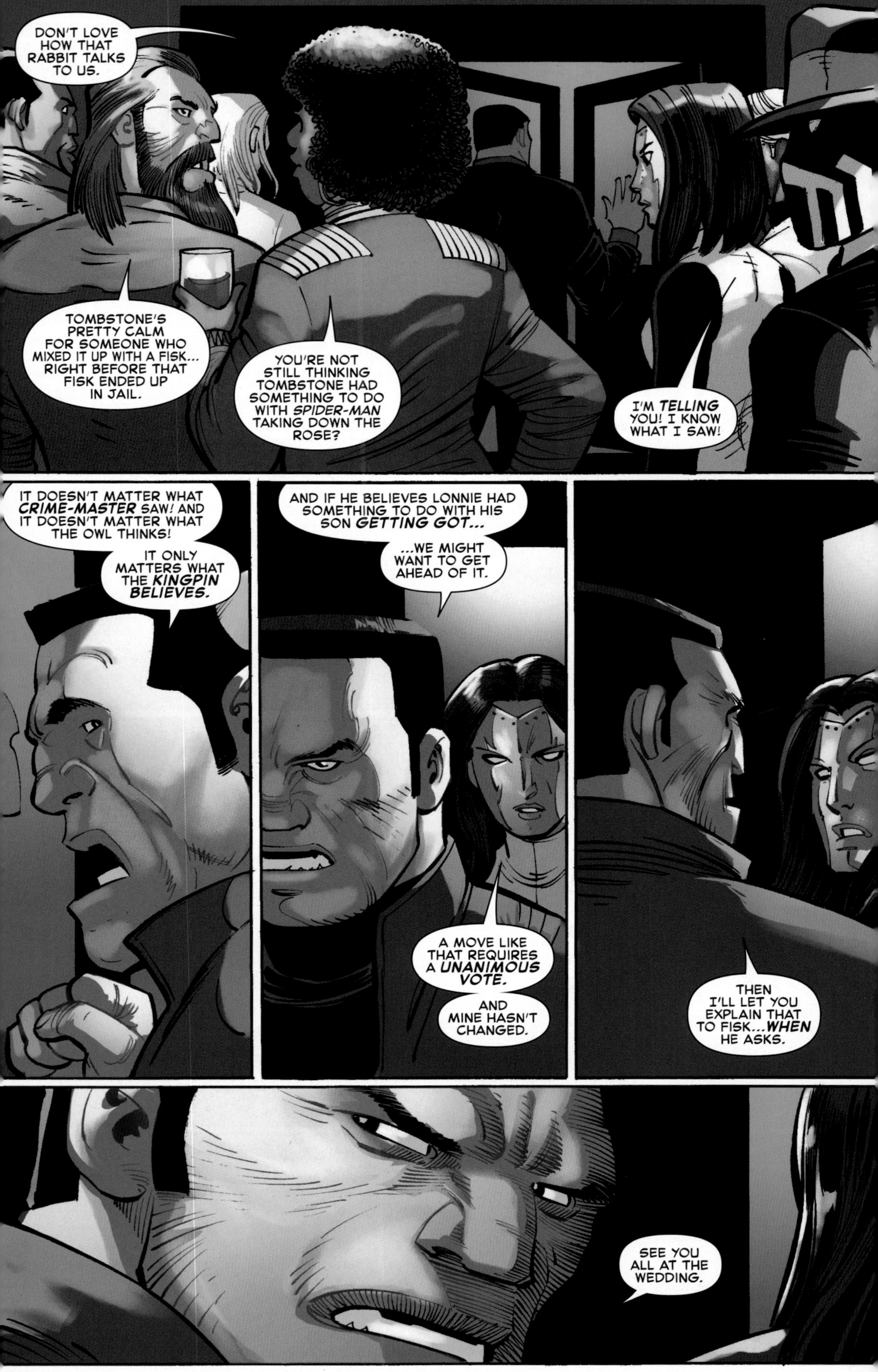
DON'T LOVE HOW THAT RABBIT TALKS TO US.
TOMBSTONE'S PRETTY CALM FOR SOMEONE WHO MIXED IT UP WITH A FISK... RIGHT BEFORE THAT FISK ENDED UP IN JAIL.
YOU'RE NOT STILL THINKING TOMBSTONE HAD SOMETHING TO DO WITH SPIDER-MAN TAKING DOWN THE ROSE?
I'M TELLING YOU! I KNOW WHAT I SAW!
IT DOESN'T MATTER WHAT CRIME-MASTER SAW! AND IT DOESN'T MATTER WHAT THE OWL THINKS!
IT ONLY MATTERS WHAT THE KINGPIN BELIEVES.
AND IF HE BELIEVES LONNIE HAD SOMETHING TO DO WITH HIS SON GETTING GOT...
...WE MIGHT WANT TO GET AHEAD OF IT.
A MOVE LIKE THAT REQUIRES A UNANIMOUS VOTE.
AND MINE HASN'T CHANGED.
THEN I'LL LET YOU EXPLAIN THAT TO FISK...WHEN HE ASKS.
SEE YOU ALL AT THE WEDDING.

CHAPTER 1:

The Last Night

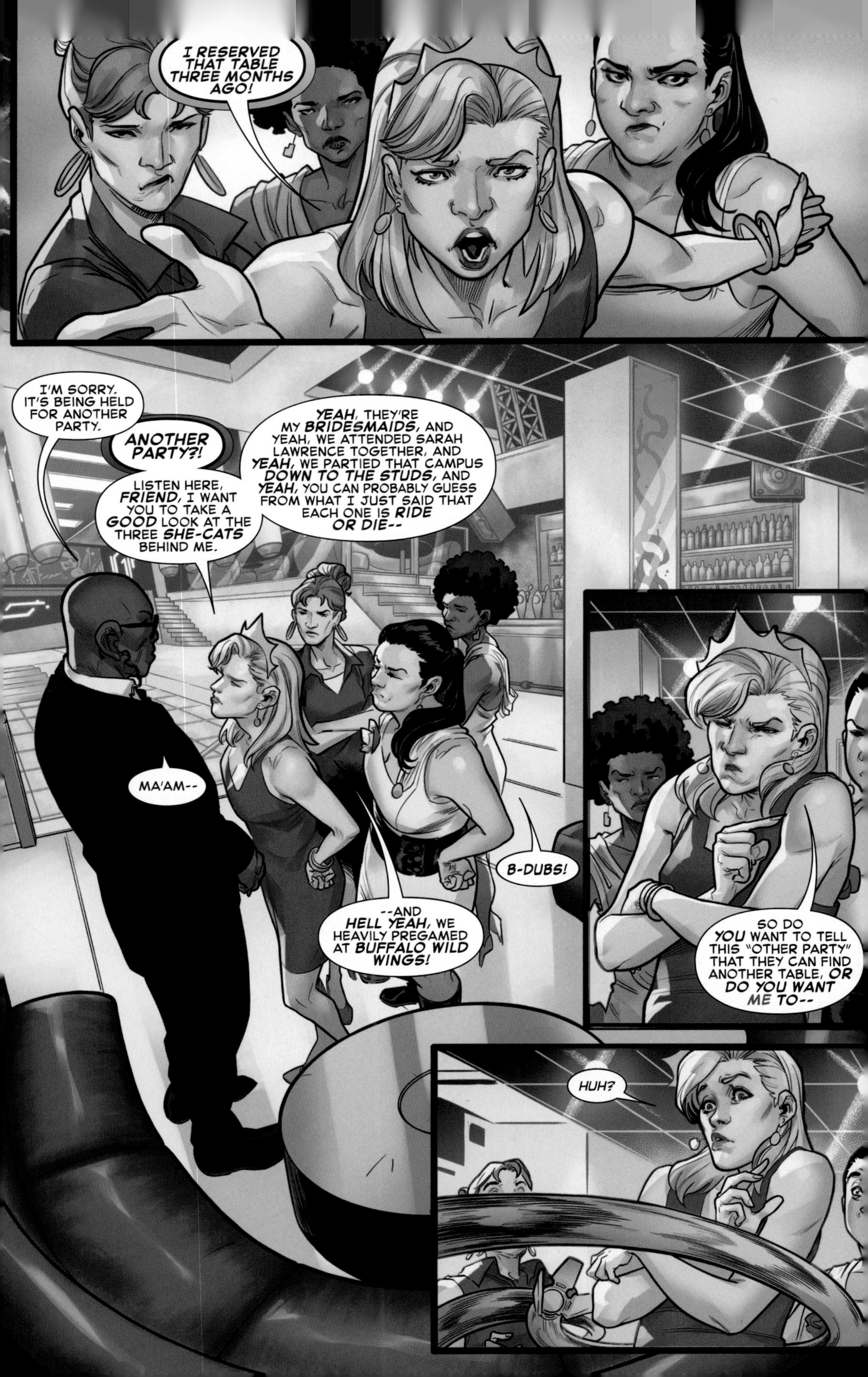
I RESERVED THAT TABLE THREE MONTHS AGO!
I'M SORRY. IT'S BEING HELD FOR ANOTHER PARTY.
ANOTHER PARTY?!
LISTEN HERE, FRIEND, I WANT YOU TO TAKE A GOOD LOOK AT THE THREE SHE-CATS BEHIND ME.
YEAH, THEY'RE MY BRIDESMAIDS, AND YEAH, WE ATTENDED SARAH LAWRENCE TOGETHER, AND YEAH, WE PARTIED THAT CAMPUS DOWN TO THE STUDS, AND YEAH, YOU CAN PROBABLY GUESS FROM WHAT I JUST SAID THAT EACH ONE IS RIDE OR DIE--
MA'AM--
--AND HELL YEAH, WE HEAVILY PREGAMED AT BUFFALO WILD WINGS!
B-DUBS!
SO DO YOU WANT TO TELL THIS "OTHER PARTY" THAT THEY CAN FIND ANOTHER TABLE, OR DO YOU WANT ME TO--
HUH?

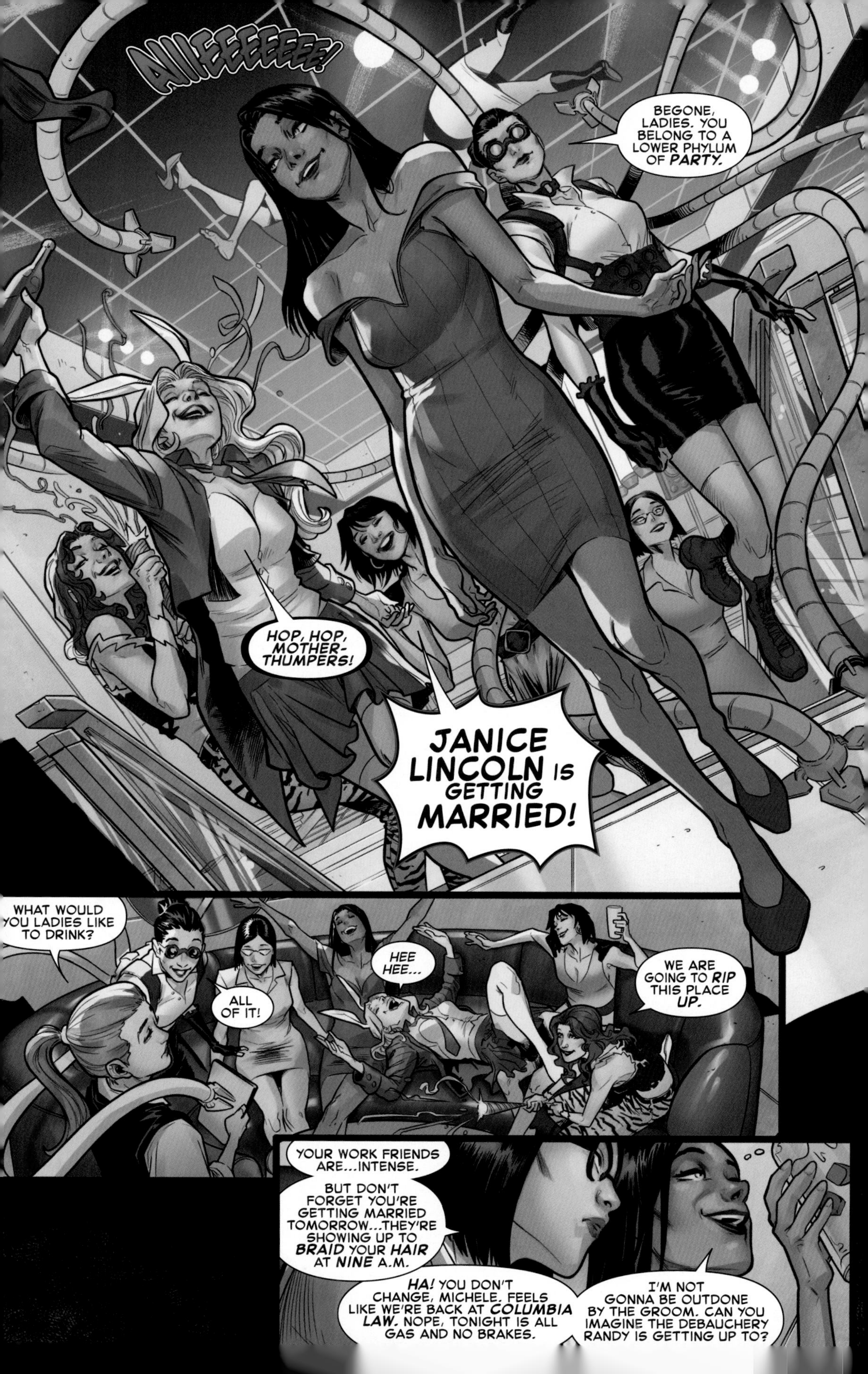
AIIEEEEEEE!
BEGONE, LADIES. YOU BELONG TO A LOWER PHYLUM OF PARTY.
HOP, HOP, MOTHER-THUMPERS!
JANICE LINCOLN IS GETTING MARRIED!
WHAT WOULD YOU LADIES LIKE TO DRINK?
ALL OF IT!
HEE HEE...
WE ARE GOING TO RIP THIS PLACE UP.
YOUR WORK FRIENDS ARE...INTENSE.
BUT DON'T FORGET YOU'RE GETTING MARRIED TOMORROW...THEY'RE SHOWING UP TO BRAID YOUR HAIR AT NINE A.M.
HA! YOU DON'T CHANGE, MICHELE. FEELS LIKE WE'RE BACK AT COLUMBIA LAW. NOPE, TONIGHT IS ALL GAS AND NO BRAKES.
I'M NOT GONNA BE OUTDONE BY THE GROOM. CAN YOU IMAGINE THE DEBAUCHERY RANDY IS GETTING UP TO?

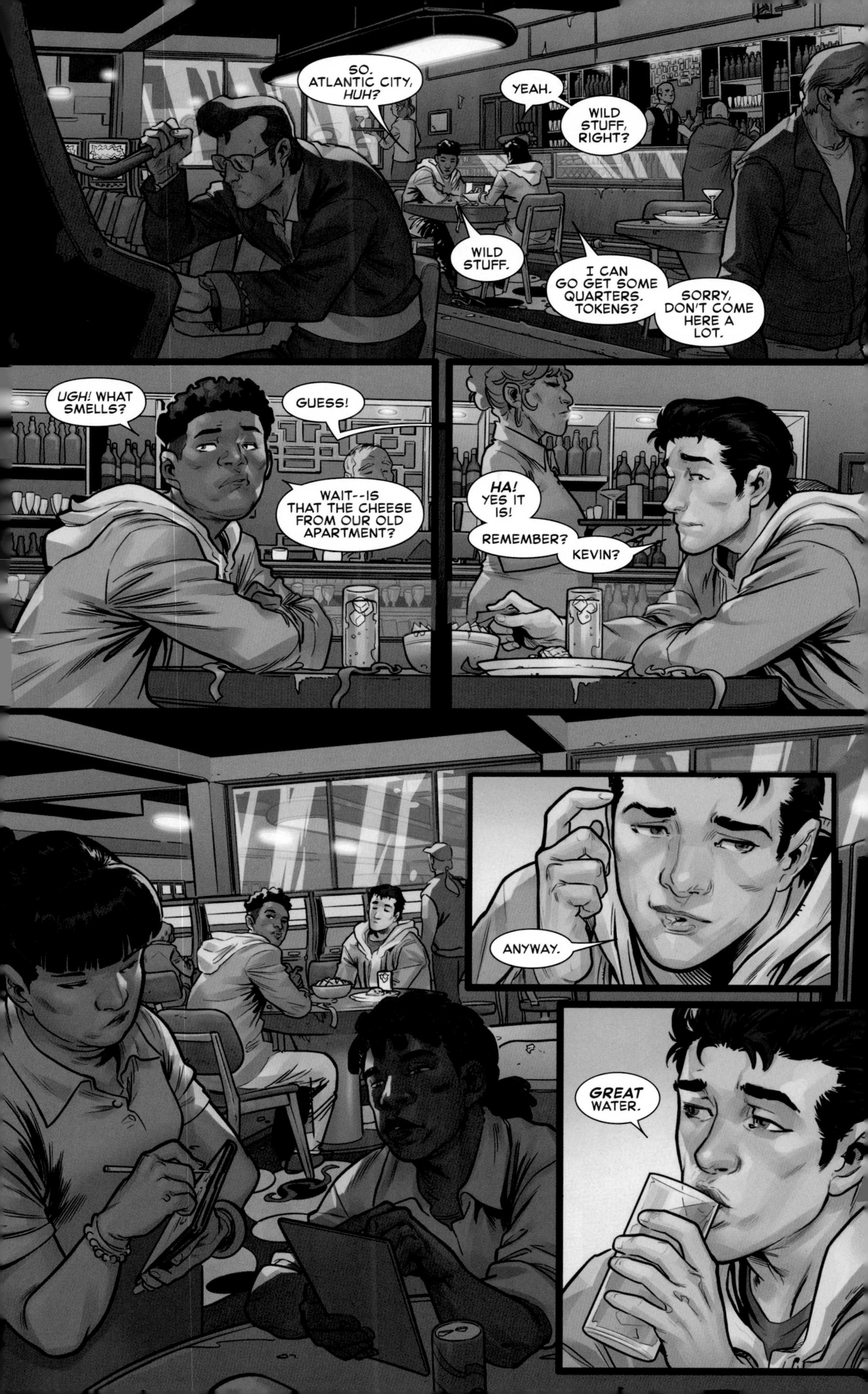
SO. ATLANTIC CITY, *HUH?*
YEAH.
WILD STUFF, RIGHT?
WILD STUFF.
I CAN GO GET SOME QUARTERS. TOKENS?
SORRY, DON'T COME HERE A LOT.
UGH! WHAT SMELLS?
GUESS!
WAIT--IS THAT THE CHEESE FROM OUR OLD APARTMENT?
HA! YES IT IS!
REMEMBER?
KEVIN?
ANYWAY.
GREAT WATER.

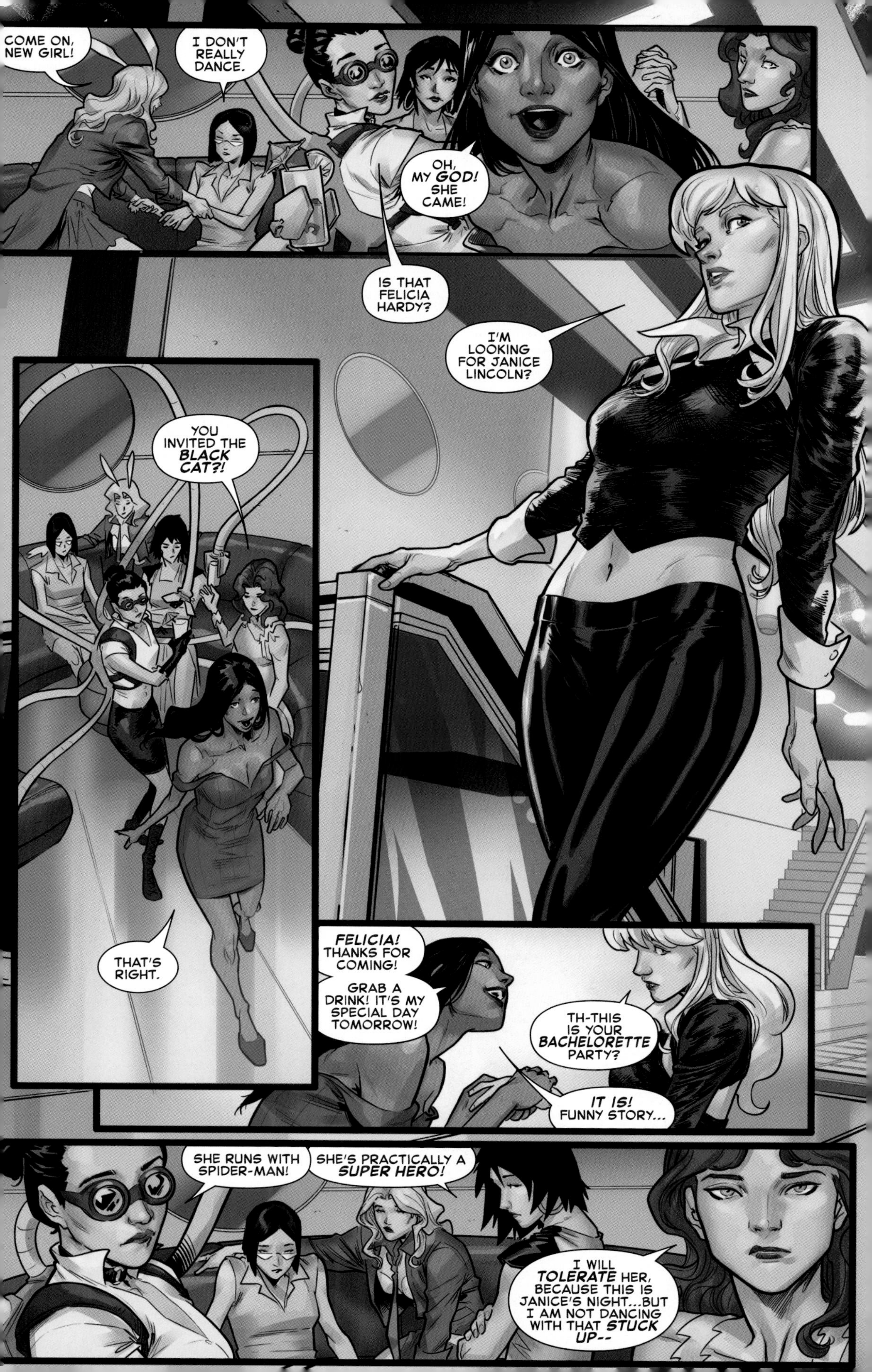
COME ON, NEW GIRL!
I DON'T REALLY DANCE.
OH, MY GOD! SHE CAME!
IS THAT FELICIA HARDY?
I'M LOOKING FOR JANICE LINCOLN?
YOU INVITED THE BLACK CAT?!
THAT'S RIGHT.
FELICIA! THANKS FOR COMING!
GRAB A DRINK! IT'S MY SPECIAL DAY TOMORROW!
TH-THIS IS YOUR BACHELORETTE PARTY?
IT IS! FUNNY STORY...
SHE RUNS WITH SPIDER-MAN!
SHE'S PRACTICALLY A SUPER HERO!
I WILL TOLERATE HER, BECAUSE THIS IS JANICE'S NIGHT...BUT I AM NOT DANCING WITH THAT STUCK UP--

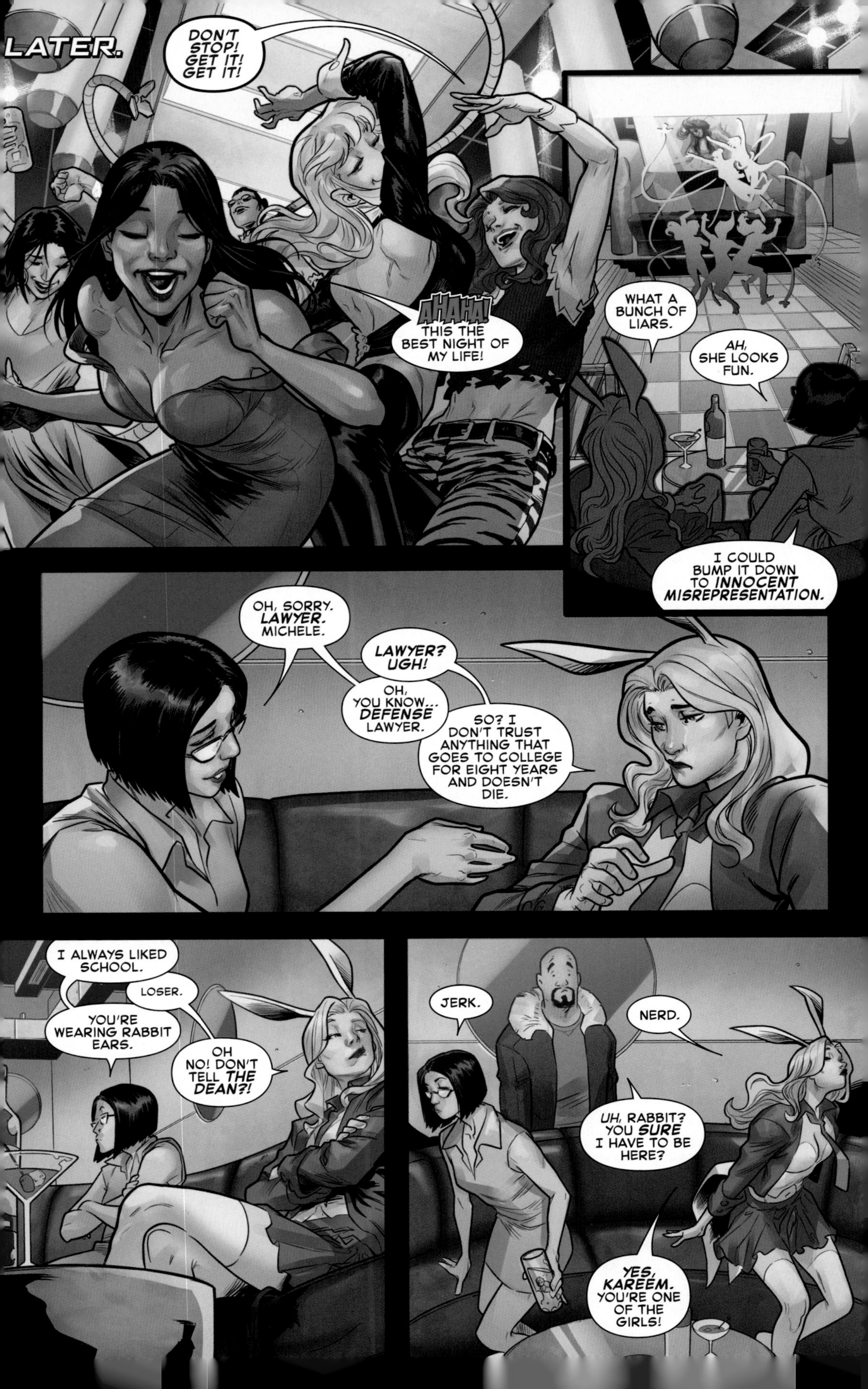
LATER.
DON'T STOP! GET IT! GET IT!
AHAHA! THIS THE BEST NIGHT OF MY LIFE!
WHAT A BUNCH OF LIARS.
AH, SHE LOOKS FUN.
I COULD BUMP IT DOWN TO INNOCENT MISREPRESENTATION.
OH, SORRY. LAWYER. MICHELE.
LAWYER? UGH!
OH, YOU KNOW... DEFENSE LAWYER.
SO? I DON'T TRUST ANYTHING THAT GOES TO COLLEGE FOR EIGHT YEARS AND DOESN'T DIE.
I ALWAYS LIKED SCHOOL.
LOSER.
YOU'RE WEARING RABBIT EARS.
OH NO! DON'T TELL THE DEAN?!
JERK.
NERD.
UH, RABBIT? YOU SURE I HAVE TO BE HERE?
YES, KAREEM. YOU'RE ONE OF THE GIRLS!

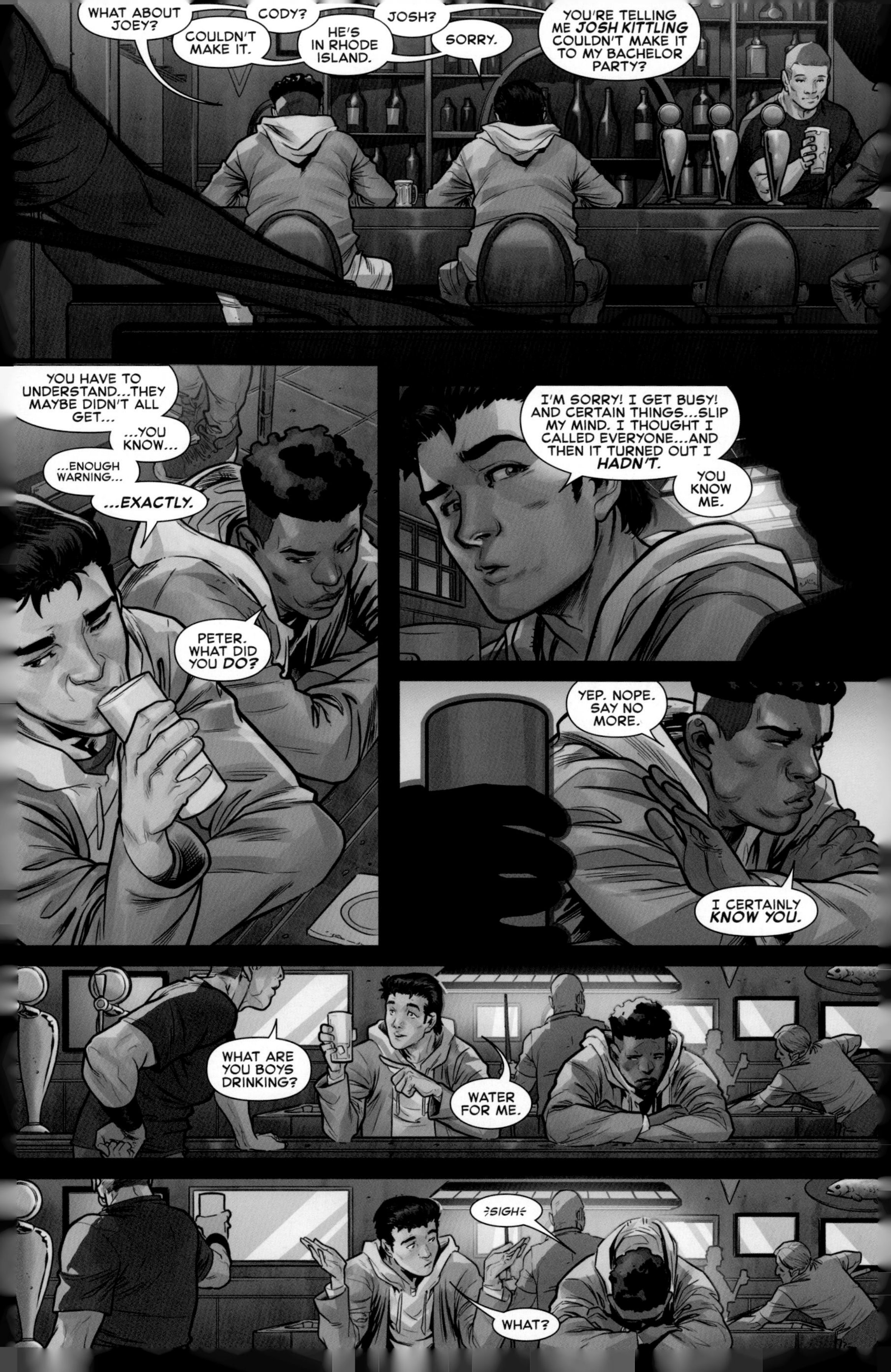
WHAT ABOUT JOEY?
COULDN'T MAKE IT.
CODY?
HE'S IN RHODE ISLAND.
JOSH?
SORRY.
YOU'RE TELLING ME JOSH KITTLING COULDN'T MAKE IT TO MY BACHELOR PARTY?
YOU HAVE TO UNDERSTAND...THEY MAYBE DIDN'T ALL GET...
...YOU KNOW...
...ENOUGH WARNING...
...EXACTLY.
PETER. WHAT DID YOU DO?
I'M SORRY! I GET BUSY! AND CERTAIN THINGS...SLIP MY MIND. I THOUGHT I CALLED EVERYONE...AND THEN IT TURNED OUT I HADN'T.
YOU KNOW ME.
YEP. NOPE. SAY NO MORE.
I CERTAINLY KNOW YOU.
WHAT ARE YOU BOYS DRINKING?
WATER FOR ME.
SIGH
WHAT?

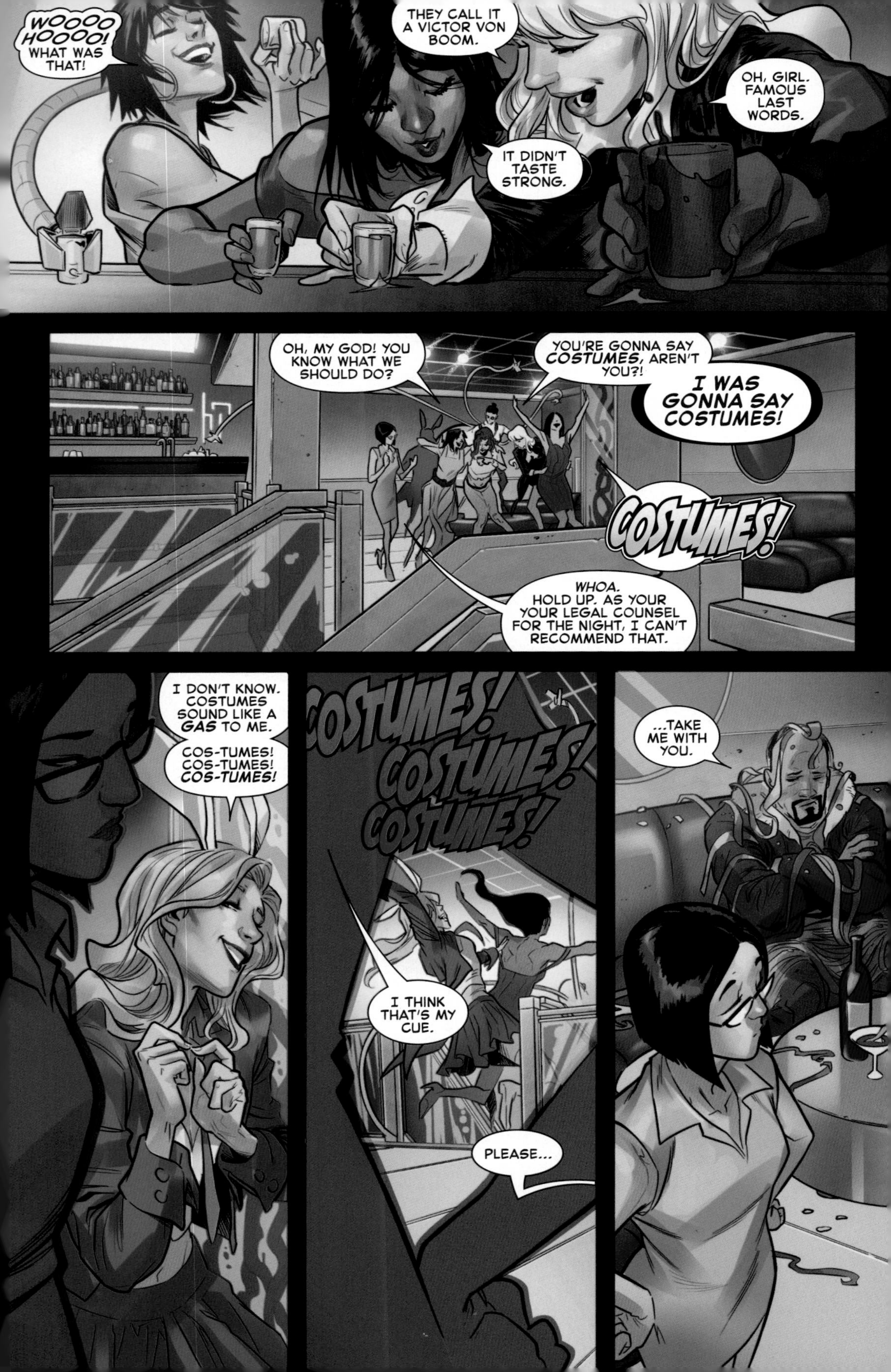
WOOOO HOOOO! WHAT WAS THAT!
THEY CALL IT A VICTOR VON BOOM.
OH, GIRL. FAMOUS LAST WORDS.
IT DIDN'T TASTE STRONG.
OH, MY GOD! YOU KNOW WHAT WE SHOULD DO?
YOU'RE GONNA SAY COSTUMES, AREN'T YOU?!
I WAS GONNA SAY COSTUMES!
COSTUMES!
WHOA. HOLD UP. AS YOUR YOUR LEGAL COUNSEL FOR THE NIGHT, I CAN'T RECOMMEND THAT.
I DON'T KNOW. COSTUMES SOUND LIKE A GAS TO ME.
COS-TUMES! COS-TUMES! COS-TUMES!
COSTUMES! COSTUMES! COSTUMES!
I THINK THAT'S MY CUE.
PLEASE...
...TAKE ME WITH YOU.

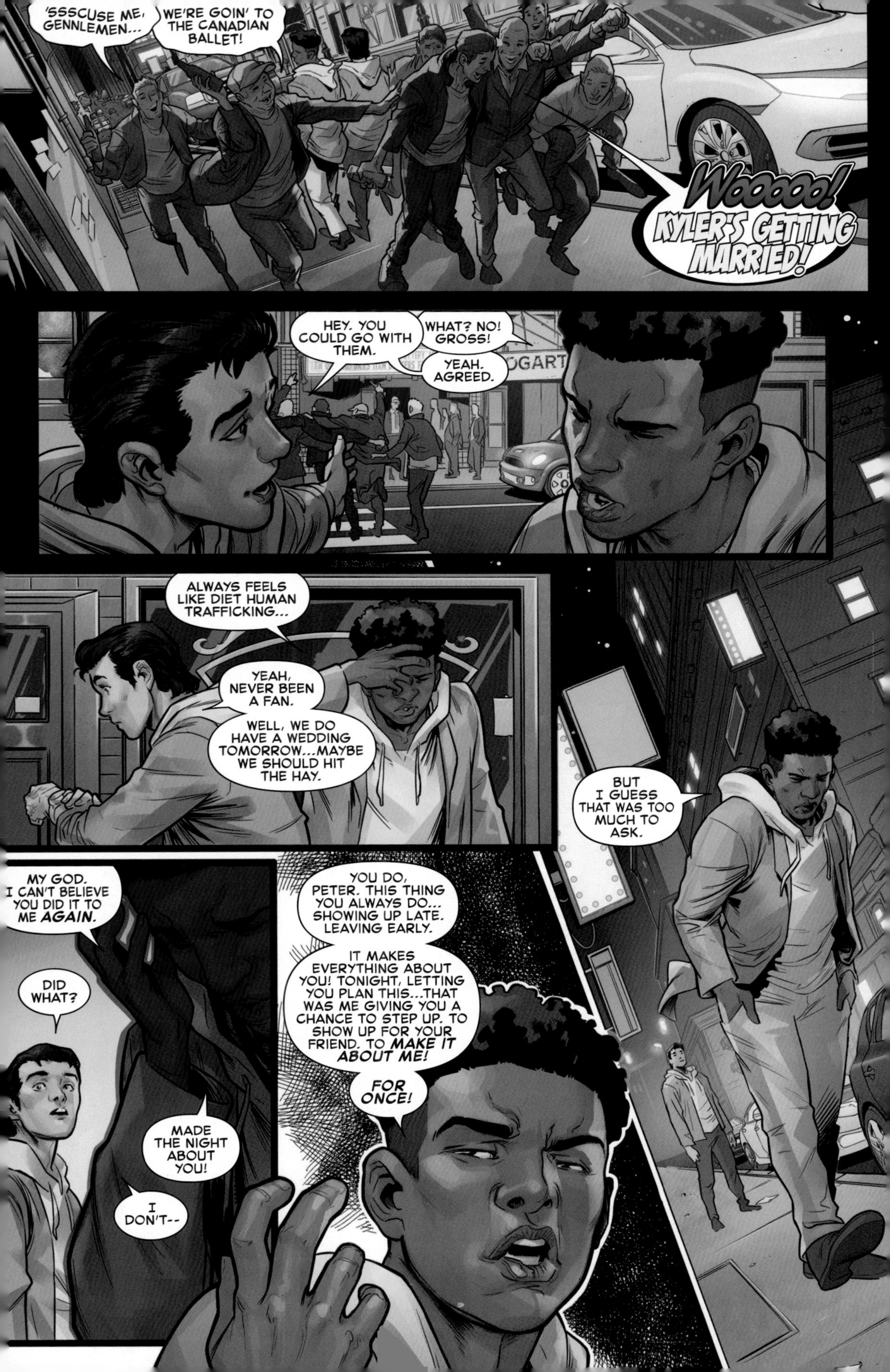
'SSSCUSE ME, GENNLEMEN...
WE'RE GOIN' TO THE CANADIAN BALLET!
WOOOOOO! KYLER'S GETTING MARRIED!
HEY. YOU COULD GO WITH THEM.
WHAT? NO! GROSS!
YEAH. AGREED.
ALWAYS FEELS LIKE DIET HUMAN TRAFFICKING...
YEAH, NEVER BEEN A FAN.
WELL, WE DO HAVE A WEDDING TOMORROW...MAYBE WE SHOULD HIT THE HAY.
BUT I GUESS THAT WAS TOO MUCH TO ASK.
MY GOD. I CAN'T BELIEVE YOU DID IT TO ME AGAIN.
DID WHAT?
MADE THE NIGHT ABOUT YOU!
I DON'T--
YOU DO, PETER. THIS THING YOU ALWAYS DO... SHOWING UP LATE. LEAVING EARLY.
IT MAKES EVERYTHING ABOUT YOU! TONIGHT, LETTING YOU PLAN THIS...THAT WAS ME GIVING YOU A CHANCE TO STEP UP. TO SHOW UP FOR YOUR FRIEND. TO MAKE IT ABOUT ME!
FOR ONCE!

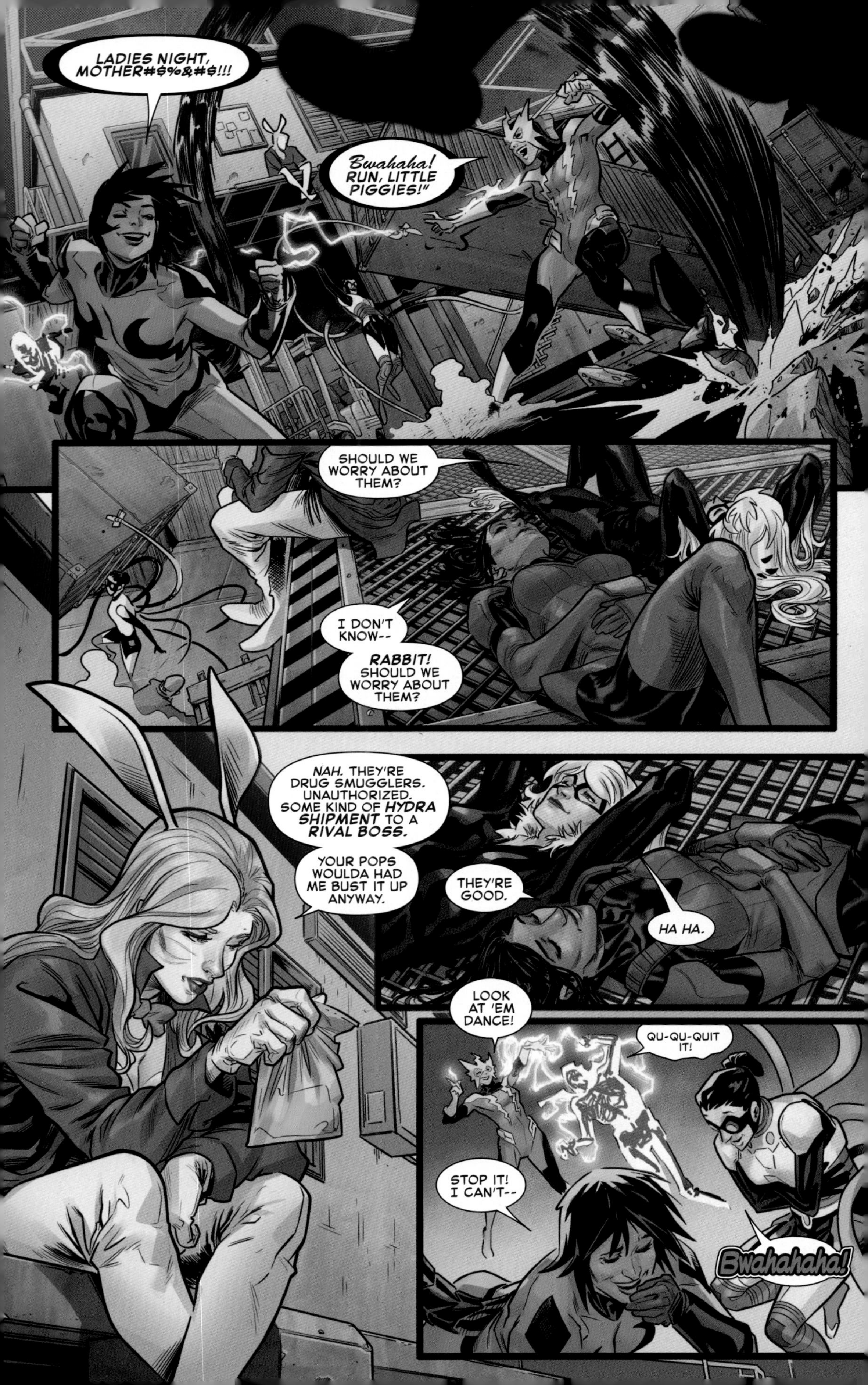

LADIES NIGHT, MOTHER#$%&#$!!!
Bwahaha! RUN, LITTLE PIGGIES!"
SHOULD WE WORRY ABOUT THEM?
I DON'T KNOW--
RABBIT! SHOULD WE WORRY ABOUT THEM?
NAH. THEY'RE DRUG SMUGGLERS. UNAUTHORIZED. SOME KIND OF HYDRA SHIPMENT TO A RIVAL BOSS.
YOUR POPS WOULDA HAD ME BUST IT UP ANYWAY.
THEY'RE GOOD.
HA HA.
LOOK AT 'EM DANCE!
QU-QU-QUIT IT!
STOP IT! I CAN'T--
Bwahahaha!

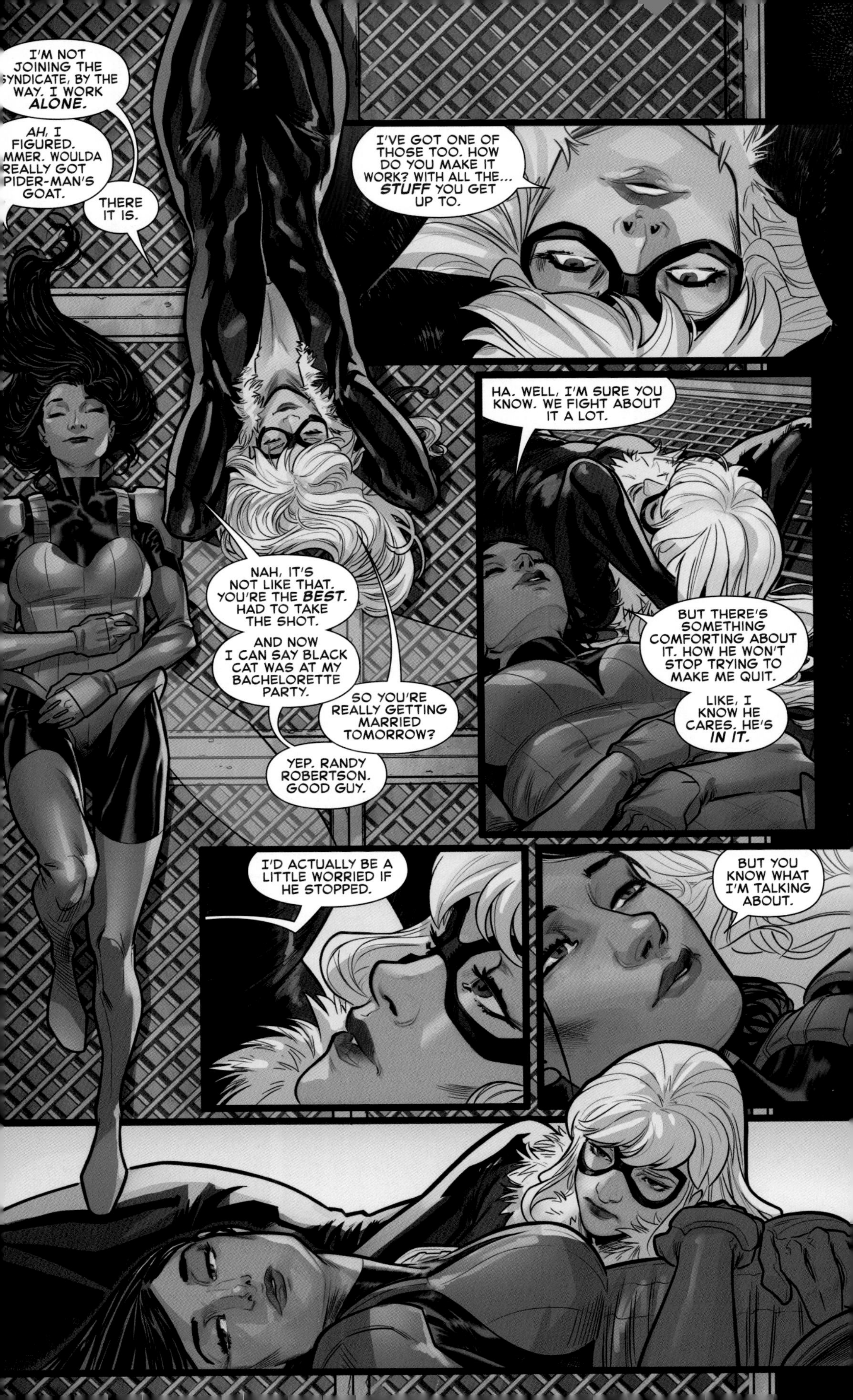
I'M NOT JOINING THE SYNDICATE, BY THE WAY. I WORK ALONE.
AH, I FIGURED. BUMMER. WOULDA REALLY GOT SPIDER-MAN'S GOAT.
THERE IT IS.
I'VE GOT ONE OF THOSE TOO. HOW DO YOU MAKE IT WORK? WITH ALL THE... STUFF YOU GET UP TO.
NAH, IT'S NOT LIKE THAT. YOU'RE THE BEST. HAD TO TAKE THE SHOT.
AND NOW I CAN SAY BLACK CAT WAS AT MY BACHELORETTE PARTY.
SO YOU'RE REALLY GETTING MARRIED TOMORROW?
YEP. RANDY ROBERTSON. GOOD GUY.
HA. WELL, I'M SURE YOU KNOW. WE FIGHT ABOUT IT A LOT.
BUT THERE'S SOMETHING COMFORTING ABOUT IT. HOW HE WON'T STOP TRYING TO MAKE ME QUIT.
LIKE, I KNOW HE CARES. HE'S IN IT.
I'D ACTUALLY BE A LITTLE WORRIED IF HE STOPPED.
BUT YOU KNOW WHAT I'M TALKING ABOUT.

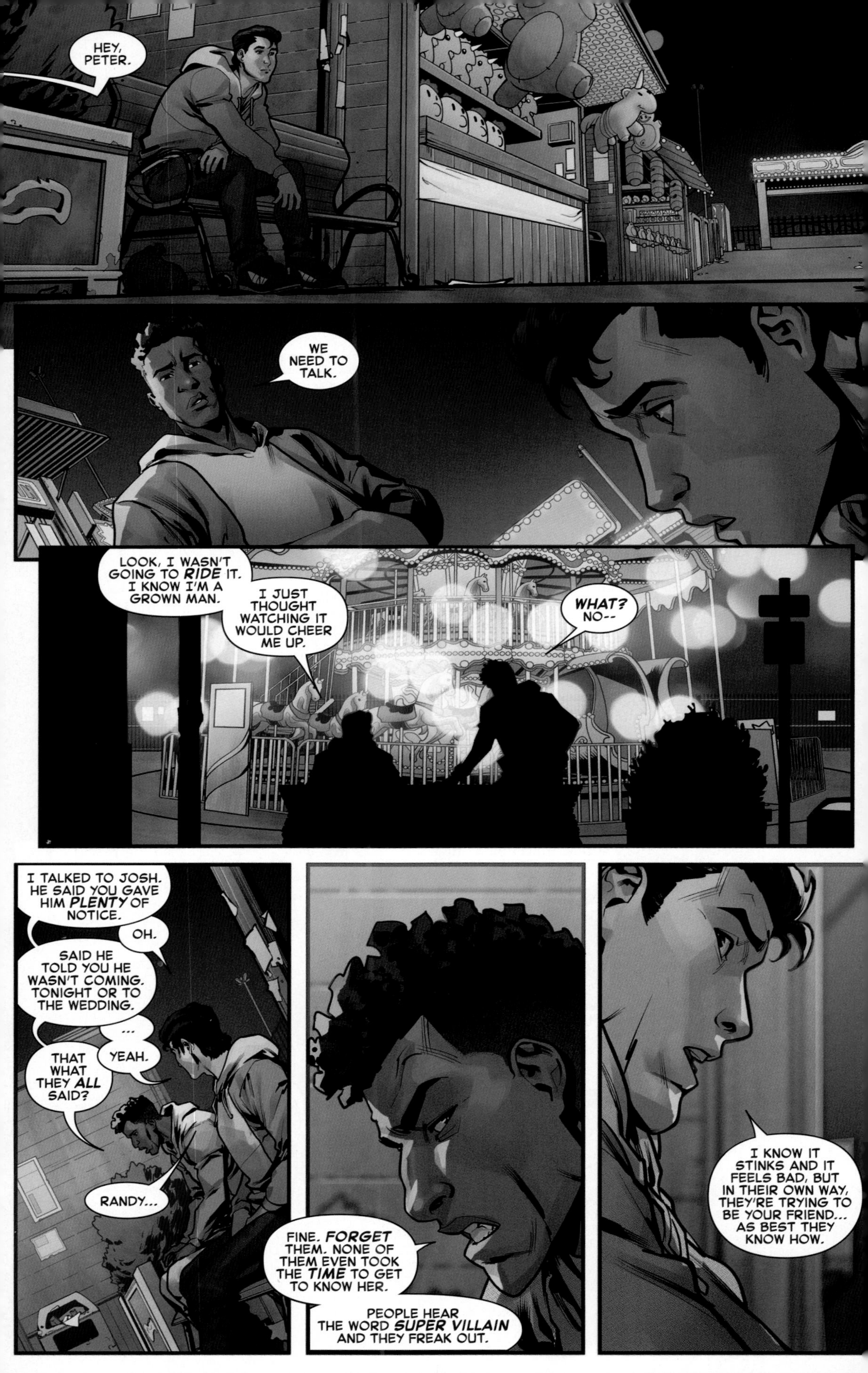
HEY, PETER.
WE NEED TO TALK.
LOOK, I WASN'T GOING TO *RIDE* IT. I KNOW I'M A GROWN MAN.
I JUST THOUGHT WATCHING IT WOULD CHEER ME UP.
WHAT? NO--
I TALKED TO JOSH. HE SAID YOU GAVE HIM *PLENTY* OF NOTICE.
OH.
SAID HE TOLD YOU HE WASN'T COMING. TONIGHT OR TO THE WEDDING.
...
YEAH.
THAT WHAT THEY *ALL* SAID?
RANDY...
FINE. *FORGET* THEM. NONE OF THEM EVEN TOOK THE *TIME* TO GET TO KNOW HER.
PEOPLE HEAR THE WORD *SUPER VILLAIN* AND THEY FREAK OUT.
I KNOW IT STINKS AND IT FEELS BAD, BUT IN THEIR OWN WAY, THEY'RE TRYING TO BE YOUR FRIEND... AS BEST THEY KNOW HOW.

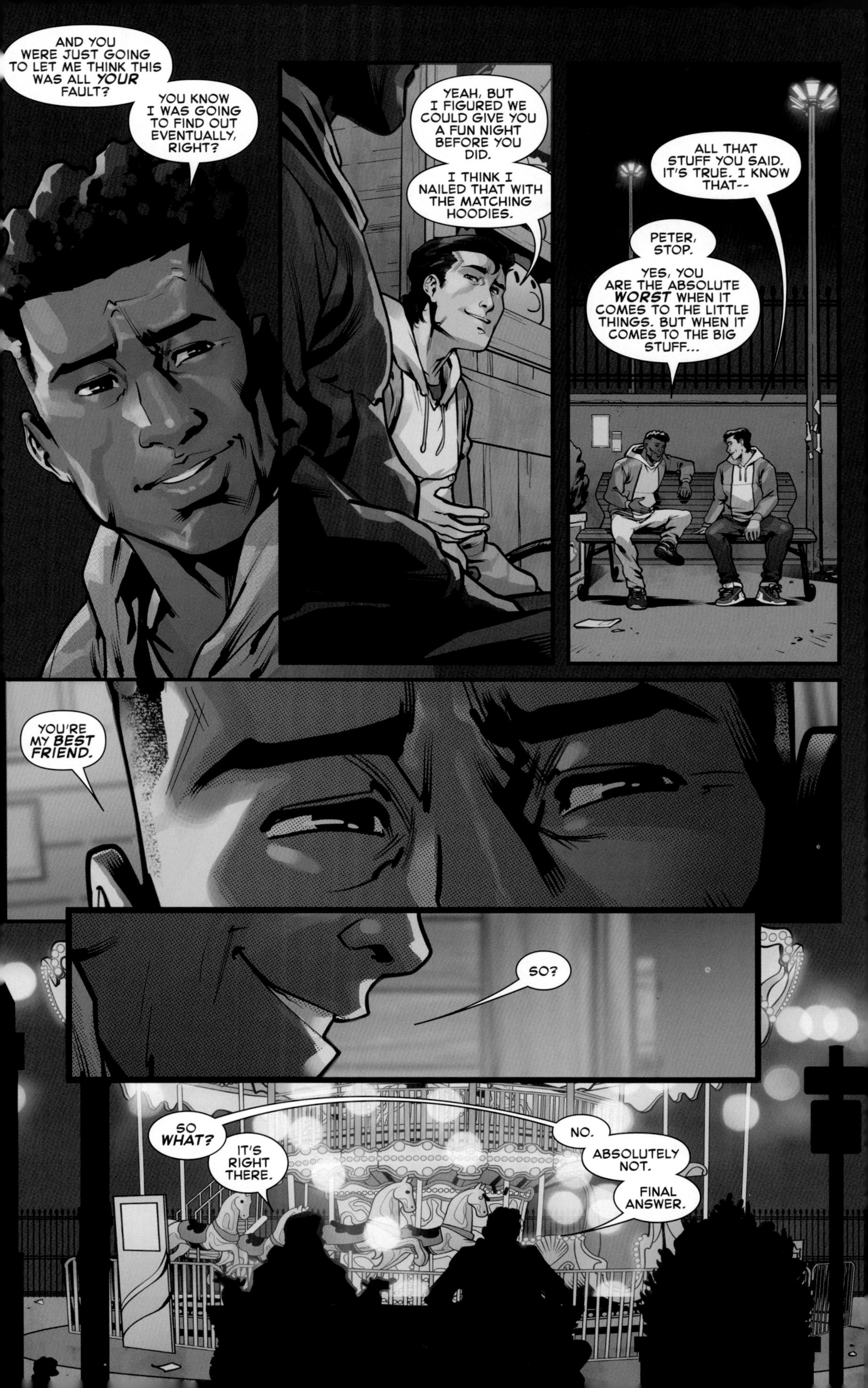
AND YOU WERE JUST GOING TO LET ME THINK THIS WAS ALL *YOUR* FAULT?
YOU KNOW I WAS GOING TO FIND OUT EVENTUALLY, RIGHT?
YEAH, BUT I FIGURED WE COULD GIVE YOU A FUN NIGHT BEFORE YOU DID.
I THINK I NAILED THAT WITH THE MATCHING HOODIES.
ALL THAT STUFF YOU SAID. IT'S TRUE. I KNOW THAT--
PETER, STOP.
YES, YOU ARE THE ABSOLUTE ***WORST*** WHEN IT COMES TO THE LITTLE THINGS. BUT WHEN IT COMES TO THE BIG STUFF...
YOU'RE MY ***BEST FRIEND.***
SO?
SO ***WHAT?***
IT'S RIGHT THERE.
NO.
ABSOLUTELY NOT.
FINAL ANSWER.

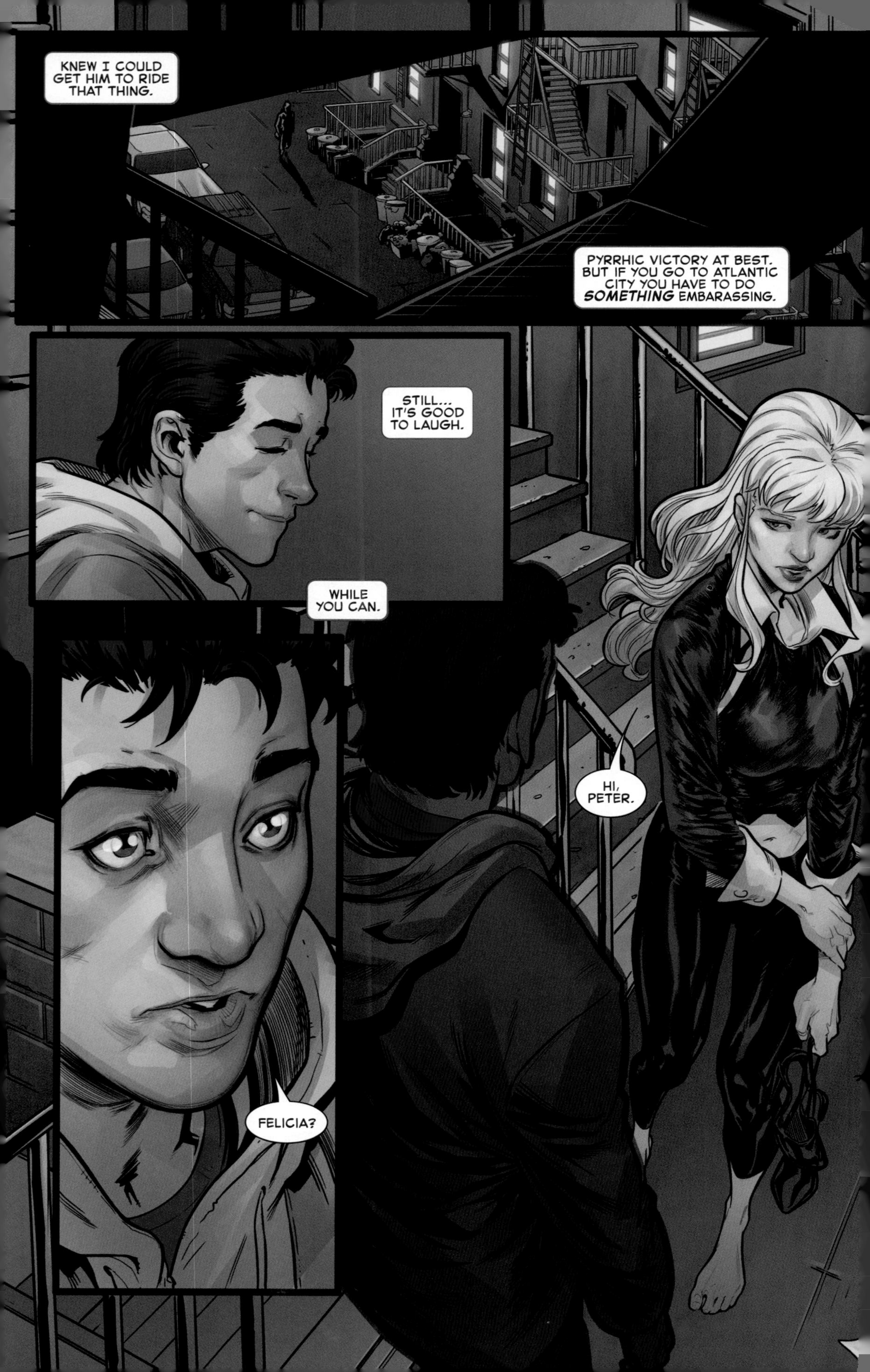

KNEW I COULD GET HIM TO RIDE THAT THING.
PYRRHIC VICTORY AT BEST. BUT IF YOU GO TO ATLANTIC CITY YOU HAVE TO DO SOMETHING EMBARASSING.
STILL... IT'S GOOD TO LAUGH.
WHILE YOU CAN.
HI, PETER.
FELICIA?

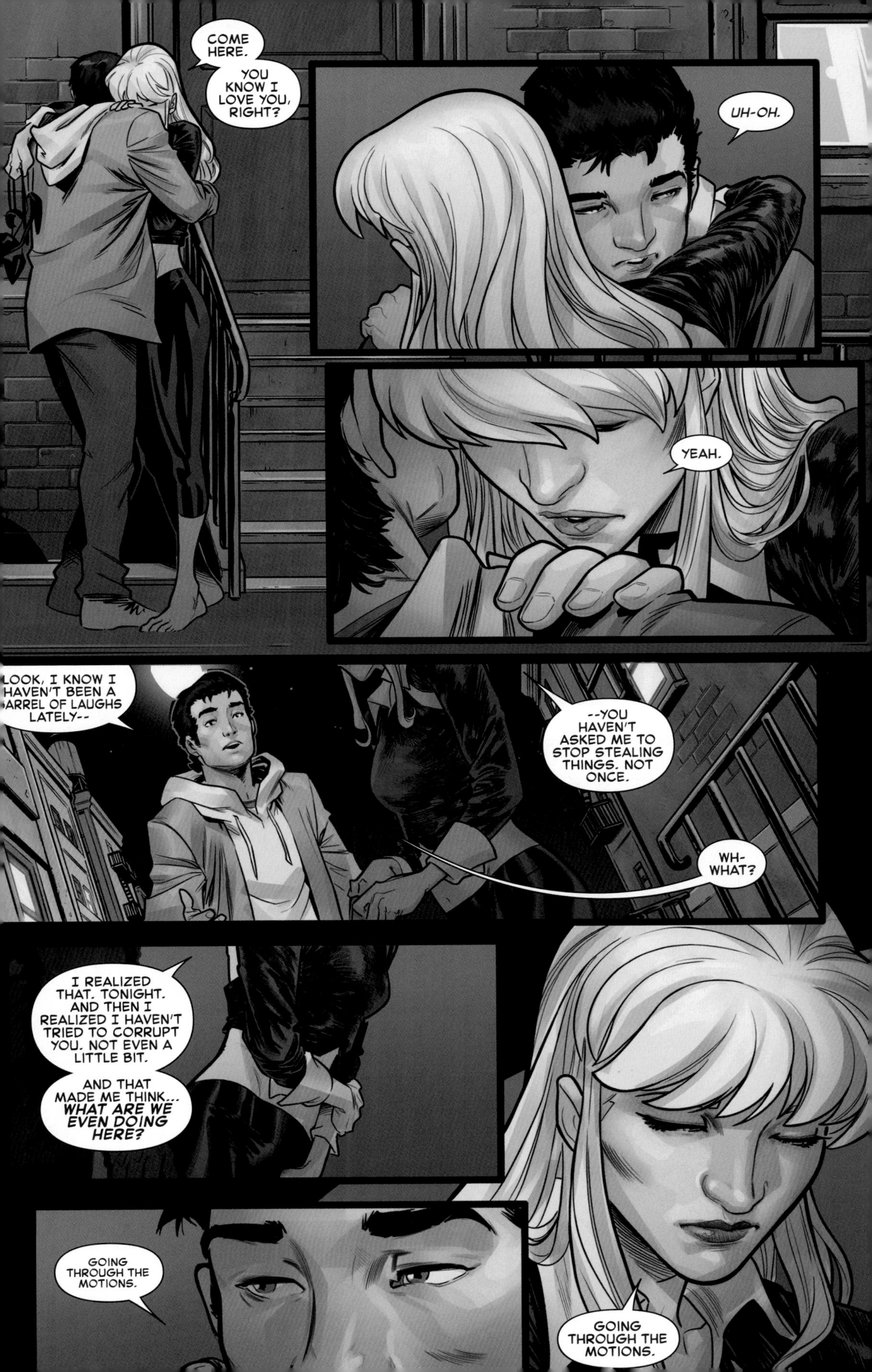
COME HERE.
YOU KNOW I LOVE YOU, RIGHT?
UH-OH.
YEAH.
LOOK, I KNOW I HAVEN'T BEEN A BARREL OF LAUGHS LATELY--
--YOU HAVEN'T ASKED ME TO STOP STEALING THINGS. NOT ONCE.
WH-WHAT?
I REALIZED THAT. TONIGHT. AND THEN I REALIZED I HAVEN'T TRIED TO CORRUPT YOU. NOT EVEN A LITTLE BIT.
AND THAT MADE ME THINK... *WHAT ARE WE EVEN DOING HERE?*
GOING THROUGH THE MOTIONS.
GOING THROUGH THE MOTIONS.

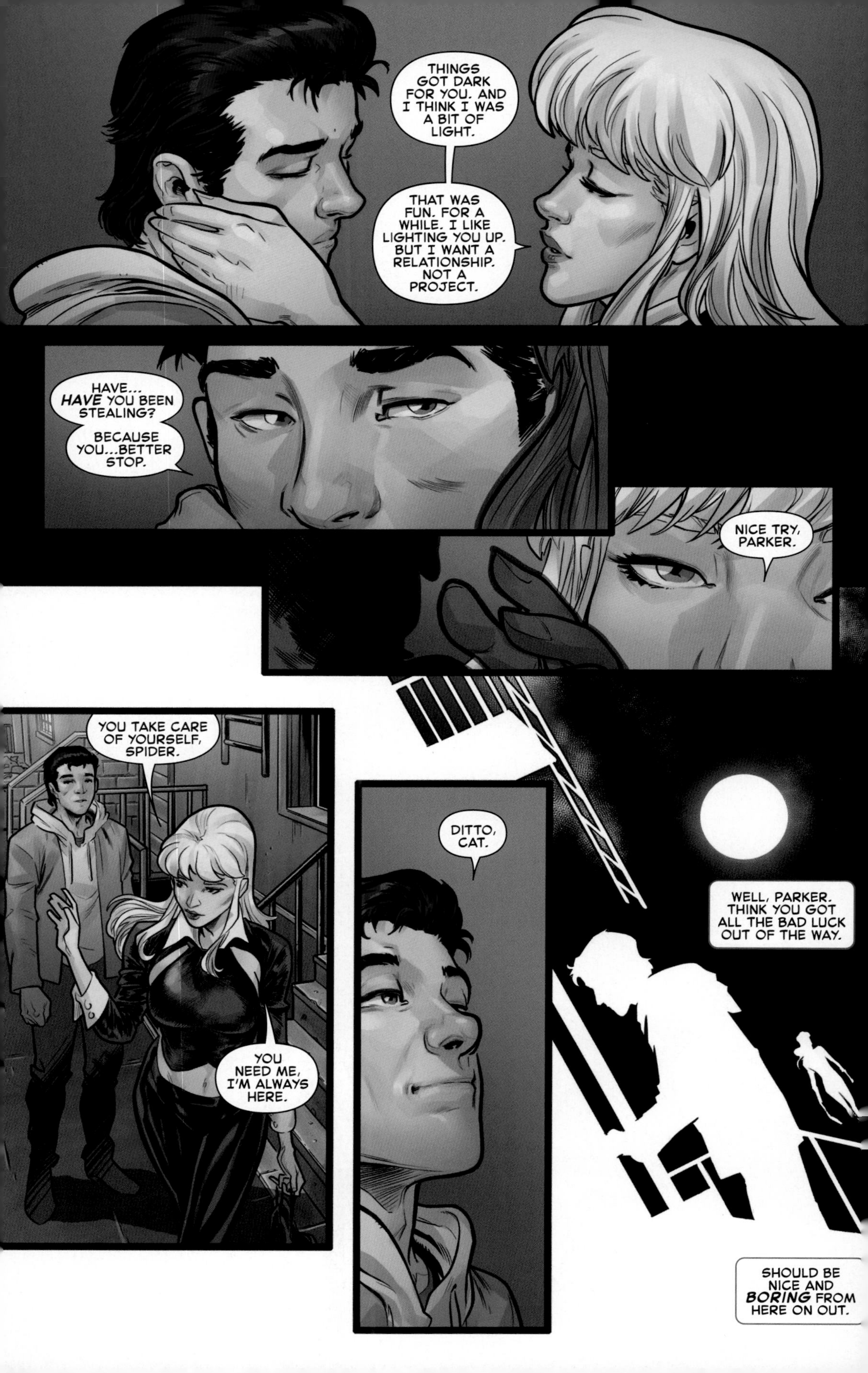

THINGS GOT DARK FOR YOU. AND I THINK I WAS A BIT OF LIGHT.
THAT WAS FUN. FOR A WHILE. I LIKE LIGHTING YOU UP. BUT I WANT A RELATIONSHIP. NOT A PROJECT.
HAVE... HAVE YOU BEEN STEALING?
BECAUSE YOU...BETTER STOP.
NICE TRY, PARKER.
YOU TAKE CARE OF YOURSELF, SPIDER.
YOU NEED ME, I'M ALWAYS HERE.
DITTO, CAT.
WELL, PARKER. THINK YOU GOT ALL THE BAD LUCK OUT OF THE WAY.
SHOULD BE NICE AND BORING FROM HERE ON OUT.

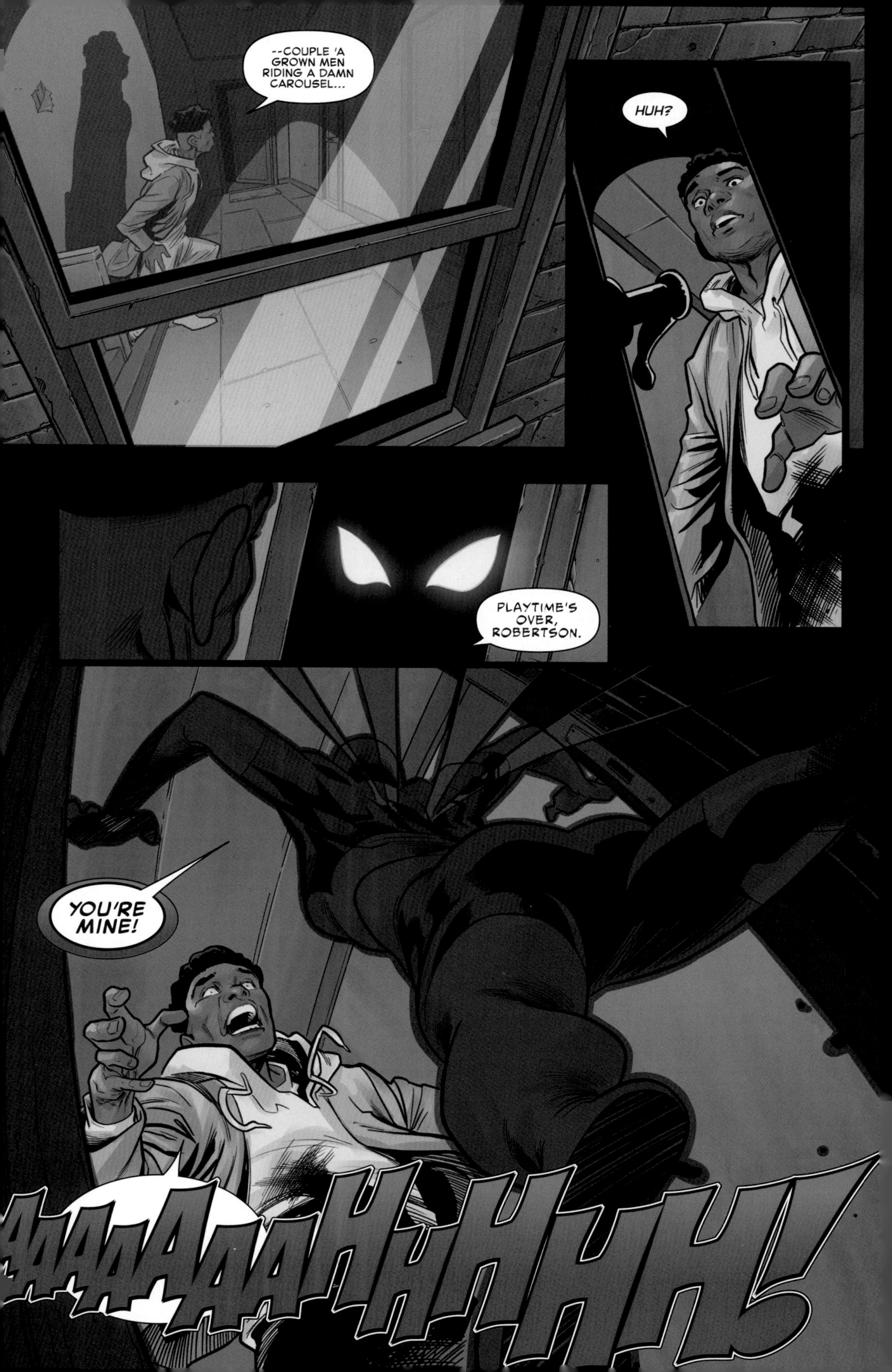
--COUPLE 'A GROWN MEN RIDING A DAMN CAROUSEL...
HUH?
PLAYTIME'S OVER, ROBERTSON.
YOU'RE MINE!
AAAAAAAHHHHHH!

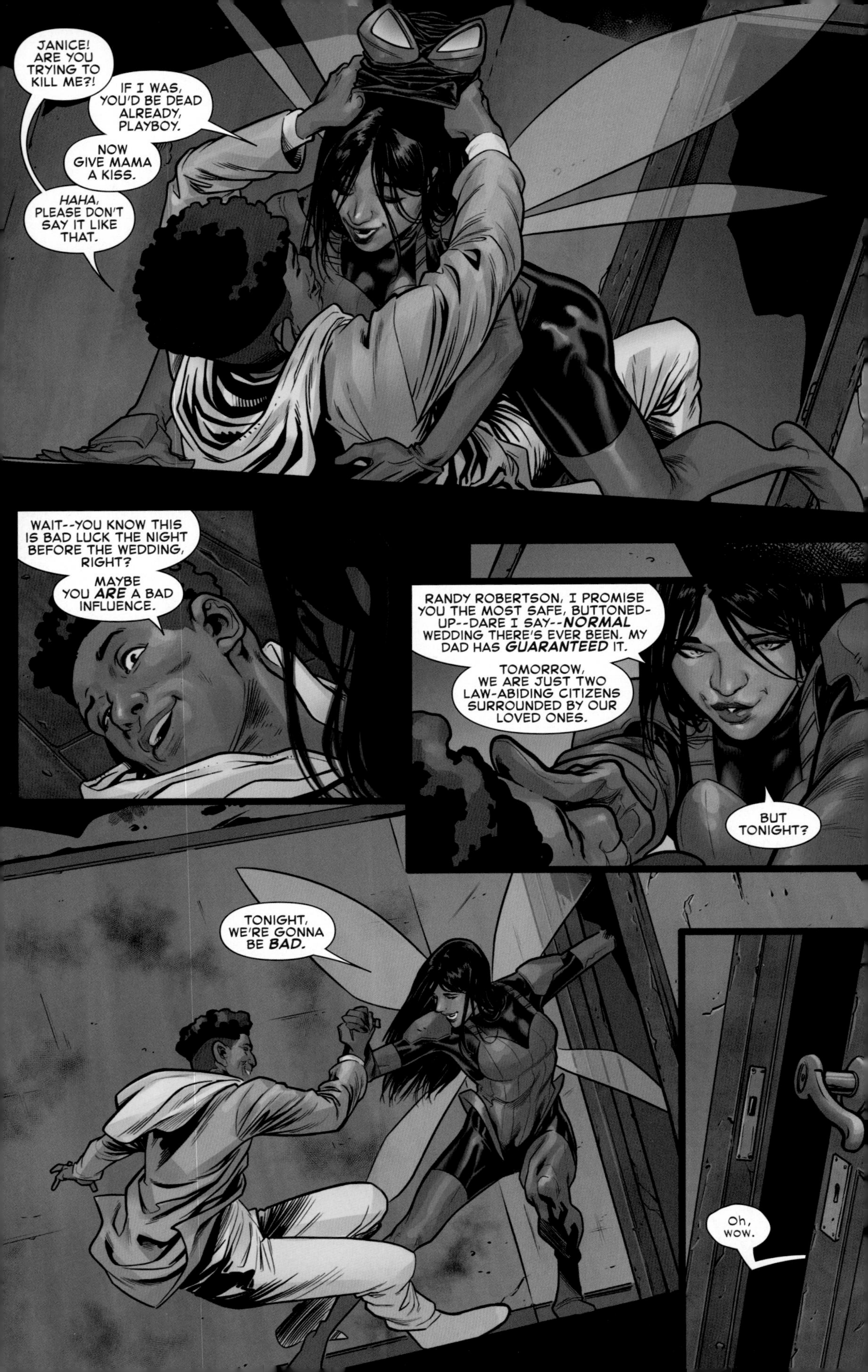
JANICE! ARE YOU TRYING TO KILL ME?!
IF I WAS, YOU'D BE DEAD ALREADY, PLAYBOY.
NOW GIVE MAMA A KISS.
HAHA, PLEASE DON'T SAY IT LIKE THAT.
WAIT--YOU KNOW THIS IS BAD LUCK THE NIGHT BEFORE THE WEDDING, RIGHT?
MAYBE YOU ARE A BAD INFLUENCE.
RANDY ROBERTSON, I PROMISE YOU THE MOST SAFE, BUTTONED-UP--DARE I SAY--NORMAL WEDDING THERE'S EVER BEEN. MY DAD HAS GUARANTEED IT.
TOMORROW, WE ARE JUST TWO LAW-ABIDING CITIZENS SURROUNDED BY OUR LOVED ONES.
BUT TONIGHT?
TONIGHT, WE'RE GONNA BE BAD.
Oh, wow.

CHAPTER 2:

The Big Day

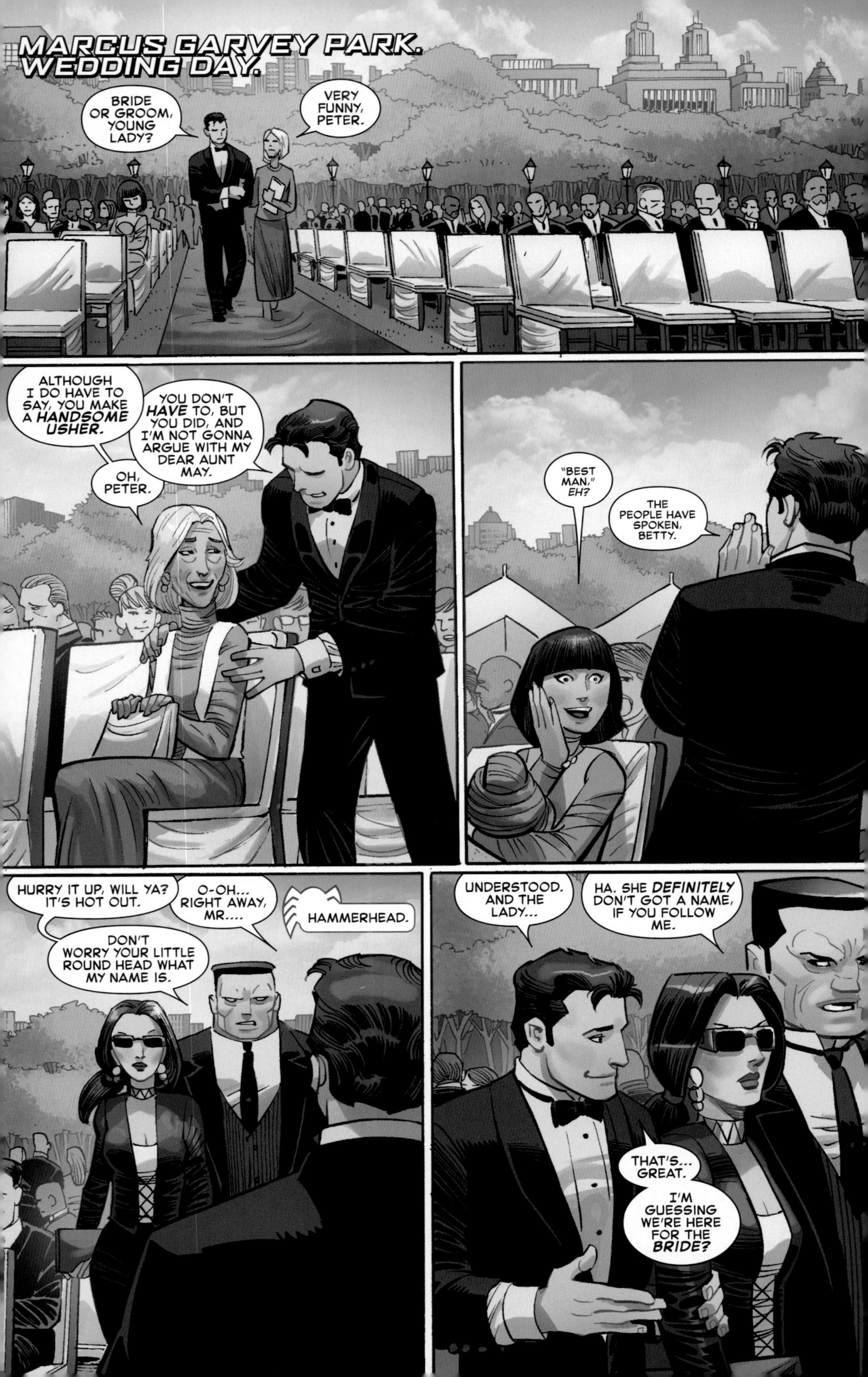
MARCUS GARVEY PARK. WEDDING DAY.
BRIDE OR GROOM, YOUNG LADY?
VERY FUNNY, PETER.
ALTHOUGH I DO HAVE TO SAY, YOU MAKE A HANDSOME USHER.
YOU DON'T HAVE TO, BUT YOU DID, AND I'M NOT GONNA ARGUE WITH MY DEAR AUNT MAY.
OH, PETER.
"BEST MAN," EH?
THE PEOPLE HAVE SPOKEN, BETTY.
HURRY IT UP, WILL YA? IT'S HOT OUT.
O-OH... RIGHT AWAY, MR....
DON'T WORRY YOUR LITTLE ROUND HEAD WHAT MY NAME IS.
HAMMERHEAD.
UNDERSTOOD. AND THE LADY...
HA. SHE DEFINITELY DON'T GOT A NAME, IF YOU FOLLOW ME.
THAT'S... GREAT.
I'M GUESSING WE'RE HERE FOR THE BRIDE?

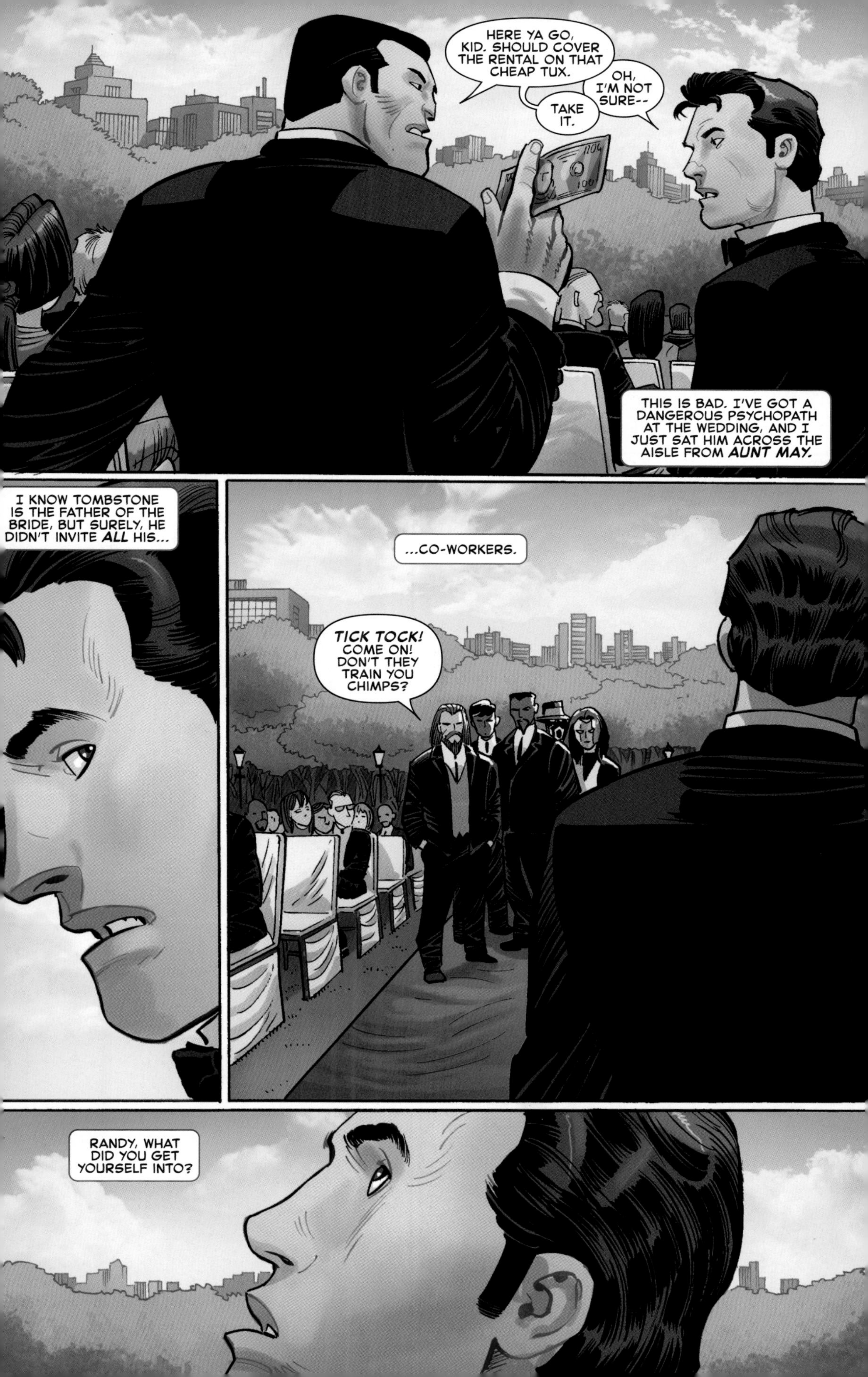
HERE YA GO, KID. SHOULD COVER THE RENTAL ON THAT CHEAP TUX.
OH, I'M NOT SURE--
TAKE IT.
THIS IS BAD. I'VE GOT A DANGEROUS PSYCHOPATH AT THE WEDDING, AND I JUST SAT HIM ACROSS THE AISLE FROM AUNT MAY.
I KNOW TOMBSTONE IS THE FATHER OF THE BRIDE, BUT SURELY, HE DIDN'T INVITE ALL HIS...
...CO-WORKERS.
TICK TOCK! COME ON! DON'T THEY TRAIN YOU CHIMPS?
RANDY, WHAT DID YOU GET YOURSELF INTO?

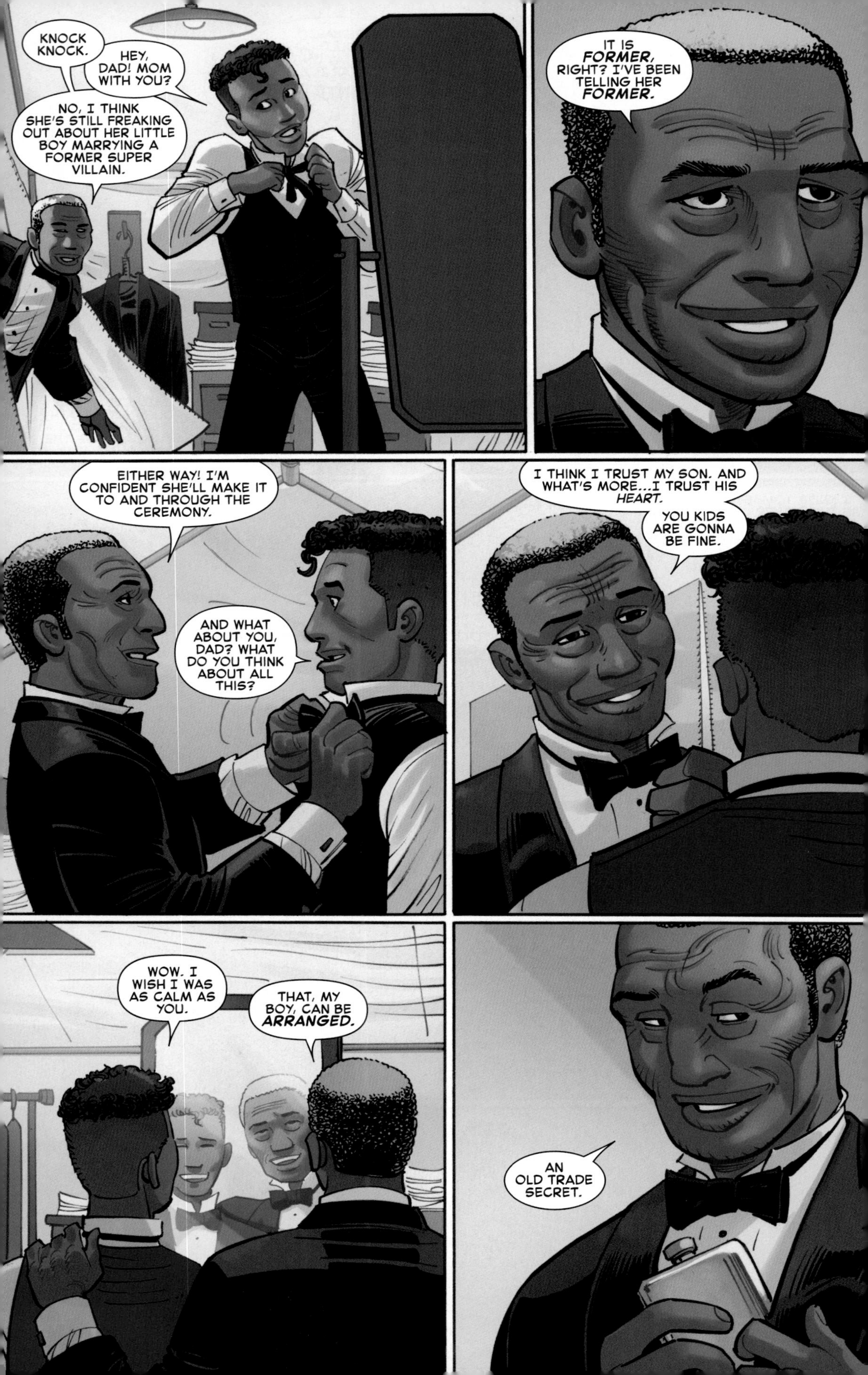
KNOCK KNOCK.
HEY, DAD! MOM WITH YOU?
NO, I THINK SHE'S STILL FREAKING OUT ABOUT HER LITTLE BOY MARRYING A FORMER SUPER VILLAIN.
IT IS *FORMER*, RIGHT? I'VE BEEN TELLING HER *FORMER*.
EITHER WAY! I'M CONFIDENT SHE'LL MAKE IT TO AND THROUGH THE CEREMONY.
AND WHAT ABOUT YOU, DAD? WHAT DO YOU THINK ABOUT ALL THIS?
I THINK I TRUST MY SON. AND WHAT'S MORE...I TRUST HIS *HEART*.
YOU KIDS ARE GONNA BE FINE.
WOW. I WISH I WAS AS CALM AS YOU.
THAT, MY BOY, CAN BE *ARRANGED*.
AN OLD TRADE SECRET.

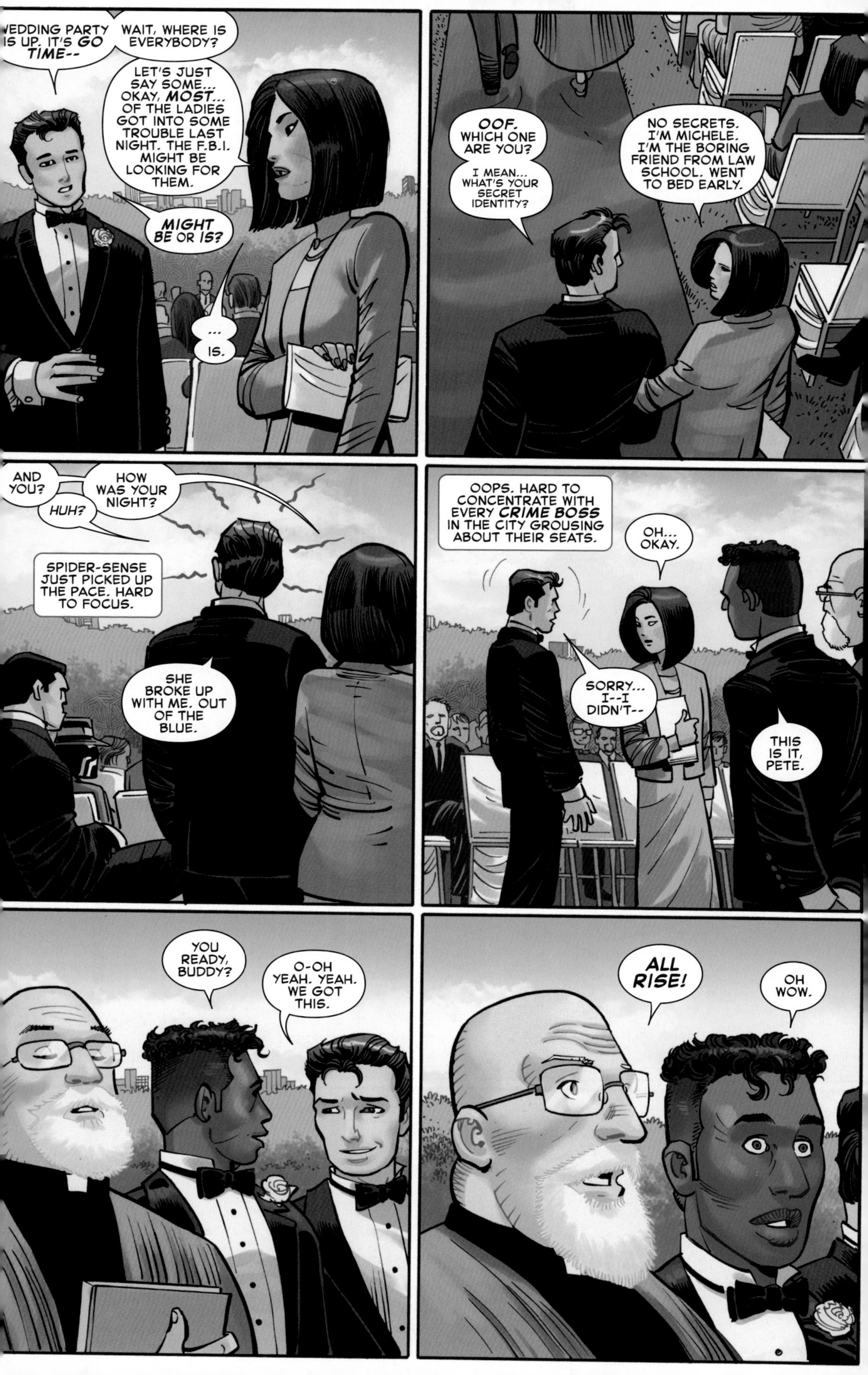
WEDDING PARTY IS UP. IT'S GO TIME--
WAIT, WHERE IS EVERYBODY?
LET'S JUST SAY SOME... OKAY, MOST... OF THE LADIES GOT INTO SOME TROUBLE LAST NIGHT. THE F.B.I. MIGHT BE LOOKING FOR THEM.
MIGHT BE OR IS?
...
IS.
OOF. WHICH ONE ARE YOU?
I MEAN... WHAT'S YOUR SECRET IDENTITY?
NO SECRETS. I'M MICHELE. I'M THE BORING FRIEND FROM LAW SCHOOL. WENT TO BED EARLY.
AND YOU?
HOW WAS YOUR NIGHT?
HUH?
SPIDER-SENSE JUST PICKED UP THE PACE. HARD TO FOCUS.
SHE BROKE UP WITH ME. OUT OF THE BLUE.
OOPS. HARD TO CONCENTRATE WITH EVERY CRIME BOSS IN THE CITY GROUSING ABOUT THEIR SEATS.
OH... OKAY.
SORRY... I--I DIDN'T--
THIS IS IT, PETE.
YOU READY, BUDDY?
O-OH YEAH. YEAH. WE GOT THIS.
ALL RISE!
OH WOW.

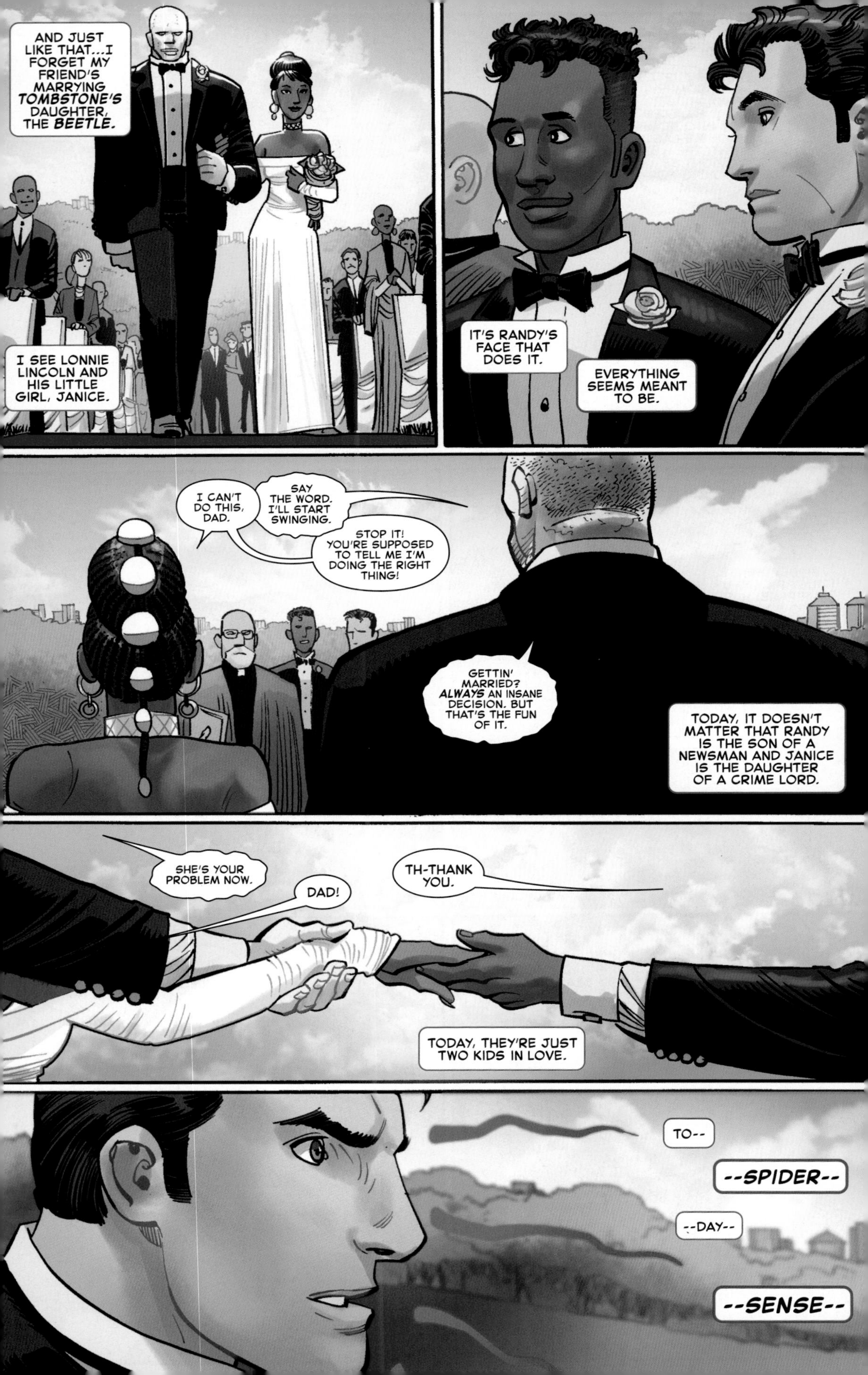
AND JUST LIKE THAT...I FORGET MY FRIEND'S MARRYING *TOMBSTONE'S* DAUGHTER, THE *BEETLE.*
I SEE LONNIE LINCOLN AND HIS LITTLE GIRL, JANICE.
IT'S RANDY'S FACE THAT DOES IT.
EVERYTHING SEEMS MEANT TO BE.
I CAN'T DO THIS, DAD.
SAY THE WORD. I'LL START SWINGING.
STOP IT! YOU'RE SUPPOSED TO TELL ME I'M DOING THE RIGHT THING!
GETTIN' MARRIED? *ALWAYS* AN INSANE DECISION. BUT THAT'S THE FUN OF IT.
TODAY, IT DOESN'T MATTER THAT RANDY IS THE SON OF A NEWSMAN AND JANICE IS THE DAUGHTER OF A CRIME LORD.
SHE'S YOUR PROBLEM NOW.
DAD!
TH-THANK YOU.
TODAY, THEY'RE JUST TWO KIDS IN LOVE.
TO--
--SPIDER--
--DAY--
--SENSE--

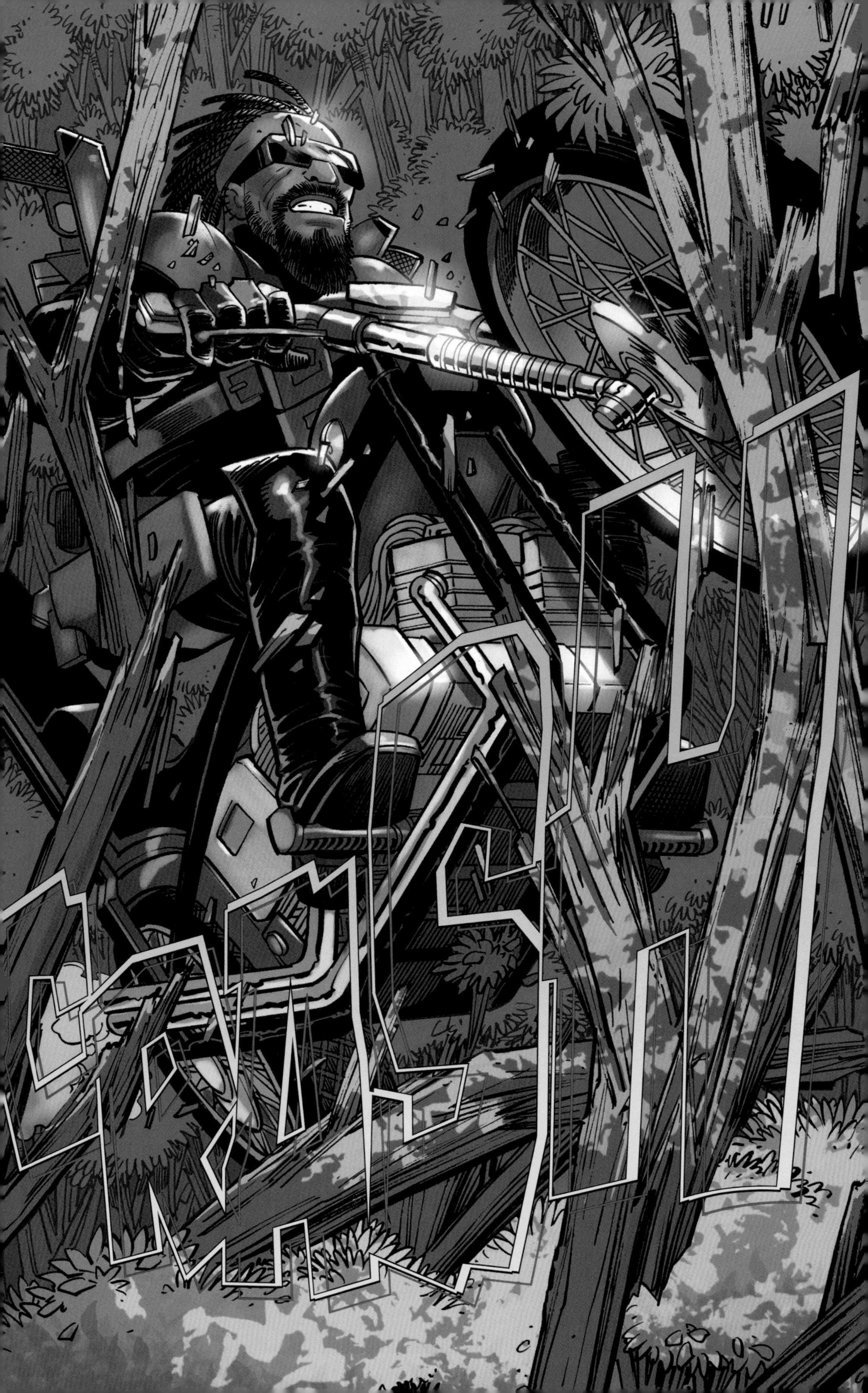

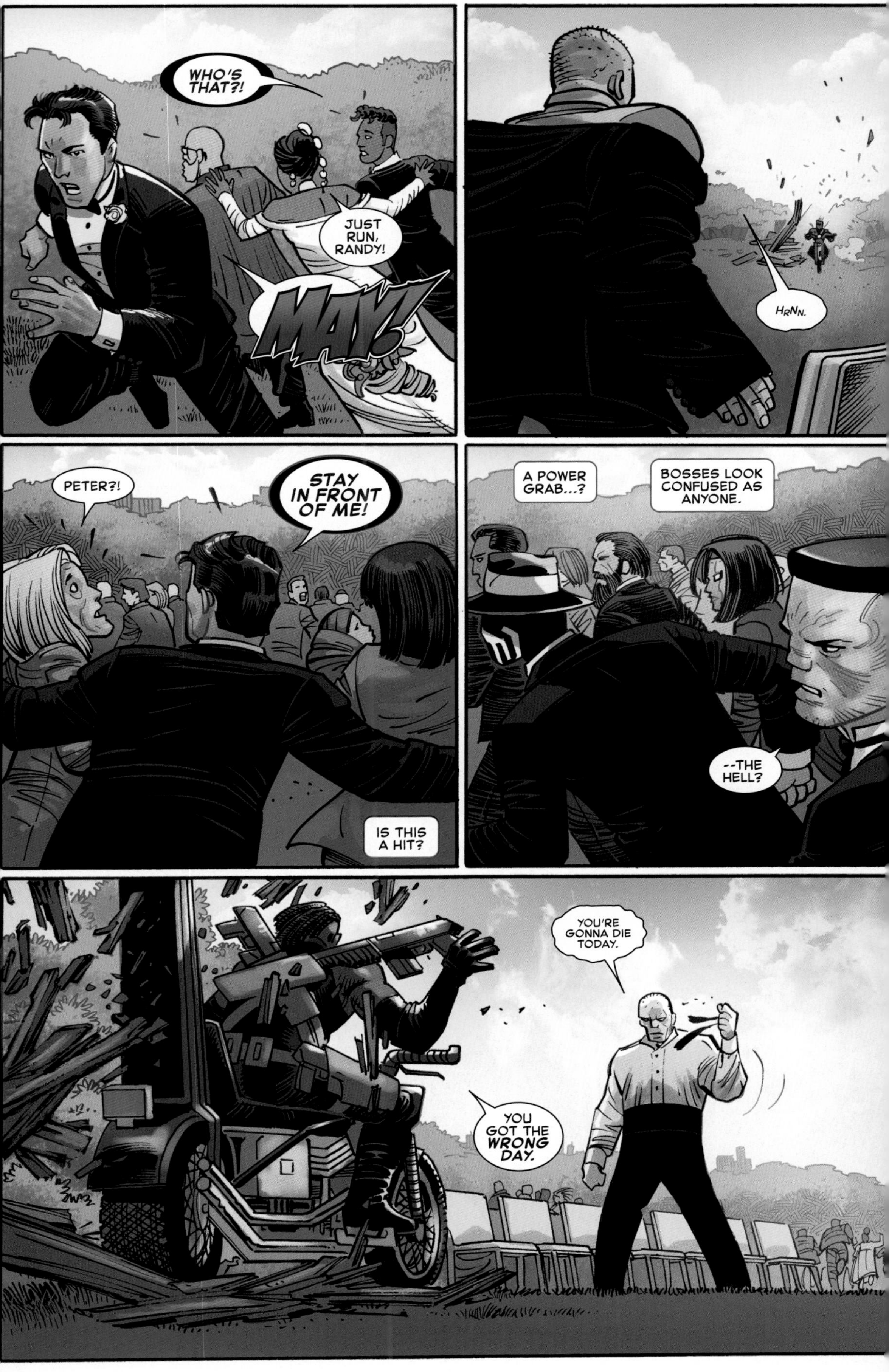

WHO'S THAT?!
JUST RUN, RANDY!
MAY!
HRNN.
PETER?!
STAY IN FRONT OF ME!
IS THIS A HIT?
A POWER GRAB...?
BOSSES LOOK CONFUSED AS ANYONE.
--THE HELL?
YOU'RE GONNA DIE TODAY.
YOU GOT THE WRONG DAY.

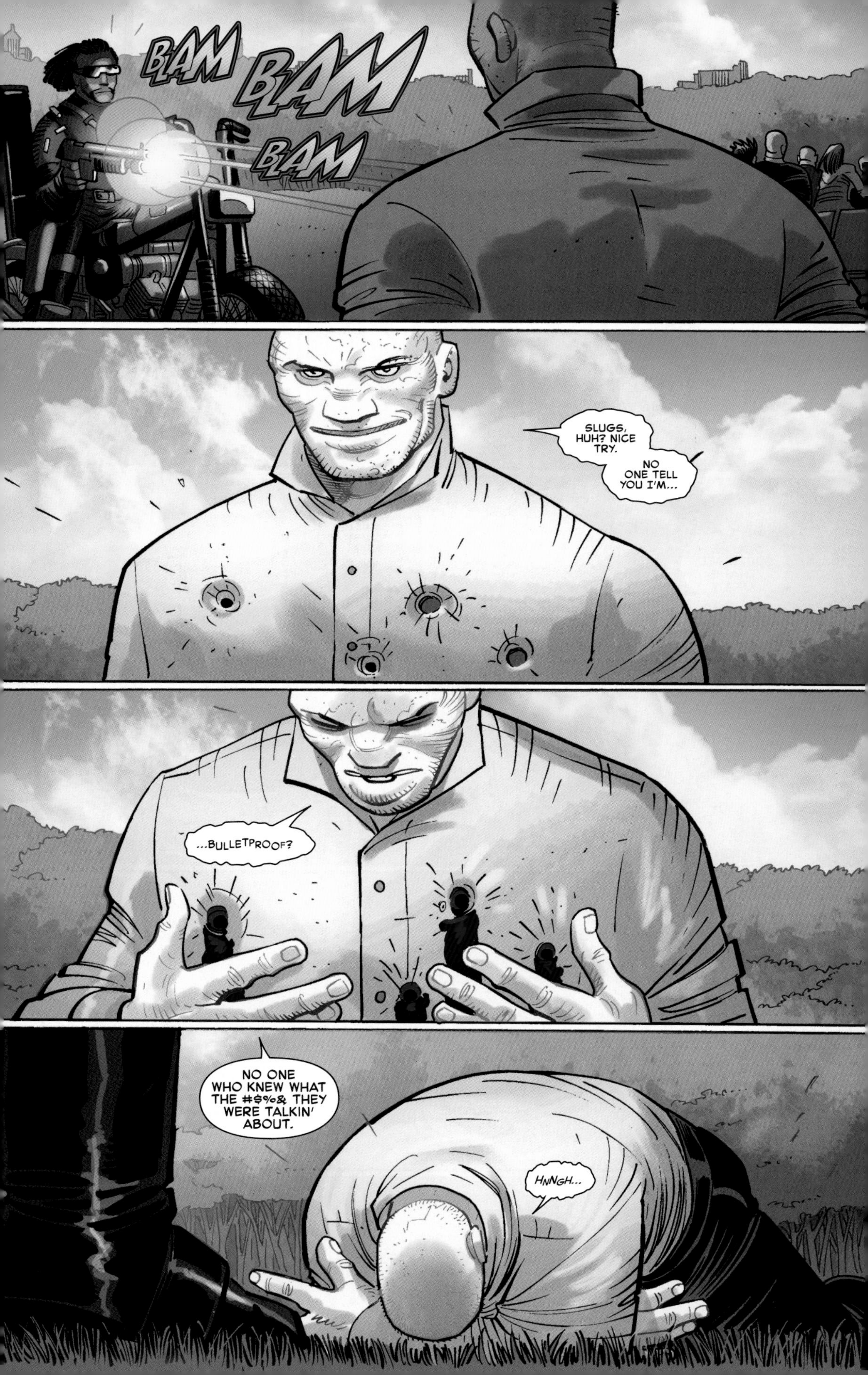
BLAM BLAM BLAM
SLUGS, HUH? NICE TRY.
NO ONE TELL YOU I'M...
...BULLETPROOF?
NO ONE WHO KNEW WHAT THE #$%& THEY WERE TALKIN' ABOUT.
HNNGH...

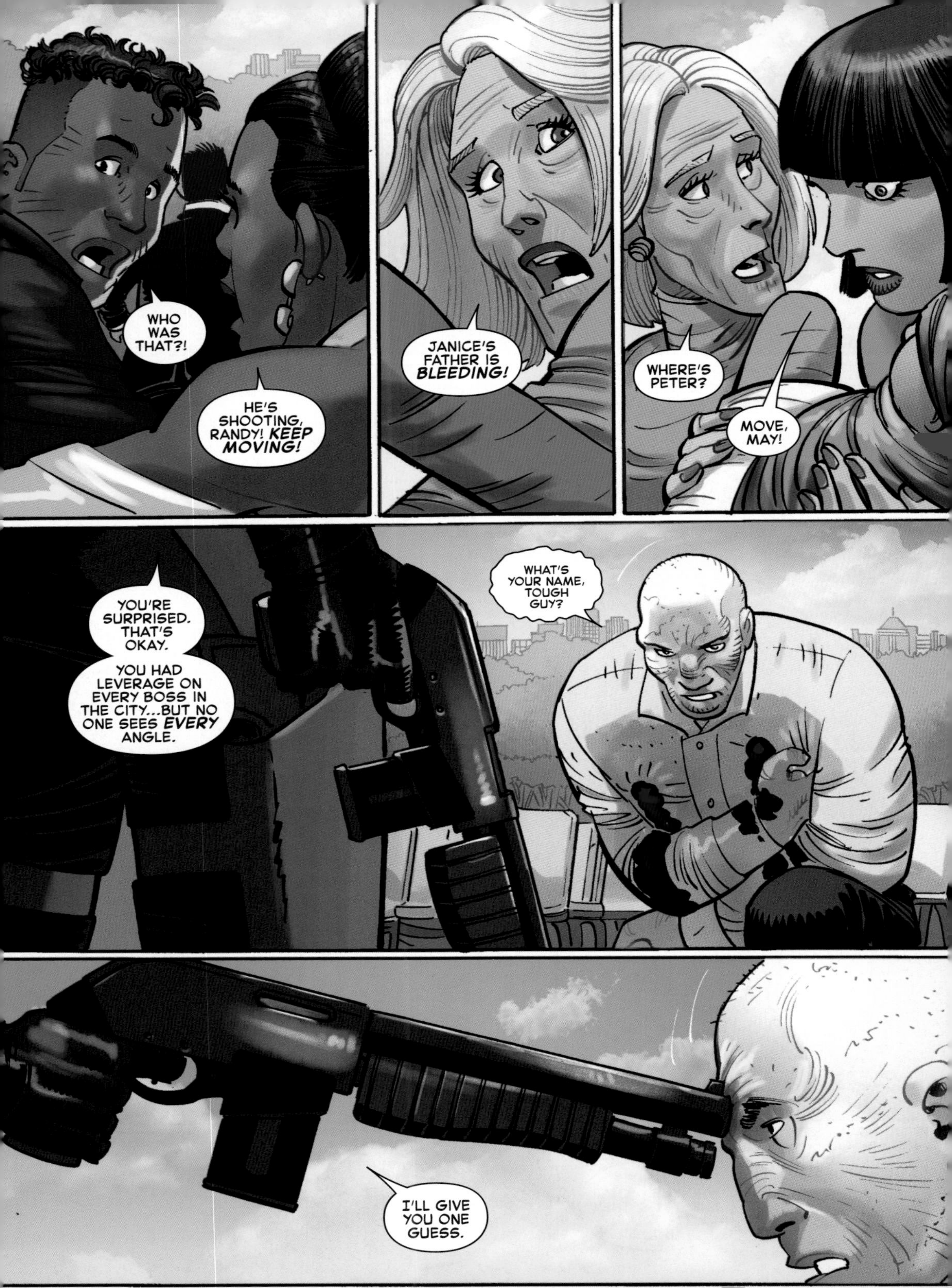
WHO WAS THAT?!
HE'S SHOOTING, RANDY! *KEEP MOVING!*
JANICE'S FATHER IS *BLEEDING!*
WHERE'S PETER?
MOVE, MAY!
WHAT'S YOUR NAME, TOUGH GUY?
YOU'RE SURPRISED. THAT'S OKAY.
YOU HAD LEVERAGE ON EVERY BOSS IN THE CITY...BUT NO ONE SEES *EVERY* ANGLE.
I'LL GIVE YOU ONE GUESS.

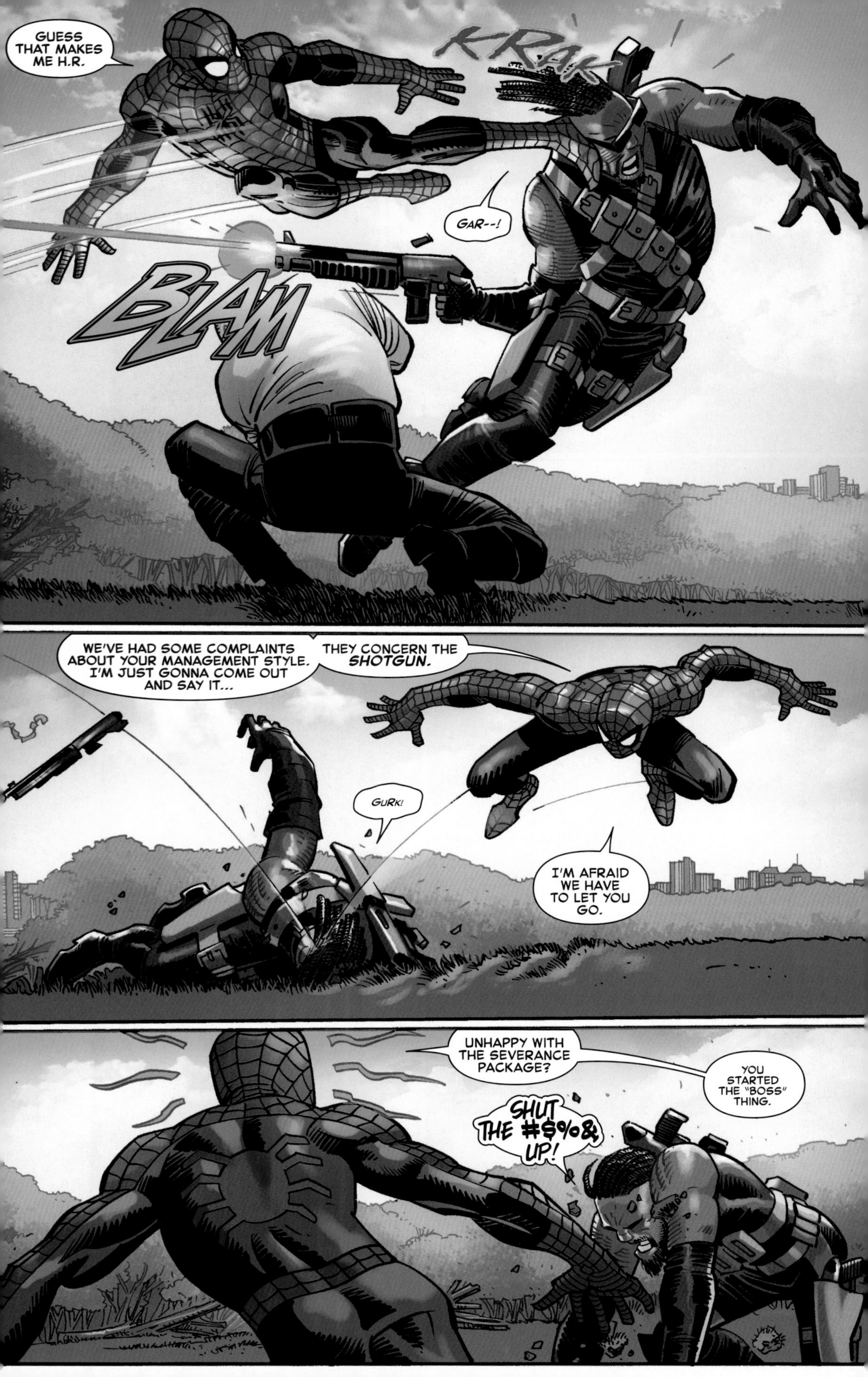
GUESS THAT MAKES ME H.R.
K-RAK
GAR--!
BLAM
WE'VE HAD SOME COMPLAINTS ABOUT YOUR MANAGEMENT STYLE. I'M JUST GONNA COME OUT AND SAY IT...
THEY CONCERN THE SHOTGUN.
GURK!
I'M AFRAID WE HAVE TO LET YOU GO.
UNHAPPY WITH THE SEVERANCE PACKAGE?
SHUT THE #$%&, UP!
YOU STARTED THE "BOSS" THING.

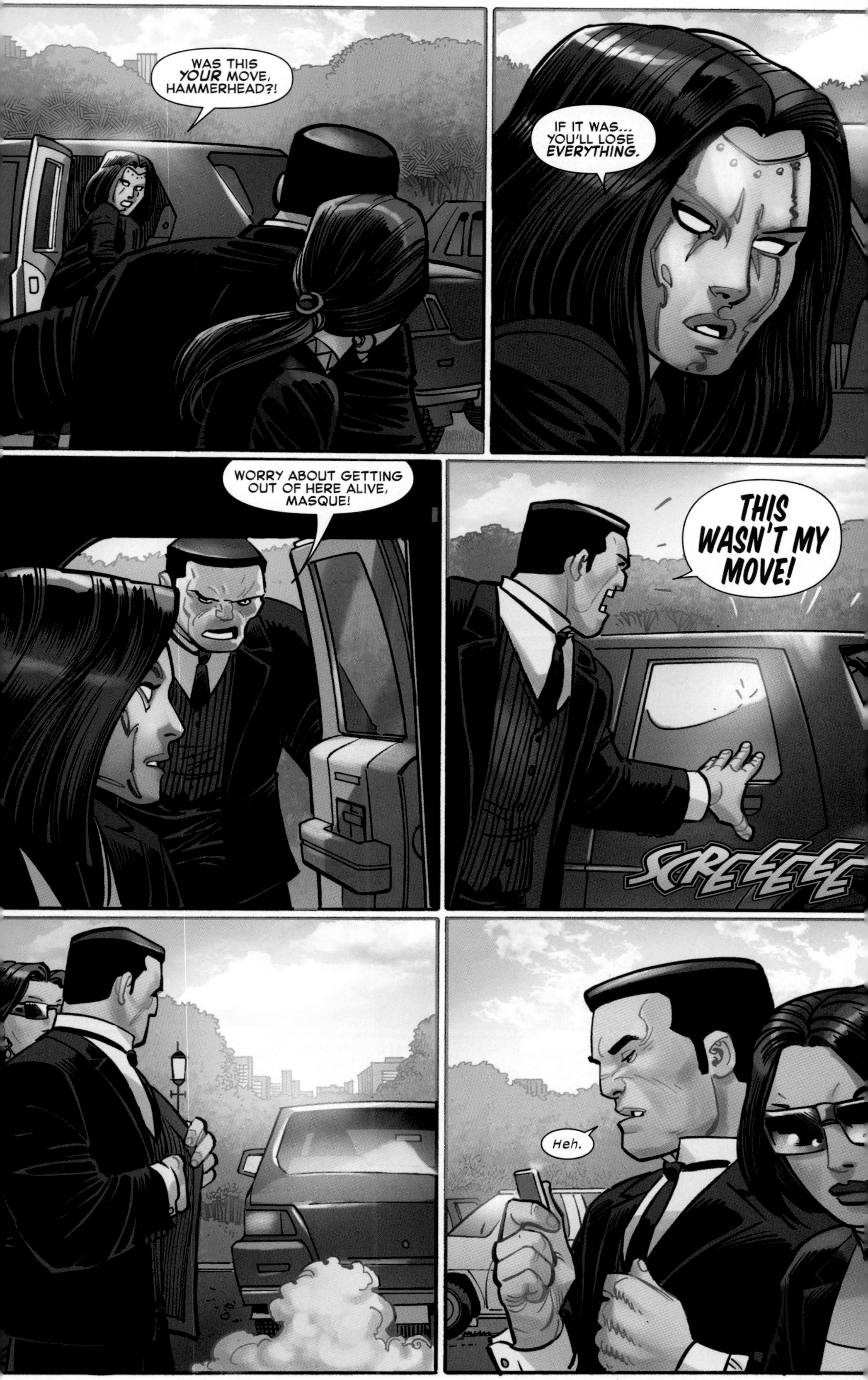
WAS THIS *YOUR* MOVE, HAMMERHEAD?!
IF IT WAS... YOU'LL LOSE *EVERYTHING.*
WORRY ABOUT GETTING OUT OF HERE ALIVE, MASQUE!
THIS WASN'T MY MOVE!
SCREEEEE
Heh.

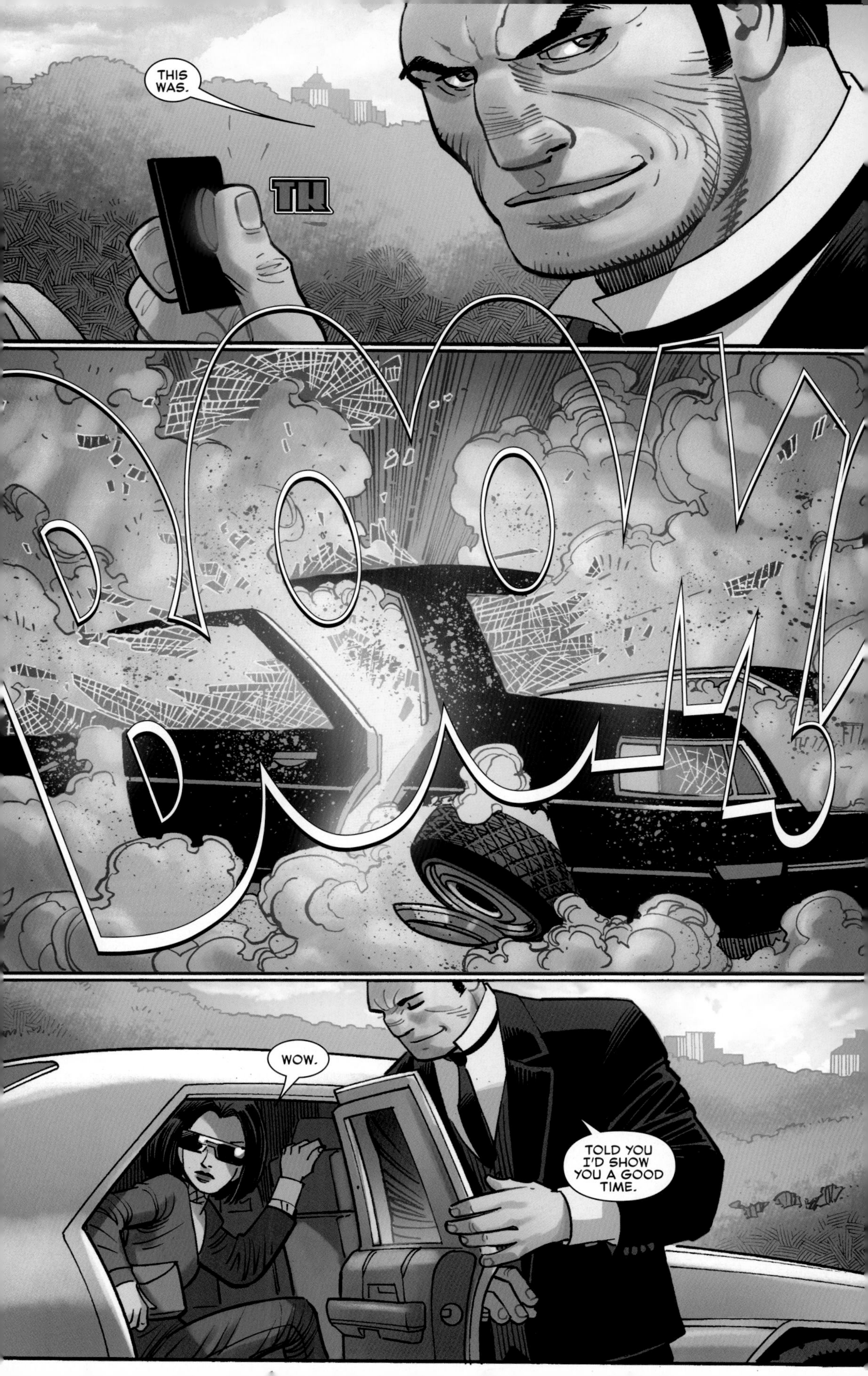
THIS WAS.
TK
DOOOM!
WOW.
TOLD YOU I'D SHOW YOU A GOOD TIME.

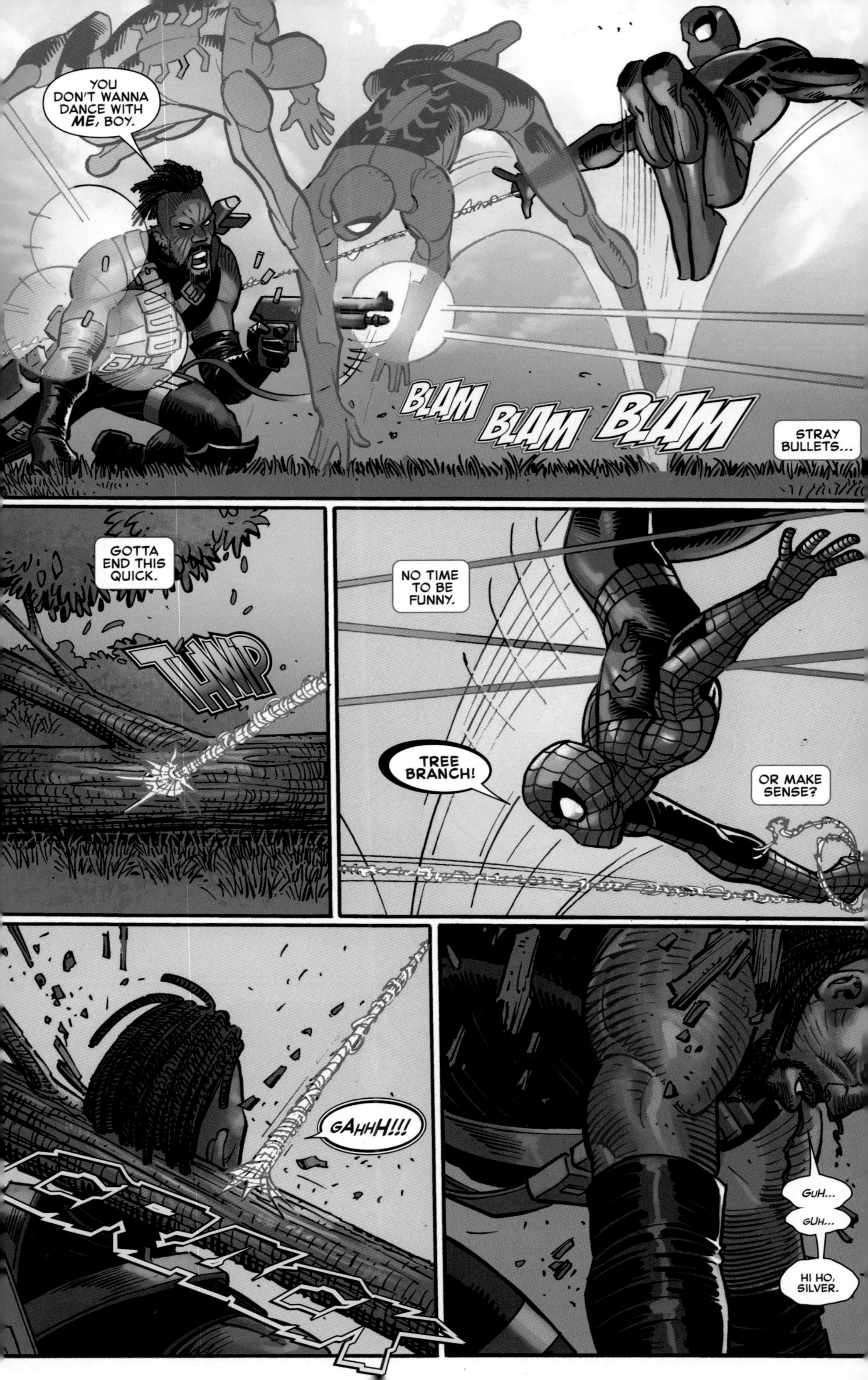
YOU DON'T WANNA DANCE WITH ME, BOY.
BLAM
BLAM
BLAM
STRAY BULLETS...
GOTTA END THIS QUICK.
THWIP
NO TIME TO BE FUNNY.
TREE BRANCH!
OR MAKE SENSE?
GAHHH!!!
GUH...
GUH...
HI HO, SILVER.

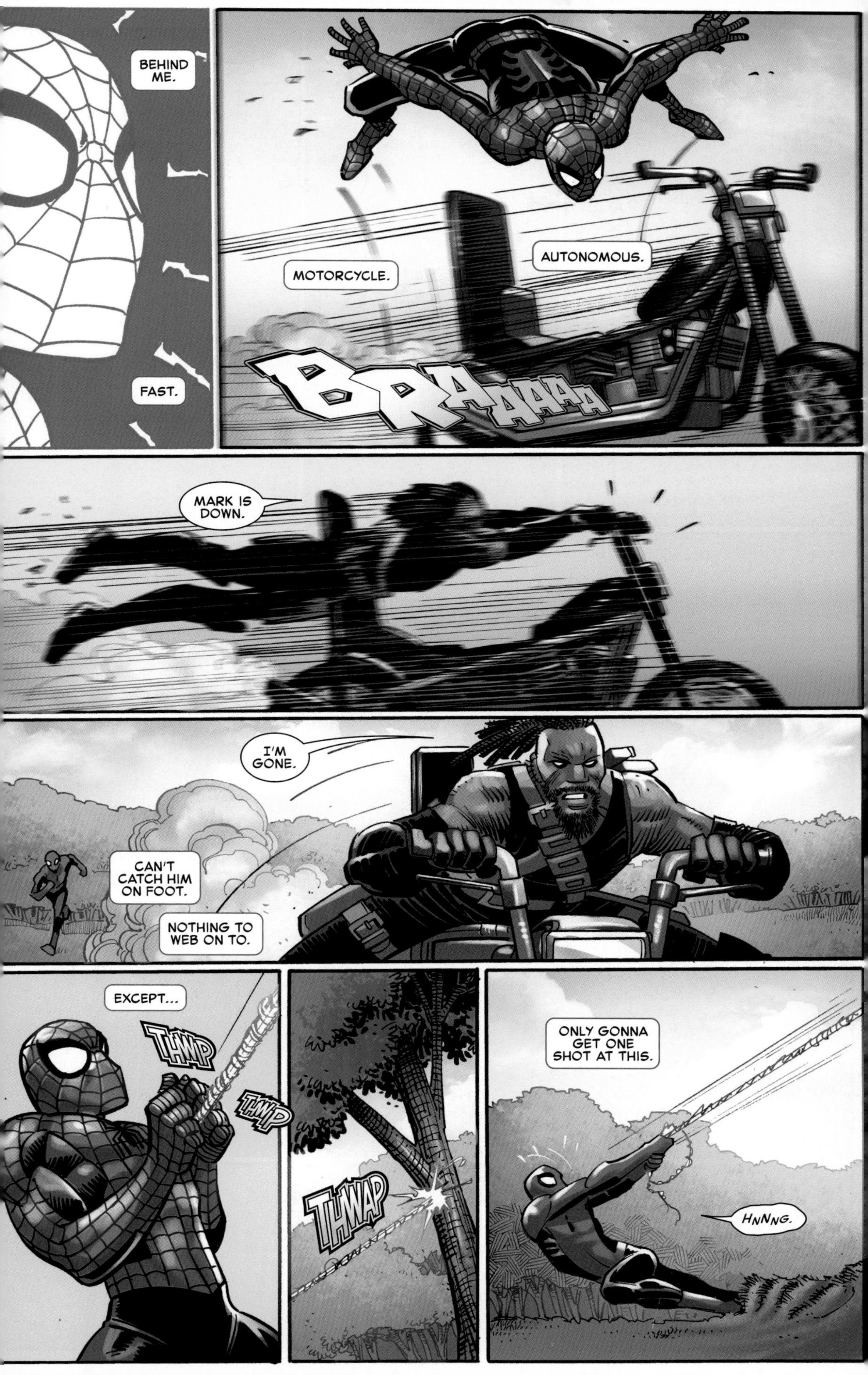
BEHIND ME.
FAST.
MOTORCYCLE.
AUTONOMOUS.
BRAAAAA
MARK IS DOWN.
I'M GONE.
CAN'T CATCH HIM ON FOOT.
NOTHING TO WEB ON TO.
EXCEPT...
THWIP
THWIP
THWAP
ONLY GONNA GET ONE SHOT AT THIS.
HNNNG.

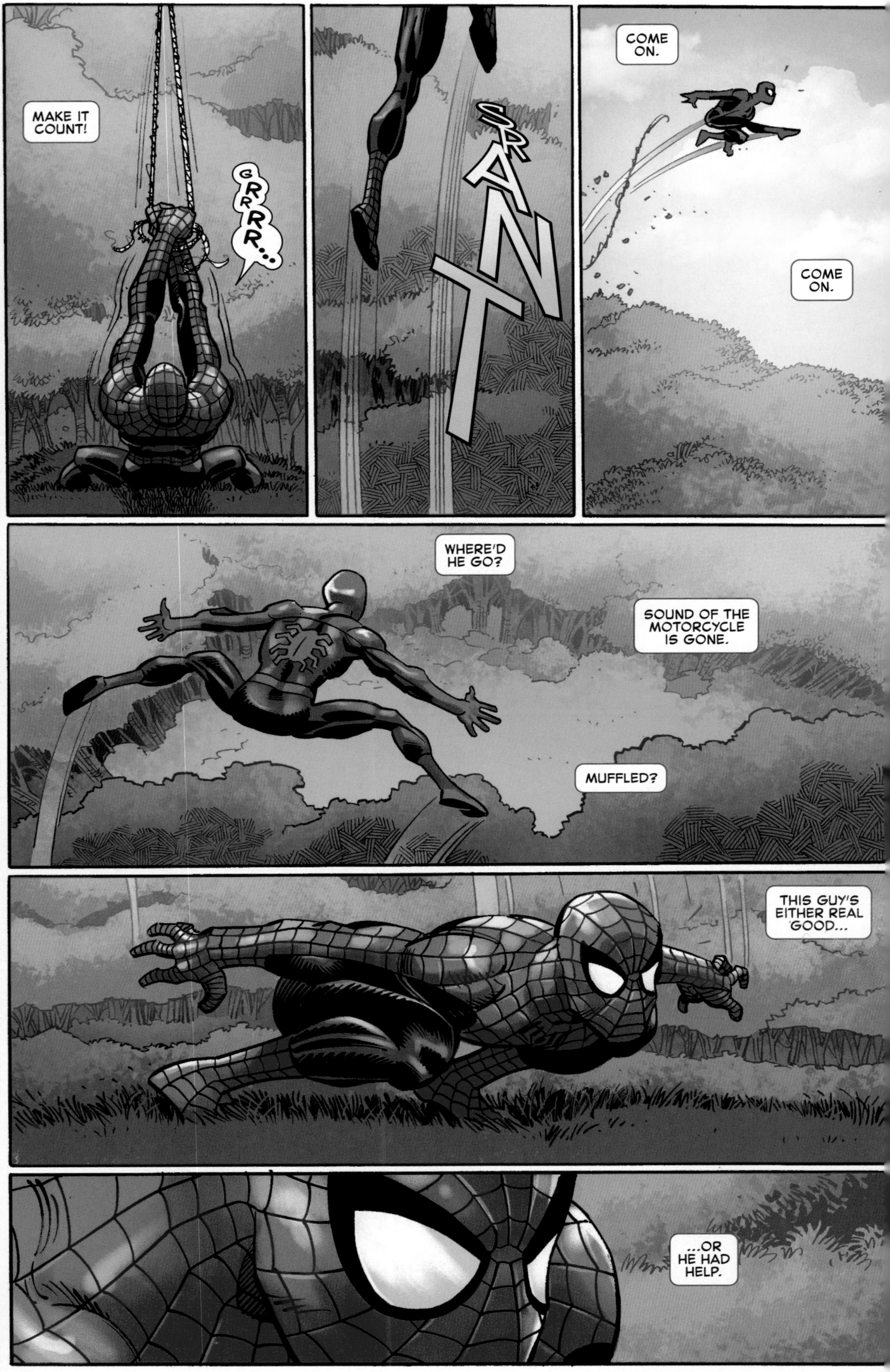
MAKE IT COUNT!
GRRRR...
SRRANT
COME ON.
COME ON.
WHERE'D HE GO?
SOUND OF THE MOTORCYCLE IS GONE.
MUFFLED?
THIS GUY'S EITHER REAL GOOD...
...OR HE HAD HELP.

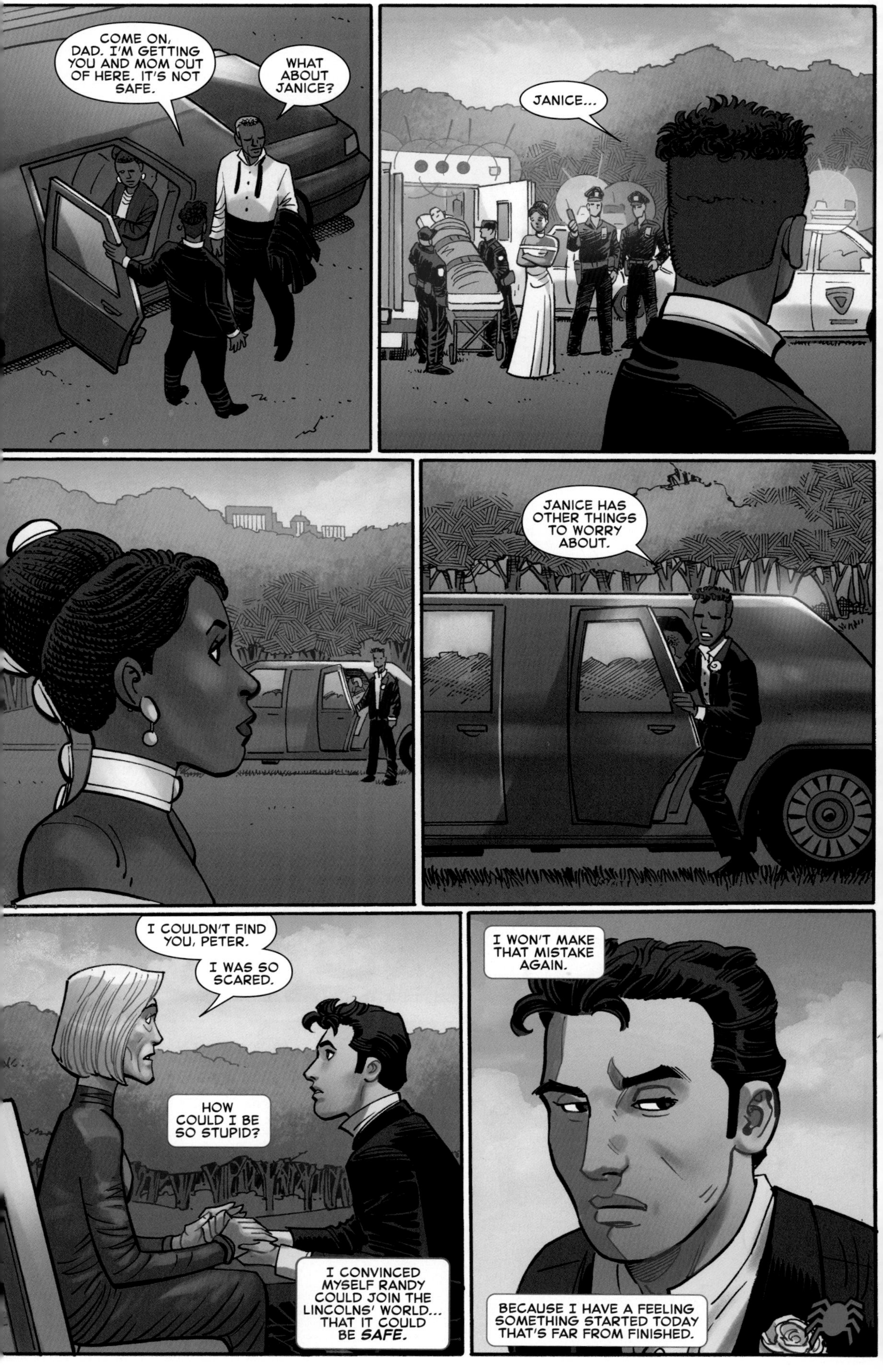
COME ON, DAD. I'M GETTING YOU AND MOM OUT OF HERE. IT'S NOT SAFE.
WHAT ABOUT JANICE?
JANICE...
JANICE HAS OTHER THINGS TO WORRY ABOUT.
I COULDN'T FIND YOU, PETER.
I WAS SO SCARED.
HOW COULD I BE SO STUPID?
I CONVINCED MYSELF RANDY COULD JOIN THE LINCOLNS' WORLD... THAT IT COULD BE SAFE.
I WON'T MAKE THAT MISTAKE AGAIN.
BECAUSE I HAVE A FEELING SOMETHING STARTED TODAY THAT'S FAR FROM FINISHED.

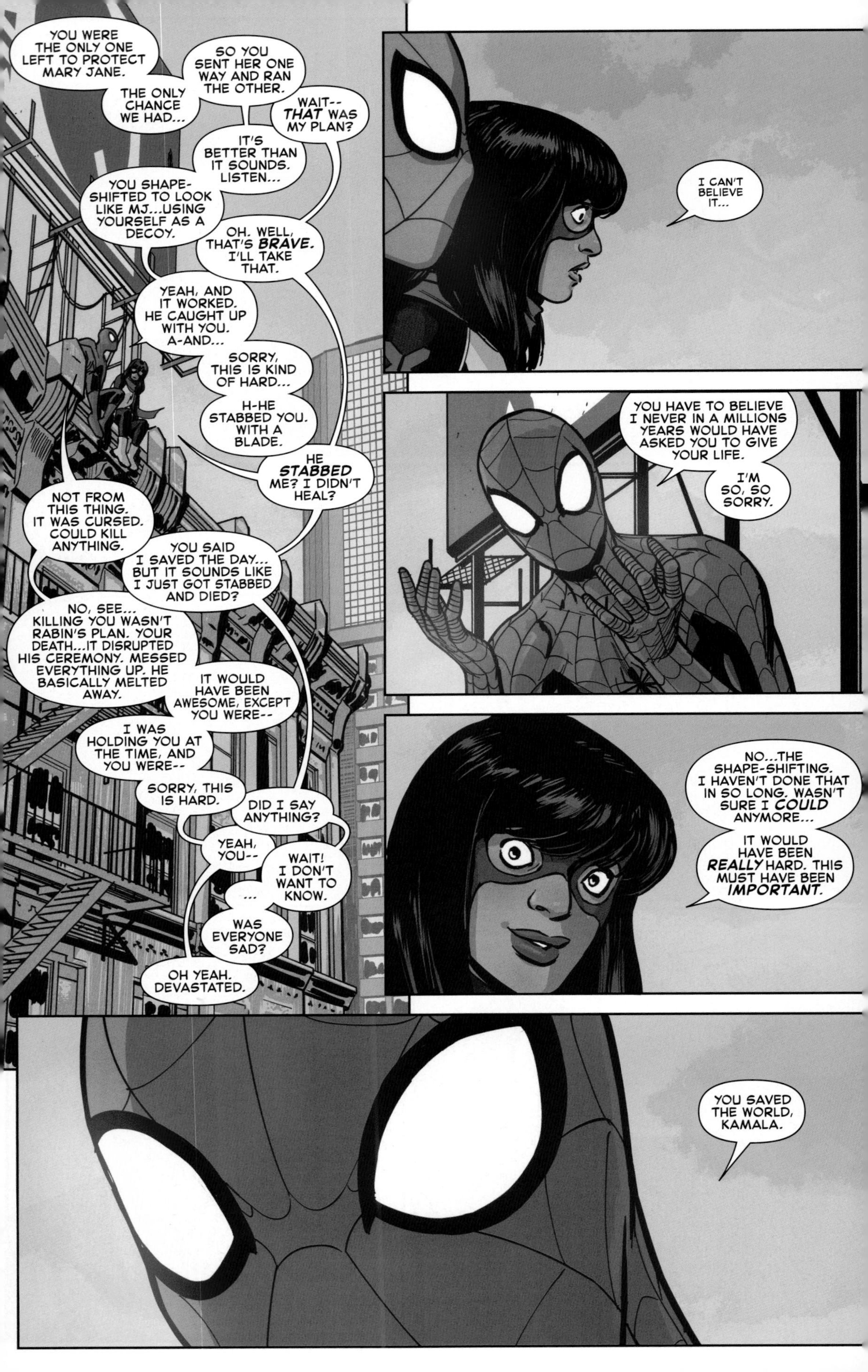
YOU WERE THE ONLY ONE LEFT TO PROTECT MARY JANE.
THE ONLY CHANCE WE HAD...
SO YOU SENT HER ONE WAY AND RAN THE OTHER.
WAIT-- THAT WAS MY PLAN?
IT'S BETTER THAN IT SOUNDS. LISTEN...
YOU SHAPE-SHIFTED TO LOOK LIKE MJ...USING YOURSELF AS A DECOY.
OH. WELL, THAT'S BRAVE. I'LL TAKE THAT.
YEAH, AND IT WORKED. HE CAUGHT UP WITH YOU. A-AND...
SORRY, THIS IS KIND OF HARD...
H-HE STABBED YOU. WITH A BLADE.
HE STABBED ME? I DIDN'T HEAL?
NOT FROM THIS THING. IT WAS CURSED. COULD KILL ANYTHING.
YOU SAID I SAVED THE DAY... BUT IT SOUNDS LIKE I JUST GOT STABBED AND DIED?
NO, SEE... KILLING YOU WASN'T RABIN'S PLAN. YOUR DEATH...IT DISRUPTED HIS CEREMONY. MESSED EVERYTHING UP. HE BASICALLY MELTED AWAY.
IT WOULD HAVE BEEN AWESOME, EXCEPT YOU WERE--
I WAS HOLDING YOU AT THE TIME, AND YOU WERE--
SORRY, THIS IS HARD.
DID I SAY ANYTHING?
YEAH, YOU--
WAIT! I DON'T WANT TO KNOW.
...
WAS EVERYONE SAD?
OH YEAH. DEVASTATED.
I CAN'T BELIEVE IT...
YOU HAVE TO BELIEVE I NEVER IN A MILLIONS YEARS WOULD HAVE ASKED YOU TO GIVE YOUR LIFE.
I'M SO, SO SORRY.
NO...THE SHAPE-SHIFTING. I HAVEN'T DONE THAT IN SO LONG. WASN'T SURE I COULD ANYMORE...
IT WOULD HAVE BEEN REALLY HARD. THIS MUST HAVE BEEN IMPORTANT.
YOU SAVED THE WORLD, KAMALA.

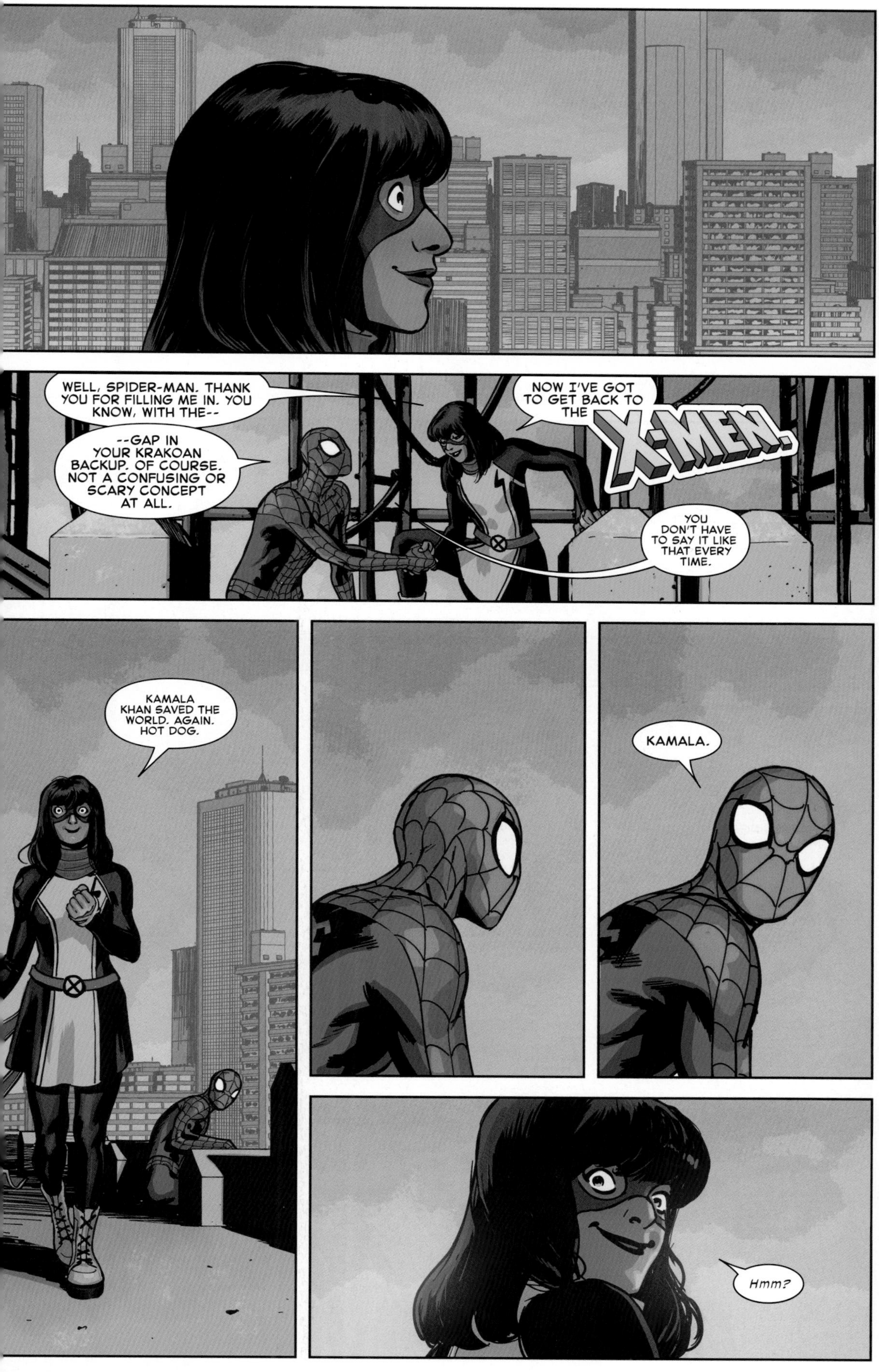
WELL, SPIDER-MAN. THANK YOU FOR FILLING ME IN. YOU KNOW, WITH THE--
--GAP IN YOUR KRAKOAN BACKUP. OF COURSE. NOT A CONFUSING OR SCARY CONCEPT AT ALL.
NOW I'VE GOT TO GET BACK TO THE
X-MEN.
YOU DON'T HAVE TO SAY IT LIKE THAT EVERY TIME.
KAMALA KHAN SAVED THE WORLD. AGAIN. HOT DOG.
KAMALA.
Hmm?

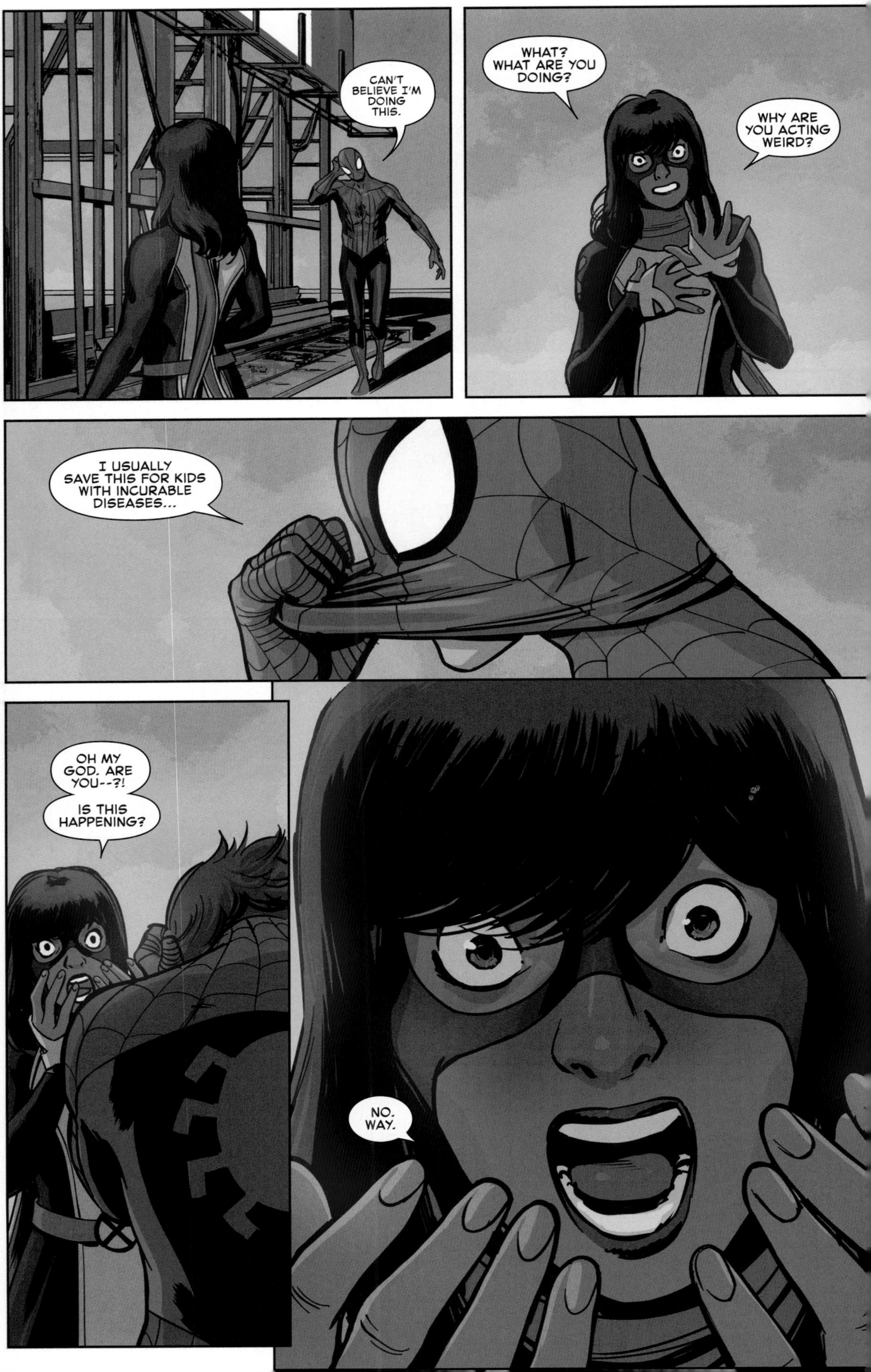
CAN'T BELIEVE I'M DOING THIS.
WHAT? WHAT ARE YOU DOING?
WHY ARE YOU ACTING WEIRD?
I USUALLY SAVE THIS FOR KIDS WITH INCURABLE DISEASES...
OH MY GOD. ARE YOU--?!
IS THIS HAPPENING?
NO. WAY.

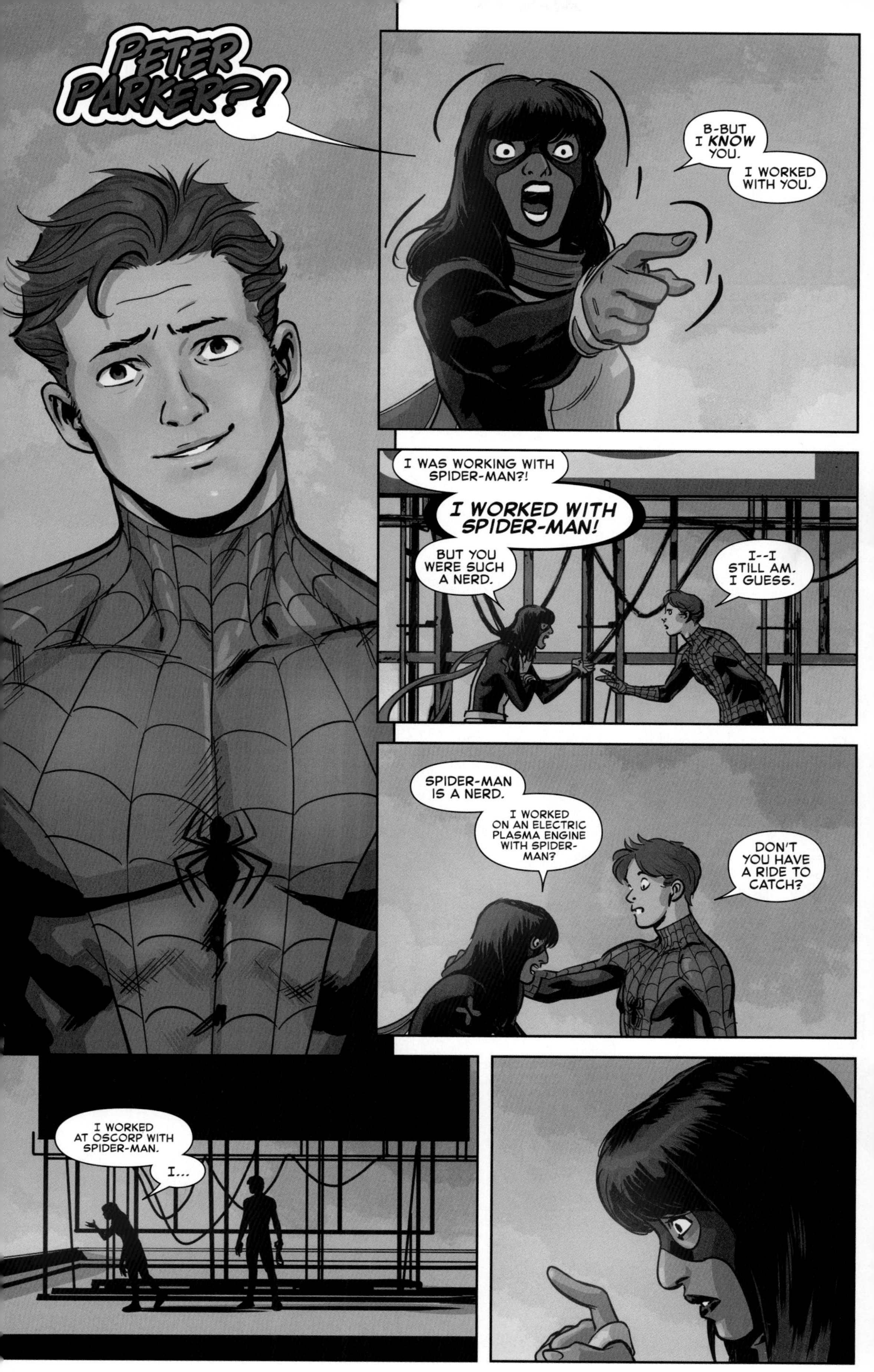
PETER PARKER?!
B-BUT I KNOW YOU.
I WORKED WITH YOU.
I WAS WORKING WITH SPIDER-MAN?!
I WORKED WITH SPIDER-MAN!
BUT YOU WERE SUCH A NERD.
I--I STILL AM. I GUESS.
SPIDER-MAN IS A NERD.
I WORKED ON AN ELECTRIC PLASMA ENGINE WITH SPIDER-MAN?
DON'T YOU HAVE A RIDE TO CATCH?
I WORKED AT OSCORP WITH SPIDER-MAN.
I...

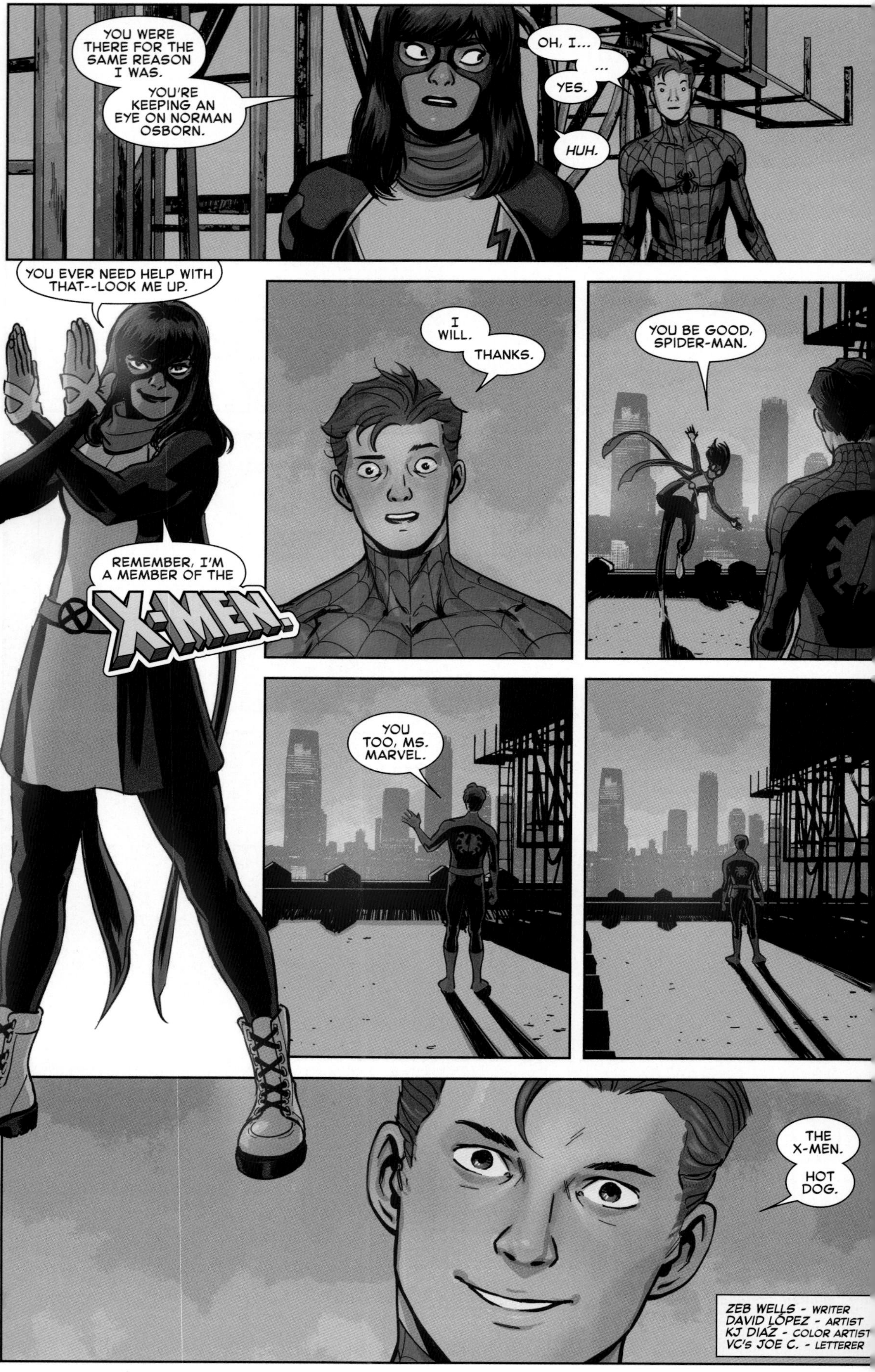
YOU WERE THERE FOR THE SAME REASON I WAS.
YOU'RE KEEPING AN EYE ON NORMAN OSBORN.
OH, I...
...
YES.
HUH.
YOU EVER NEED HELP WITH THAT--LOOK ME UP.
REMEMBER, I'M A MEMBER OF THE
X-MEN.
I WILL.
THANKS.
YOU BE GOOD, SPIDER-MAN.
YOU TOO, MS. MARVEL.
THE X-MEN.
HOT DOG.
ZEB WELLS - WRITER
DAVID LÓPEZ - ARTIST
KJ DIAZ - COLOR ARTIST
VC'S JOE C. - LETTERER

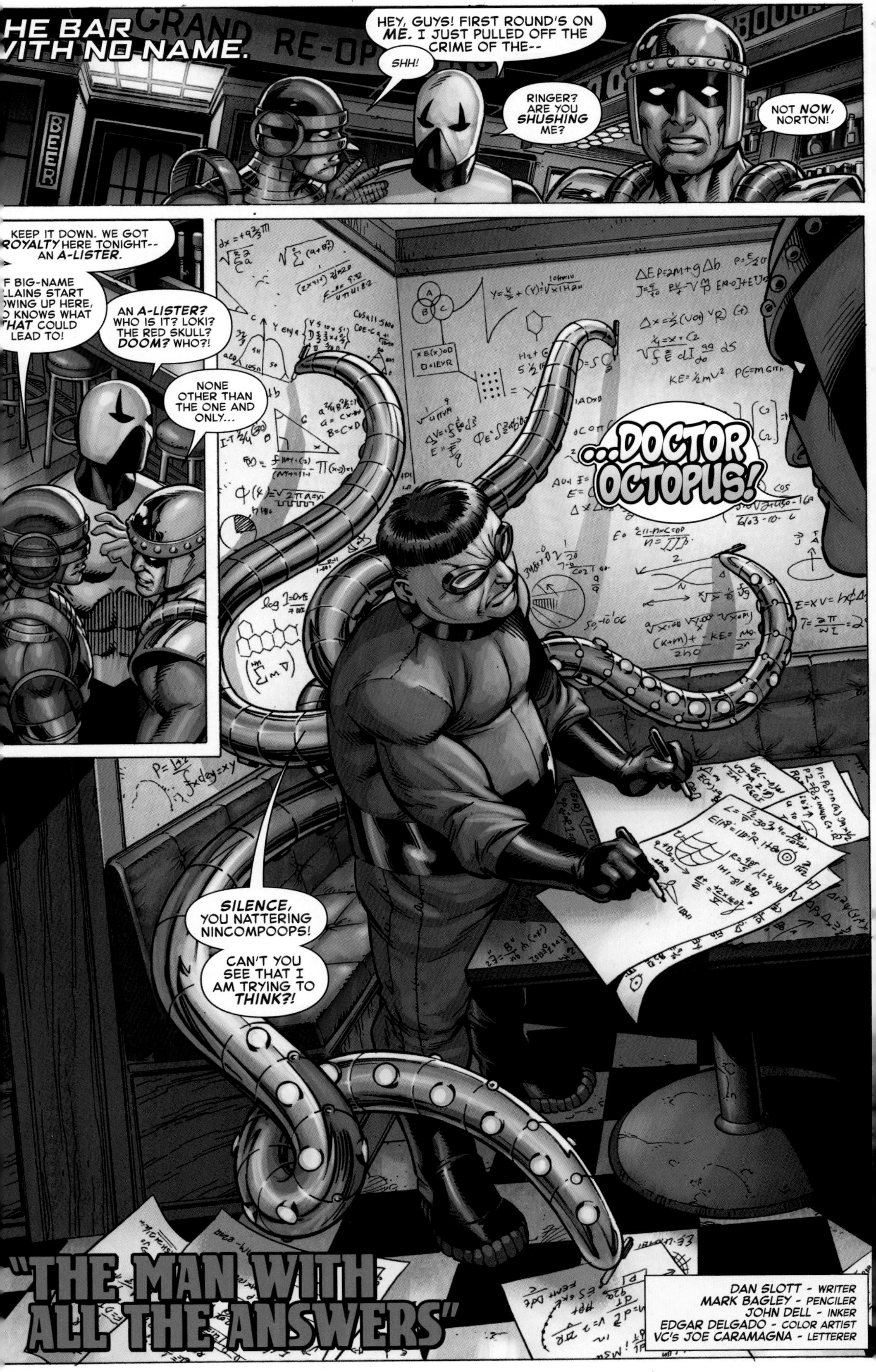
HE BAR VITH NO NAME.
GRAND RE-OP
BEER
HEY, GUYS! FIRST ROUND'S ON ME. I JUST PULLED OFF THE CRIME OF THE--
SHH!
RINGER? ARE YOU SHUSHING ME?
NOT NOW, NORTON!
KEEP IT DOWN. WE GOT ROYALTY HERE TONIGHT-- AN A-LISTER.
F BIG-NAME LLAINS START OWING UP HERE, O KNOWS WHAT THAT COULD LEAD TO!
AN A-LISTER? WHO IS IT? LOKI? THE RED SKULL? DOOM? WHO?!
NONE OTHER THAN THE ONE AND ONLY...
...DOCTOR OCTOPUS!
SILENCE, YOU NATTERING NINCOMPOOPS!
CAN'T YOU SEE THAT I AM TRYING TO THINK?!
"THE MAN WITH ALL THE ANSWERS"
DAN SLOTT - WRITER
MARK BAGLEY - PENCILER
JOHN DELL - INKER
EDGAR DELGADO - COLOR ARTIST
VC's JOE CARAMAGNA - LETTERER

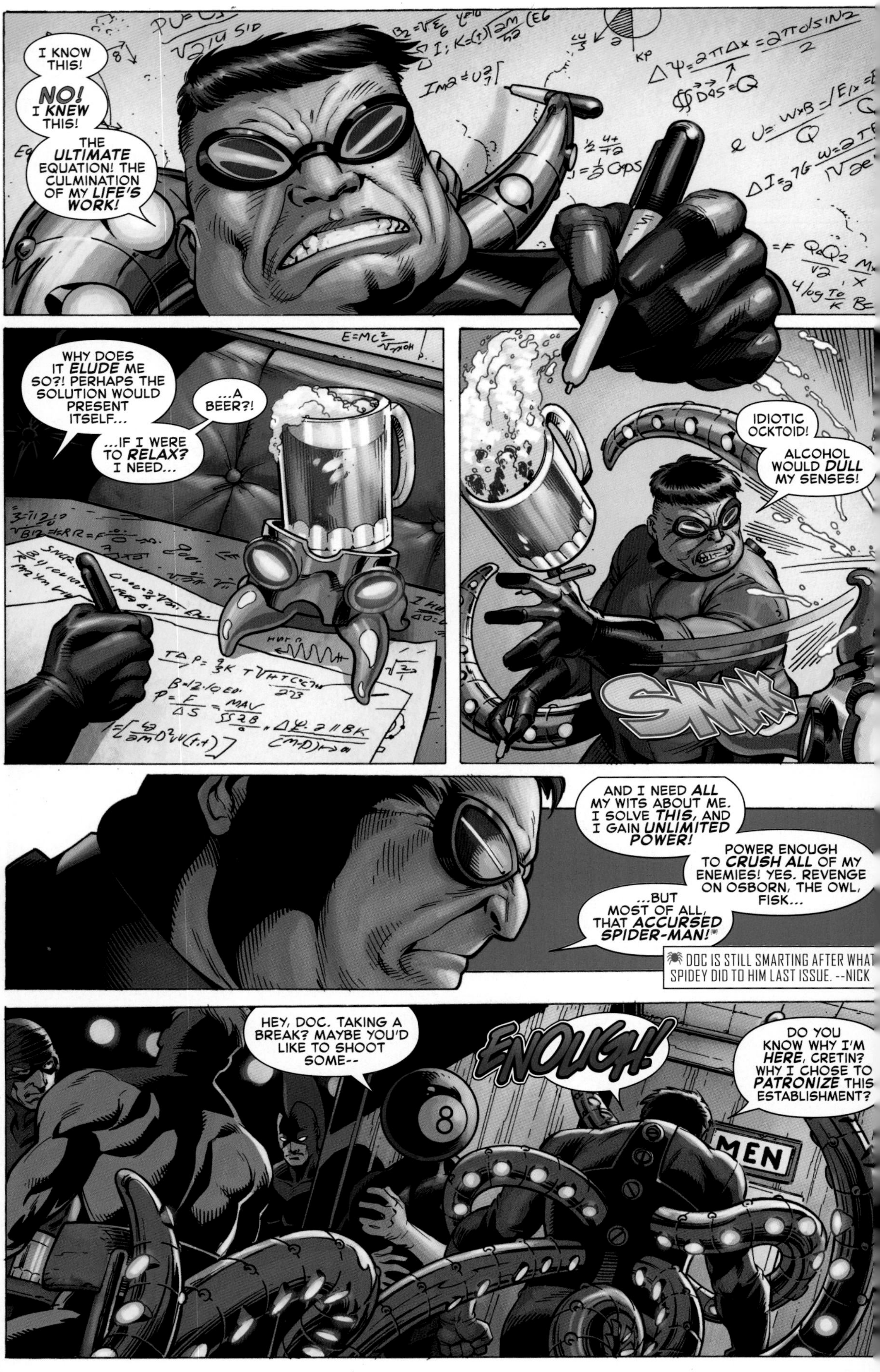
I KNOW THIS!
NO! I KNEW THIS!
THE ULTIMATE EQUATION! THE CULMINATION OF MY LIFE'S WORK!
WHY DOES IT ELUDE ME SO?! PERHAPS THE SOLUTION WOULD PRESENT ITSELF...
...IF I WERE TO RELAX? I NEED...
...A BEER?!
IDIOTIC OCKTOID!
ALCOHOL WOULD DULL MY SENSES!
SMAK
AND I NEED ALL MY WITS ABOUT ME. I SOLVE THIS, AND I GAIN UNLIMITED POWER!
POWER ENOUGH TO CRUSH ALL OF MY ENEMIES! YES. REVENGE ON OSBORN, THE OWL, FISK...
...BUT MOST OF ALL, THAT ACCURSED SPIDER-MAN!
DOC IS STILL SMARTING AFTER WHAT SPIDEY DID TO HIM LAST ISSUE. --NICK
HEY, DOC. TAKING A BREAK? MAYBE YOU'D LIKE TO SHOOT SOME--
ENOUGH!
DO YOU KNOW WHY I'M HERE, CRETIN? WHY I CHOSE TO PATRONIZE THIS ESTABLISHMENT?
MEN

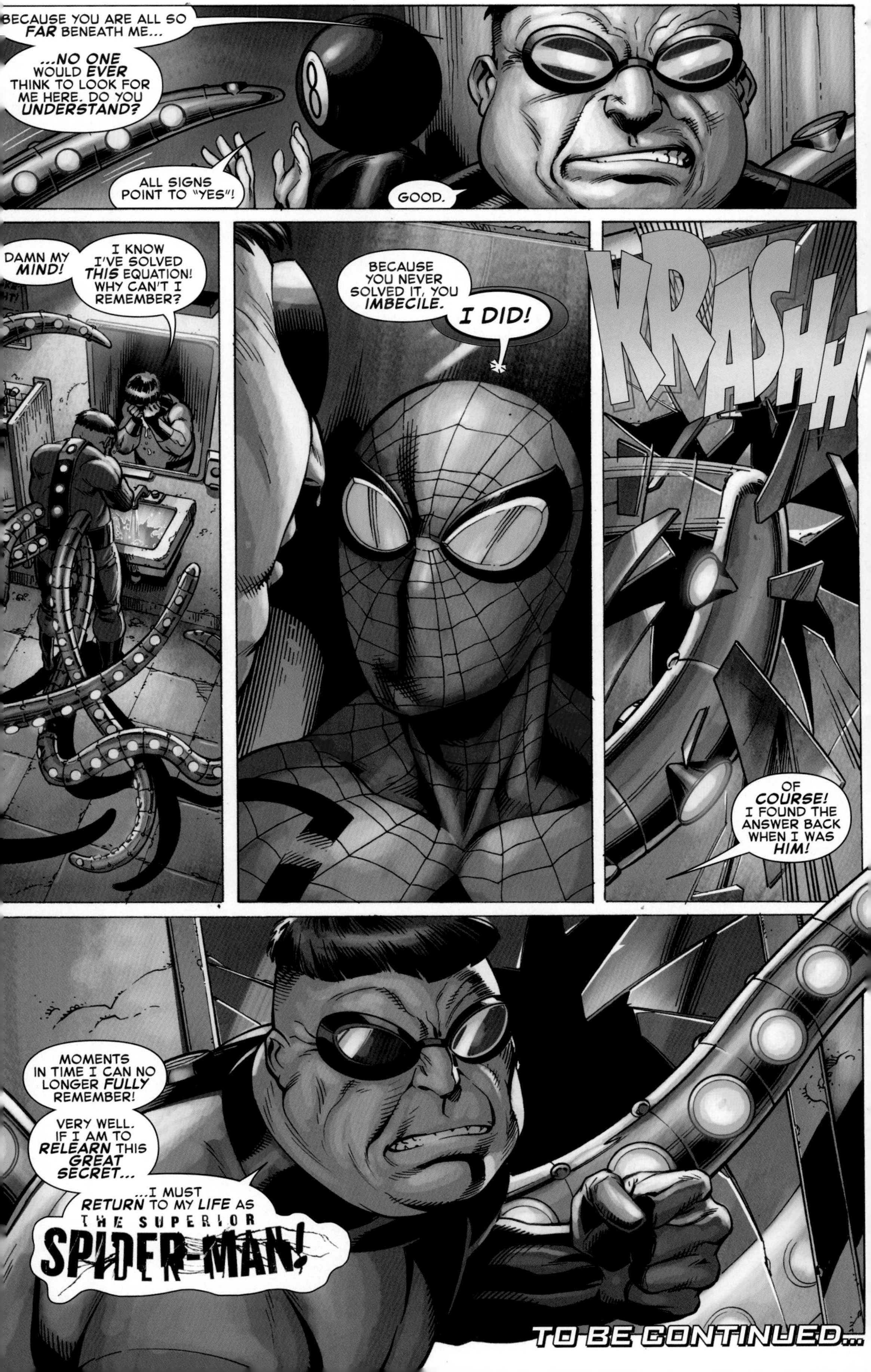
BECAUSE YOU ARE ALL SO FAR BENEATH ME...
...NO ONE WOULD EVER THINK TO LOOK FOR ME HERE. DO YOU UNDERSTAND?
ALL SIGNS POINT TO "YES"!
GOOD.
DAMN MY MIND!
I KNOW I'VE SOLVED THIS EQUATION! WHY CAN'T I REMEMBER?
BECAUSE YOU NEVER SOLVED IT, YOU IMBECILE.
I DID!
KRASHH
OF COURSE! I FOUND THE ANSWER BACK WHEN I WAS HIM!
MOMENTS IN TIME I CAN NO LONGER FULLY REMEMBER!
VERY WELL. IF I AM TO RELEARN THIS GREAT SECRET...
...I MUST RETURN TO MY LIFE AS THE SUPERIOR SPIDER-MAN!
TO BE CONTINUED...

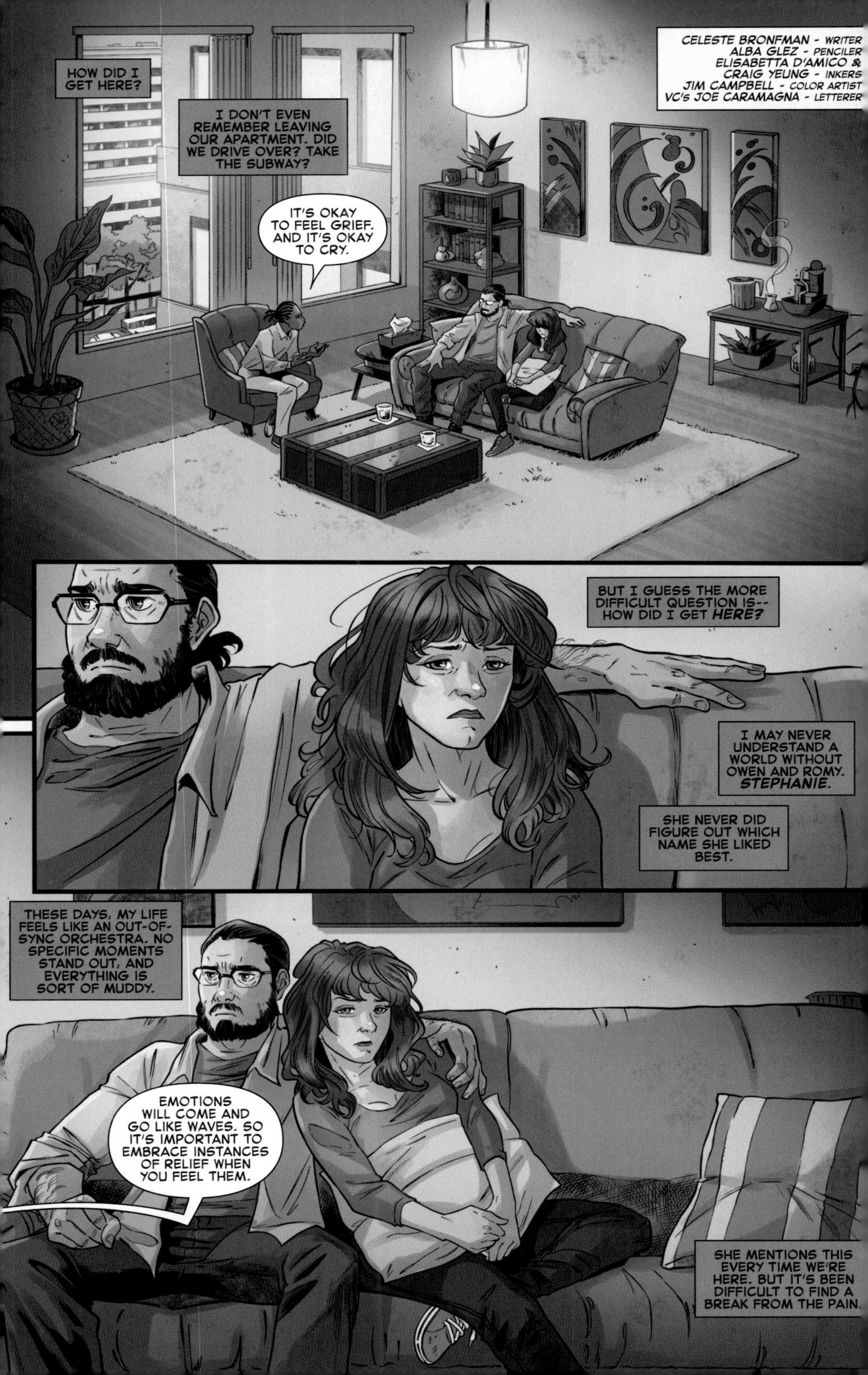
CELESTE BRONFMAN - WRITER
ALBA GLEZ - PENCILER
ELISABETTA D'AMICO &
CRAIG YEUNG - INKERS
JIM CAMPBELL - COLOR ARTIST
VC's JOE CARAMAGNA - LETTERER
HOW DID I GET HERE?
I DON'T EVEN REMEMBER LEAVING OUR APARTMENT. DID WE DRIVE OVER? TAKE THE SUBWAY?
IT'S OKAY TO FEEL GRIEF. AND IT'S OKAY TO CRY.
BUT I GUESS THE MORE DIFFICULT QUESTION IS-- HOW DID I GET *HERE?*
I MAY NEVER UNDERSTAND A WORLD WITHOUT OWEN AND ROMY. ***STEPHANIE.***
SHE NEVER DID FIGURE OUT WHICH NAME SHE LIKED BEST.
THESE DAYS, MY LIFE FEELS LIKE AN OUT-OF-SYNC ORCHESTRA. NO SPECIFIC MOMENTS STAND OUT, AND EVERYTHING IS SORT OF MUDDY.
EMOTIONS WILL COME AND GO LIKE WAVES. SO IT'S IMPORTANT TO EMBRACE INSTANCES OF RELIEF WHEN YOU FEEL THEM.
SHE MENTIONS THIS EVERY TIME WE'RE HERE. BUT IT'S BEEN DIFFICULT TO FIND A BREAK FROM THE PAIN.

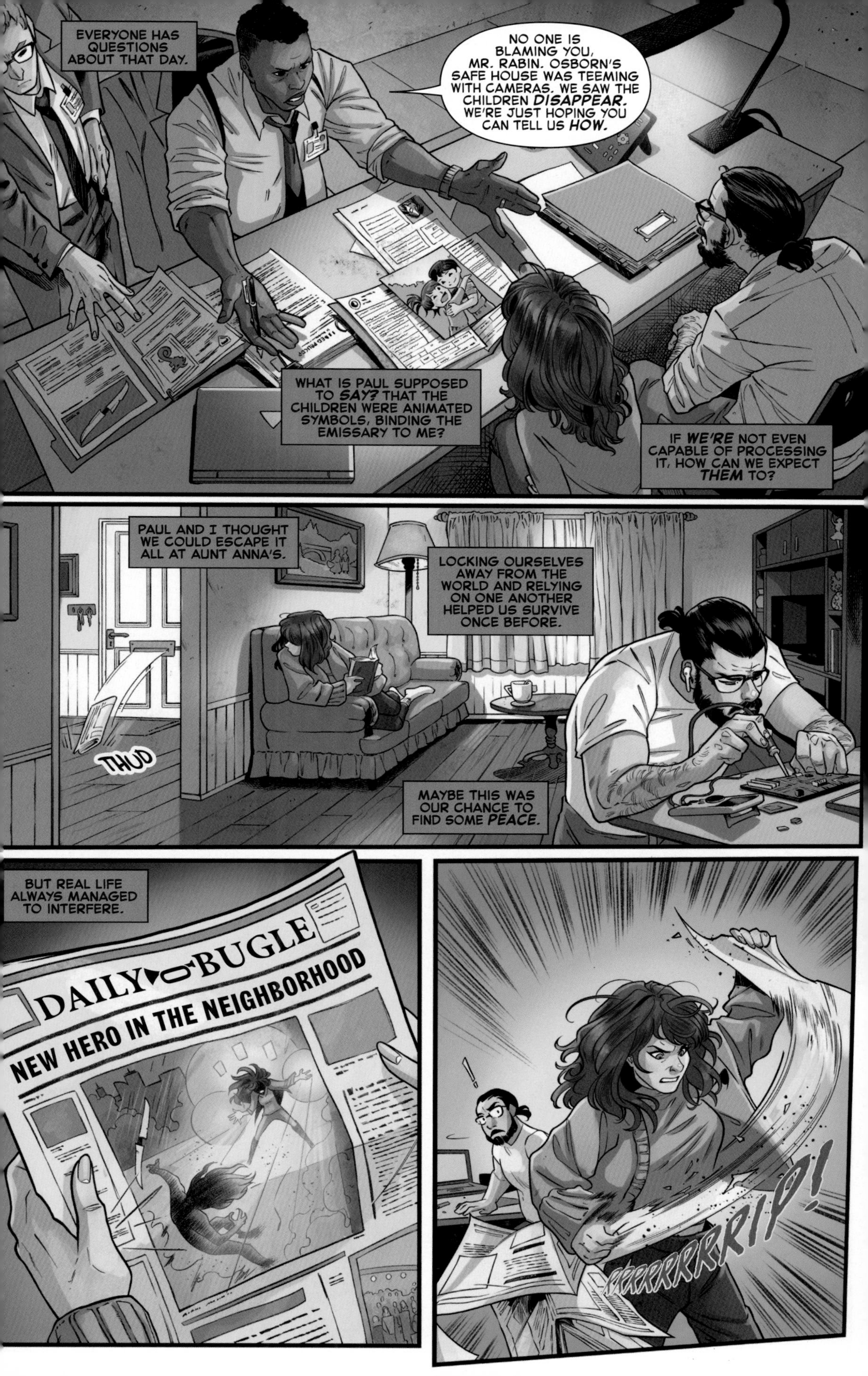

EVERYONE HAS QUESTIONS ABOUT THAT DAY.
NO ONE IS BLAMING YOU, MR. RABIN. OSBORN'S SAFE HOUSE WAS TEEMING WITH CAMERAS. WE SAW THE CHILDREN DISAPPEAR. WE'RE JUST HOPING YOU CAN TELL US HOW.
WHAT IS PAUL SUPPOSED TO SAY? THAT THE CHILDREN WERE ANIMATED SYMBOLS, BINDING THE EMISSARY TO ME?
IF WE'RE NOT EVEN CAPABLE OF PROCESSING IT, HOW CAN WE EXPECT THEM TO?
PAUL AND I THOUGHT WE COULD ESCAPE IT ALL AT AUNT ANNA'S.
LOCKING OURSELVES AWAY FROM THE WORLD AND RELYING ON ONE ANOTHER HELPED US SURVIVE ONCE BEFORE.
THUD
MAYBE THIS WAS OUR CHANCE TO FIND SOME PEACE.
BUT REAL LIFE ALWAYS MANAGED TO INTERFERE.
DAILY BUGLE
NEW HERO IN THE NEIGHBORHOOD
!
RRRRRRRRRIP!

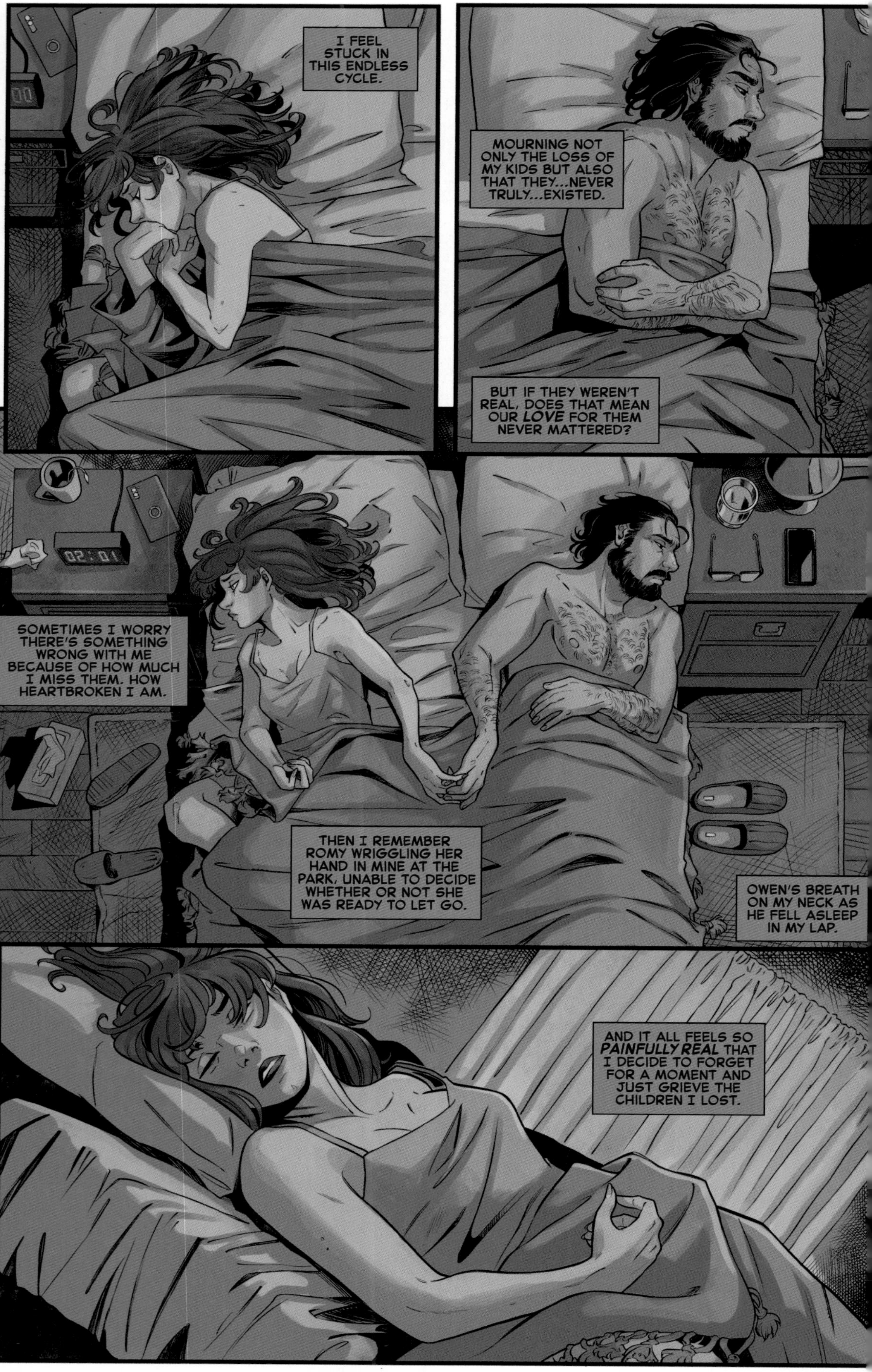
I FEEL STUCK IN THIS ENDLESS CYCLE.
MOURNING NOT ONLY THE LOSS OF MY KIDS BUT ALSO THAT THEY...NEVER TRULY...EXISTED.
BUT IF THEY WEREN'T REAL, DOES THAT MEAN OUR LOVE FOR THEM NEVER MATTERED?
02:01
SOMETIMES I WORRY THERE'S SOMETHING WRONG WITH ME BECAUSE OF HOW MUCH I MISS THEM. HOW HEARTBROKEN I AM.
THEN I REMEMBER ROMY WRIGGLING HER HAND IN MINE AT THE PARK, UNABLE TO DECIDE WHETHER OR NOT SHE WAS READY TO LET GO.
OWEN'S BREATH ON MY NECK AS HE FELL ASLEEP IN MY LAP.
AND IT ALL FEELS SO PAINFULLY REAL THAT I DECIDE TO FORGET FOR A MOMENT AND JUST GRIEVE THE CHILDREN I LOST.

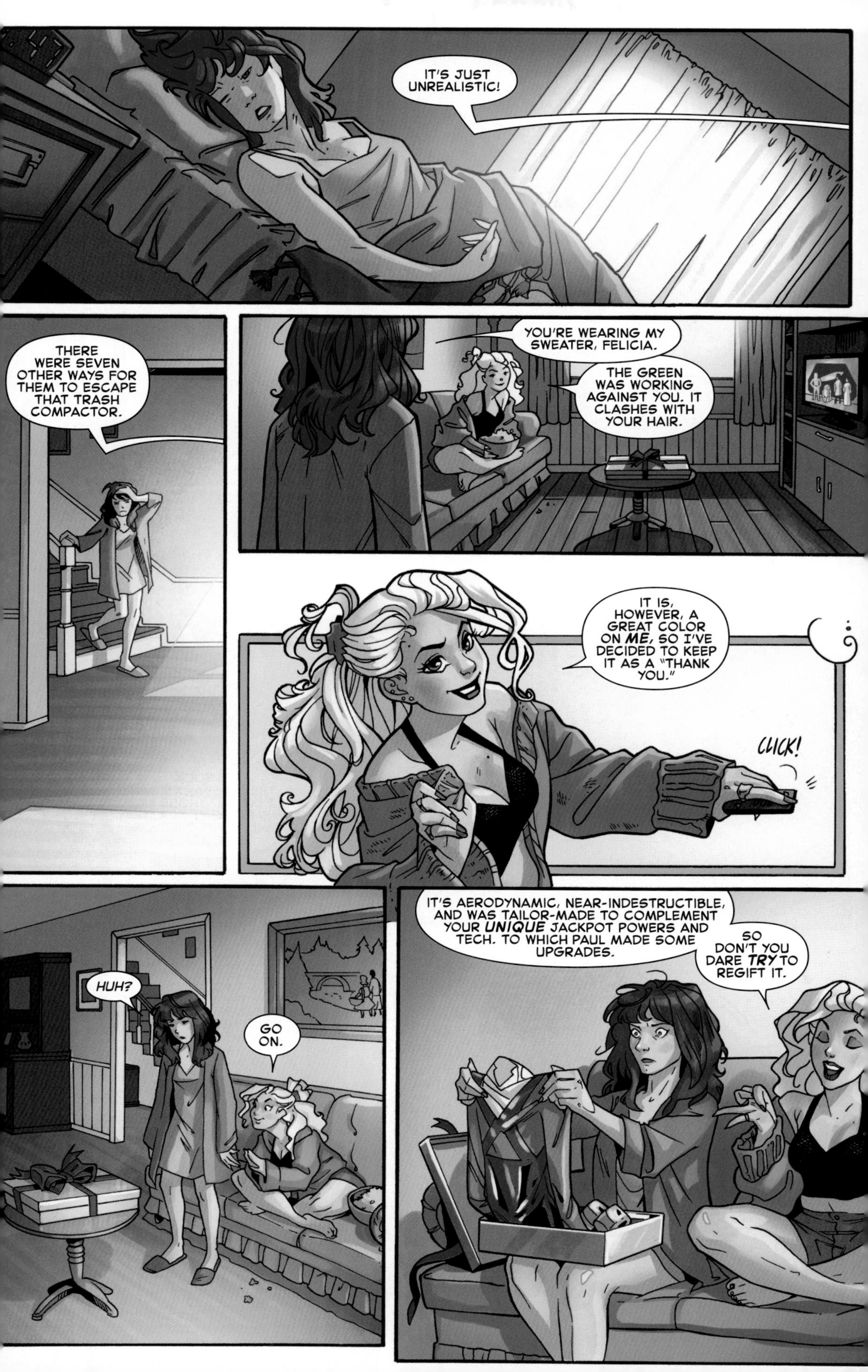
IT'S JUST UNREALISTIC!
THERE WERE SEVEN OTHER WAYS FOR THEM TO ESCAPE THAT TRASH COMPACTOR.
YOU'RE WEARING MY SWEATER, FELICIA.
THE GREEN WAS WORKING AGAINST YOU. IT CLASHES WITH YOUR HAIR.
IT IS, HOWEVER, A GREAT COLOR ON *ME*, SO I'VE DECIDED TO KEEP IT AS A "THANK YOU."
CLICK!
HUH?
GO ON.
IT'S AERODYNAMIC, NEAR-INDESTRUCTIBLE, AND WAS TAILOR-MADE TO COMPLEMENT YOUR *UNIQUE* JACKPOT POWERS AND TECH. TO WHICH PAUL MADE SOME UPGRADES.
SO DON'T YOU DARE *TRY* TO REGIFT IT.

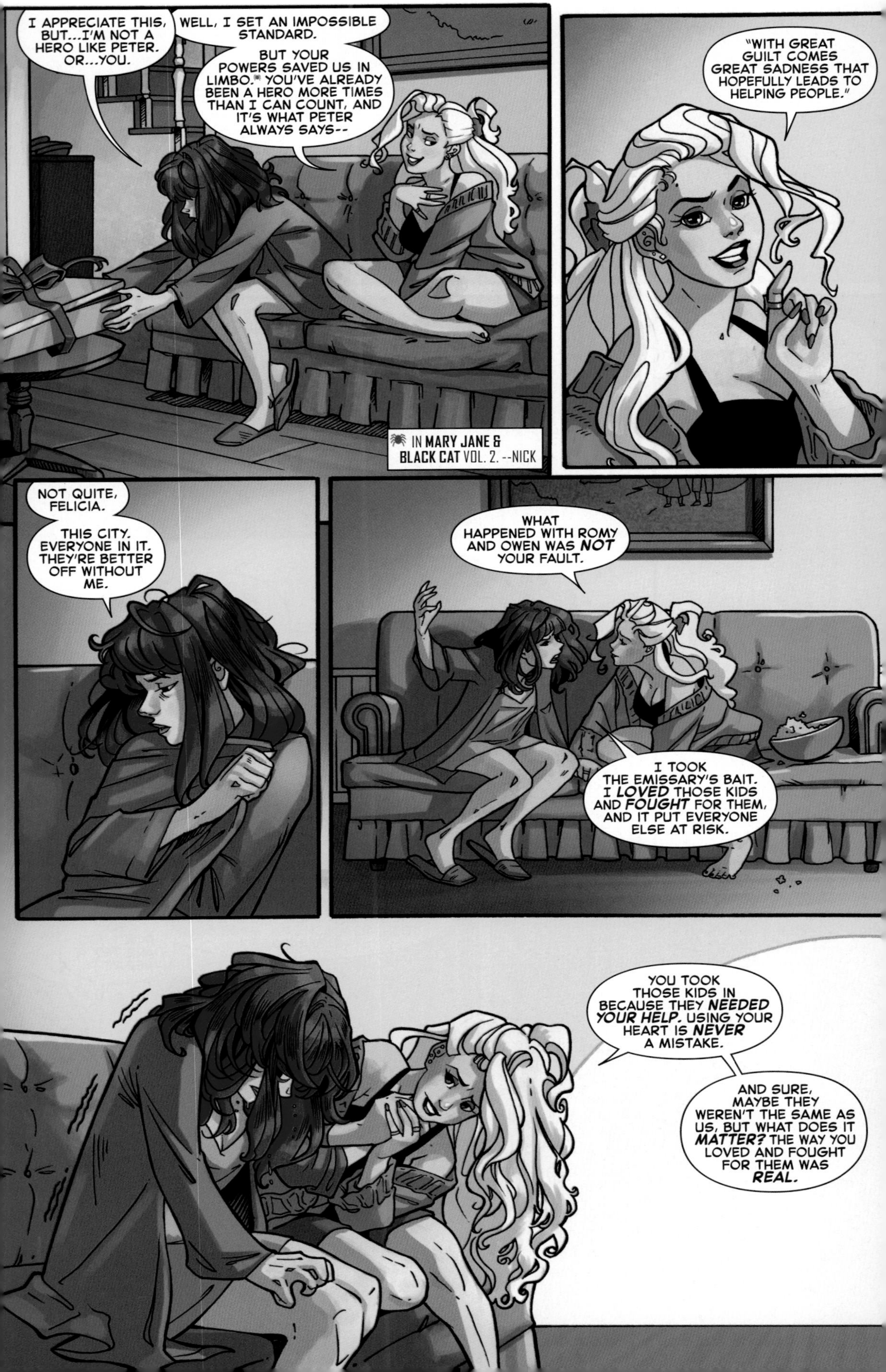
I APPRECIATE THIS, BUT...I'M NOT A HERO LIKE PETER. OR...YOU.
WELL, I SET AN IMPOSSIBLE STANDARD.
BUT YOUR POWERS SAVED US IN LIMBO.* YOU'VE ALREADY BEEN A HERO MORE TIMES THAN I CAN COUNT, AND IT'S WHAT PETER ALWAYS SAYS--
* IN MARY JANE & BLACK CAT VOL. 2. --NICK
"WITH GREAT GUILT COMES GREAT SADNESS THAT HOPEFULLY LEADS TO HELPING PEOPLE."
NOT QUITE, FELICIA.
THIS CITY. EVERYONE IN IT. THEY'RE BETTER OFF WITHOUT ME.
WHAT HAPPENED WITH ROMY AND OWEN WAS NOT YOUR FAULT.
I TOOK THE EMISSARY'S BAIT. I LOVED THOSE KIDS AND FOUGHT FOR THEM, AND IT PUT EVERYONE ELSE AT RISK.
YOU TOOK THOSE KIDS IN BECAUSE THEY NEEDED YOUR HELP. USING YOUR HEART IS NEVER A MISTAKE.
AND SURE, MAYBE THEY WEREN'T THE SAME AS US, BUT WHAT DOES IT MATTER? THE WAY YOU LOVED AND FOUGHT FOR THEM WAS REAL.

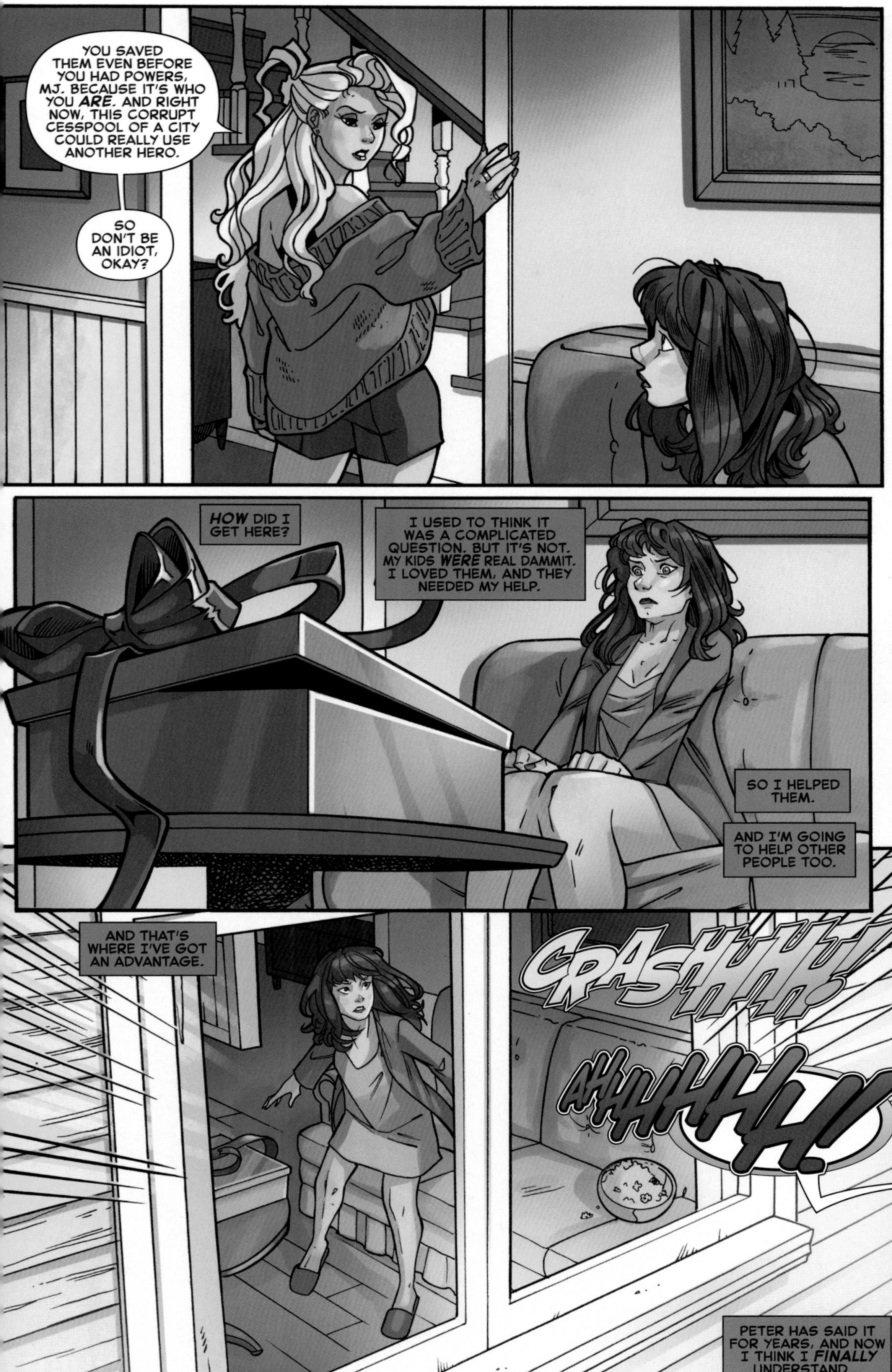
YOU SAVED THEM EVEN BEFORE YOU HAD POWERS, MJ. BECAUSE IT'S WHO YOU *ARE*. AND RIGHT NOW, THIS CORRUPT CESSPOOL OF A CITY COULD REALLY USE ANOTHER HERO.
SO DON'T BE AN IDIOT, OKAY?
HOW DID I GET HERE?
I USED TO THINK IT WAS A COMPLICATED QUESTION. BUT IT'S NOT. MY KIDS *WERE* REAL DAMMIT. I LOVED THEM, AND THEY NEEDED MY HELP.
SO I HELPED THEM.
AND I'M GOING TO HELP OTHER PEOPLE TOO.
AND THAT'S WHERE I'VE GOT AN ADVANTAGE.
CRASHHH!
AHHHHHH!!
PETER HAS SAID IT FOR YEARS, AND NOW I THINK I *FINALLY* UNDERSTAND...

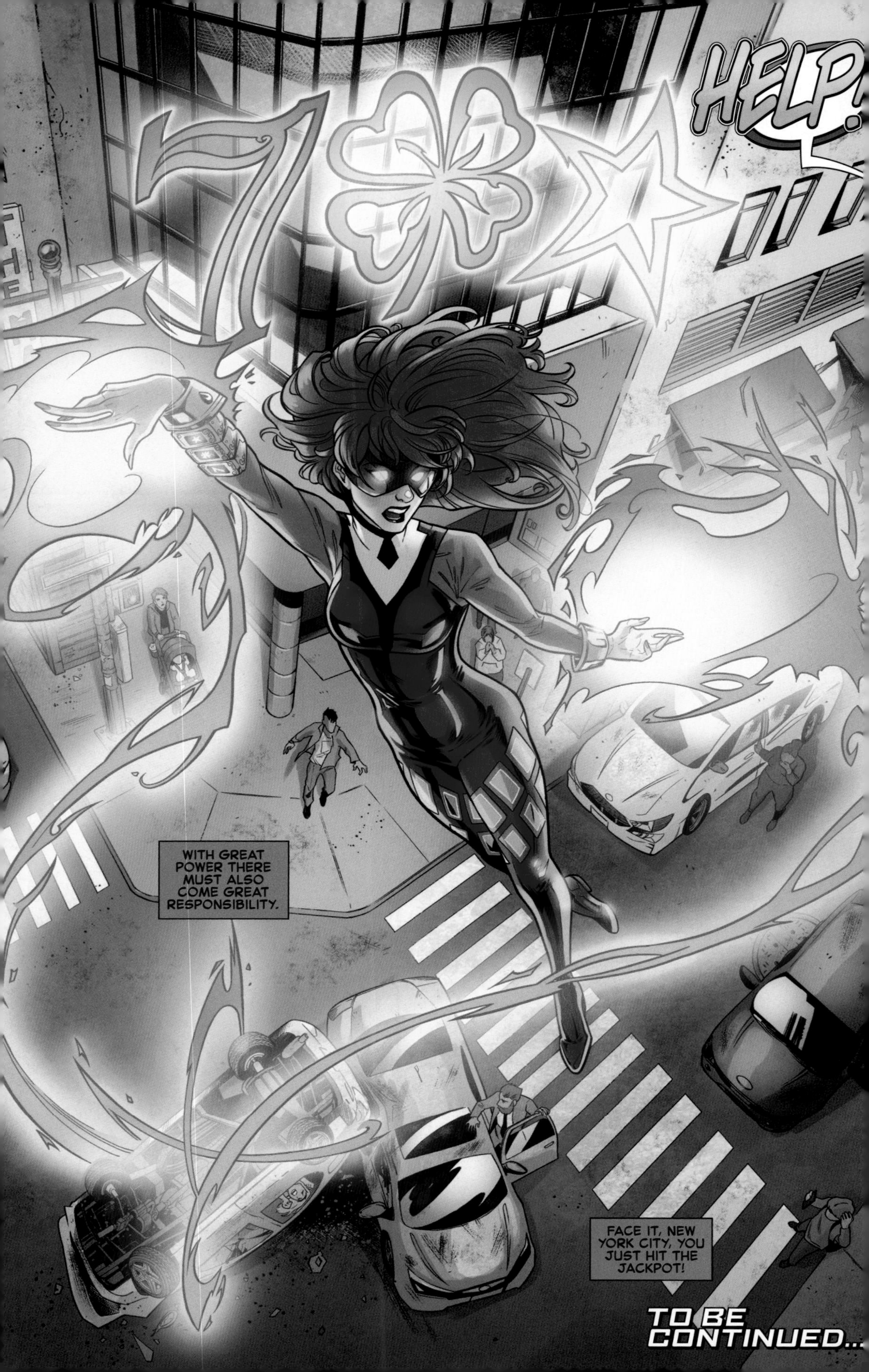
HELP!
WITH GREAT POWER THERE MUST ALSO COME GREAT RESPONSIBILITY.
FACE IT, NEW YORK CITY, YOU JUST HIT THE JACKPOT!
TO BE CONTINUED...

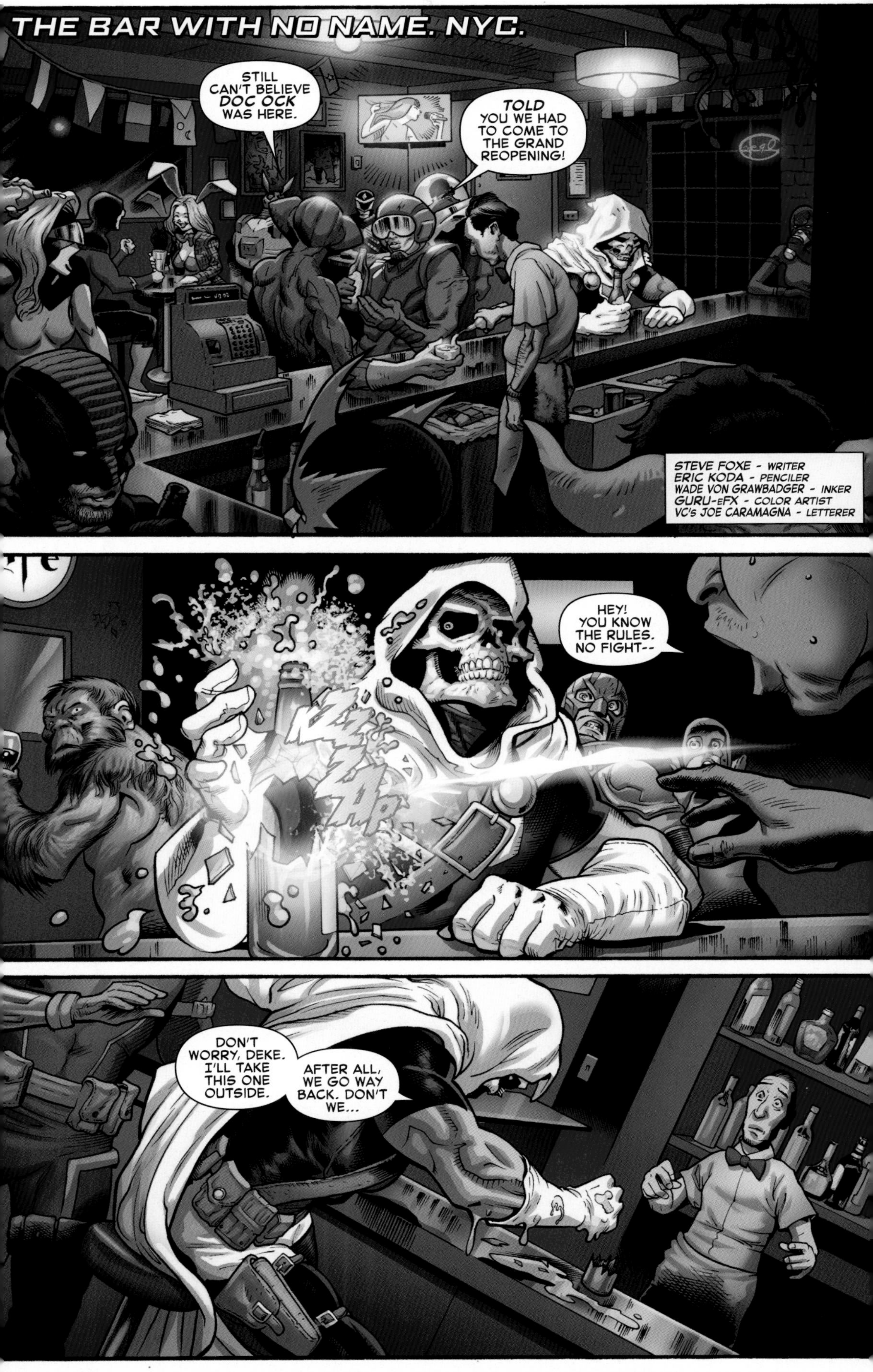
THE BAR WITH NO NAME. NYC.
STILL CAN'T BELIEVE DOC OCK WAS HERE.
TOLD YOU WE HAD TO COME TO THE GRAND REOPENING!
STEVE FOXE - WRITER
ERIC KODA - PENCILER
WADE VON GRAWBADGER - INKER
GURU-eFX - COLOR ARTIST
VC's JOE CARAMAGNA - LETTERER
HEY! YOU KNOW THE RULES. NO FIGHT--
DON'T WORRY, DEKE. I'LL TAKE THIS ONE OUTSIDE.
AFTER ALL, WE GO WAY BACK. DON'T WE...

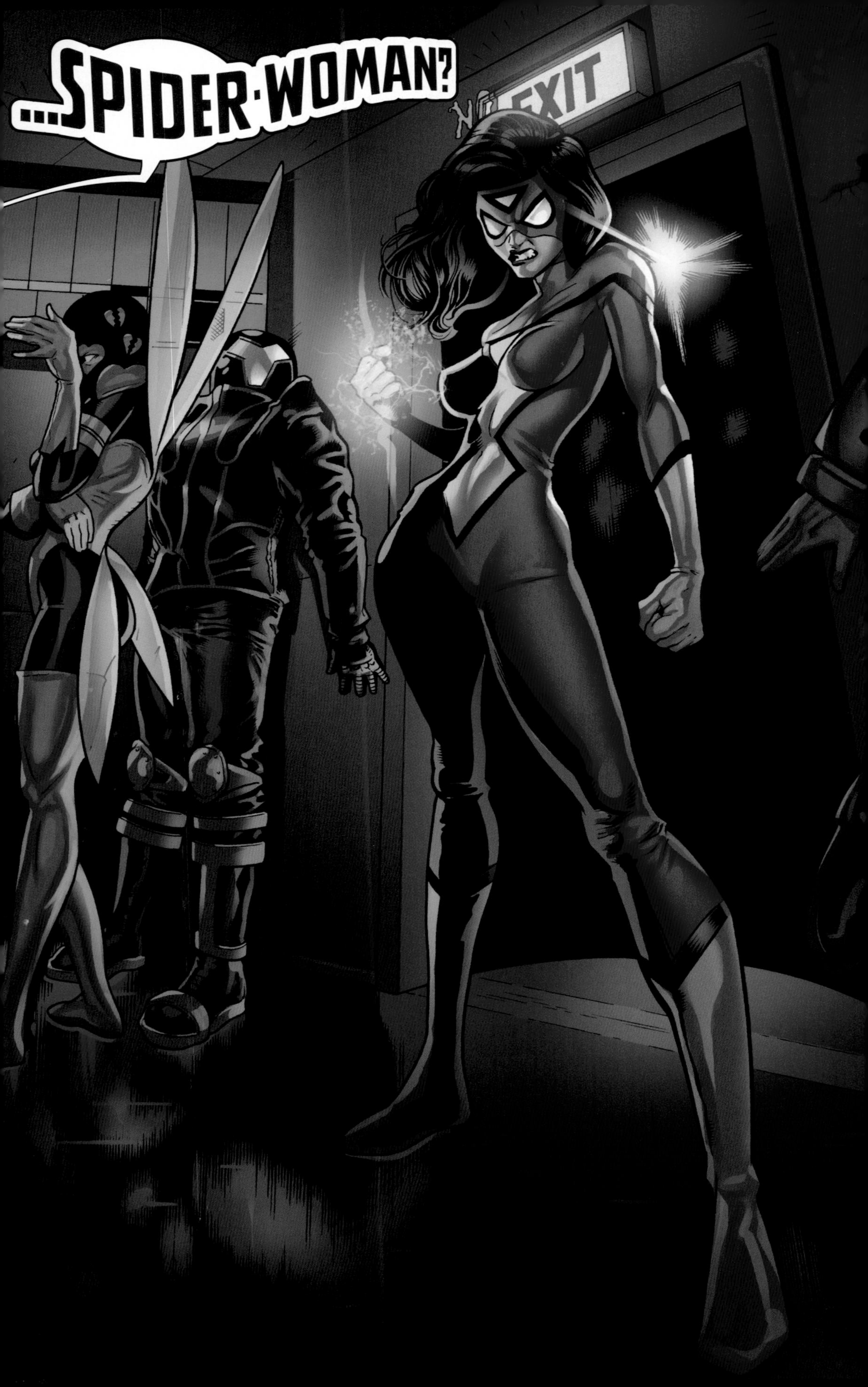
...SPIDER-WOMAN?
EXIT

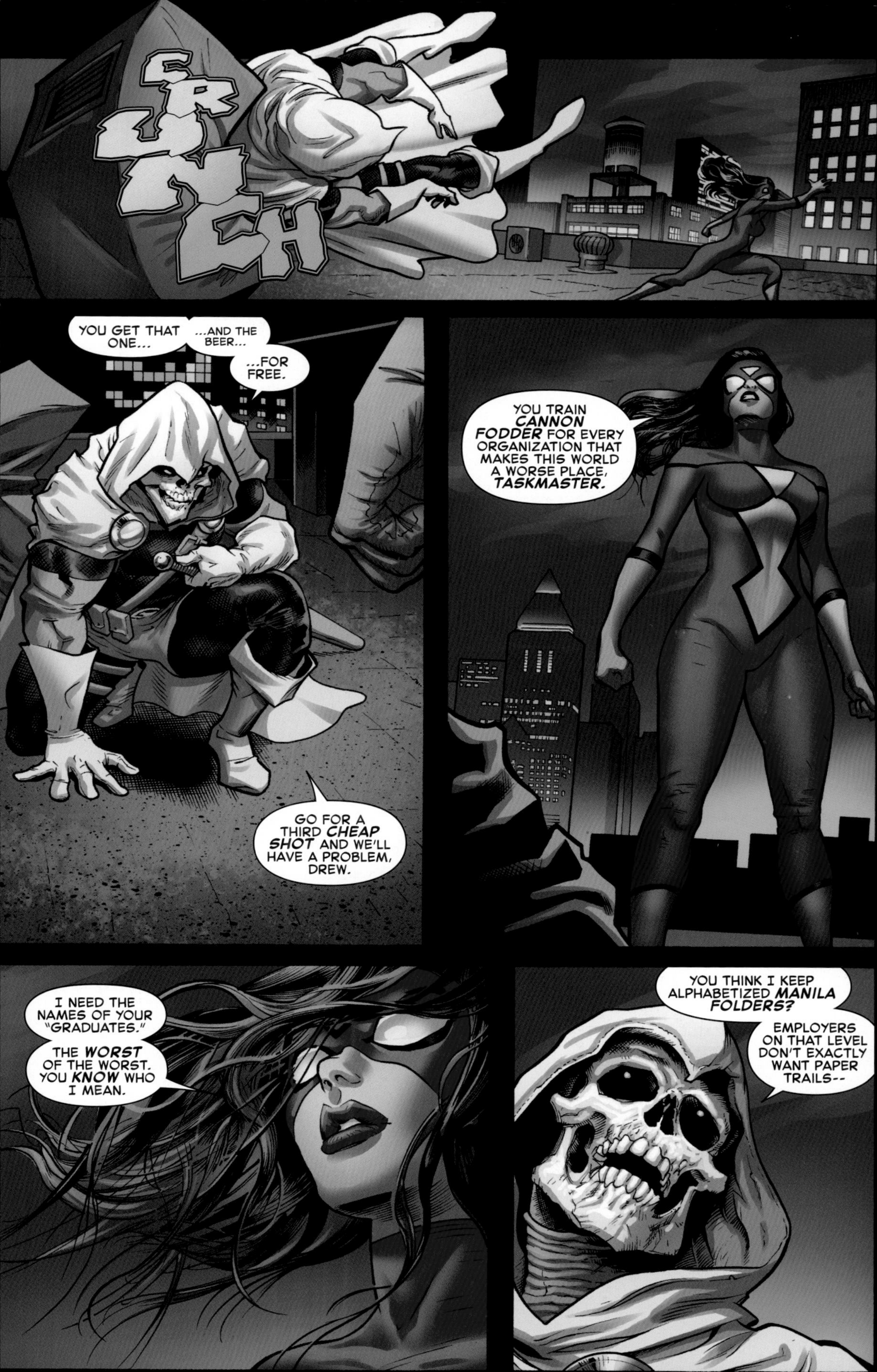
CRUNCH
YOU GET THAT ONE...
...AND THE BEER...
...FOR FREE.
GO FOR A THIRD *CHEAP SHOT* AND WE'LL HAVE A PROBLEM, DREW.
YOU TRAIN *CANNON FODDER* FOR EVERY ORGANIZATION THAT MAKES THIS WORLD A WORSE PLACE, *TASKMASTER.*
I NEED THE NAMES OF YOUR "GRADUATES."
THE *WORST* OF THE WORST. YOU *KNOW* WHO I MEAN.
YOU THINK I KEEP ALPHABETIZED *MANILA FOLDERS?*
EMPLOYERS ON THAT LEVEL DON'T EXACTLY WANT PAPER TRAILS--

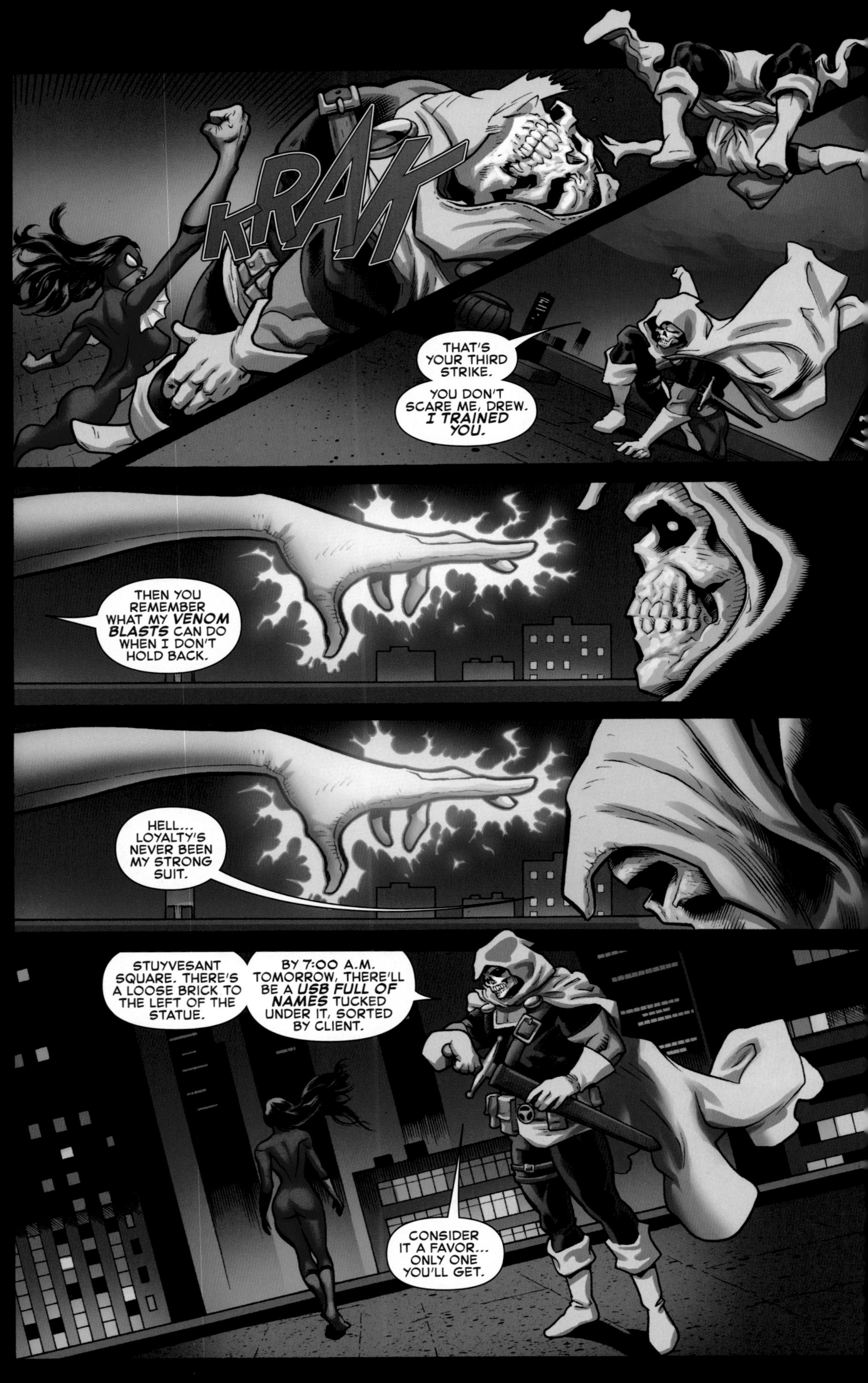
KRAK
THAT'S YOUR THIRD STRIKE.
YOU DON'T SCARE ME, DREW. I TRAINED YOU.
THEN YOU REMEMBER WHAT MY VENOM BLASTS CAN DO WHEN I DON'T HOLD BACK.
HELL... LOYALTY'S NEVER BEEN MY STRONG SUIT.
STUYVESANT SQUARE. THERE'S A LOOSE BRICK TO THE LEFT OF THE STATUE.
BY 7:00 A.M. TOMORROW, THERE'LL BE A USB FULL OF NAMES TUCKED UNDER IT, SORTED BY CLIENT.
CONSIDER IT A FAVOR... ONLY ONE YOU'LL GET.

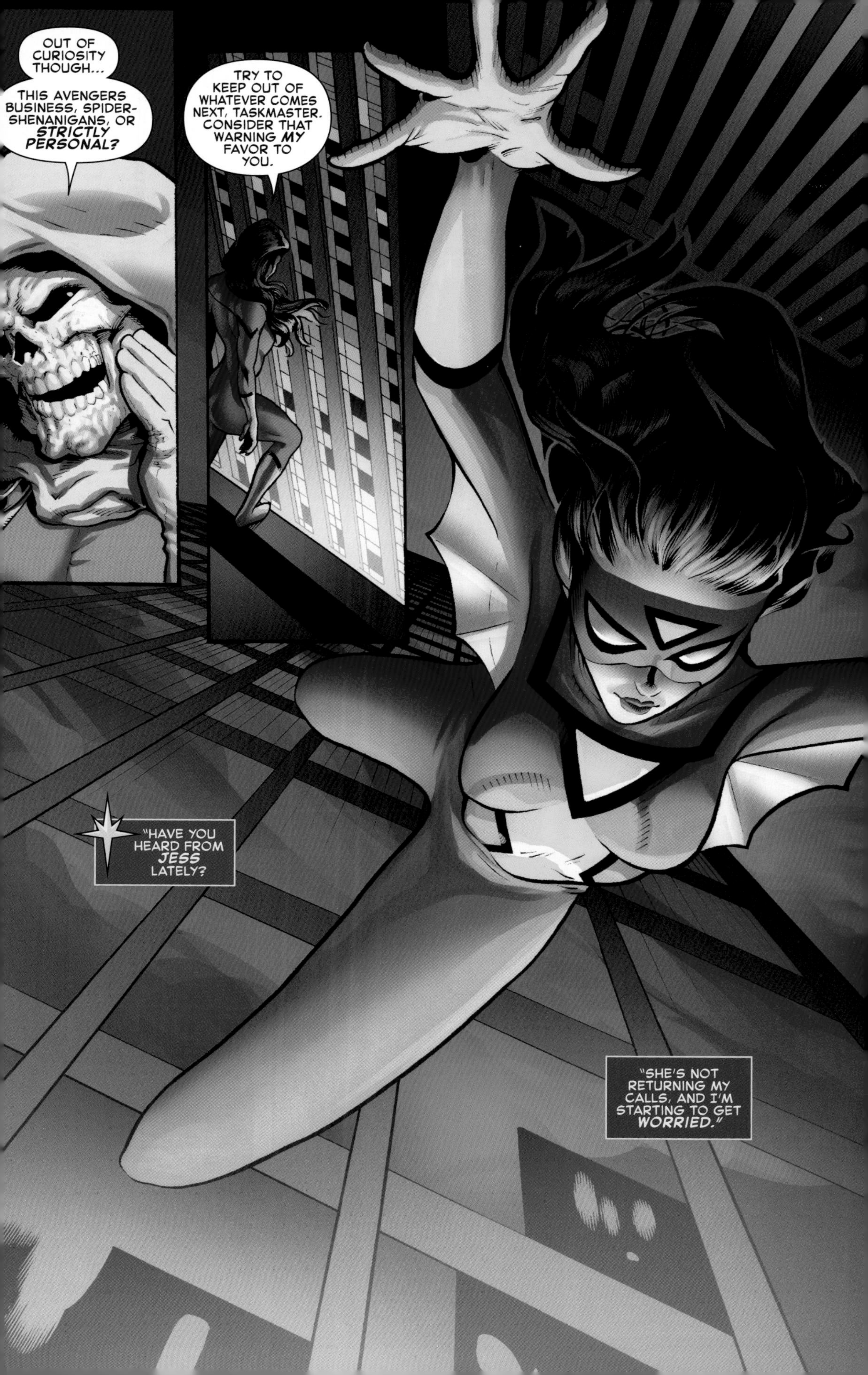
OUT OF CURIOSITY THOUGH...
THIS AVENGERS BUSINESS, SPIDER-SHENANIGANS, OR STRICTLY PERSONAL?
TRY TO KEEP OUT OF WHATEVER COMES NEXT, TASKMASTER. CONSIDER THAT WARNING MY FAVOR TO YOU.
"HAVE YOU HEARD FROM JESS LATELY?
"SHE'S NOT RETURNING MY CALLS, AND I'M STARTING TO GET WORRIED."

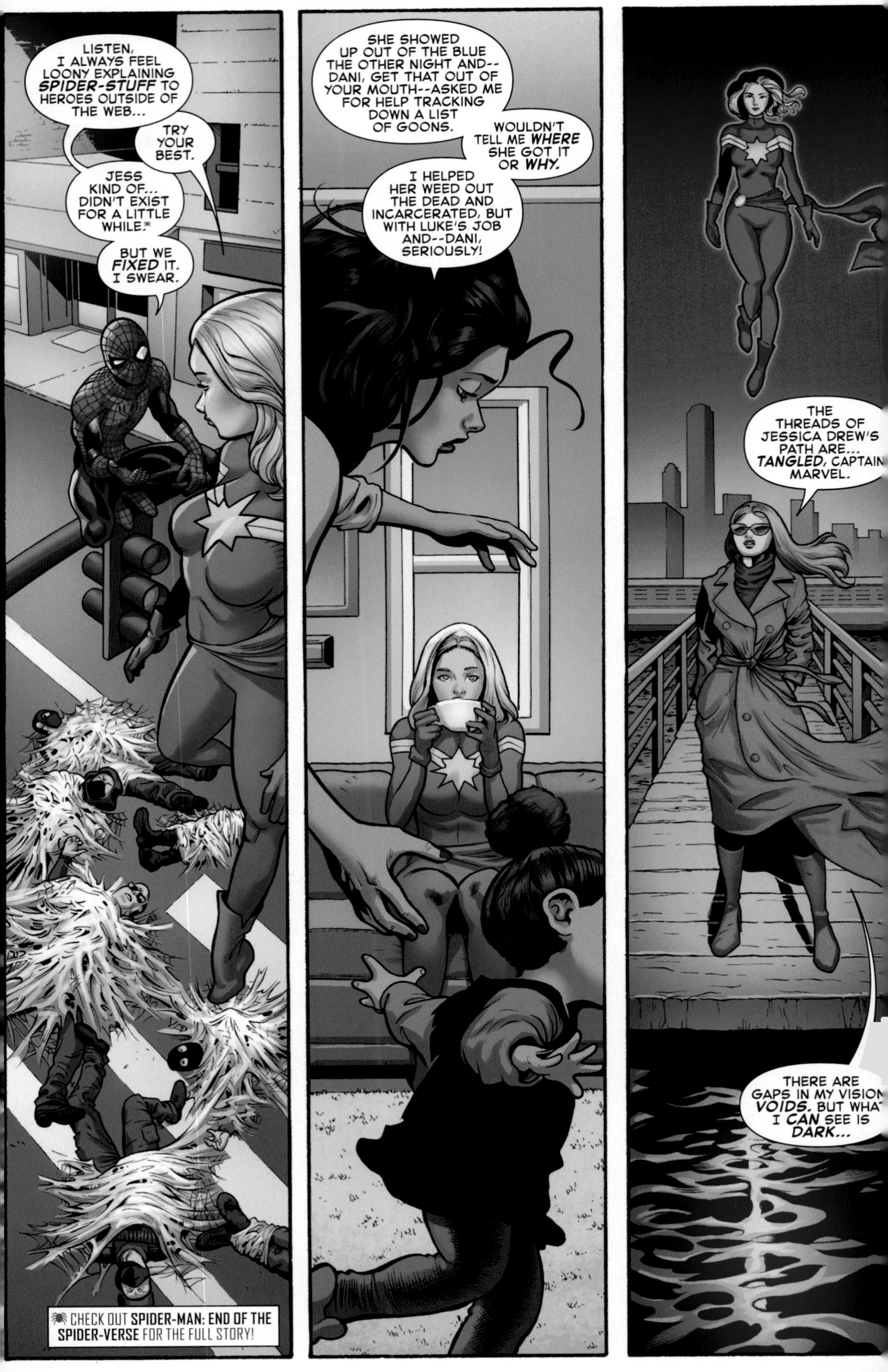
LISTEN, I ALWAYS FEEL LOONY EXPLAINING SPIDER-STUFF TO HEROES OUTSIDE OF THE WEB...
TRY YOUR BEST.
JESS KIND OF... DIDN'T EXIST FOR A LITTLE WHILE.*
BUT WE FIXED IT. I SWEAR.
*CHECK OUT SPIDER-MAN: END OF THE SPIDER-VERSE FOR THE FULL STORY!
SHE SHOWED UP OUT OF THE BLUE THE OTHER NIGHT AND--DANI, GET THAT OUT OF YOUR MOUTH--ASKED ME FOR HELP TRACKING DOWN A LIST OF GOONS.
WOULDN'T TELL ME WHERE SHE GOT IT OR WHY.
I HELPED HER WEED OUT THE DEAD AND INCARCERATED, BUT WITH LUKE'S JOB AND--DANI, SERIOUSLY!
THE THREADS OF JESSICA DREW'S PATH ARE... TANGLED, CAPTAIN MARVEL.
THERE ARE GAPS IN MY VISION VOIDS. BUT WHAT I CAN SEE IS DARK...

"...AND VIOLENT."

TOLD YOU I HAD THE HOOKUP, MAN. A FREE SAMPLE OF THE NEW FORMULA, ON THE HOU--

SLAM

ISAAC TATE. AGE THIRTY-FIVE.

TASKMASTER TRAINED YOU--AND NOT TO PUSH #$%& TO KIDS ON THE STREET.

NO ONE GETS TO JST WALK AWAY FROM THE MONSTERS YOU WORKED FOR.

OOF!

THEN YOU KNOW-- hhhh--THAT I'LL DIE BEFORE I TELL YOU ANYTHING.

WAIT, WHAT ARE YOU--?

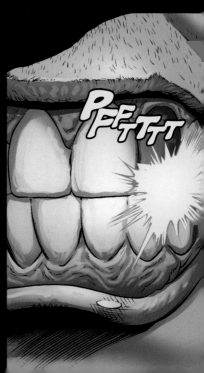

PFFTTTT

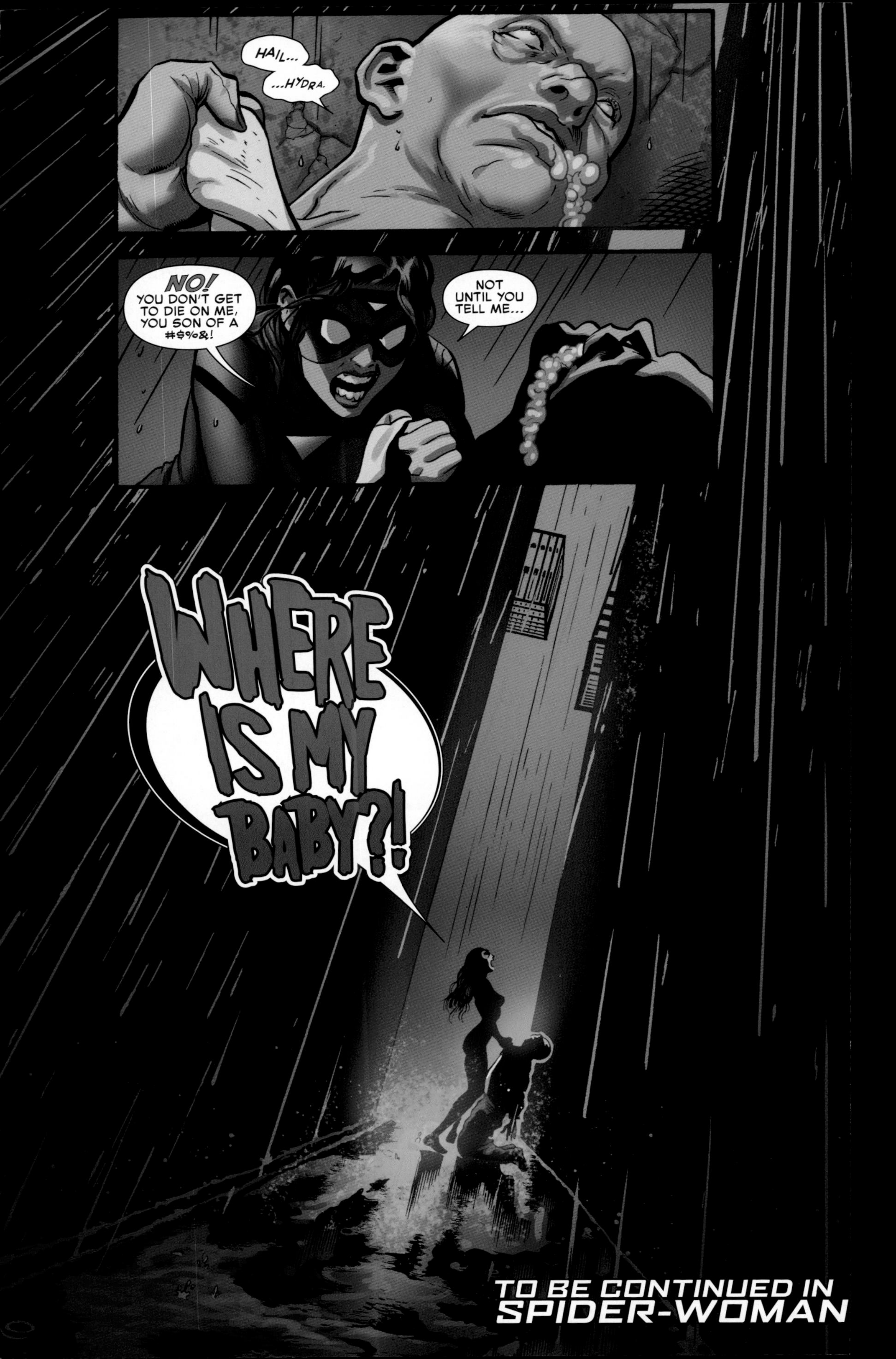
HAIL...
...HYDRA.
NO! YOU DON'T GET TO DIE ON ME, YOU SON OF A #$%&!
NOT UNTIL YOU TELL ME...
WHERE IS MY BABY?!
TO BE CONTINUED IN SPIDER-WOMAN

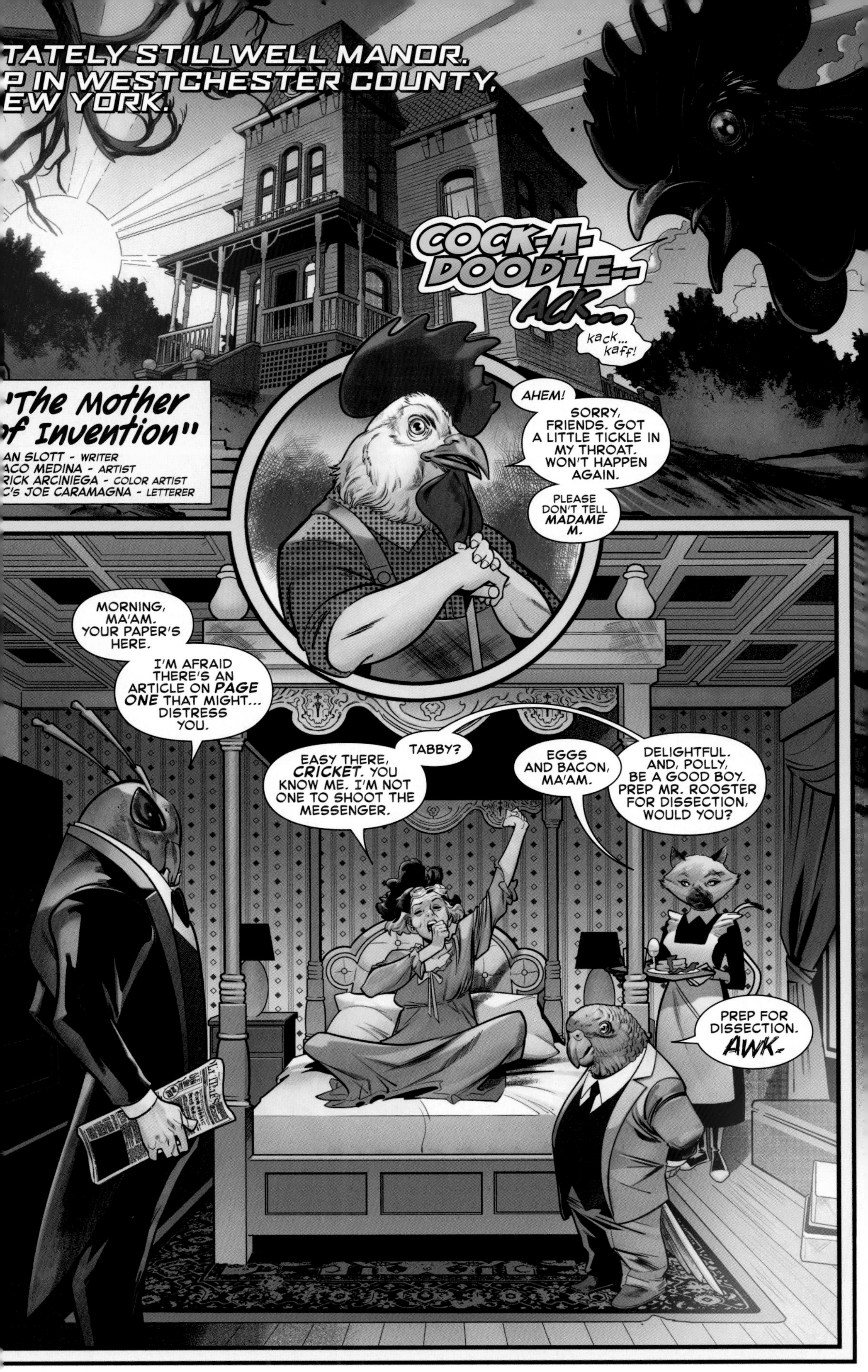
TATELY STILLWELL MANOR. P IN WESTCHESTER COUNTY, EW YORK.
COCK-A-DOODLE--ACK...
kack... kaff!
"The Mother of Invention"
AN SLOTT - WRITER
ACO MEDINA - ARTIST
RICK ARCINIEGA - COLOR ARTIST
C's JOE CARAMAGNA - LETTERER
AHEM!
SORRY, FRIENDS. GOT A LITTLE TICKLE IN MY THROAT. WON'T HAPPEN AGAIN.
PLEASE DON'T TELL MADAME M.
MORNING, MA'AM. YOUR PAPER'S HERE.
I'M AFRAID THERE'S AN ARTICLE ON PAGE ONE THAT MIGHT... DISTRESS YOU.
EASY THERE, CRICKET. YOU KNOW ME. I'M NOT ONE TO SHOOT THE MESSENGER.
TABBY?
EGGS AND BACON, MA'AM.
DELIGHTFUL. AND, POLLY, BE A GOOD BOY. PREP MR. ROOSTER FOR DISSECTION, WOULD YOU?
PREP FOR DISSECTION. AWK-

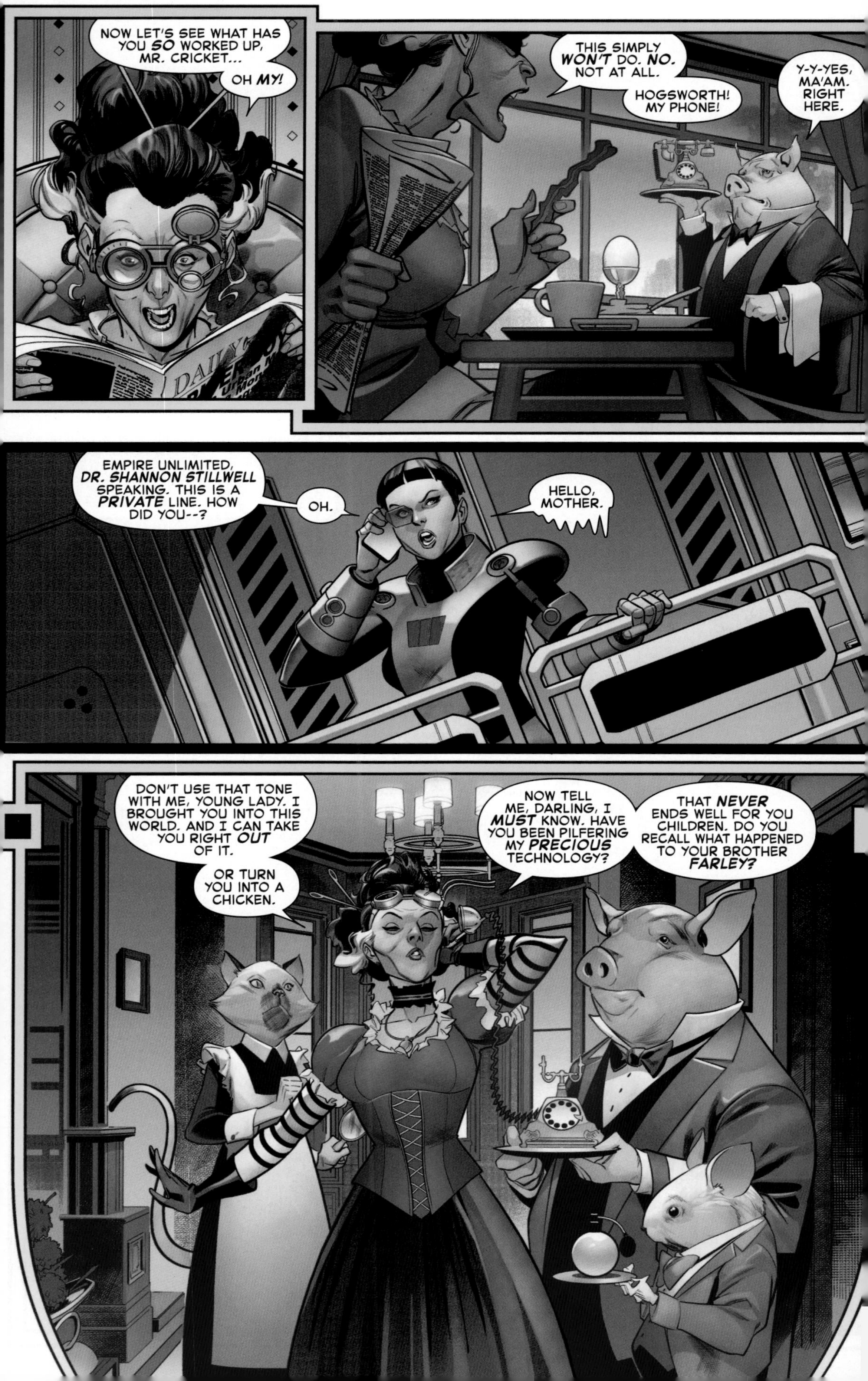
NOW LET'S SEE WHAT HAS YOU *SO* WORKED UP, MR. CRICKET...
OH *MY!*
THIS SIMPLY *WON'T* DO. *NO.* NOT AT ALL.
HOGSWORTH! MY PHONE!
Y-Y-YES, MA'AM. RIGHT HERE.
EMPIRE UNLIMITED, *DR. SHANNON STILLWELL* SPEAKING. THIS IS A *PRIVATE* LINE. HOW DID YOU--?
OH.
HELLO, MOTHER.
DON'T USE THAT TONE WITH ME, YOUNG LADY. I BROUGHT YOU INTO THIS WORLD. AND I CAN TAKE YOU RIGHT *OUT* OF IT.
OR TURN YOU INTO A CHICKEN.
NOW TELL ME, DARLING, I *MUST* KNOW. HAVE YOU BEEN PILFERING MY *PRECIOUS* TECHNOLOGY?
THAT *NEVER* ENDS WELL FOR YOU CHILDREN. DO YOU RECALL WHAT HAPPENED TO YOUR BROTHER *FARLEY?*

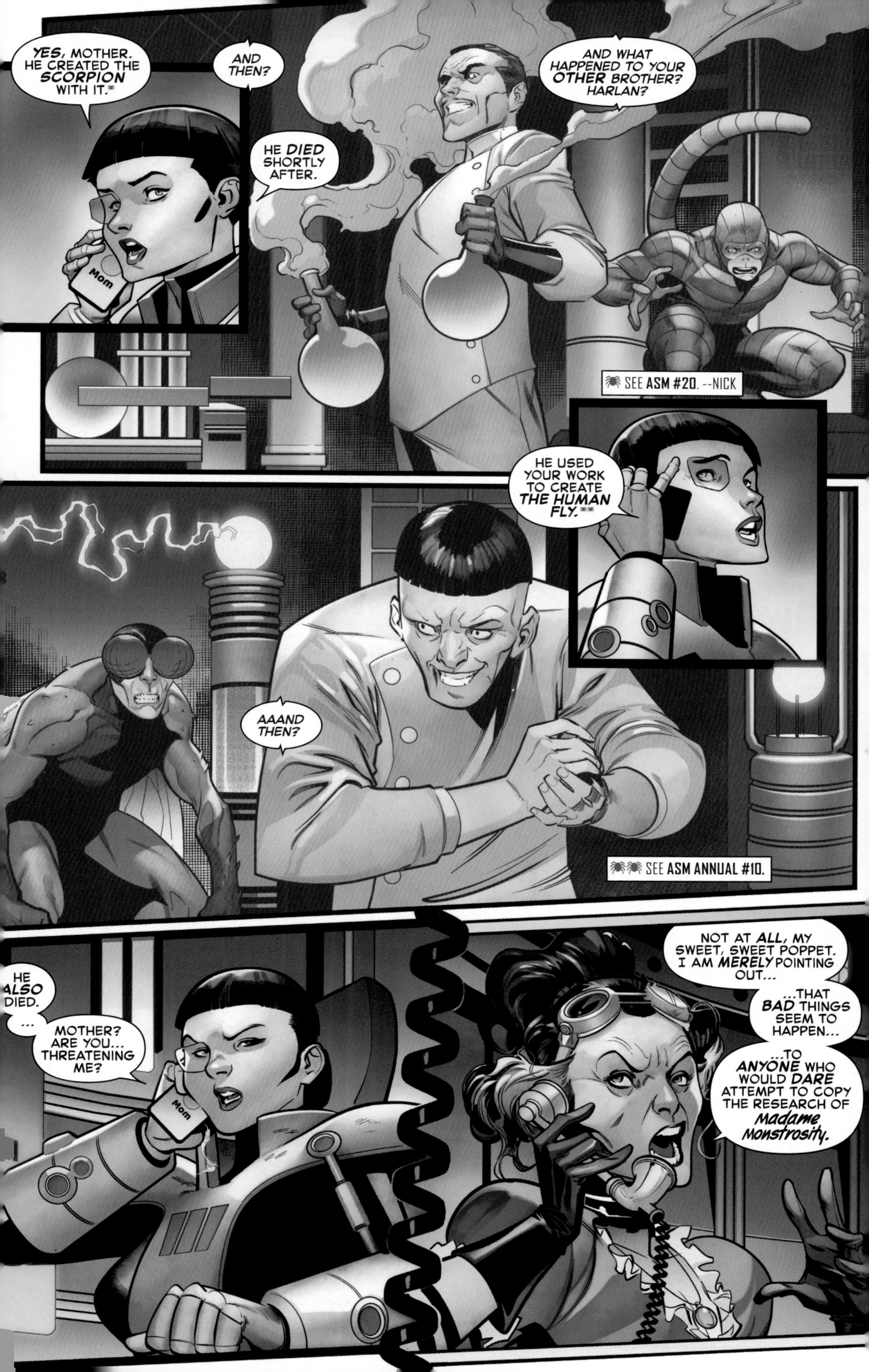
YES, MOTHER. HE CREATED THE SCORPION WITH IT.*
AND THEN?
HE DIED SHORTLY AFTER.
AND WHAT HAPPENED TO YOUR OTHER BROTHER? HARLAN?
SEE ASM #20. --NICK
HE USED YOUR WORK TO CREATE THE HUMAN FLY.**
AAAND THEN?
SEE ASM ANNUAL #10.
HE ALSO DIED.
...
MOTHER? ARE YOU... THREATENING ME?
Mom
NOT AT ALL, MY SWEET, SWEET POPPET. I AM MERELY POINTING OUT...
...THAT BAD THINGS SEEM TO HAPPEN...
...TO ANYONE WHO WOULD DARE ATTEMPT TO COPY THE RESEARCH OF Madame Monstrosity.

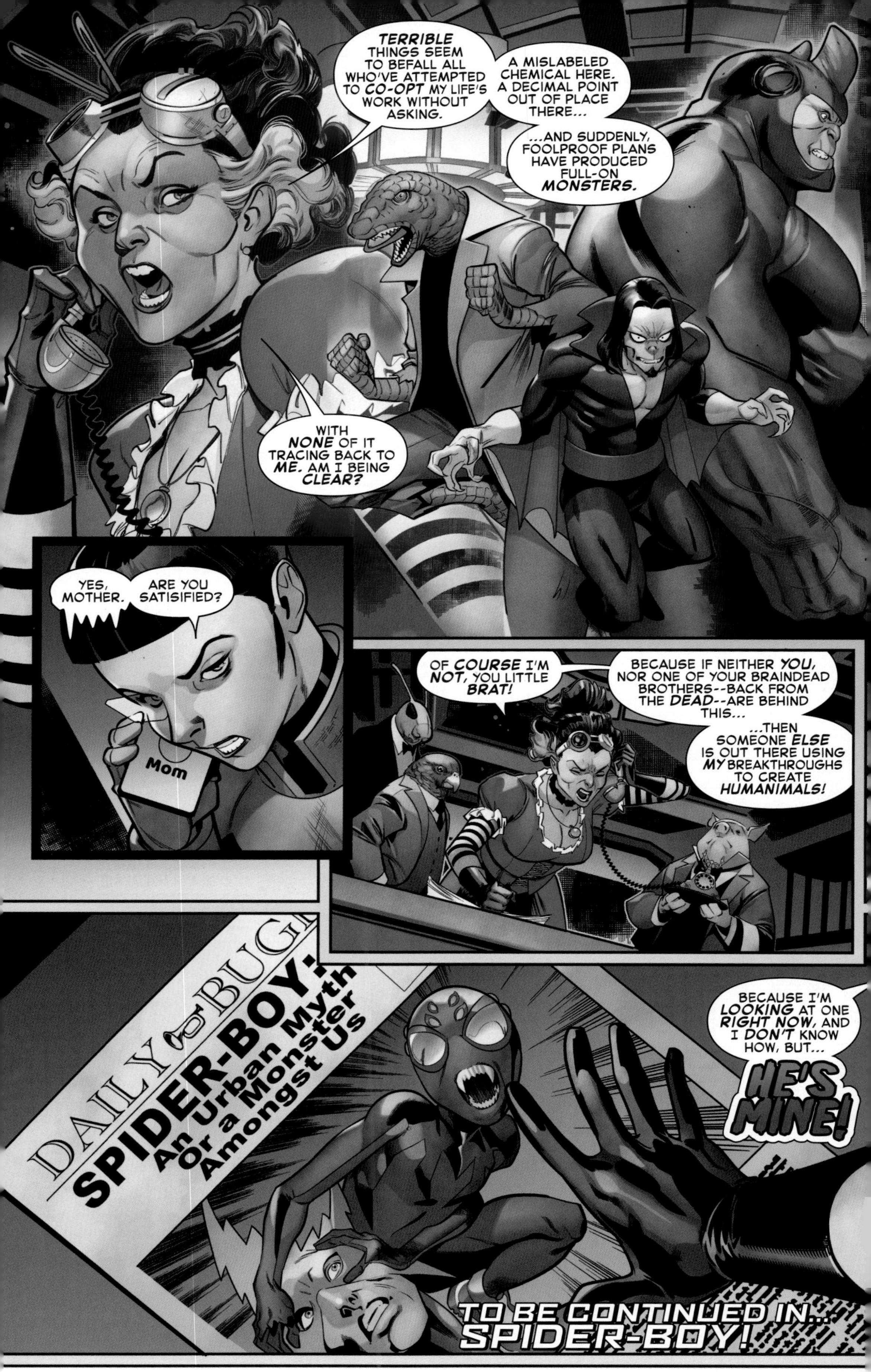
TERRIBLE THINGS SEEM TO BEFALL ALL WHO'VE ATTEMPTED TO CO-OPT MY LIFE'S WORK WITHOUT ASKING.
A MISLABELED CHEMICAL HERE. A DECIMAL POINT OUT OF PLACE THERE...
...AND SUDDENLY, FOOLPROOF PLANS HAVE PRODUCED FULL-ON MONSTERS.
WITH NONE OF IT TRACING BACK TO ME. AM I BEING CLEAR?
YES, MOTHER.
ARE YOU SATISIFIED?
Mom
OF COURSE I'M NOT, YOU LITTLE BRAT!
BECAUSE IF NEITHER YOU, NOR ONE OF YOUR BRAINDEAD BROTHERS--BACK FROM THE DEAD--ARE BEHIND THIS...
...THEN SOMEONE ELSE IS OUT THERE USING MY BREAKTHROUGHS TO CREATE HUMANIMALS!
DAILY BUGL
SPIDER-BOY: An Urban Myth Or a Monster Amongst Us
BECAUSE I'M LOOKING AT ONE RIGHT NOW, AND I DON'T KNOW HOW, BUT...
HE'S MINE!
TO BE CONTINUED IN... SPIDER-BOY!

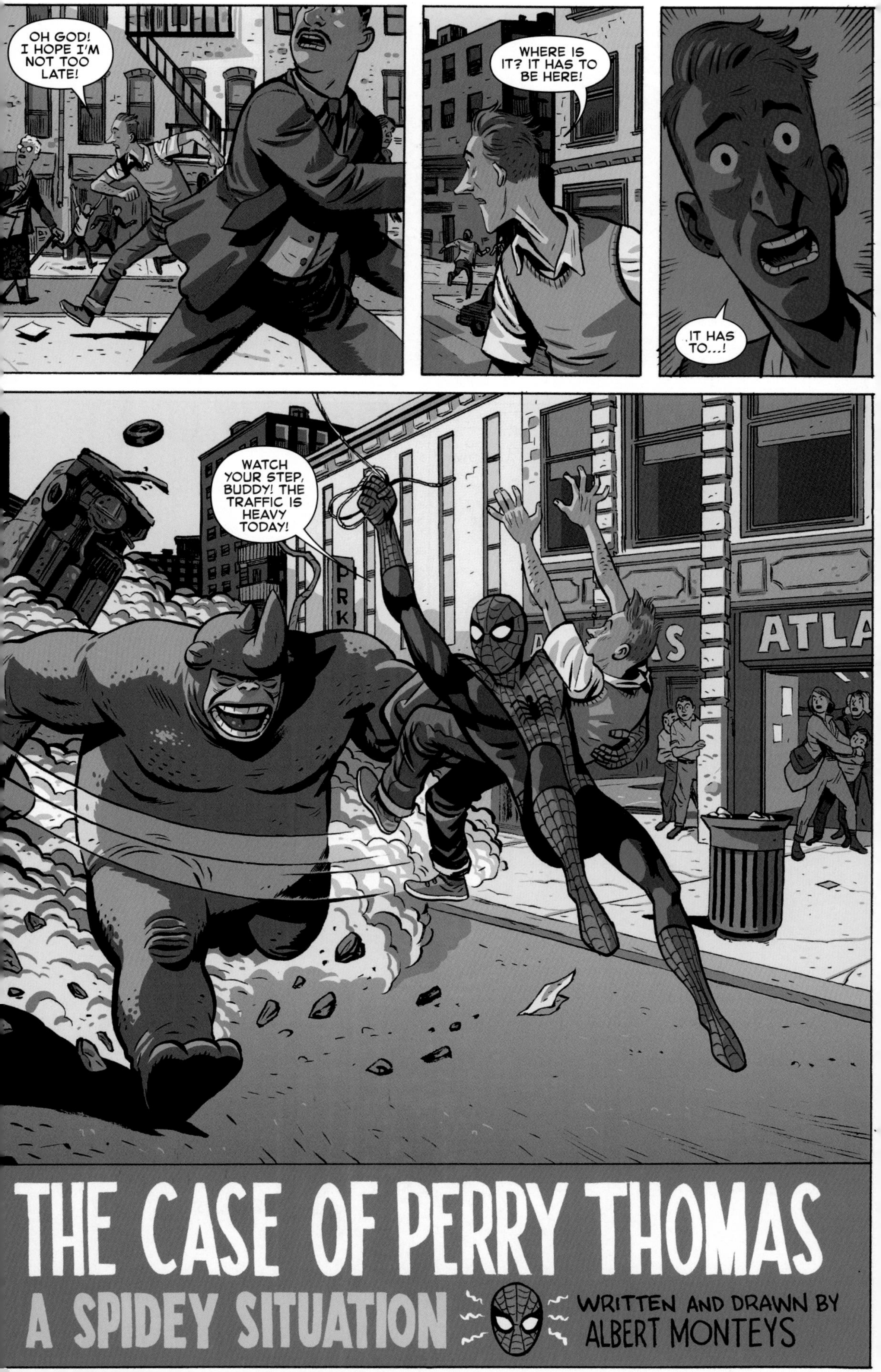
OH GOD! I HOPE I'M NOT TOO LATE!
WHERE IS IT? IT HAS TO BE HERE!
IT HAS TO...!
WATCH YOUR STEP, BUDDY! THE TRAFFIC IS HEAVY TODAY!
THE CASE OF PERRY THOMAS
A SPIDEY SITUATION
WRITTEN AND DRAWN BY ALBERT MONTEYS

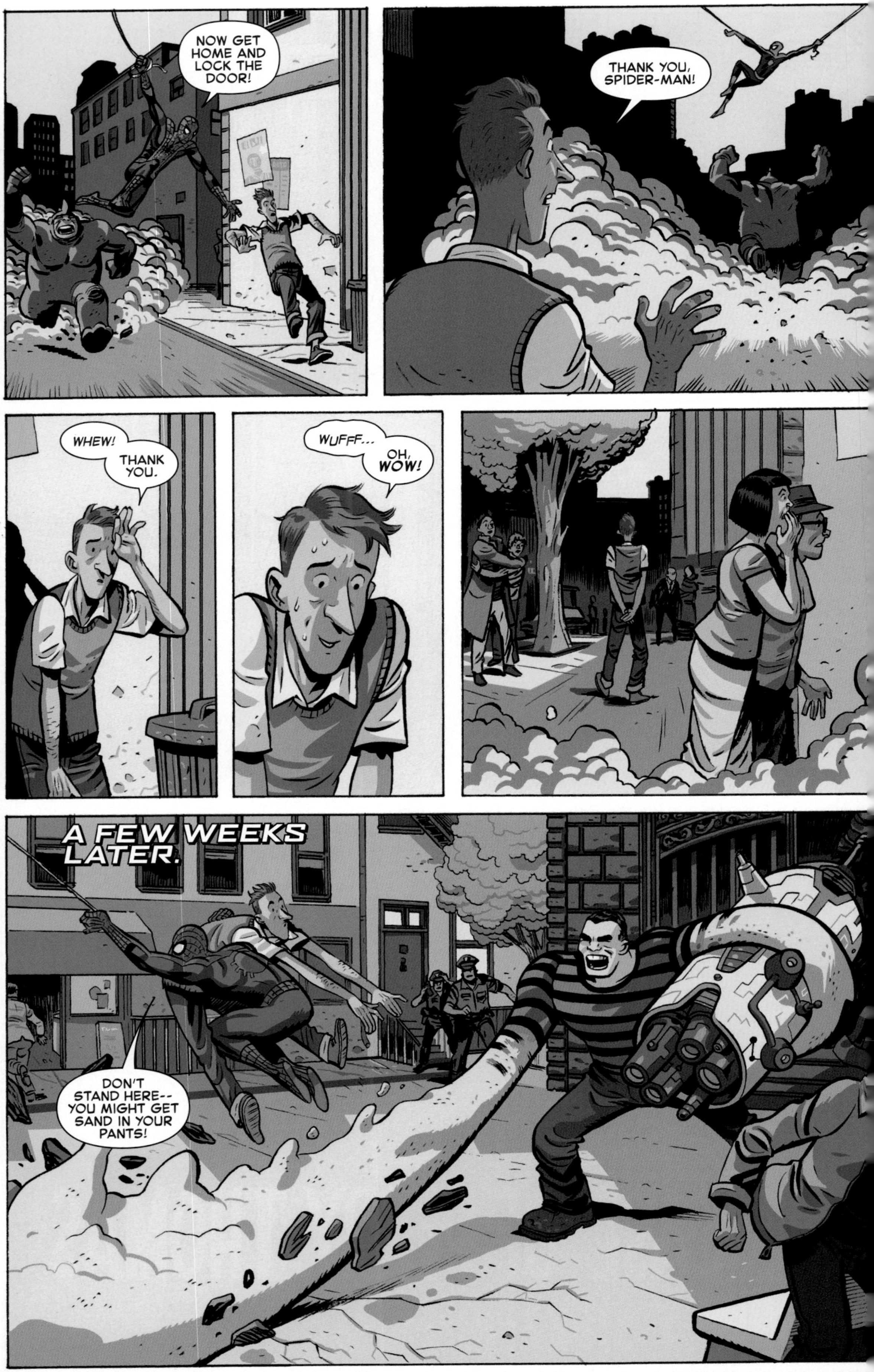
NOW GET HOME AND LOCK THE DOOR!
THANK YOU, SPIDER-MAN!
WHEW!
THANK YOU.
WUFFF...
OH, WOW!
A FEW WEEKS LATER.
DON'T STAND HERE-- YOU MIGHT GET SAND IN YOUR PANTS!

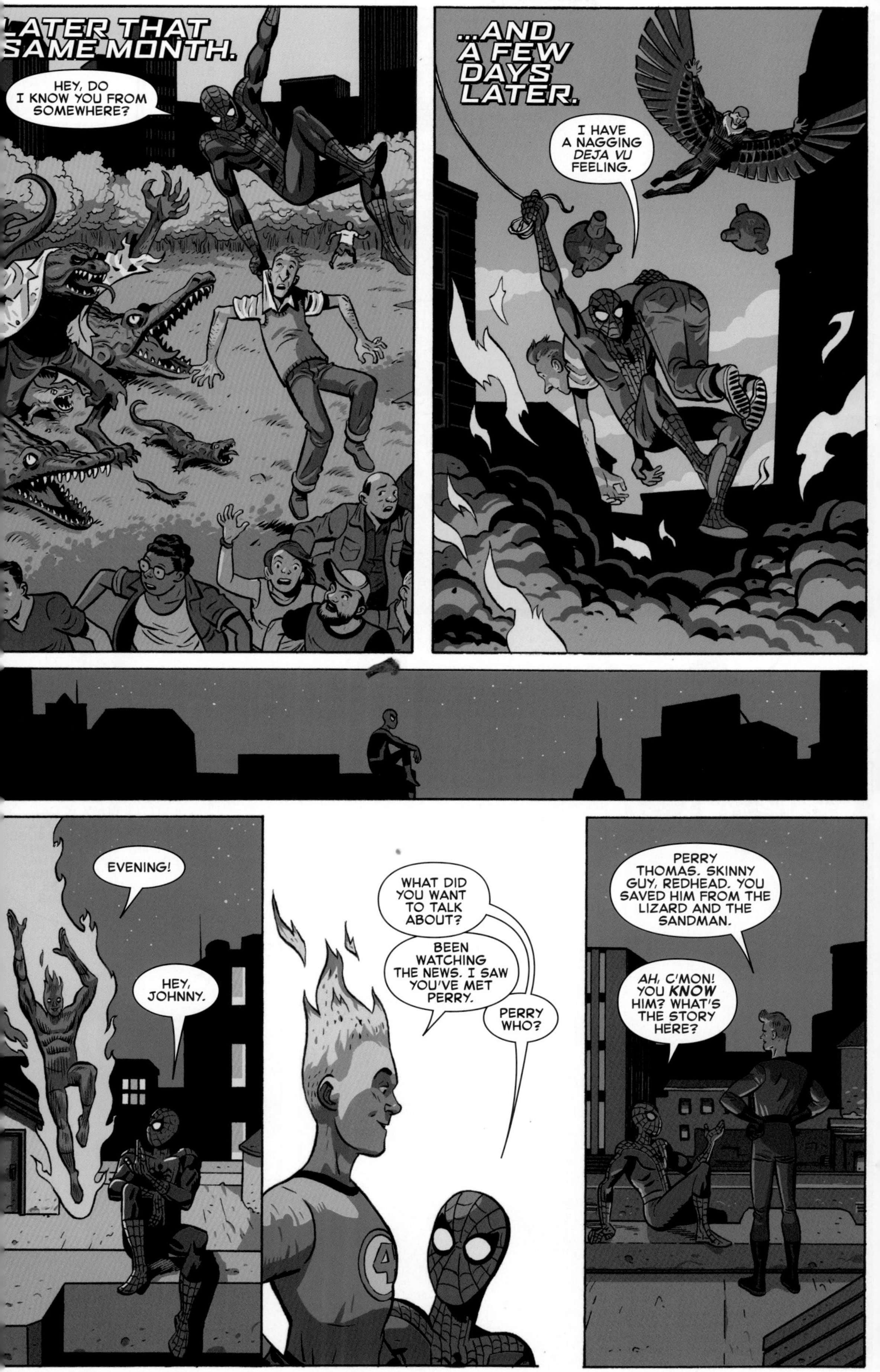
LATER THAT SAME MONTH.
HEY, DO I KNOW YOU FROM SOMEWHERE?
...AND A FEW DAYS LATER.
I HAVE A NAGGING *DEJA VU* FEELING.
EVENING!
HEY, JOHNNY.
WHAT DID YOU WANT TO TALK ABOUT?
BEEN WATCHING THE NEWS. I SAW YOU'VE MET PERRY.
PERRY WHO?
PERRY THOMAS. SKINNY GUY, REDHEAD. YOU SAVED HIM FROM THE LIZARD AND THE SANDMAN.
AH, C'MON! YOU ***KNOW*** HIM? WHAT'S THE STORY HERE?

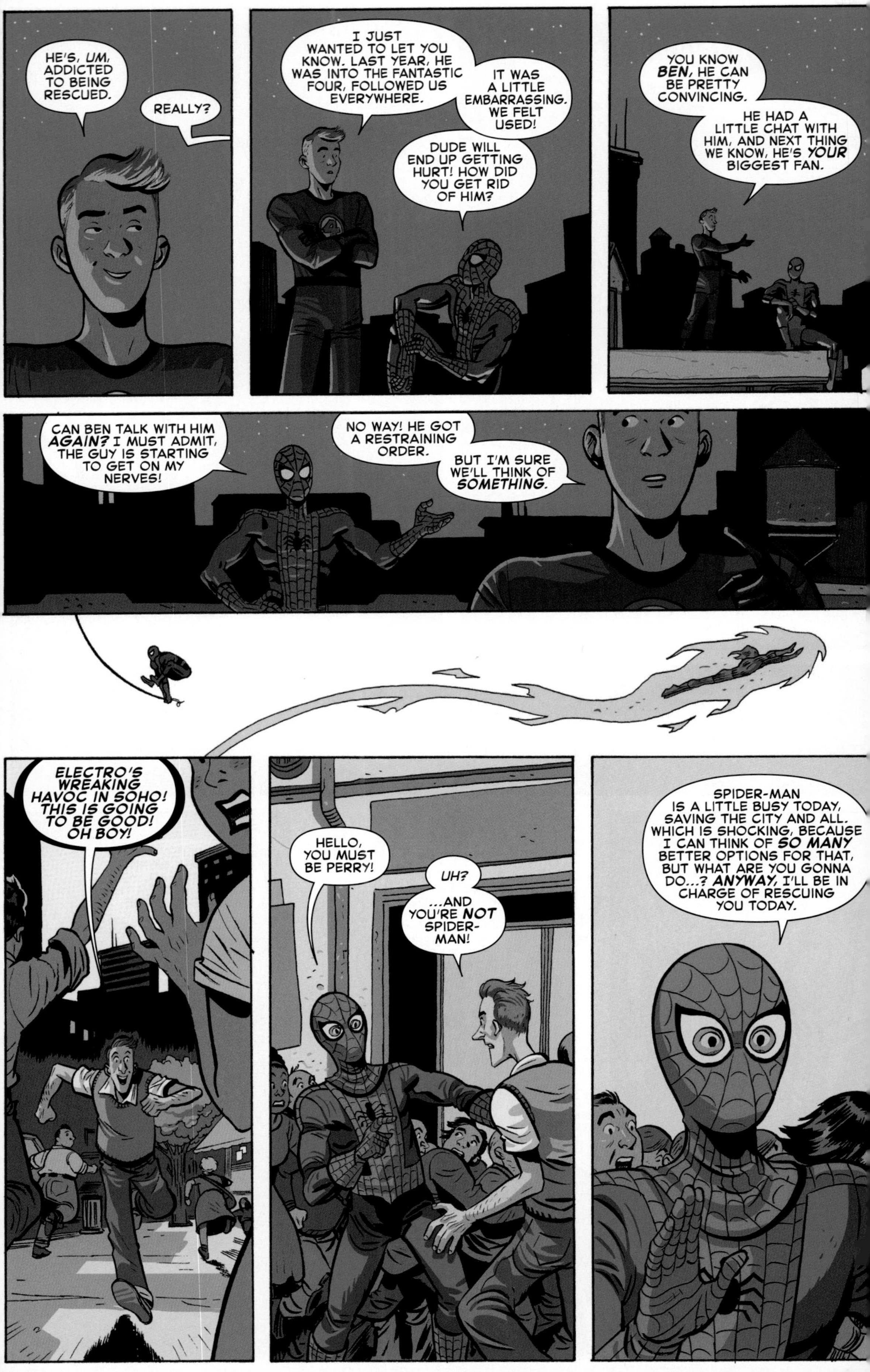
HE'S, UM, ADDICTED TO BEING RESCUED.
REALLY?
I JUST WANTED TO LET YOU KNOW. LAST YEAR, HE WAS INTO THE FANTASTIC FOUR, FOLLOWED US EVERYWHERE.
IT WAS A LITTLE EMBARRASSING. WE FELT USED!
DUDE WILL END UP GETTING HURT! HOW DID YOU GET RID OF HIM?
YOU KNOW BEN, HE CAN BE PRETTY CONVINCING.
HE HAD A LITTLE CHAT WITH HIM, AND NEXT THING WE KNOW, HE'S YOUR BIGGEST FAN.
CAN BEN TALK WITH HIM AGAIN? I MUST ADMIT, THE GUY IS STARTING TO GET ON MY NERVES!
NO WAY! HE GOT A RESTRAINING ORDER.
BUT I'M SURE WE'LL THINK OF SOMETHING.
ELECTRO'S WREAKING HAVOC IN SOHO! THIS IS GOING TO BE GOOD! OH BOY!
HELLO, YOU MUST BE PERRY!
UH?
...AND YOU'RE NOT SPIDER-MAN!
SPIDER-MAN IS A LITTLE BUSY TODAY, SAVING THE CITY AND ALL. WHICH IS SHOCKING, BECAUSE I CAN THINK OF SO MANY BETTER OPTIONS FOR THAT, BUT WHAT ARE YOU GONNA DO...? ANYWAY, I'LL BE IN CHARGE OF RESCUING YOU TODAY.

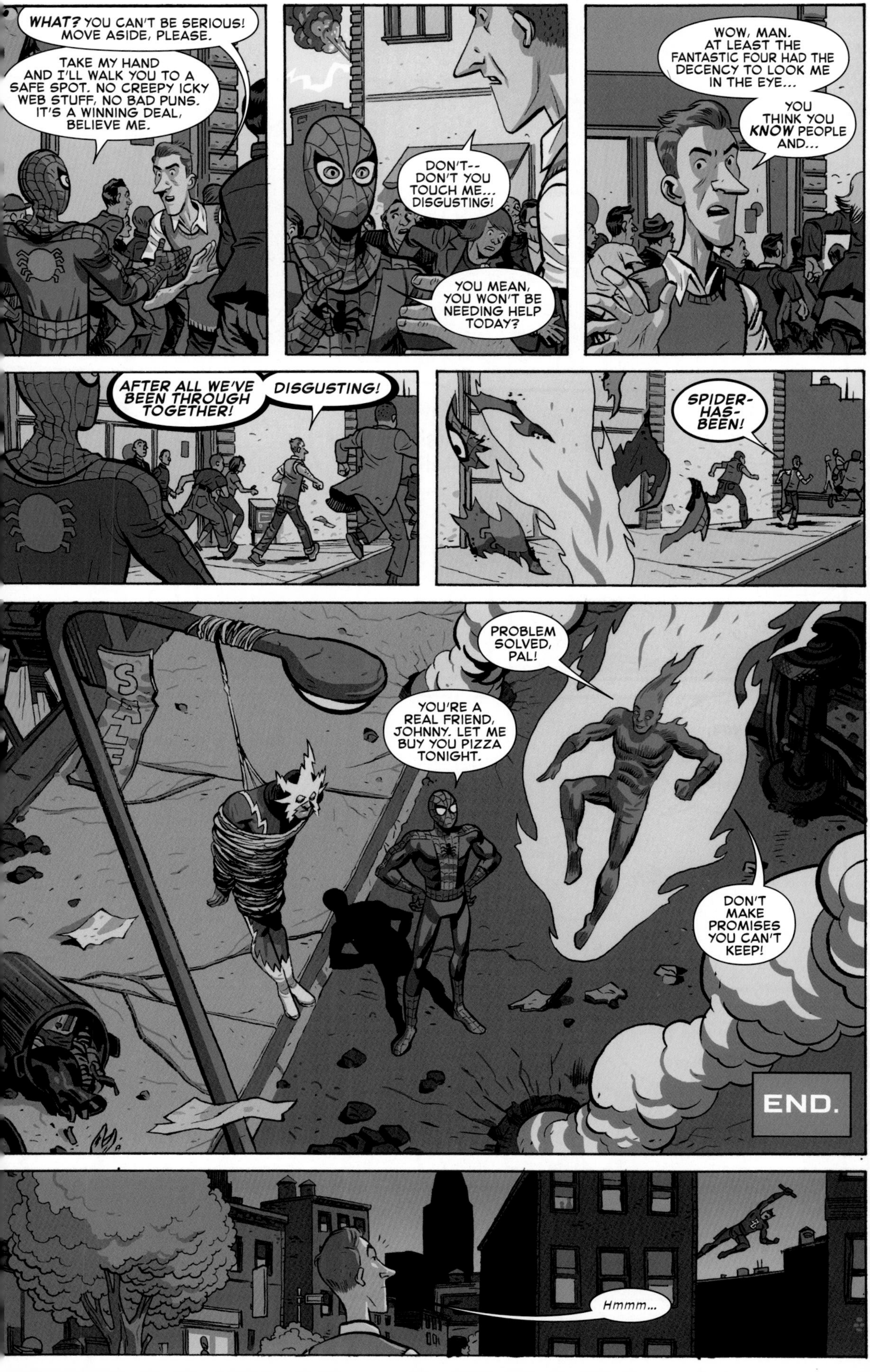
WHAT? YOU CAN'T BE SERIOUS! MOVE ASIDE, PLEASE.
TAKE MY HAND AND I'LL WALK YOU TO A SAFE SPOT. NO CREEPY ICKY WEB STUFF, NO BAD PUNS. IT'S A WINNING DEAL, BELIEVE ME.
DON'T-- DON'T YOU TOUCH ME... DISGUSTING!
YOU MEAN, YOU WON'T BE NEEDING HELP TODAY?
WOW, MAN. AT LEAST THE FANTASTIC FOUR HAD THE DECENCY TO LOOK ME IN THE EYE...
YOU THINK YOU KNOW PEOPLE AND...
AFTER ALL WE'VE BEEN THROUGH TOGETHER!
DISGUSTING!
SPIDER-HAS-BEEN!
SALE
PROBLEM SOLVED, PAL!
YOU'RE A REAL FRIEND, JOHNNY. LET ME BUY YOU PIZZA TONIGHT.
DON'T MAKE PROMISES YOU CAN'T KEEP!
END.
Hmmm...

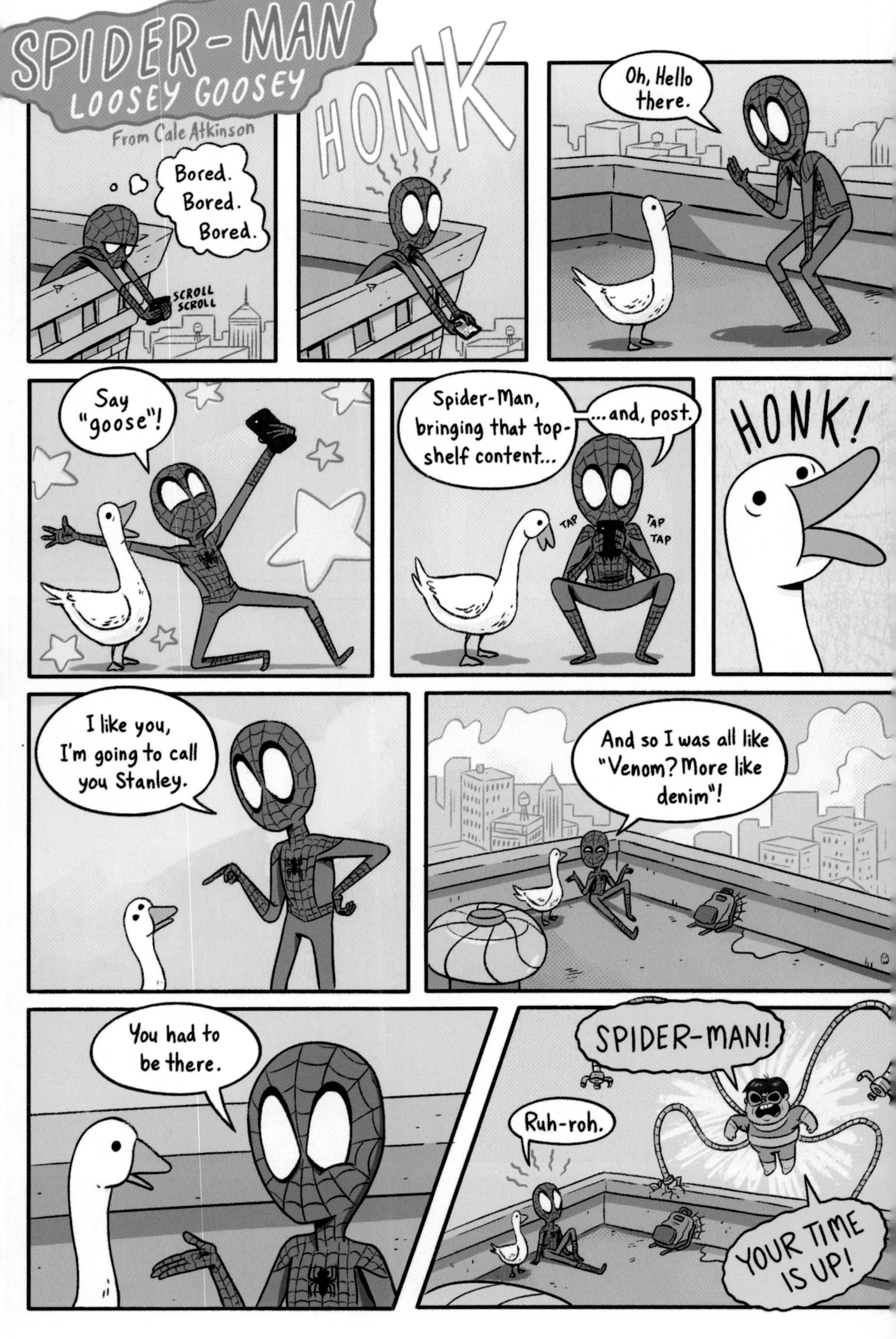
SPIDER-MAN
LOOSEY GOOSEY
From Cale Atkinson
Bored. Bored. Bored.
SCROLL SCROLL
HONK
Oh, Hello there.
Say "goose"!
Spider-Man, bringing that top-shelf content...
...and, post.
TAP
TAP TAP
HONK!
I like you, I'm going to call you Stanley.
And so I was all like "Venom? More like denim"!
You had to be there.
SPIDER-MAN!
Ruh-roh.
YOUR TIME IS UP!

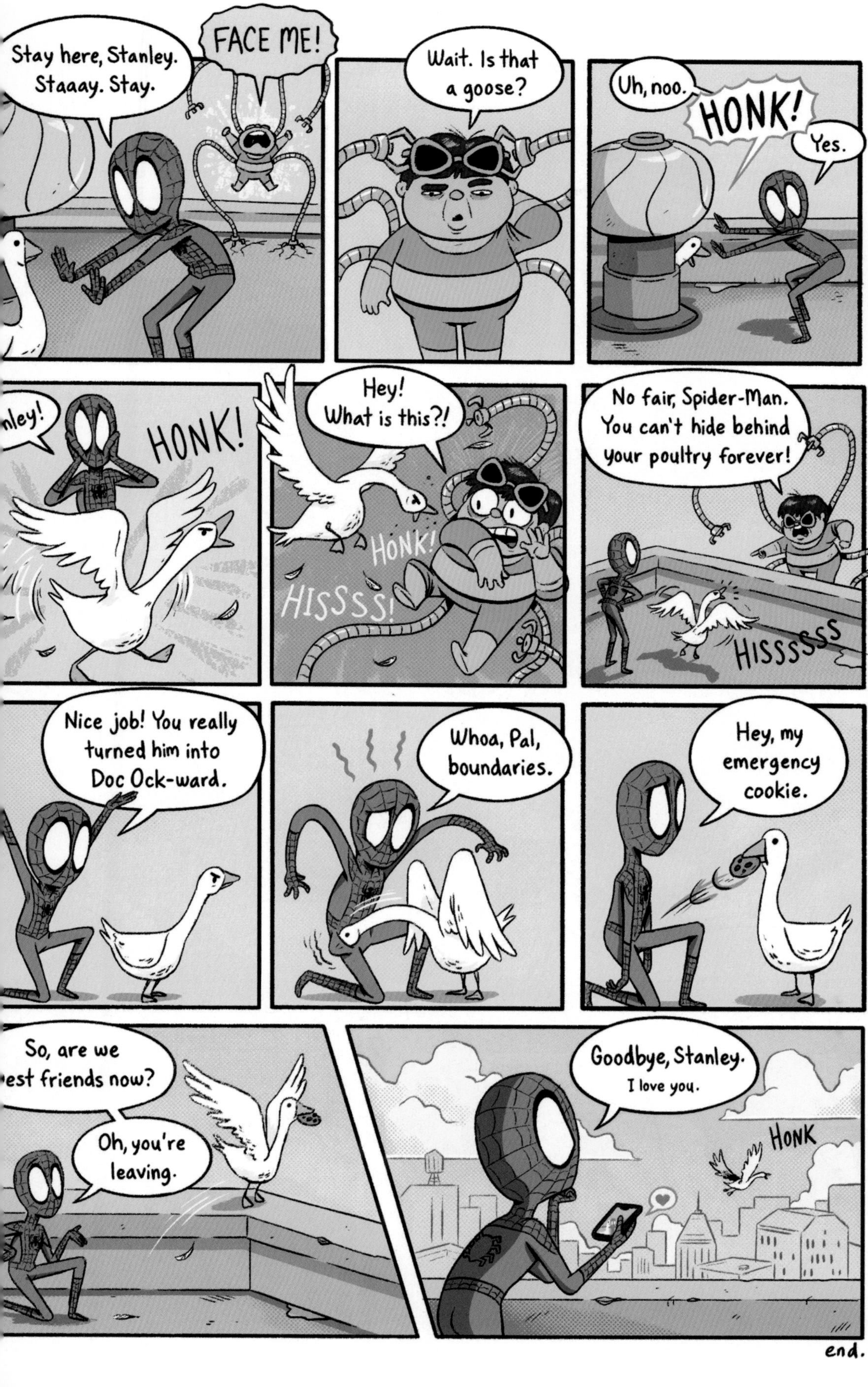

Stay here, Stanley. Staaay. Stay.
FACE ME!
Wait. Is that a goose?
Uh, noo.
HONK!
Yes.
nley!
HONK!
Hey! What is this?!
HONK!
HISSSS!
No fair, Spider-Man. You can't hide behind your poultry forever!
HISSSSSS
Nice job! You really turned him into Doc Ock-ward.
Whoa, Pal, boundaries.
Hey, my emergency cookie.
So, are we est friends now?
Oh, you're leaving.
Goodbye, Stanley. I love you.
HONK

end.

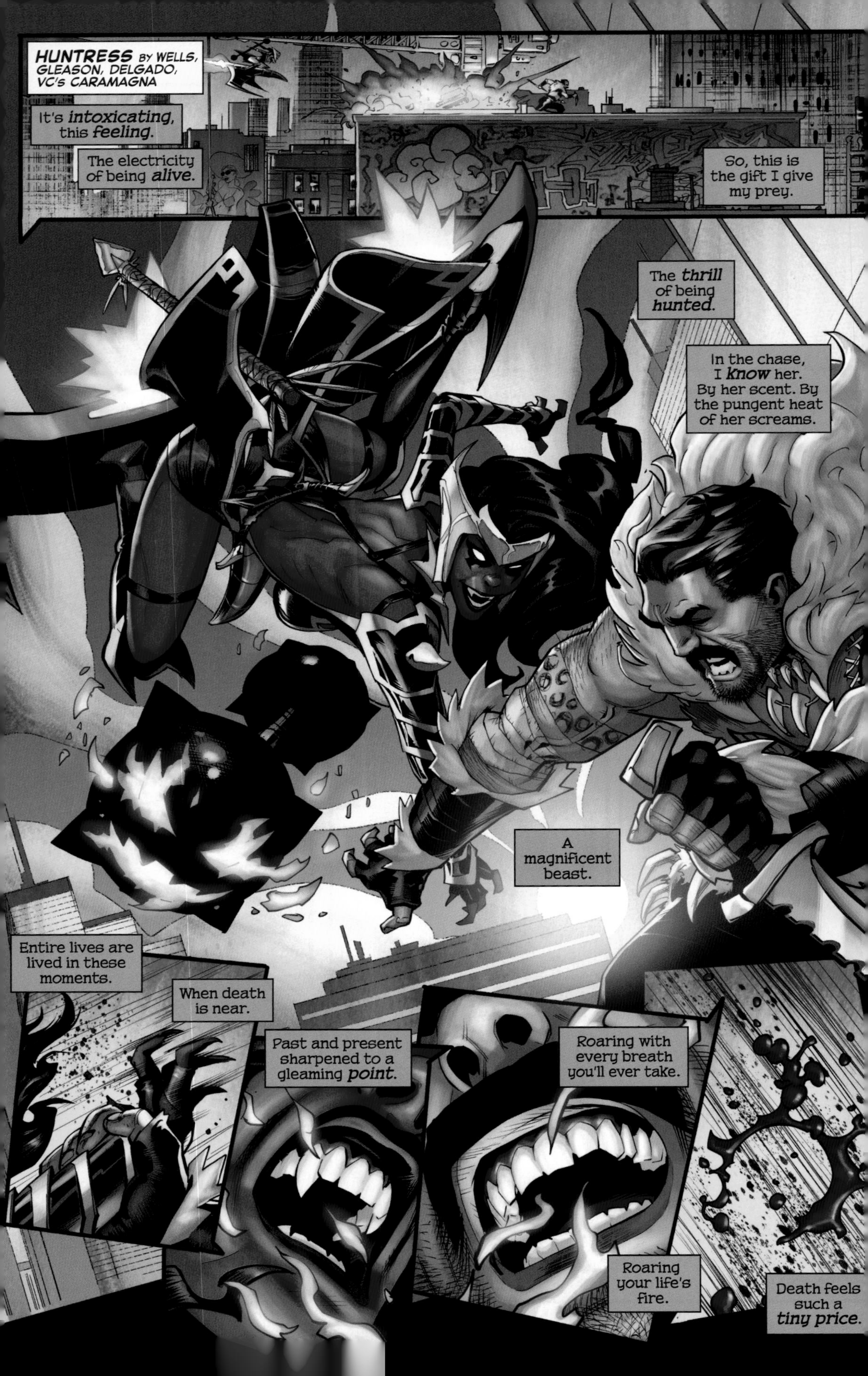
HUNTRESS BY WELLS, GLEASON, DELGADO, VC's CARAMAGNA
It's intoxicating, this feeling.
The electricity of being alive.
So, this is the gift I give my prey.
The thrill of being hunted.
In the chase, I know her. By her scent. By the pungent heat of her screams.
A magnificent beast.
Entire lives are lived in these moments.
When death is near.
Past and present sharpened to a gleaming point.
Roaring with every breath you'll ever take.
Roaring your life's fire.
Death feels such a tiny price.

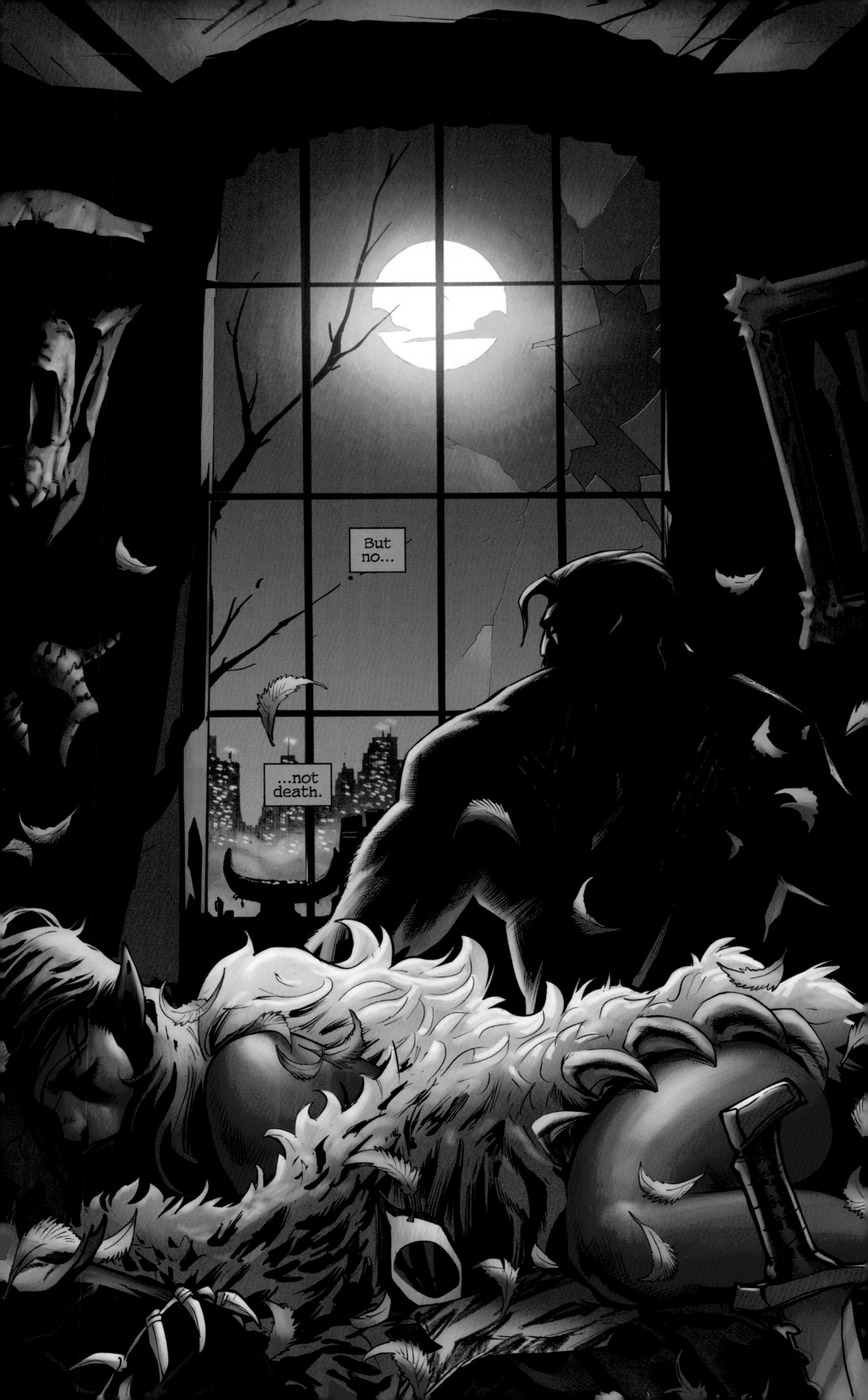

But no...
...not death.

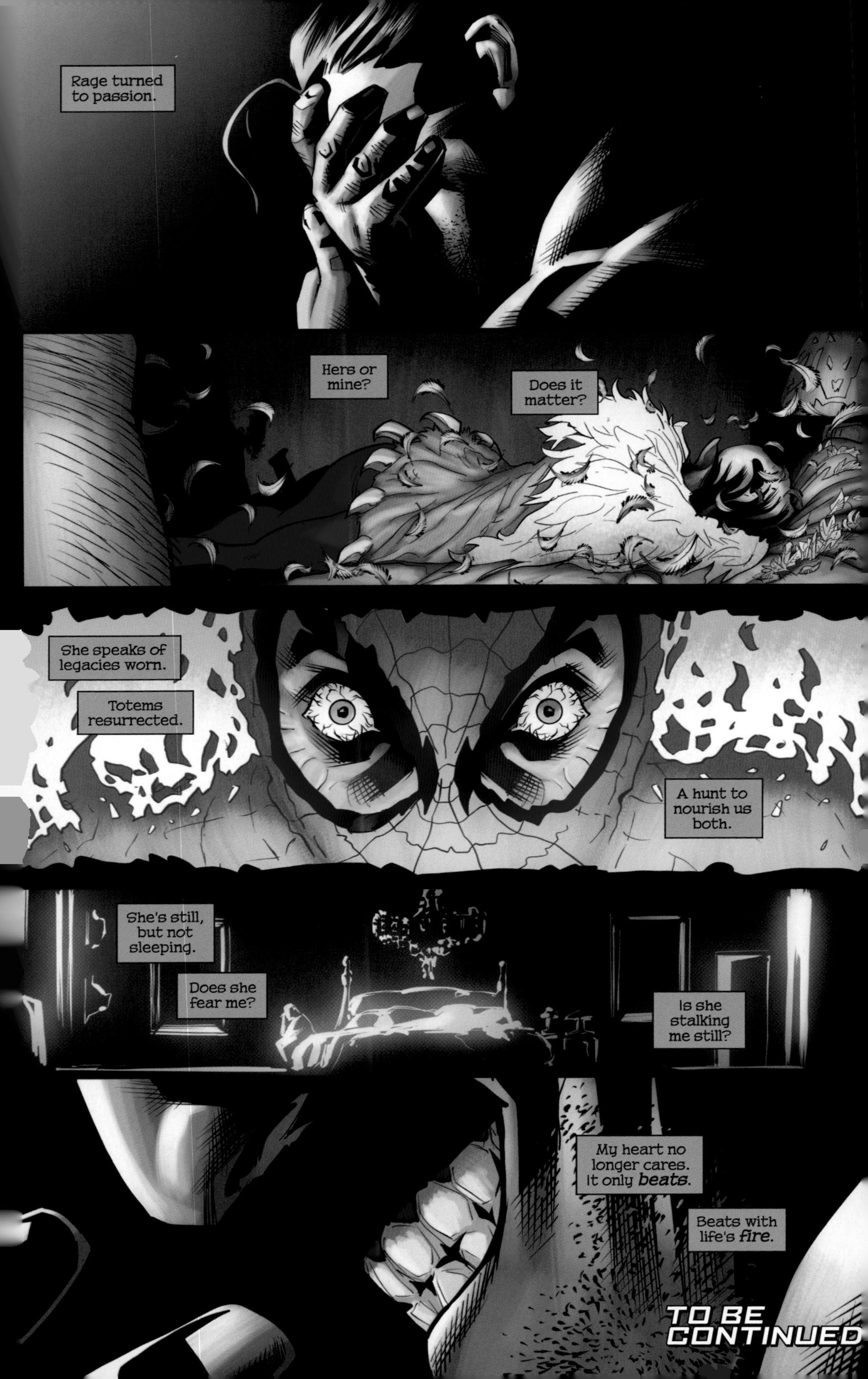
Rage turned to passion.
Hers or mine?
Does it matter?
She speaks of legacies worn.
Totems resurrected.
A hunt to nourish us both.
She's still, but not sleeping.
Does she fear me?
Is she stalking me still?
My heart no longer cares. It only *beats*.
Beats with life's *fire*.
TO BE CONTINUED

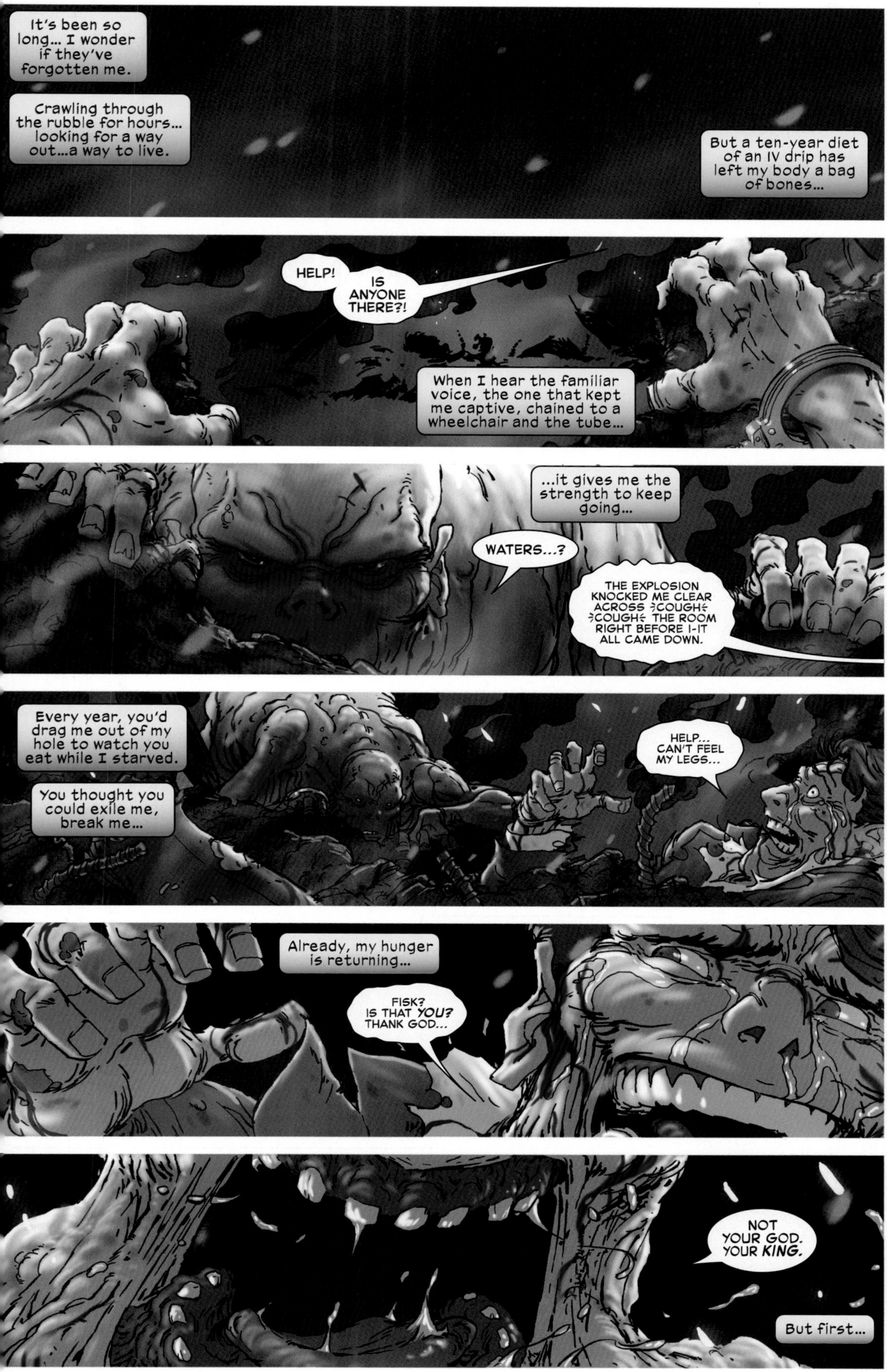

It's been so long... I wonder if they've forgotten me.
Crawling through the rubble for hours... looking for a way out...a way to live.
But a ten-year diet of an IV drip has left my body a bag of bones...
HELP!
IS ANYONE THERE?!
When I hear the familiar voice, the one that kept me captive, chained to a wheelchair and the tube...
...it gives me the strength to keep going...
WATERS...?
THE EXPLOSION KNOCKED ME CLEAR ACROSS *COUGH* *COUGH* THE ROOM RIGHT BEFORE I-IT ALL CAME DOWN.
Every year, you'd drag me out of my hole to watch you eat while I starved.
You thought you could exile me, break me...
HELP... CAN'T FEEL MY LEGS...
Already, my hunger is returning...
FISK? IS THAT YOU? THANK GOD...
NOT YOUR GOD. YOUR KING.
But first...

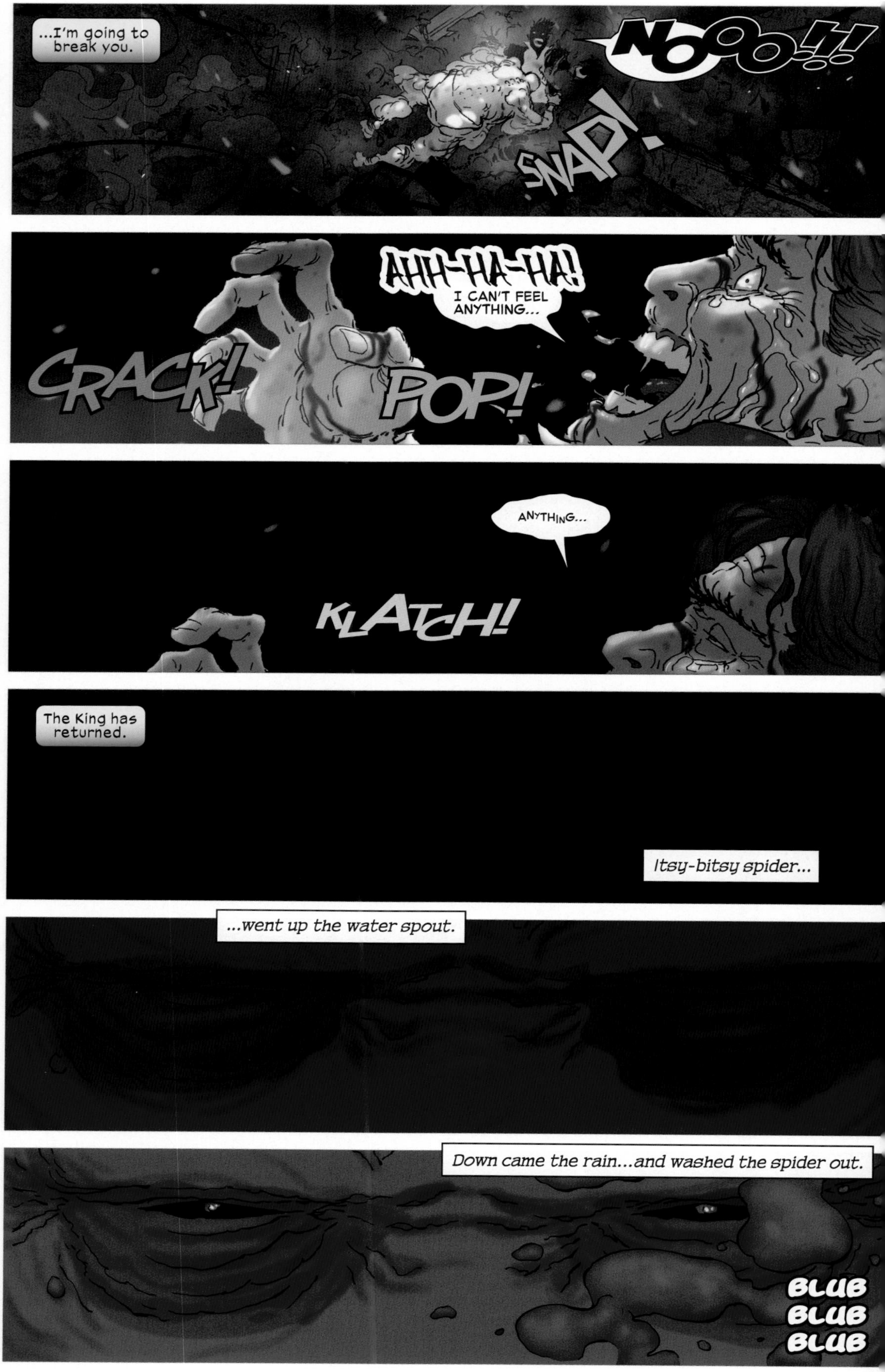

...I'm going to break you.
NOOOO!!!
SNAP!
AHH-HA-HA!
I CAN'T FEEL ANYTHING...
CRACK!
POP!
ANYTHING...
KLATCH!
The King has returned.
Itsy-bitsy spider...
...went up the water spout.
Down came the rain...and washed the spider out.
BLUB
BLUB
BLUB

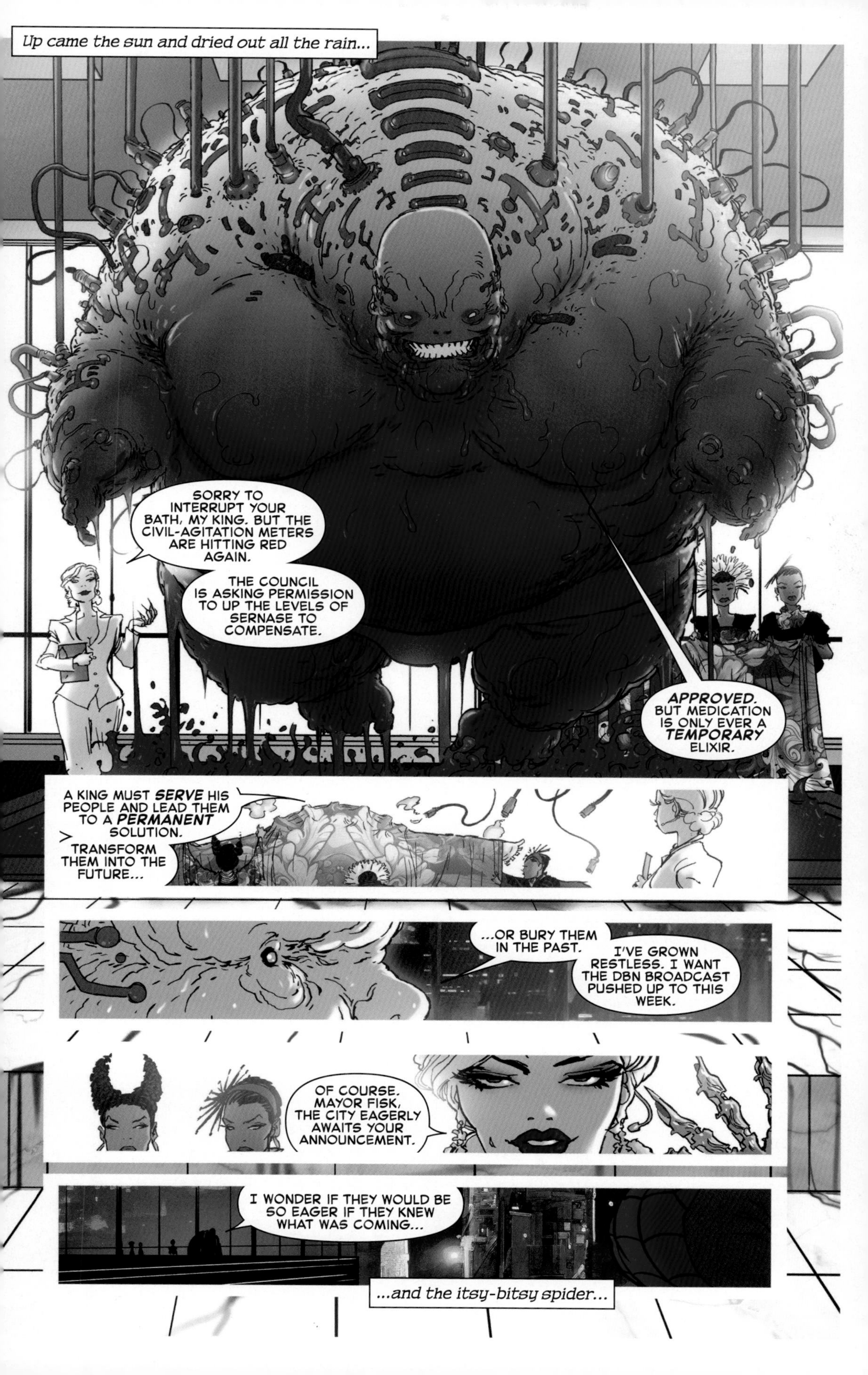
Up came the sun and dried out all the rain...
SORRY TO INTERRUPT YOUR BATH, MY KING. BUT THE CIVIL-AGITATION METERS ARE HITTING RED AGAIN.
THE COUNCIL IS ASKING PERMISSION TO UP THE LEVELS OF SERNASE TO COMPENSATE.
APPROVED. BUT MEDICATION IS ONLY EVER A TEMPORARY ELIXIR.
A KING MUST SERVE HIS PEOPLE AND LEAD THEM TO A PERMANENT SOLUTION.
TRANSFORM THEM INTO THE FUTURE...
...OR BURY THEM IN THE PAST.
I'VE GROWN RESTLESS. I WANT THE DBN BROADCAST PUSHED UP TO THIS WEEK.
OF COURSE. MAYOR FISK, THE CITY EAGERLY AWAITS YOUR ANNOUNCEMENT.
I WONDER IF THEY WOULD BE SO EAGER IF THEY KNEW WHAT WAS COMING...
...and the itsy-bitsy spider...

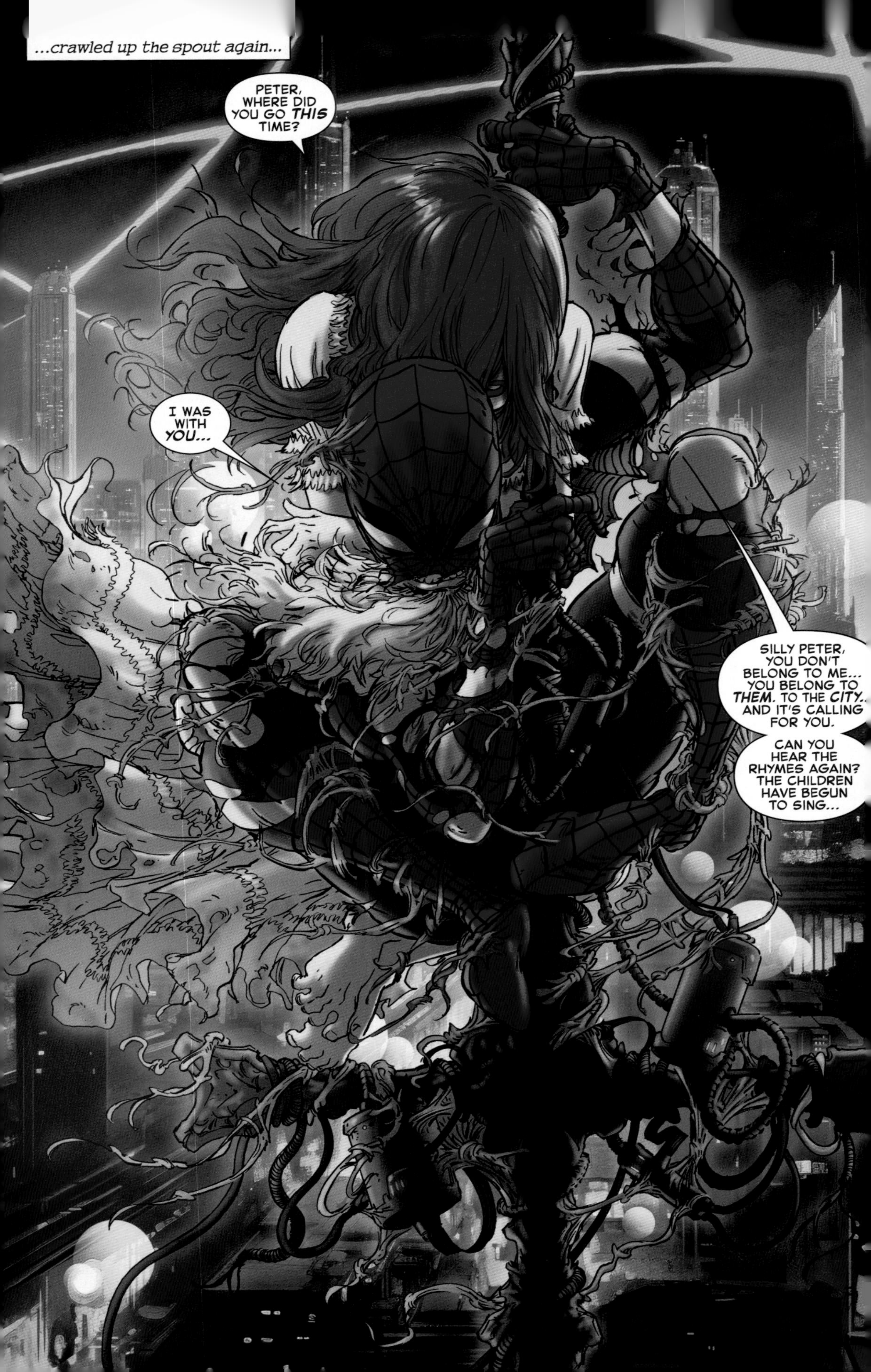

...crawled up the spout again...
PETER, WHERE DID YOU GO THIS TIME?
I WAS WITH YOU...
SILLY PETER, YOU DON'T BELONG TO ME... YOU BELONG TO THEM. TO THE CITY. AND IT'S CALLING FOR YOU.
CAN YOU HEAR THE RHYMES AGAIN? THE CHILDREN HAVE BEGUN TO SING...

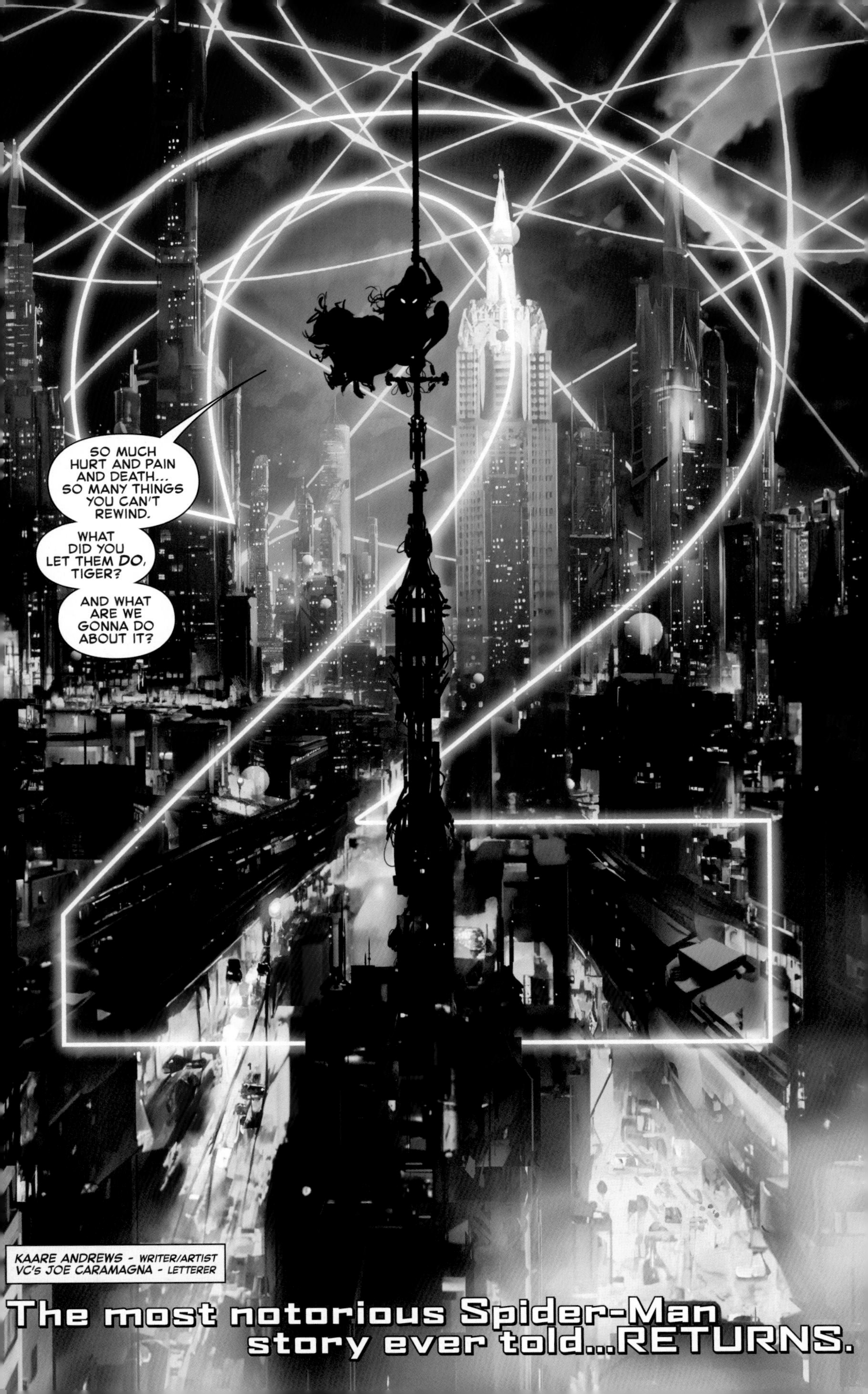
SO MUCH HURT AND PAIN AND DEATH... SO MANY THINGS YOU CAN'T REWIND.
WHAT DID YOU LET THEM DO, TIGER?
AND WHAT ARE WE GONNA DO ABOUT IT?
KAARE ANDREWS - WRITER/ARTIST
VC's JOE CARAMAGNA - LETTERER
The most notorious Spider-Man story ever told...RETURNS.

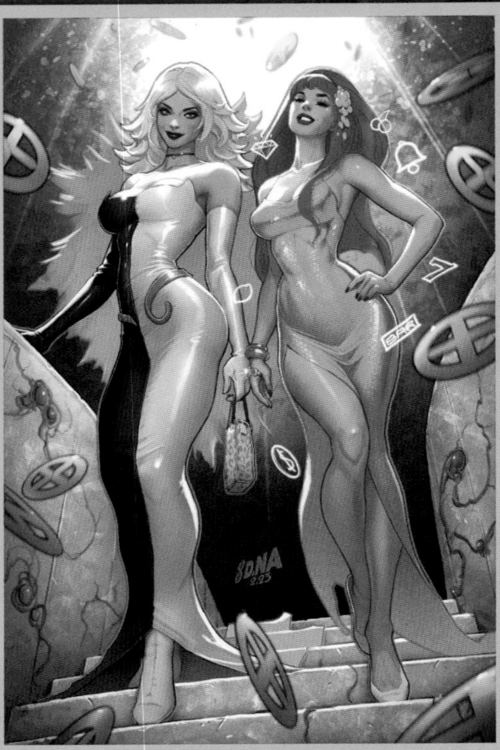

David Nakayama
#29 HELLFIRE GALA VARIANT

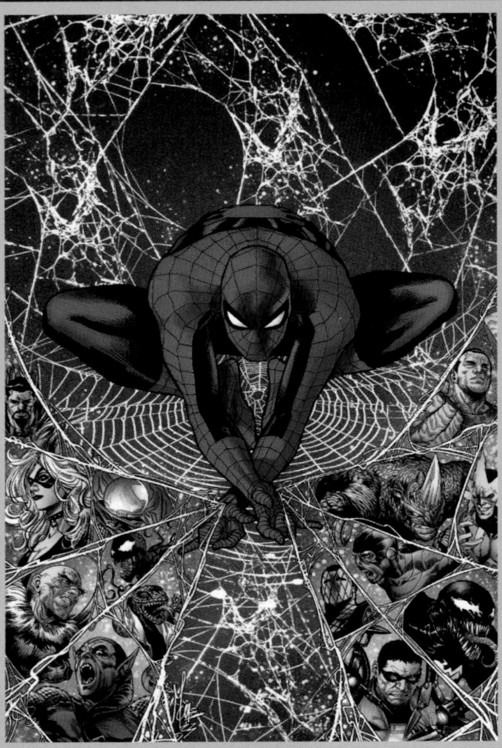

Marco Checchetto & Richard Isanove
#29 VARIANT

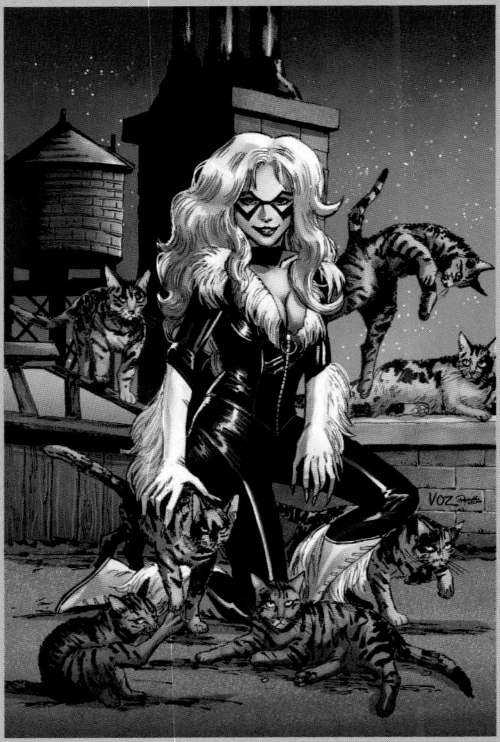

Mike Vosburg & Rachelle Rosenberg
#30 VARIANT

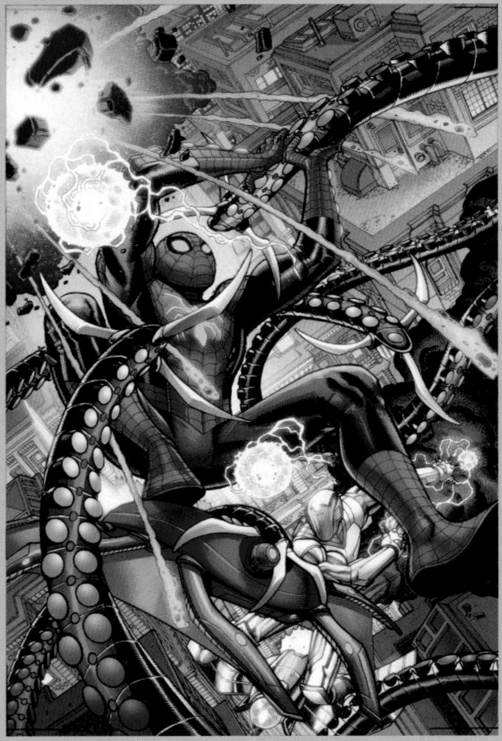

Nick Bradshaw & Rachelle Rosenberg
#30 VARIANT

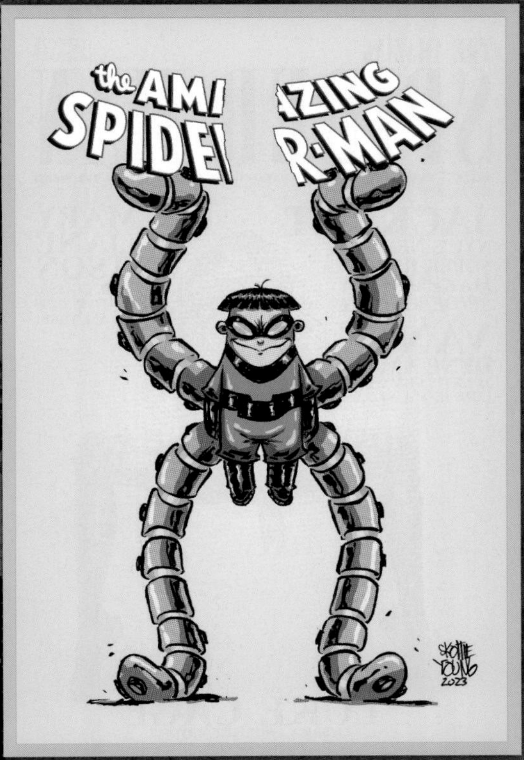
the AMI
AZING
SPIDE
R-MAN

Skottie Young
#30 VARIANT

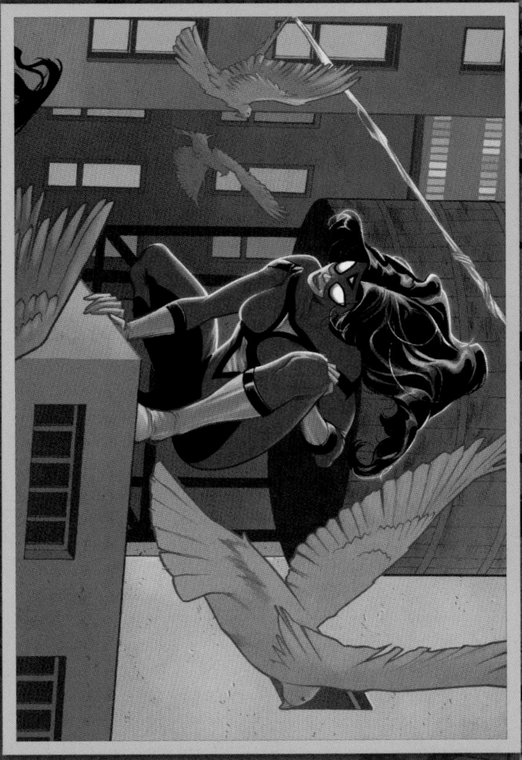

Elena Casagrande & Jordie Bellaire
#31 WOMEN OF MARVEL VARIANT

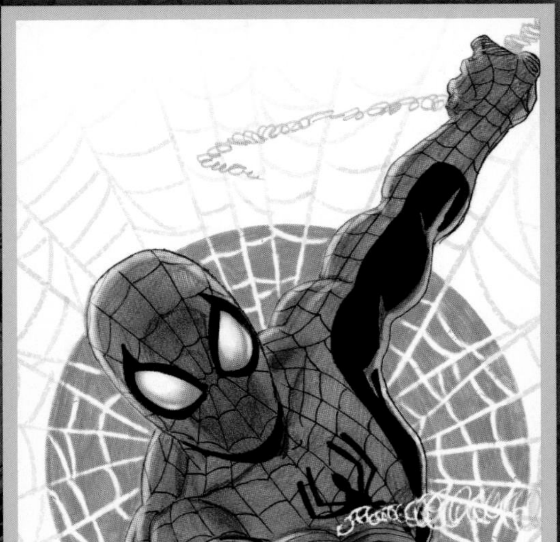

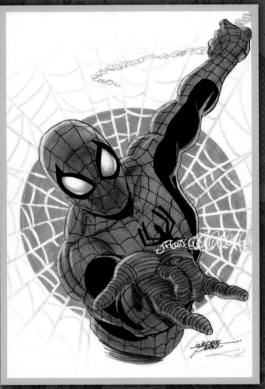

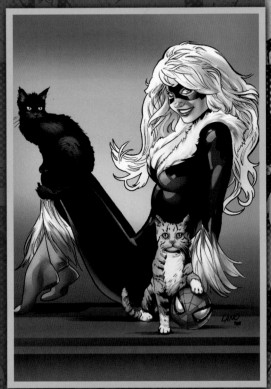

George Pérez & Alex Sinclair
#31 VARIANT

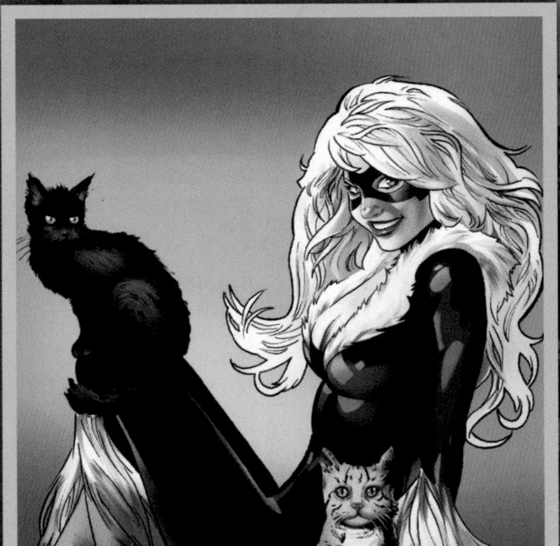

Greg Land & Frank D'Armata
#31 VARIANT

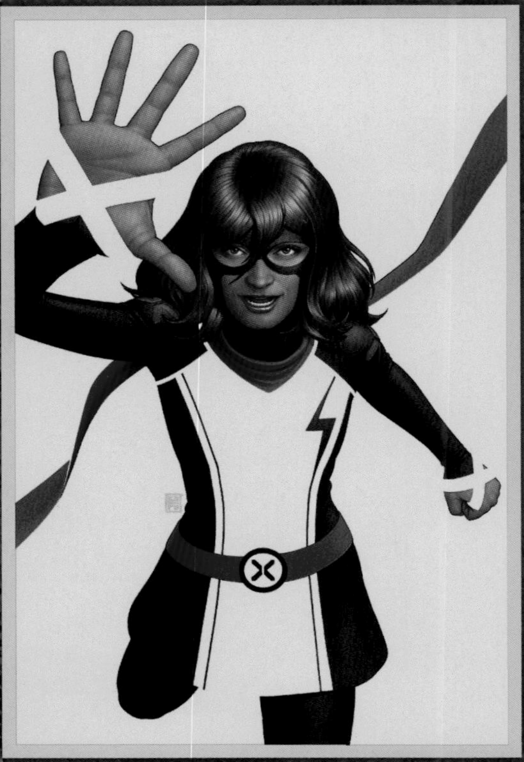

John Tyler Christopher

#31 NEGATIVE SPACE VARIANT

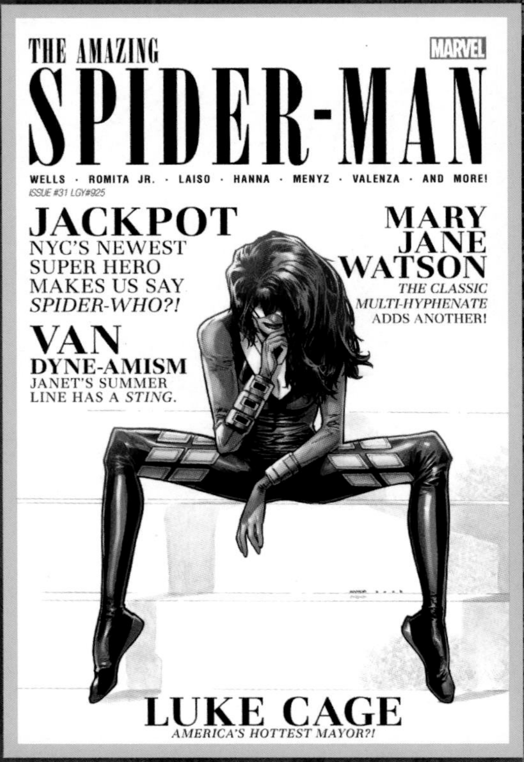
THE AMAZING
SPIDER-MAN
MARVEL
WELLS · ROMITA JR. · LAISO · HANNA · MENYZ · VALENZA · AND MORE!
ISSUE #31 LGY#925
JACKPOT
NYC'S NEWEST SUPER HERO MAKES US SAY SPIDER-WHO?!
VAN DYNE-AMISM
JANET'S SUMMER LINE HAS A STING.
MARY JANE WATSON
THE CLASSIC MULTI-HYPHENATE ADDS ANOTHER!
LUKE CAGE
AMERICA'S HOTTEST MAYOR?!

Humberto Ramos & Edgar Delgado

#31 2ND PRINTING VARIANT

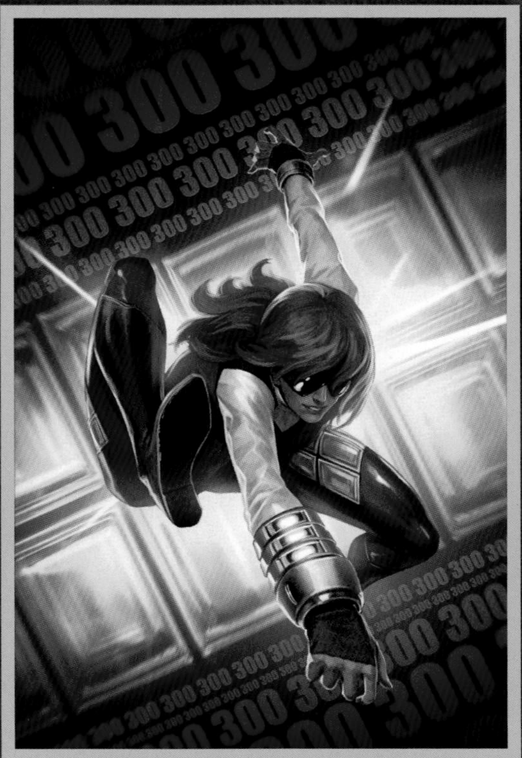

Skan

#31 2ND PRINTING VARIANT